LOCAL AUTHORITY LIABILITY
THIRD EDITION

LOCAL AUTHORITY LIABILITY

THIRD EDITION

General Editors:

John Morrell, Solicitor, Weightmans

and

His Honour Judge Richard Foster

JORDANS

2005

Published by
Jordan Publishing Limited
21 St Thomas Street, Bristol BS1 6JS

British Library Cataloguing-in-Publication Data

A catalogue record for this book is available from the British Library.

ISBN 0 85308 942 6

Typeset by MFK-Mendip, Frome, Somerset
Printed in Great Britain by Antony Rowe Limited

Contributors

JOHN MORRELL is a partner in Weightmans, specialising in liability claims against local authorities. He has dealt with a number of the leading cases involving local authorities, including *Murphy v Brentwood District Council, X (Minors) v Bedfordshire County Council, Phelps v London Borough of Hillingdon, Delaware Mansions Limited v City of Westminster* and *Adams v Bracknell Forest Borough Council.*

His Honour Judge RICHARD FOSTER is a Circuit Judge on the South Eastern Circuit and a Deputy High Court Judge. He was previously a partner in Vizard Oldham and later Weightmans. He handled a number of the leading cases involving local authorities including *X (Minors) v Bedfordshire County Council* and *Fowles v Bedfordshire County Council.*

His Honour Judge ADRIAN COOPER practised at the Bar until 2004 when he became a Circuit Judge on the South Eastern Circuit. For the previous 20 years a large part of his time was taken up with claims made against local authorities, many of which are cited in this book. Prior to his appointment, he had been a Recorder of the Crown Court since 1993.

BERNARD DOHERTY is a Barrister at 39 Essex Street. He practises in the fields of personal injuries, professional negligence and commercial work. In addition, he writes and lectures regularly on various aspects on the law of torts.

EDWARD FAULKS QC is Head of Chambers at No 1 Serjeants' Inn. He has been instructed in many of the leading cases on the liability of local authorities. He is a Recorder of the Crown Court and former Chairman of the Professional Negligence Bar Association.

GARY HAY is a partner in Weightmans and heads the firm's employment law unit. A keen advocate, he represents clients in employment tribunals involving claims of race, sex and disability discrimination. He is legal adviser to ALARM, the association for risk managers in the public sector.

MARK WHITTAKER is a partner in Weightmans and managing partner of the firm's London office. He specialises in the defence of liability claims on behalf of insurers and defendants. Cases which he has handled include *Ancell v McDermott*, one of the leading cases on the civil liability of police forces.

Foreword to the first edition

This is a book written by specialists. It deals with a specialist subject. It is written for specialists. I know of no other single book which deals exclusively with this subject. It will therefore be of great value to all those who have to deal either directly or indirectly with claims involving local authorities.

Both the general editors and two of the contributors are partners in the well-known firm of Vizards. It is a sign of the increasingly litigious age in which we live that each of those partners works in what is known as the 'Local Authority Claims Unit'. That Vizards have found it necessary to establish a specialist unit to handle litigation involving local authorities tells its own story. I am afraid the position is unlikely to improve. This being so, it is important that we deal as effectively as possible with litigation in which they are involved.

Local authorities differ from other defendants in that they are public bodies which are responsible for local government. At the same time, they carry on many activities which are also carried on by private bodies and private individuals. For example, as an employer, many of their duties and potential liabilities are not dissimilar to those of a private employer. The position is very much the same in relation to their liability for torts which they commit as occupiers of properties or landlords. On the other hand, there are areas, such as the provision of social services, the environment, education and highways, where local authorities have responsibilities which are not usually found in the private sector or where the responsibilities of local authorities differ from those in the private sector. This can often be the result of legislation.

When the responsibilities of local authorities are mirrored by those in the private sector, the law is very much the same whether the proposed defendant is a public authority or a private individual. Obviously, it is when this book is dealing with subjects where the legal situation of local authorities is distinct from that of private individuals that it will be of particular value to most of its readers. However, it does not restrict itself to those areas. The book would be of little value if it did. Very sensibly, it adopts a comprehensive approach. However, while doing so, the contributors have selected for citation in the text mainly decisions of the courts involving local authorities. This will be an approach which will be welcomed by the readers since the decisions are more likely to deal with the problems of readers. In the case of many subjects, it should not have been difficult to find the cases to cite involving local authorities. In a great many areas of the law, it is cases involving local authorities which are the leading cases. There are, however, aspects of the subject where there is no obvious case decided by the High Court which deals with the point. It is here that the practical experience of the contributors is important. It enables them to refer to decisions of other courts of first instance of which the generalist might well be unaware. As to these cases, it is important to recognise that they provide useful illustrations but are not authoritative if the views on the law they contain are challenged.

Local Authority Liability does not directly examine the liability of local authorities under public law. It is primarily litigation which can result in local authorities having to pay damages under private law with which it is concerned. It, therefore, complements rather than provides a substitute for textbooks on local government and judicial review. It does, however, take into account the potential impact of the Human Rights Act 1998. That Act is now unlikely to be brought into force until the year 2000. When it does come into force, it will not only have a dramatic effect upon the public law liability of local authorities but their private law liability as well. All the subjects dealt with in this book will be affected to a dramatic extent as a result of the Act coming into force. The full impact will not be appreciated straight away. The interval gives us a very important opportunity to prepare. Local authorities will be liable for damages if the local authority acts in a way which is 'incompatible with a Convention right' (Clause 6.1 of the Human Rights Bill). A full examination of that impact will no doubt have to be included in the second edition of this book. In the meantime, it is beneficial that the first edition deals with the potential impact.

One subject with which this book does not deal, there is no reason why it should, is the huge cost to local authorities of claims which are made against them. In many areas, for example, housing, litigation absorbs a deeply worrying proportion of the total budget which local authorities are in a position to spend on that area of their activities. As is well known, one objective of the forthcoming reforms of civil procedure is to ensure that, wherever possible, litigation is avoided and where it is not avoided, it is resolved at a much earlier stage than happens at present. If the change of culture which this involves takes place, it will be very beneficial to local authorities, their insurers and the public as a whole.

In order to achieve the necessary change of approach, those on both sides of the dispute have to be able to make a realistic assessment of what would be the probable outcome of a case if it had to be finally determined by the courts. Among the many reasons for welcoming the first edition of *Local Authority Liability* is the fact that, in relation to litigation involving local authorities, it will assist the legal advisors of both plaintiffs and defendants to make that realistic assessment.

THE RT HON THE LORD WOOLF
Master of the Rolls
October 1998

Foreword to the second edition

The activities of local authorities affect us all, individually and every day. As highway authorities they repair the roads and pavements, as education authorities they run the schools, as planning authorities they permit or refuse new houses and shops, offices and factories. They have profound responsibilities for the welfare of children, they have far-reaching obligations to provide accommodation for the homeless, they maintain registers of local land charges.

When things go wrong the legal liability of local authorities is often a matter of complexity. Negligence, nuisance, breach of statutory duty, occupier's liability and misfeasance in public office are some of the possible torts involved. The law in these areas is not always clear. Negligence is one obvious example. Moreover, practitioners are still feeling their way with regard to the Human Rights Act 1998 and its impact on local authorities as public authorities.

Traditionally these various heads of liability are dealt with in separate books, or in separate chapters of a book covering the whole field of the law of tort. Already several books have been written on the implications of the Human Rights Act, again covering the whole subject. In the past, those concerned with tortious claims in damages against local authorities, for this book is mainly concerned with such claims, had to go hunting in these works of general application for the principles and court decisions, particularly concerning local authorities.

This is no longer necessary. The present book, now in its second edition, performs the valuable service of setting out, in summary form, the relevant law on these varied topics so far as they impinge on local authorities. The need for this service is shown by the success of the first edition of *Local Authority Liability*. Busy practitioners, advising clients who may have claims against local authorities or advising local authorities, would do well to start here. This is a book they should have on their bookshelves.

LORD NICHOLLS OF BIRKENHEAD
House of Lords
September 2001

Foreword to the third edition

The liability of local authorities in tort has been for many years a troublesome area of the law. This is partly due, as Lord Woolf pointed out in his preface to the first edition of this book, to their amphibious nature both as corporate persons doing things which might equally be done by private persons, such as occupying land and letting property, and as public authorities performing statutory duties and exercising statutory powers. No doubt this sometimes gives rise to conceptual problems about the interaction between statute and common law. But another reason for the growth of litigation against local authorities, illustrated by the need for three editions of this book within six years (compare the 44 years during which there have been three editions of *Buckley on the Companies Acts*), is that local authorities often have powers which would have enabled them to take steps which would or might have avoided the risk of damage. Has the claimant's property been flooded by a heavy downpour which overwhelms the capacity of the stormwater drains? The drainage authority could have prevented it by building bigger drains. Has a car driver been injured on account of going too fast? The highway authority might have prevented it by signs telling her to go slow. Has a swimmer injured himself swimming in a local authority's pond? The authority could have prevented it by putting up barbed wire to keep him out. All these things are true, but they all cost money, and some of them involve having to stop people doing things that they want to do, like swimming in ponds or playing football in the playground.

Judicial attitudes to these claims have varied, reflecting both changes in fashion and the personal predilections of judges. Some see only the plight of the claimant, perhaps seriously injured, facing what may be a lifetime on the meagre benefits offered by the social security system. They reason that the local authority has money, the law of negligence is pretty much of a lottery anyway, and so why should compensation not be paid? Others are impressed by the problems of local authorities having to decide whether to reduce the education budget to fund the road budget or the cost of safety measures in the recreation budget, to say nothing of the ever-increasing demands of the litigation department. And then there are the protests of other citizens, who find their swimming pools shut, the gravel paths in their parks replaced with slip-free resin compound, and a forest of signs warning them of remote and obvious risks.

It is therefore not surprising that the law in this area is complex and not always consistent. As in previous editions, this book provides excellent assistance to enable practitioners to find their way: well organised, comprehensive and above all, lucidly written. I commend it to the profession.

LORD HOFFMANN
House of Lords
January 2005

Preface

Local authorities face a wide range of claims because of the extent of their activities. They operate as highway authorities and occupiers. They have roles in education and social care, and as employers. In preparing the third edition of *Local Authority Liability* we have been able to consider the truth of the popularly held view that local authorities, in particular, are facing an increasing number of claims because of a 'compensation culture'.

It is true that local authorities have been at the forefront of the development in the law of tort. We are fortunate to have practised in this area of law. The Human Rights Act 1998 has now been in force for four years. Although it has not had a substantial impact on the cases which we consider in this book, nevertheless its effect is to be seen in, for example, *JD & Others v East Berkshire Community Health and Others* in the approach to the duty of care of social workers.

In the second edition we dealt with *Phelps v London Borough of Hillingdon* which confirmed the existence of a duty of care on teachers to respond to the educational needs of children, something which would not have been recognised more than ten years ago. Since the publication of the second edition of our book, the courts have been able to put the decision in *Phelps* into practice and, in general, they have adopted a restrictive approach to the liability of teachers.

In *Sutherland v Hatton* the Court of Appeal has given guidance in claims alleging psychiatric injury due to stress at work, in general terms endorsed by the House of Lords in *Barber v Somerset County Council*, which has tended to emphasise the difficulty in establishing liability against employers.

Finally, in *Tomlinson v Congleton Borough Council*, which has been followed in a number of cases, the House of Lords has reminded us that failure to remove an identified risk does not automatically give rise to liability. There is always a risk of accidents arising out of the 'joie de vivre of the young' and the law should not impose a 'grey and dull safety regime on everyone'.

We would like to thank those who have contributed to this book, namely: Mark Whittaker and Gary Hay, Partners at Weightmans, and from the Bar, Edwards Faulks QC and Bernard Doherty, as well as Adrian Cooper, now a Circuit Judge on the South Eastern Circuit. We must also thank all who have given assistance with research and typing, particularly Katrina Lindop and Rachel Jeffs. Finally, our families who, again, have had to allow us time to review the developing case-law to include in this third edition.

As always a line has to be drawn and, accordingly, this book reflects cases decided and effective before 30 November 2004.

JOHN MORRELL
RICHARD FOSTER

Contents

Table of Cases

Table of Statutes

References are to paragraph numbers.

Table of Statutory Instruments

Table of European Material

References are to paragraph numbers.

Guidance

Treaties

Table of Abbreviations

ABI	Association of British Insurers
ECHR	European Convention for the Protection of Human Rights and Fundamental Freedoms (European Convention on Human Rights)
EPA 1990	Environmental Protection Act 1990
GLA	Greater London Authority
HSE	Health & Safety Executive
IPC	integrated pollution control
LAAPC	local authority air pollution control
LLCA 1975	Local Land Charges Act 1975
MOD	Ministry of Defence
PCE	perchloroethane
TUPE	Transfer of Undertakings (Protection of Employment) Regulations 1981

Chapter 1

INTRODUCTION TO DUTIES OWED BY LOCAL AUTHORITIES

INTRODUCTION

1.1   To consider the duties owed by local authorities it is now necessary not only to consider the general principles which have been developed by the courts over a considerable period of time, but also to look at how far these general principles have been affected, or added to, by the Human Rights Act 1998. The Act came into force on 2 October 2000, and introduced the Convention for the Protection of Human Rights and Fundamental Freedoms into UK law. This chapter deals with the general principles which have been developed by the courts. The Human Rights Act 1998 will be considered in more detail in Chapter 2.

NEGLIGENCE

The basic rule

1.2   In order to establish negligence, it is necessary for a claimant to establish three requirements:

(1)   the defendant owed him a duty of care the scope of which includes avoidance of the damage in fact suffered;
(2)   the defendant was in breach of that duty;
(3)   the claimant has suffered damage by reason of that breach.

1.3   In considering the first requirement, the courts have examined the activities of local authorities in a number of cases over the last 25 years.

1.4   The modern law of negligence by which the courts decide whether a particular situation gives rise to a duty of care in law can be traced back to *Donoghue v Stevenson*.[1] In that case, Lord Atkin formulated his famous 'neighbour' principle as follows:

> 'You must take reasonable care to avoid acts or omissions which you can reasonably foresee would be likely to injure a neighbour. Who, then, in law is my neighbour? The answer seems to be – persons who are so closely and directly affected by my act that I ought reasonably to have them in contemplation as being so affected when I am directing my mind to the acts or omissions which are called in question.'

---

1   [1932] AC 562.

1.5   It is important to note that the duty of care in *Donoghue v Stevenson* is a duty to avoid acts or omissions which a defendant can reasonably foresee will be likely to cause personal injury or damage to the property of persons who are closely and directly affected by the defendant's conduct.

1.6   In *Dorset Yacht Co Ltd v Home Office*,[1] Lord Reid relied upon the principle in *Donoghue v Stevenson* when holding that prison officers owed a duty of care in respect of the custody of young offenders to owners of nearby property likely to be damaged if the prisoners escaped. Damage to yachts was caused by the young offenders who escaped from custody due to the negligence of the prison officers.

Negligent statements

1.7   In *Hedley Byrne v Heller & Partners*,[2] the House of Lords extended the duty of care from negligent acts or omissions which cause physical damage, to negligent statements causing pure economic loss, namely financial loss suffered by a claimant, which is not connected with and does not flow from damage to his own person or property.

1.8   To some extent, the duty of care established by the House of Lords in *Hedley Byrne v Heller & Partners* has been restricted to cases where there has been an actual or quasi-contractual or professional relationship between the parties. Furthermore, it has been taken to establish liability in respect of negligent statements as opposed to the negligent performance of services. As will be seen below, the House of Lords has now explained the scope of this duty on the basis of assumption of a particular or general responsibility.[3]

Assumption of responsibility

1.9   In *Spring v Guardian Assurance plc*[4] and *Henderson v Merrett Syndicates Ltd*,[5] Lord Goff explained the concept of 'assumption of responsibility' when establishing the existence of a duty of care on the defendants. The *Spring* case concerned the liability of an employer when giving a reference for one of his former employees. The *Henderson* case involved the liability of underwriting agents to certain Lloyd's Names. Assumption of responsibility was viewed either as a test additional to the three tests laid down in *Caparo*,[6] or a way of establishing whether the three-stage test had been met. The position has now been explained further in *Phelps v London Borough of Hillingdon*,[7] a case concerned with the duties of educational psychologists and teachers to their pupils, which is dealt with at greater length in Chapter 4. Lord Slynn clarified the position by confirming that the 'assumption of responsibility' test is objective, not subjective, and does not mean that the defendant must actually assume responsibility:

---

1   [1970] AC 1004.
2   [1963] 2 All ER 575.
3   See *Henderson v Merrett Syndicates Ltd* [1995] 2 AC 145.
4   [1995] 2 AC 296.
5   [1995] 2 AC 145.
6   See para **1.21** et seq.
7   [2000] 3 WLR 776.

'It is sometimes said that there has to be an assumption of responsibility by the person concerned. That phrase can be misleading in that it can suggest that the professional person must knowingly and deliberately accept responsibility. It is, however, clear that the test is an objective one (*Henderson v Merrett Syndicates Ltd*). The phrase means simply that the law recognises that there is a duty of care. It is not so much that responsibility is assumed as that it is recognised or imposed by the law.'

1.10 In both *Spring* and *Henderson*, Lord Goff referred to the duty of care for negligent statements established in *Hedley Byrne v Heller & Partners*,[1] but he made it clear that liability could arise out of the provision of services.

Local authorities and assumption of responsibility

1.11 Following the decision in *Murphy v Brentwood District Council*,[2] in which it was held that *Anns v Merton London Borough Council*[3] had been wrongly decided, the courts have turned to the *Hedley Byrne* principle to decide whether local authorities owe a duty of care in claims for economic loss. This is discussed at greater length in Chapter 9.

1.12 The courts recognised a *Hedley Byrne*-type duty resting on local authorities in 1970 in the case of *Ministry of Housing and Local Government v Sharp*.[4] The defendant, who was responsible for the local land charges registry, negligently issued a certificate which failed to specify that a local land charge was held over the land by the plaintiff. A prospective purchaser bought the land in reliance upon the clear certificate and the provisions of the registration scheme. This meant that the plaintiff's charge was unenforceable. The Court of Appeal held that the defendant was liable to the plaintiff for the value of the lost charge. Lord Denning MR justified his decision on the ground that:

'The very object of the registration system is to secure (the encumbrancer) against loss. The system breaks down utterly if he is left to bear the loss himself.'

1.13 Although Lord Denning MR did not refer to the case, both the other members of the Court of Appeal referred to *Hedley Byrne* in their judgments. It can be argued that *Sharp* went beyond *Hedley Byrne* since, unlike *Hedley Byrne*, the negligent statement was not made to the plaintiff. On the other hand, the conveyancing system is such that the defendant must have known that the negligently produced certificate would come into the hands of a purchaser of the property even though he did not know the identity of the particular purchaser.

1.14 The nature of the duty owed by local authorities has been considered by the courts in cases such as *Tidman v Reading Borough Council*,[5] a case in which the local authority was asked to give advice as to whether planning permission was required for a particular change of use, and *Welton v North Cornwall District Council*,[6] where a local authority environmental health officer had required the owners of a guest house to carry out works purportedly to comply with the Food Safety Act 1990. In *Welton*,

---

1   [1963] 2 All ER 575.
2   [1991] 1 AC 398.
3   [1978] AC 728.
4   [1970] 2 QB 223.
5   [1994] 3 PLR 72. See also para **9.55**.
6   [1997] 1 WLR 570. See also paras **9.12–9.14**.

Rose LJ considered whether the existence of statutory enforcement duties provided any ground for excluding a *Hedley Byrne* duty. He identified three categories of conduct to which the existence of the local authority's statutory enforcement duties might have given rise, as follows:

(1) conduct specifically directed to statutory enforcement such as the institution of proceedings before the magistrates or the service of an improvement notice. In the light of Lord Browne-Wilkinson's comments in *X (Minors) v Bedfordshire County Council*,[1] there will be no duty of care at common law if such a duty would be inconsistent with or have tendency to discourage due performance of the statutory duty;

(2) the offering of an advisory service. Insofar as this was part of the local authority's system for discharging its statutory duties, liability would be excluded so as not to impede performance of those duties, but an advisory service was capable of giving rise to a duty of care if it went beyond performance of statutory duty;

(3) conduct (which the judge clearly considered to exist in *Welton*) which went well beyond the powers provided by the legislation.

1.15 It is clear, however, that the Court of Appeal did not consider that the mere existence of statutory powers and duties could provide a reason for holding that no *Hedley Byrne* duty could arise. In the case of *Harris v Evans and Health and Safety Executive*[2] the Court of Appeal expressed some difficulty in understanding how it was possible to come to the conclusion that the plaintiff's claim in *Welton* based on the principles in *Hedley Byrne* was 'incontrovertible'. For more detailed analysis of these decisions see Chapter 9.

1.16 A further example of a situation where a *Hedley Byrne* duty has been held to exist is *T (A Minor) v Surrey County Council*,[3] a case in which a local authority social worker negligently informed a mother that there was no reason why her baby should not be placed with a child minder who had come under suspicion of physically abusing a baby previously placed in her care. Scott Baker J held that the local authority was liable for the injuries caused by the child minder to the baby since the circumstances placed the case entirely within the *Hedley Byrne* principle. It is arguable that the decision can be justified as falling within the category of 'assumption of responsibility' identified by Lord Goff.[4] This decision was reached before *X (Minors) v Bedfordshire County Council* was decided in the House of Lords. Whilst it is not easy to reconcile with *X (Minors)*, cases since then suggest that *T v Surrey County Council* might still be decided the same way.[5]

Novel duties of care

1.17 In the 1970s, starting probably with the *Dorset Yacht* case, the courts found themselves faced with novel situations to which it seemed that the principles laid down in *Donoghue v Stevenson* and *Hedley Byrne v Heller & Partners* did not apply.

---

1   [1995] 2 AC 633.
2   [1998] 1 WLR 1285 and see paras **9.15–9.20**.
3   [1994] 4 All ER 577.
4   See para **1.9**.
5   See Chapter 3.

In *Anns v Merton London Borough Council*,[1] the House of Lords had to decide whether a duty of care existed in the novel circumstances before it and the principles to be applied.

Lord Wilberforce established the following two-stage test:

> 'First one has to ask whether, as between the alleged wrongdoer and the person who has suffered damage there is sufficient relationship of proximity or neighbourhood such that, in the reasonable contemplation of the former, carelessness on his part may be likely to cause damage to the latter, in which case a prima facie duty of care arises.

> Secondly, if the first question is answered affirmatively, it is necessary to consider whether there are any considerations which ought to negative, or reduce or limit the scope of the duty or the class of person to whom it is owed or the damages to which a breach of it may give rise.'

1.18 The courts applied Lord Wilberforce's two-stage test, for a short but nevertheless expensive period for local authorities and other defendants. During this period the courts were ready to find that a duty of care existed in what hitherto had seemed unlikely circumstances. The high-water mark of this approach was the House of Lords' decision in *Junior Books Ltd v Veitchi Co Ltd*,[2] where a sub-contractor was found liable to the employer for laying flooring which was defective, but not dangerous. As will be seen below, this decision was a major extension of the principle in *Donoghue v Stevenson* under which liability can arise only where a latent defect in a building results in personal injury or damage to property and not where the owner of the building knows the full extent of the defect before any such damage is caused and incurs expenditure on its repair.

1.19 The move away from Lord Wilberforce's two-stage test began with the House of Lords' decision in *Peabody Donation Fund Governors v Sir Lindsay Parkinson & Co Ltd*,[3] where Lord Keith, referring to the *Dorset Yacht* case and more particularly to Lord Wilberforce's two-stage test, said as follows:

> 'There has been a tendency in some recent cases to treat these passages as being themselves of a definitive character. This is a temptation which should be resisted. The true question in each case is whether the particular Defendant owed to the particular Plaintiff a duty of care having the scope which is contended for, and whether he was in breach of that duty with consequent cost to the Plaintiff. A relationship of proximity in Lord Atkin's sense (*Donoghue v Stevenson*) must exist before any duty of care can arise, but the scope of the duty must depend on all the circumstances of the case.'

Incremental development of new duties of care

1.20 The move away from Lord Wilberforce's two-stage test was completed by the House of Lords' decision in *Murphy v Brentwood District Council*[4] when Lord Keith quoted with approval the view of Brennan J in the case of *Sutherland Shire Council v Heyman*[5] delivered in the High Court of Australia when he had said:

---

1 [1978] AC 728.
2 [1983] AC 520.
3 [1985] AC 210.
4 [1991] AC 398.
5 (1985) 60 ALR 1.

'It is preferable, in my view, that the law should develop novel categories of negligence incrementally and by analogy with established categories rather than by a massive extension of a prima facie duty of care restrained only by indefinable "considerations" which ought to negative or reduce or limit the scope of the duty or the class of person to whom it is owed.'

'The three-stage approach'

1.21 The culmination of the consideration by the House of Lords of the so-called 'three-stage' approach was *Caparo Industries Plc v Dickman*[1] when Lord Bridge summarised the position as follows:

'What emerges is that, in addition to the foreseeability of damage, necessary ingredients of any situation giving rise to a duty of care are that there should exist between the party owing the duty and the party to whom it is owed a relationship characterised by the law as one of "proximity" or "neighbourhood" and that the situation should be one in which the Court considers it fair, just and reasonable that the law should impose a duty of a given scope on the one party for the benefit of the other.'

1.22 The three elements required are therefore as follows:

(1) foreseeability of damage;
(2) a relationship of 'proximity' or 'neighbourhood' between the parties;
(3) that it is fair, just and reasonable that the law should impose a duty in the circumstances giving rise to the case.

1.23 The three-stage approach was followed by the House of Lords in *Marc Rich & Co AG v Bishop Rock Marine Co Ltd*,[2] where it was alleged that a ship surveyor, employed by the defendant, had acted negligently when recommending that a damaged ship should continue its voyage. The ship continued its voyage with loss of cargo belonging to the plaintiff. Their Lordships held that it was settled law that the elements of foreseeability and proximity as well as considerations of fairness, justice and reasonableness applied to cases of direct physical damage as well as indirect physical or economic loss. Accordingly, even assuming, without deciding the point, that there was sufficient proximity between the cargo owners and the surveyor, nevertheless it would not be fair, just and reasonable to impose a duty of care because of the result it would have on ship surveyors and international trade.

1.24 The existence of a duty of care cannot be established like the product of a mathematical equation. It must always be borne in mind that the law is not like mathematics. Ultimately, a judicial decision is required to decide whether a duty of care exists in a particular set of circumstances. An example is *Perrett v Collins*,[3] at first sight a case similar to *Marc Rich*. The defendant was a member of a flying club and constructed his own light aircraft. During the course of construction the aircraft was inspected to confirm that it was airworthy. The inspector was appointed by the flying club. The claimant was a passenger in the aircraft when it crashed. The Court of Appeal decided that the inspector and the flying club both owed a duty of care to the claimant. The claimant was, or ought to have been, in their contemplation, and their involvement gave them a measure of control over, and responsibility for, a dangerous

---

1   [1990] 2 AC 605.
2   [1995] 3 All ER 307.
3   [1998] 2 Lloyds Rep 255.

situation which was liable to injure the claimant. The difference between this case and *Marc Rich* was that it was an action for personal injury. Hobhouse LJ said:

> 'Once proximity is established by reference to the test which I have identified, none of the more sophisticated criteria which have to be used in relation to allegations of liability for mere economic loss need to be applied in relation to personal injury, nor have they been in the decided cases.'

Buxton LJ considered the question whether it was fair, just and reasonable to impose a duty of care and concluded that it was. The certification of airworthiness was intended to protect those who might be injured if an aircraft was certified as fit to fly when it was not. The fact that the flying club was not a commercial undertaking, and might have to pass on increased insurance costs to the detriment of small aircraft operators, was no reason to decide against imposing a duty of care.

1.25 *Perrett v Collins* was considered by the Court of Appeal in *Watson v British Boxing Board of Control*,[1] another case where the defendant was in an inspection or overseeing role. The claimant, a professional boxer, sustained a severe head injury while engaged in a fight which took place in accordance with the rules established by the defendant Board. There was a delay in providing medical attention which made the claimant's condition more serious than had he been treated immediately. The peculiar features of the case were, first that it was not concerned with a duty to avoid causing personal injury, but to ensure that personal injuries already sustained were properly treated, and secondly, that it was not the Board which administered treatment. Its role was to make regulations imposing on others the duty to provide proper facilities and administer proper treatment to those injured. Dealing with proximity, the Court of Appeal observed that the authorities appear to distinguish between cases where there can be said to have been an assumption of responsibility to an individual on the part of the defendant and those cases where the defendant has accepted the role (usually under statutory powers or duty) of protecting the community in general from foreseeable dangers. The latter category, such as *Capital and Counties Plc and Others v Hampshire County Council and Others*,[2] where a fire brigade was held to be under no common law duty to answer a call for help or, having done so, to exercise reasonable skill and care to extinguish the fire, tend to be cases where the court considers that there is insufficient proximity and therefore no duty of care owed. In the former category, for example, *Kent v Griffiths*,[3] where an ambulance service was held to owe a duty of care to respond within a reasonable time to a particular patient, there will be a duty of care. Lord Phillips MR summarised the position:

> '[The authorities] support the proposition that the act of undertaking to cater for the medical needs of a victim of illness or injury will generally carry with it a duty to exercise reasonable care in addressing those needs. While this may not be true of the volunteer who offers assistance at the scene of an accident, it will be true of a body whose purpose is or includes the provision of such assistance.'

It will be noted that this was a case where the court was considering a personal injury and the question of a duty owed to an individual rather than the community at large.

---

1   [2001] 2 WLR 1256.
2   [1997] 2 All ER 865 and see Chapter 10.
3   [2000] 2 WLR 1158 and see para **10.59**.

The Court of Appeal adopted a similar approach in *Sandhar and Another v Department of Transport, Environment and the Regions*[1] when deciding that case.

'Fair, just and reasonable' – 'public policy'

1.26 This is the third stage in deciding whether a duty of care exists, as set out in *Caparo Industries Plc v Dickman*.[2] The first two tests, namely foreseeability and proximity, depend upon the facts of a given case. The decision whether it is fair, just and reasonable to impose a duty of care in a given set of circumstances is one where the courts perform a policy-making role, although sometimes they decide that policy is a matter for Parliament. The courts in this country have been used to deciding policy issues, usually on the basis of submissions, and often on hearing defendants' applications to strike out claims as showing no cause of action, such applications being heard without evidence. *X (Minors)* and *Barrett*[3] were two such cases. The decision of the European Court of Human Rights in *Osman v United Kingdom*[4] has influenced the way in which the domestic courts approach policy arguments, although that case must now be considered in the light of the European Court's decision in *Z and Others v United Kingdom*[5] which will be considered below.

1.27 The traditional approach to policy questions is illustrated by cases such as *Hill v Chief Constable of West Yorkshire*[6] and *Capital and Counties Plc and Others v Hampshire County Council and Others*.[7] In *Hill* it was alleged that the police had been negligent by failing to apprehend Peter Sutcliffe, the 'Yorkshire Ripper', and that this had led to the death of his last victim. The House of Lords held that public policy required that the police should not be liable for failure to apprehend the perpetrator of crimes and so protect members of the public who might be his future victims. Lord Keith said:

> 'In some cases the imposition of liability may lead to the exercise of a function being carried on in a detrimentally defensive frame of mind.'

And later:

> 'A great deal of police time, trouble and expense might be expected to have to be put into the preparation of the defence to the action and the attendance of witnesses at the trial. The result would be a significant diversion of police manpower and attention from their most important function, that of the suppression of crime.'

In *Capital and Counties* the Court of Appeal had to consider the liability of the fire brigade arising out of its fire-fighting activities. The Court refused to grant immunity to the fire brigade on public policy grounds and, in so doing, disagreed with arguments that, inter alia, a finding of liability against the fire brigade would lead to defensive fire-fighting, would open the floodgates of litigation and would act as a distraction from fire-fighting.

---

1   [2004] EWCA Civ 1440, and see para 7.
2   [1990] 2 AC 605 and see para **1.21**.
3   *Barrett v Enfield London Borough Council* [1999] 2 FLR 426.
4   [1999] 1 FLR 193.
5   [2001] 2 FLR 612 and see para **1.31**.
6   [1989] AC 53 and see Chapter 10.
7   [1997] 2 All ER 865 and see Chapter 10.

1.28 The so-called 'floodgates' argument which failed in the *Capital and Counties* case had succeeded in the Court of Appeal in *Osman v Ferguson*.[1] This is significant because it was *Osman* which subsequently came before the European Court of Human Rights in *Osman v United Kingdom*.[2] In *Osman v Ferguson* it was alleged that the police had been negligent in failing to apprehend someone who was harassing the Osman family, committing acts of criminal damage and behaving in an unusual and irrational manner. Eventually the police decided to arrest the individual, however, before they could do so he killed a member of the Osman family and another person. Relying on the decision in *Hill* the Court of Appeal struck out the Osmans' claim. The European Court of Human Rights decided that there had been a breach of Art 6(1) of the European Convention on Human Rights which provides:

> 'In the determination of his civil rights and obligations . . . everyone is entitled to a fair and public hearing within a reasonable time by an independent and impartial tribunal established by law.'

The court considered that the conferring of what it described as a 'blanket immunity' on the police for their acts and omissions during the investigation and suppression of crime amounted to an unjustifiable restriction on the claimant's right to have a determination of his or her claim on the merits. Significantly, and this is relevant to the domestic courts' consideration of policy issues, the European Court, referring to policy considerations, said:

> 'It must be open to a domestic court to have regard to the presence of other public interest considerations which pull in the opposite direction to the application of the rule.'

1.29 The effect of the *Osman* decision has been a reluctance on the part of courts to strike out claims on the basis that the claimant has failed to show that his case discloses a duty of care owed by the defendant. An example is the approach of Lord Browne-Wilkinson in *Barrett v Enfield London Borough Council*[3] when he said:

> 'In view of the decision in the *Osman* case it is now difficult to foretell what would be the result in the present case if we were to uphold the striking out order. It seems to me that it is at least probable that the matter would then be taken to Strasbourg. That court, applying its decision in the *Osman* case if it considers it to be correct, would say that we had deprived the plaintiff of his right to have the balance struck between the hardship suffered by him and the damage to be done to the public interest in the present case if an order were to be made against the defendant council.'

It should be noted, however, that in *Jarvis v Hampshire County Council*[4] the Court of Appeal considered that a claim could still be struck out if it was clear and obvious that there was no real prospect of success. Further, in *Palmer v Tees Health Authority*,[5] the Court of Appeal struck out the claim on the basis that *Osman* and *Barrett* did not preclude a court from holding as a matter of law that there was no proximity established on the pleaded facts.

---

1   [1993] 4 All ER 344.
2   [1999] 1 FLR 193.
3   [1999] 2 FLR 426.
4   [2000] ELR 36.
5   [2000] PIQR 1.

1.30   The *Osman* decision has been criticised.[1] Nevertheless, as a result of the decision, it has been suggested that any argument to exclude liability for policy reasons will need to be established by evidence. For example, Lord Slynn in *Phelps v London Borough of Hillingdon*[2] said:

> 'I accept that, as was said in *X (Minors)*, there may be cases where to recognise such a vicarious liability on the part of the authority may so interfere with the performance of the local education authority's duties that it would be wrong to recognise any liability on the part of the authority. It must, however, be for the local authority to establish that: it is not to be presumed, and I anticipate that the circumstances where it could be established would be exceptional.'

The apparent effect of *Osman*, and the approach adopted by the House of Lords in *Barrett*, has been the suggestion that the courts will decide fewer cases on the basis of the existence, or otherwise, of a duty and will concentrate more on whether there has been a breach of duty. An example is *Larner v Solihull Metropolitan Borough Council*,[3] where the Court of Appeal, having noted that the House of Lords had been influenced by *Osman*, preferred to decide that there had been no breach of duty by the council rather than holding that s 39 of the Road Traffic Act 1988 did not give rise to a duty of care. *Larner* has now been disapproved by the House of Lords in *Gorringe v Calderdale Metropolitan Borough Council*.[4] Lord Hoffmann commented that, because the Court of Appeal had left open the possibility of claims under s 39 of the Road Traffic Act 1988, the highway authority in *Gorringe* had been obliged to provide a considerable amount of documentation and evidence, had had to go through a 6-day trial, and had been subjected to judicial criticism for its approach to the litigation. This would have been avoided had the Court of Appeal in *Larner* correctly decided that s 39 of the Road Traffic Act 1988 could not give rise to a common law duty of care.

1.31   The apparent reluctance to strike out claims for policy reasons must be reconsidered in the light of *Z and Others v United Kingdom*[5] where the European Court of Human Rights was considering the earlier House of Lords' decision in *X (Minors) v Bedfordshire County Council*. The case is considered in more detail in paras **2.23–2.33**. It is, however, important to note that the European Court, in the course of its judgment, said:

> 'The Court considers that its reasoning in the *Osman* judgment was based on an understanding of the law of negligence ... which has to be reviewed in the light of the clarifications subsequently made by the domestic courts and notably in the House of Lords.'

The Court referred to Article 6 of the European Convention on Human Rights and noted that this can be relied upon by anyone who considers that he has not had the possibility of submitting his claim to a 'fair and public hearing'. The Court noted that the House of Lords' decision in *X (Minors)* had ended the case without the factual matters being determined on evidence, but then said:

---

1   See, eg, Lord Hoffmann 'Human Rights and the House of Lords' (1999) 62 MLR 159.
2   [2000] 3 WLR 776.
3   [2001] LGR 255.
4   [2004] UKHL 15, [2004] 2 All ER 326.
5   [2001] 2 FLR 612.

'However, if as a matter of law, there was no basis for the claim, the hearing of evidence would have been an expensive and time-consuming process which would not have provided the Applicants with any remedy as its conclusion. There is no reason to consider the striking out procedure which rules on the existence of sustainable causes of action as per se offending the principle of access to court.'

It is therefore submitted that the reluctance of the domestic courts, following *Osman*, to strike out claims as disclosing no cause of action in negligence may disappear. Courts may, however, still allow claims to proceed under s 6 of the Human Rights Act 1998 (see Chapter 2).

1.32 Confirmation that courts no longer consider that the striking out procedure offends against Article 6 of the European Convention on Human Rights is to be found in *JD and Others v East Berkshire Community Health NHS Trust and Others*.[1] Claims for negligence arising out of the taking into care of children whose parents were accused of abuse had been struck out at first instance. The Court of Appeal was invited to decide that the claims should not have been struck out as this would violate Article 6. The Court of Appeal reviewed the decisions in *Osman* and *Z and Others* and decided that the result of the latter decision was that the striking out procedure does not violate Article 6. Lord Phillips MR, commenting on the three appeals under consideration, said:

'They do not concern an area where it is difficult to draw a line between procedural and substantive rules of law. They are concerned with the application of a fundamental principle of our common law of negligence. In performing their accepted function of tailoring the law of negligence to new factual situations, the courts will not recognise a duty of care unless it is "fair just and reasonable" that such a duty should exist – see *Caparo*. The procedure that has given rise to these appeals involves determining, by way of preliminary issues, whether the test of what is "fair just and reasonable" applied with respect for a case precedent which our law requires, precludes the existence of a duty of care, even if all the facts alleged by the claimants are established. Those preliminary issues have reached the Court of Appeal and may well reach the House of Lords. No violation of article 6 is involved in this procedure, as the Strasbourg court expressly recognised in *Z and Others v United Kingdom* and *TP and KM v United Kingdom*.'

Local authorities' 'liabilities' arising out of the performance of statutory duties

1.33 In applying the principle set out above to the cases involving local authorities, the courts have had to come to the terms with the fact that a local authority performs functions assigned to it by Parliament, either by way of the discharge of statutory duties, or the exercise of statutory powers. In the latter case, the authority has a discretion as to whether it should act. A clear example of this is to be found in *Anns v Merton London Borough Council*,[2] which concerned the liability of a local authority building inspector for negligence in carrying out inspections of foundation trenches dug before they were filled with concrete to form the foundations. It was clear that the local authority was not under a statutory duty to carry out any inspections. However, the court held that where it decided to exercise the statutory power to inspect

---

1   [2003] EWCA Civ 1151, [2004] QB 558.
2   [1978] AC 728.

foundation trenches, a local authority owed a duty to exercise reasonable care in so doing. As will be seen below, *Anns* has been overruled by the House of Lords who held that it had been wrongly decided although not specifically on this point.[1]

1.34   The liability of local authorities in the performance of their statutory functions has been the subject of considerable analysis by the courts in recent years and has been considered by the House of Lords in at least four major cases over the last 6 years, namely:

> *X (Minors) v Bedfordshire County Council*[2]
> *Stovin v Wise*[3]
> *Barrett v Enfield London Borough Council*[4]
> *Phelps v London Borough of Hillingdon*.[5]

The facts of each of the above cases will be considered in greater detail in later chapters.[6]

X (Minors) v Bedfordshire County Council

1.35   The House of Lords, in fact, heard five cases together. In the first two cases their Lordships were concerned with alleged negligence on the part of local authorities as a result of their failure to exercise powers under the Children and Young Persons Act 1969, the Child Care Act 1980 and the Children Act 1989. In the other three cases there were claims for breaches of duties arising under the Education Acts 1944 and 1981. It was alleged that the local authorities had failed to provide appropriate education for children with special needs.

1.36   In the leading speech, Lord Browne-Wilkinson set out general principles to determine the circumstances in which a common law duty of care would arise from the exercise of statutory powers or duties. He dealt with three circumstances as follows:

(i) Actions for breach of statutory duty simpliciter (ie irrespective of carelessness)

1.37   Lord Browne-Wilkinson considered that this did not give rise to any difficulty. The subsequent cases referred to in para **1.34** appear to confirm this. The courts are used to answering the question whether a breach of statutory duty gives rise to a private law cause of action. They do so by construction of the relevant statute and consideration whether, first, the statutory duty was imposed for the protection of a limited class of the public and, second, Parliament intended to confer on members of that class a private right of action for breach of duty, in which case a private law cause of action will arise. If the statute itself contains provisions for enforcement of the duty, this will normally indicate that no private law cause of action arises. Lord Browne-Wilkinson pointed out that in relation to the claims against the social services departments their Lordships had not been referred to any case:

---

1   *Murphy v Brentwood District Council* [1991] 1 AC 398 and see para **1.61**.
2   [1995] 3 All ER 353.
3   [1996] 3 All ER 801.
4   [1999] 2 FLR 426.
5   [2000] 3 WLR 776.
6   *X (Minors)* and *Barrett* in Chapter 3, *Phelps* in Chapter 4 and *Stovin* in Chapter 7.

'... where it had been held that statutory provisions establishing a regulatory system of general welfare for the public at large had been held to give rise to a private right of action.'

All the claims against the social services departments were struck out. Although the negligence claims against the education authorities were not struck out in their entirety (see Chapter 4), the claims for breach of statutory duty in these cases were.

(ii) The careless performance of a statutory duty in the absence of any other common law right

1.38   Lord Browne-Wilkinson considered that the simple assertion of the careless exercise of a statutory power or duty was not sufficient to establish a cause of action. To succeed, the claimant had to show that the circumstances were such as to raise a duty of care at common law. His Lordship commented that confusion had arisen from the speech of Lord Blackburn in *Geddis v Proprietors of Bann Reservoir*:[1]

> 'For I take it, without citing cases, that it is now thoroughly well established that no action will lie for doing that which the legislature has authorised, if it be done without negligence, although it does occasion damage to anyone; but an action does lie for doing that which the legislature has authorised, if it be done negligently.'

Lord Browne-Wilkinson explained *Geddis* as deciding that the careless exercise by the defendant of a statutory duty or power provides no defence to a claim by a claimant based on a free-standing common law cause of action, with which his Lordship then went on to deal.

(iii) A common law duty of care arising from the imposition or performance of statutory functions

1.39   Lord Browne-Wilkinson, in the first part of his analysis, drew a distinction between:

(a)   cases in which it is alleged that the authority owes a duty of care in the manner in which it exercises its statutory discretion; and

(b)   cases in which a duty of care is alleged to arise from the manner in which the duty has been performed or the power exercised in practice.

This distinction was also noted by Lord Slynn in *Barrett v Enfield London Borough Council*.[2]

1.40   Lord Browne-Wilkinson continued his analysis in *X (Minors)* by confirming that, both in principle and from decided cases, if the decisions of the local authority complained of fall within the ambit of a discretion given by Parliament as to the way in which a statutory function is to be performed those decisions cannot be actionable in common law. On the other hand, however, if the decision complained of is so unreasonable that it falls outside the ambit of discretion conferred upon the local authority there can be a duty. His Lordship referred to the decision in the *Dorset Yacht* case where Lord Reid had said:

---

1   (1878) 3 App Cas 430.
2   [1999] 2 FLR 426.

'But there must come a stage when the discretion is exercised so carelessly or unreasonably that there has been no real exercise of the discretion which Parliament has conferred. The person purporting to exercise his discretion has acted in abuse or excess of his power. Parliament cannot be supposed to have granted immunity to persons who do that.'

1.41   If a decision complained of falls outside the statutory discretion then it can (but not necessarily will) give rise to a common law liability. Lord Browne-Wilkinson went on to point out that if the factors relevant to the exercise of the discretion include matters of policy, the courts cannot adjudicate on such policy matters and therefore cannot reach the conclusion that the decision was outside the ambit of the statutory discretion. In *Barrett*, Lord Slynn agreed:

'On this basis, if an authority acts wholly within its discretion – i.e. it is doing what Parliament said it can do, even if it has to choose between several alternatives open to it, then there can be no liability in negligence'.

On the other hand, if the claimant alleges carelessness not in the taking of a discretionary decision to do some act, but in the practical manner in which that act is performed, the question whether a duty of care exists falls to be considered on the usual principles discussed in paras **1.21–1.25**.

1.42   In *X (Minors)*, Lord Browne-Wilkinson stated that the question whether there is a common law duty should be considered carefully by reference to the statutory framework within which the acts complained of were done. He put it as follows:

'... in my judgment, a common law duty of care cannot be imposed on a statutory duty if the observance of such common law duty of care would be inconsistent with, or have a tendency to discourage, the due performance by the local authority of its statutory duties.'

This was echoed by Lord Slynn in *Barrett* although he then went on to consider the courts' approach not only to the question of the existence of a duty of care, but also to the question of breach of any such duty of care:

'Both in deciding whether particular issues are justiciable and whether if a duty of care is owed, it has been broken, the Court must have regard to the statutory context and to the nature of the tasks involved. The mere fact that something has gone wrong or that a mistake has been made, or that someone has been inefficient does not mean that there was a duty to be careful or that such duty has been broken. Much of what has to be done in this area involves the balancing of delicate and difficult factors and Courts should not be too ready to find in these situations that there has been negligence by staff who are largely skilled and dedicated.'

It is clear that Lord Slynn took the view in *Barrett* that in deciding whether a local authority was in breach of any duty of care owed as a result of the exericse of a statutory function, its staff were entitled to rely on the principle stated in *Bolam v Friern Hospital Management Committee*.[1]

1.43   In summarising the approach to be adopted by the courts in deciding whether there is a duty of care on a local authority arising out of the imposition or performance of statutory functions, Lord Browne-Wilkinson, in *X (Minors)*, said that the questions to be answered were as follows:

---

1   [1957] 1 WLR 582, and see para **4.89**.

'(a) Is the negligence relied upon negligence in the exercise of a statutory discretion involving policy considerations: if so the claim will pro tanto fail as being non-justiciable;

(b) were the acts alleged to give rise to the cause of action within the ambit of discretion conferred on the local authority; if not,

(c) is it appropriate to impose on the local authority a common law duty of care?'

1.44 In *Barrett*, Lord Slynn considered whether an answer to the question of the existence of a duty of care was to be found in the distinction between 'policy' on the one hand and 'operational acts' on the other. He considered that while this distinction might be a guide, policy and operational acts are too closely linked to provide an absolute test. Referring to the tests as guides in deciding the question, Lord Slynn said:

'The greater the element of policy involved, the wider the area of discretion accorded, the more likely it is that the matter is not justiciable so that no action in negligence can be brought.'

1.45 Lord Slynn considered that it was not necessary, before a claim could be brought in negligence for an act done in pursuance of the exercise of a discretion, for it to be shown that the local authority behaved so unreasonably as to amount to an abuse of power. He summarised his view as follows:

'A claim of negligence in the taking of a decision to exercise a statutory discretion is likely to be barred, unless it is wholly unreasonable so as not to be a real exercise of the discretion, or if it involves the making of a policy decision involving the balancing of different public interests ...'

Significantly, on the facts of *Barrett* (which will be looked at in Chapter 3), Lord Slynn went on as follows:

'... acts done pursuant to the lawful exercise of the discretion can, however, in my view be subject to a duty of care, even if some element of discretion is involved.'

This was similar to Lord Browne-Wilkinson's view in *X (Minors)*.

1.46 Further clarification from the House of Lords is now to be found in *Gorringe v Calderdale Metropolitan Borough Council*.[1] Their Lordships decided that a highway authority owed no statutory or common law duty to a motorist when it had failed to paint warning signs on the highway in advance of a potentially dangerous stretch of road. Lord Hoffmann contrasted cases attempting to impose upon local authorities a common law duty to act based solely on the existence of a broad public law duty with cases in which public authorities have actually carried out activities or entered into relationships or undertaken responsibilities which give rise to a common law duty of care. In the second type of case:

'The fact that the public authority acted pursuant to a statutory power or public duty does not necessarily negative the existence of a duty.'

1.47 In *Barrett v Enfield London Borough Council*,[2] the plaintiff claimed that when he was taken into care, the council assumed parental responsibilities over him and so came under a duty of care in respect of the way he was treated. The House of Lords

---

1 [2004] UKHL 15, [2004] 2 All ER 326.
2 [1999] 3 WLR 79.

had refused to strike out that action. Commenting on the *Barrett* decision, Lord Hoffmann, in *Gorringe*, said:

> 'The plaintiff did not rely upon a common law duty of care generated by the existence of statutory powers. It is true that the council only assumed parental responsibility because of its statutory powers or duties, but the fact was that it did so. It was that which the plaintiff alleged gave rise to the duty. The statutory powers and duties might have provided the council with defences in respect of its specific acts or omissions, but that could not be decided without an investigation of the facts.'

1.48 Similarly, commenting on *Phelps v London Borough of Hillingdon*,[1] Lord Hoffmann said:

> 'The council relied on the fact that it had provided the psychologist pursuant to its public law duties which were not actionable in private law. But the House held that the duty of care did not depend upon the statute. It arose because the psychologist had impliedly undertaken to exercise proper professional skill in diagnosis, in the same way as a doctor provided by the National Health Service. The fact that the doctor/patient relationship was brought into being pursuant to public law duties was irrelevant except so far as the statute provided a defence. The House decided that no such defence had been established.'

Stovin v Wise[2]

1.49 It is relevant to consider *Stovin v Wise*, the facts of which are considered in more detail in Chapter 7. The claim against the highway authority arose out of an accident at a road junction, caused by a visibility problem, known to the highway authority, which could have been solved by the removal of part of a bank of earth on railway land adjacent to the road. The argument against the highway authority was that the accident would have been avoided had the highway authority required the removal of part of the bank. The existence of the statutory power was said to create a 'proximity' between the highway authority and the highway user which would not otherwise exist. By a majority of 3:2, the House of Lords decided in favour of the highway authority, and on the question of when a duty of care arises from the existence, but non-exercise, of a statutory power, Lord Hoffmann said:

> 'In summary therefore, I think that the minimum pre-conditions for basing a duty of care upon the existence of a statutory power, if it can be done at all, are first that it would in the circumstances have been irrational not to have exercised the power, so that there was in effect a public law duty to act, and secondly there are exceptional grounds for holding that the policy of the statute requires compensation to be paid to persons who suffer loss because their power was not exercised.'

1.50 Lord Hoffmann has now given further consideraton to the decision in *Stovin* in *Gorringe v Calderdale Metropolitan Borough Council*.[3] In *Stovin* the council had done nothing which, apart from statute, would have attracted a common law duty of care. The only basis on which the council could be liable was that Parliament had entrusted it with general responsibility for the highways and had given it the power to improve them and to take other measures for the safety of highway users. The relevant question was to ask whether, in conferring such powers, Parliament could be taken to have intended to create a common law duty of care:

---

1   [2000] 3 WLR 776.
2   [1996] AC 923, [1996] 3 WLR 388.
3   [2004] UKHL 15, [2004] 2 All ER 326.

'If the statute does not create a private right of action, it would be, to say the least, unusual if the mere existence of the statutory duty could generate a common law duty of care.'

This was why the majority of the House of Lords in *Stovin v Wise* had come to the conclusion that the council owed no duty to road users which could in any circumstances have required it to improve the intersection.

1.51 Lord Hoffmann was, however, concerned that a misunderstanding seemed to have arisen because their Lordships had gone on to discuss, in the alternative, the nature of any duty which might be said to exist. They had suggested that liability could arise if it was irrational, in a public law sense, not to exercise the statutory power to do the work. Commenting on this, Lord Hoffmann, in *Gorringe*, said:

'The suggestion that there might exceptionally be a case in which a breach of public law duty could found a private law right of action has proved controversial and it may have been ill-advised to speculate upon such matters.'

1.52 Lord Hoffmann considered that *Gorringe* should be decided on the principles set out in *Stovin*:

'My Lords, in this case the council is not alleged to have done anything to give rise to a duty of care. The complaint is that it did nothing. Section 39 is the sole ground upon which it is alleged to have had a common law duty to act. In my opinion the statute could not have created such a duty. The action must therefore fail.'

Economic loss

1.53 The courts have always been reluctant to award damages for what has been called 'pure economic loss' in cases of negligence arising out of the principle in *Donoghue v Stevenson*, although such losses are recoverable in cases arising under the principle of *Hedley Byrne v Heller & Partners*. The first question that arises is the meaning of 'pure economic loss'. In *Clerk and Lindsell on Torts*[1] the definition is expressed as follows:

'Pure economic loss refers to financial loss suffered by a claimant which is unconnected with, and does not flow from, damage to his own person or property.'

1.54 The case of *Spartan Steel & Alloys Ltd v Martin & Co (Contractors) Ltd*[2] was one in which the defendants cut through an electricity cable serving the plaintiffs' factory at which stainless steel alloys were manufactured, cutting off the electricity supply. As there was a danger that molten metal in the furnace might solidify and cause damage, the plaintiffs poured oxygen onto the molten metal and removed it from the furnace, thus reducing its value to the plaintiffs. If the supply of electricity had not been cut off, the plaintiffs would have made a profit on another four 'melts' which would have been put into the furnace before the electricity was reconnected.

1.55 The Court of Appeal held that the defendants were liable in respect of the physical damage to the 'melt' which was removed from the furnace, and the loss of profit on it because that loss was consequential on the physical damage. However, the defendants were not liable for the loss of profit on the other four 'melts' because no remedy was available in respect of economic loss unconnected with physical damage.

---

1   *Clerk and Lindsell on Torts* 18th edn (Sweet & Maxwell, 2000), para 7.84.
2   [1973] 1 QB 27.

1.56 Lord Denning MR noted that the courts had declined to allow recovery of economic loss in earlier cases, basing their decisions either on the defendant owing no duty or on the damage being too remote. He noted, however, that it was difficult to establish a precise test and was inclined to view the matter as one of policy as follows:

> 'At bottom, I think that the question of recovering economic loss is one of policy. Whenever the courts draw a line to mark out the bounds of duty, they do it as a matter of policy so as to limit the responsibility of the defendant. Whenever the courts set bounds to the damages recoverable – saying that they are, or are not, too remote – they do it as a matter of policy so as to limit the liability of the defendant.'

Lawton LJ also found it difficult to reconcile, on any logical basis, the various decisions relating to the recovery of damages for economic loss.

1.57 Economic loss has been considered more recently in the case of *London Waste Ltd v Amec Civil Engineering Ltd*.[1] Judge Hicks QC (sitting as an Official Referee) confirmed that where the defendant negligently damages property belonging to a third party (eg an electricity cable belonging to an electricity company) and the plaintiff suffers economic loss because of a dependence on that property or its owner, the general rule is that no duty is owed to the plaintiff in such a situation. Having decided that such a rule existed, the judge then followed cases such as *Spartan Steel & Alloys Ltd*, holding that the plaintiff was entitled to the cost of physical damage to plant, but not the costs of transport and disposal of excess waste or the loss of income from the plaintiff's electricity generating plant.

1.58 The question of economic loss also arose in the House of Lords' decision in *Murphy v Brentwood District Council*,[2] a case in which the House of Lords decided that the earlier cases of *Dutton v Bognor Regis Urban District Council*[3] and *Anns v Merton London Borough Council*[4] had been wrongly decided.

1.59 In *Dutton v Bognor Regis Urban District Council*, the Court of Appeal held that a local authority building control department, when considering drawings for approval under the bye-laws (subsequently the building regulations) and when carrying out inspections of the work on site, principally when inspecting trenches prior to the pouring of concrete for foundations, owed a duty to future owners and occupiers of the property to take reasonable care and that the negligent approval of foundations which resulted in a house being built and being put on the market with a hidden defect likely to cause injury to a future purchaser was a breach of that duty. This decision was upheld by the House of Lords in *Anns v Merton London Borough Council*.

1.60 Lord Denning MR justified his decision in *Dutton* by saying that otherwise:

> 'It would mean that, if the inspector negligently passes the house as properly built, and it collapses and injures a person, the Council are liable, but, if the owner discovers the defect in time to repair it – and he does repair it – the Council are not liable. This is an impossible distinction. They are liable in either case.'

---

1 (1997) 53 Con LR 66.
2 [1991] 1 AC 398.
3 [1982] 1 QB 373.
4 [1978] AC 728.

1.61 Lord Denning's 'impossible distinction' was nevertheless one which the law had recognised since *Donoghue v Stevenson*. It took almost 20 years until the decision in *Murphy v Brentwood District Council*[1] before the House of Lords showed that Lord Denning had been wrong to refer to his 'impossible distinction'. Lord Keith said:

> 'There can be no doubt that, whatever the rationale, a person who is injured through consuming or using a product the defective nature of which he is well aware, has no remedy against the manufacturer. In the case of a building, it is right to accept that a careless building is liable on the principle of *Donoghue v Stevenson* where a latent defect results in physical injury to anyone, whether owner, occupier, visitor or passer-by, or to the property of any such person. But that principle is not apt to bring home liability towards an occupier who knows the full extent of the defect yet continues to occupy the building.'

1.62 The *Murphy* decision, following the earlier decision in *D & F Estates Limited v Church Commissioners for England*,[2] decided that if the hidden defect in a building was discovered before any personal injury or damage to property other than the building itself occurred the loss was an economic loss which could not be recovered from the local authority. The decision left open the question whether or not liability would extend to physical damage to *other property* or to persons caused by the defective building. However, in *Tesco Stores Limited v Wards Construction (Investment) Ltd and Others*[3] the court struck out a claim against a local authority for the cost of fixtures, fittings and stock which had been damaged when a supermarket was damaged by a fire allegedly caused by a breach of the building regulations. The *Murphy* decision was also followed in *Bellefield Computer Services Limited and Others v E Turner & Sons Limited*[4] when Bell J held that an internal dividing wall, intended to be fire compartment wall, was an integral part of the whole structure of the building. A fire started and spread from one side of the internal wall to the other; however, the judge held that in the absence of a contractual or special relationship of proximity, the builder was not liable for the cost of repairs to and cleaning of the building, as well as loss of profit and increased costs of working caused by the fire damage to the building.

1.63 An attempt to distinguish *Murphy* was made in *Hamble Fisheries Limited v L Gardner & Sons Limited*.[5] The manufacturers of engines sold their entire business to the defendants. Subsequently the defendants began to receive reports that a fault was developing in the engines. About one year later a boat's engine failed, as a result of which the boat had to be towed to safety. The owners of the boat claimed the cost of repairs to the engine and loss of earnings from the defendants, arguing that they owed a duty to warn boat owners about the defective nature of the engines. They argued that in *Murphy* the House of Lords had recognised that a relationship 'akin to contract' could give rise to a duty of care not to cause economic loss. The Court of Appeal disagreed and Tuckey LJ said:

---

1   [1991] 1 AC 398.
2   [1988] 2 All ER 992.
3   (1996) 76 BLR 94.
4   [2000] BLR 97.
5   [1999] 2 Lloyd's Rep 1.

'My review of the authorities shows that the general rule is that a manufacturer in the position of the respondents owes no duty of care to avoid economic loss. Exceptionally he may be under such a duty if he assumes responsibility to his customers in a situation which is akin to contract. That duty may include a duty to warn, but it would be much more difficult to infer in the case of mere silence than in the case of misrepresentation. Reliance by the customer is relevant to whether there has been an assumption of responsibility and essential as to causation.'

Liability to owners of neighbouring properties for acts by third parties

1.64 In *Perl (P) (Exporters) Ltd v Camden London Borough Council*,[1] it was alleged that the London Borough of Camden had allowed its premises to remain empty and unsecured, as a result of which intruders gained access through the council's property and stole items from the neighbouring property owned by the plaintiffs. It was argued by the plaintiffs that the local authority should have foreseen that if it failed to secure its empty premises, thieves would be able to gain access to their property through the local authority's premises. The Court of Appeal held that the London Borough of Camden did not owe a duty of care in the absence of any special relationship of control existing between itself and the thieves.

1.65 The Court of Appeal considered the House of Lords' decision in *Home Office v Dorset Yacht Co Ltd*,[2] where the House of Lords had held the Home Office liable for the acts of third parties, namely the young borstal offenders who escaped and caused damage to yachts moored in a nearby harbour. The Court of Appeal considered that the *Dorset Yacht* decision had been based on the special relationship which existed between the prison officers, employed by the Home Office, and the young offenders. As Oliver LJ put it:

'What gave rise to the duty in the Dorset Yacht case was the special relationship which existed between the Defendants and the persons who inflicted the damage, in as much as the Defendants had both the statutory right and the statutory duty to exercise control over those persons.'

1.66 In *Lamb v Camden London Borough*,[3] the plaintiff's property had been damaged by escaping water from a water main in the road to the extent that the property had to be vacated. It was unoccupied for some months while arrangements were being made by the plaintiff for repairs to be carried out, and during this period squatters entered the plaintiff's property and did considerable damage. The local authority admitted liability in nuisance and the Court of Appeal had to consider whether the damage caused by the squatters was recoverable from the council. It held that the damage was too remote. Although Lord Denning MR expressed the view that it was a matter of policy, Oliver LJ considered that reasonable foreseeability was the appropriate test for remoteness of damage following the House of Lords' decision in *Dorset Yacht*. Somewhat graphically Oliver LJ expressed his views as follows:

'... the question is not what is foreseeable merely as a possibility, but what would the reasonable man actually foresee if he thought about it ...'

and later:

---

1   [1983] 3 All ER 161.
2   [1970] 2 All ER 294.
3   [1981] 2 All ER 408.

'I confess that I find it inconceivable that the reasonable man, wielding his pick in the road in 1973, could be said reasonably to foresee that puncturing the water main would fill the Plaintiff's house with uninvited guests in 1974 ...'

1.67 A contrary decision is that in *Ward v Cannock Chase District Council*.[1] The local authority owned the property next door to the plaintiff's house. Vandals entered the council's property, which had been left vacant, and caused damage which eventually resulted in the collapse of the rear wall of the council's property and damage to the roof of the plaintiff's house. The council agreed to carry out repairs to his house but failed to do so. As a result, the plaintiff obtained an injunction from the local county court requiring the council to carry out repairs to his house within 14 days. By this time the council had rehoused the plaintiff as a result of the condition of the property. Vandals broke into the plaintiff's house and removed parts of the building which deteriorated to the extent that the council served a dangerous structure notice and then demolished part of the house. At the same time, thieves removed various chattels from the house. The plaintiff claimed damages for the value of the stolen goods together with either diminution in value or the cost of repairs.

1.68 The council admitted negligence, but contested the action on the basis that the damage resulting from the acts of thieves and vandals was not recoverable as these were unforeseeable intervening acts of independent third parties for which the council could not be held liable. Scott J found in favour of the plaintiff on the basis that it was reasonably foreseeable that if the adjoining house were to collapse, serious damage might occur to the plaintiff's property and thieves might then break in. There was a chain of causation leading from the council's breach of duty to damage to the plaintiff's house: such damage was not too remote. On the other hand, the damage to and theft of the plaintiff's chattels was too remote because it was to be expected that the plaintiff would have taken steps to safeguard them. The theft was not a likely result of the council's breach of duty.

1.69 The judge considered the decisions in *Lamb v Camden London Borough* and *Perl (P) (Exporters) Ltd v Camden London Borough Council* and decided that the appropriate test was one of remoteness of damage. He considered that there was nothing in the *Lamb* case which obliged him to come to the same conclusion. Unlike the vandalism in the *Lamb* case which might have been foreseen as a possibility, the vandalism to the plaintiff's house should have been foreseen as 'highly likely'. It is perhaps significant to note that the judge was unimpressed by the actions of the Cannock Chase District Council which, he felt, were not in the same category as the negligent breaking of the water main in the *Lamb* case.

1.70 The House of Lords considered liability to owners of neighbour properties for acts by third parties in *Smith v Littlewoods Organisation Ltd*.[2] The defendant owned a cinema which had been left empty pending development. As a result of vandalism in the empty cinema there was a fire which damaged the plaintiff's property. Their Lordships considered that the liability of a property owner to his neighbours in the circumstances depends on the facts, but that it was rare that liability would arise. Lord Goff identified two circumstances in which liability might arise:

---

1   [1985] 3 All ER 537.
2   [1987] AC 241.

(a) where the defendant negligently causes, or permits to be created, a source of danger and it is reasonably foreseeable that third parties may interfere and cause damage to the plaintiff;

(b) where the defendant has knowledge or means of knowledge, that the third party has created or started a fire and the defendant fails to take steps to stop the fire damaging his neighbours' property.

On the facts in *Smith* Lord Goff decided that there was no liability on the defendant because the cinema was not an obvious fire risk and it had no knowledge of any previous vandalism. Lord Goff also considered that *Perl* had been rightly decided:

> 'I remain of the opinion that to impose a general duty on occupiers to take reasonable care to prevent others from entering their property would impose an unreasonable burden on ordinary households and an unreasonable curb upon the ordinary enjoyment of their property ...'

1.71 It should be noted that in *Clark Fixing Ltd and Another v Dudley Metropolitan Borough Council*,[1] the Court of Appeal expressly followed *Smith* when deciding, on the facts of the case, that the defendant's property, with its timber-constructed roof, was an obvious fire risk, that the defendant had known of previous fires, and accordingly that the defendant was liable for the damage caused to the claimants by a fire started by vandals.

NUISANCE

Nature of nuisance

1.72

> 'Nuisance is an act or omission which is an interference, disturbance or annoyance to, a person in the exercise or enjoyment of:
>
> a)   a right belonging to him as a member of the public, when it is a public nuisance or
> b)   his ownership or occupation of land or of some easement, profit or other right used or enjoyed in connection with land, when it is a private nuisance.'[2]

1.73 In *Hunter and Others v Canary Wharf Ltd*,[3] various persons living near the Canary Wharf Tower in Docklands alleged nuisance against London Docklands Development Corporation arising out of interference with television reception and dust and noise during construction. Lord Lloyd categorised private nuisance as follows:

> 'Private nuisances are of three kinds. They are:
>
> i)   nuisance by encroachment on a neighbour's land;
> ii)   nuisance by direct physical injury to a neighbour's land;
> iii)   nuisance by interference with neighbour's quiet enjoyment of his land.'

1.74 Nuisance under category (iii) above was considered by the Court of Appeal in *Lippiatt and Another v South Gloucester County Council*[4] where the claimants

---

1   (Unreported) 12 December 2001.
2   *Clerk and Lindsell on Torts* 18th edn (Sweet & Maxwell, 2000), para 19.01.
3   [1997] 2 All ER 426.
4   [2000] QB 51.

complained about the activities of travellers who were being allowed to occupy land owned by the council. They were not the council's tenants and the court considered that they were trespassers or, possibly, licensees of the council. The activities complained of took place off the council's land and generally on the claimants' land. The Court of Appeal had to consider whether the activities amounted to a private nuisance as a matter of law. In deciding in favour of the claimants, the Court of Appeal drew support from what Lord Goff had said in *Hunter*:

> 'Indeed, for an action in private nuisance to lie in respect of interference with the plaintiff's enjoyment of his land, it will generally arise from something emanating from the defendant's land. Such an emanation may take many forms – noise, dirt, fumes, obnoxious smell, vibration and such like. Occasionally activities on the defendant's land are in themselves so offensive to neighbours as to constitute an actionable nuisance, as in *Thompson-Schwab v Costaki*[1] where the sight of prostitutes and their clients entering and leaving neighbouring premises was held to fall in that category. Such cases must however be relatively rare.'

Applying the above to the facts in *Lippiatt*, Evans LJ said:

> 'The principle, as stated by Lord Goff ... is that as a general rule some form of "emanation" from the defendant's land is required. On analysis, what "emanated" in the present case was the travellers themselves. I do not find this form of emanation difficult to accept. If it was somehow excluded from the definition of a nuisance, then any number of examples come to mind where the distinction would be artificial in the extreme. Keeping fierce dogs and allowing them to roam would be a nuisance; taking them onto a neighbour's land and releasing them there would not.'

1.75 In *Arscott and Others v The Coal Authority and Another*,[2] a case concerned with flooding allegedly caused by works carried out by the defendant, Tuckey LJ noted three overlapping themes running through cases on nuisance, namely:

(a) the notion of a *natural* use of land;
(b) the notion of a *reasonable* use of land;
(c) the requirement of reasonable foreseeability of damage.

Referring to the cases on nuisance, Tuckey LJ identified:

> 'A bias in favour of natural user, subject to its being no more than reasonably enjoyed; a bias (effectively a conclusive rule) against non-natural user where that involved the escape of something noxious onto a neighbour's land; a bias against the harbouring of a danger, a hazard, on one's own and where the hazard is natural or man-made. And in no case will there be liability without reasonable foreseeability of damage.'

1.76 In *Hunter*, the House of Lords made it clear that private nuisance is an action in respect of damage to the land itself and that the measure of damages, at least as a starting point, will be the diminution in the value of the land. It was argued in *Hunter* that in the case of nuisance in the third category, the right to bring an action was not confined to those with a proprietary interest but extended to everyone who occupied the property as their home, which could include a lodger or an au pair. Their Lordships concluded that each member of family did not have a separate cause of action and that there was no more than one potential cause of action for each home involved.

---

1   [1956] 1 WLR 335.
2   [2004] EWCA Civ 892, (unreported) 13 July 2004 and see para **8.12**.

1.77 In *Hunter* the House of Lords also discussed damages and made it clear that, even in circumstances where there might be no diminution in value (eg in a case involving the effect of smoke from a neighbouring factory), there would be a loss of amenity value as long as the nuisance lasted; but that loss of amenity value was the same whether the land was occupied by one person or four.

Reasonableness and foreseeability as elements in nuisance

1.78 In cases involving nuisance brought about by things naturally on the land following *Davey v Harrow Corporation,*[1] it appeared to be the law that foreseeability was not a necessary ingredient. In that case, which involved damage to a neighbour's house caused by the encroachment of tree roots, the Court of Appeal held:

> 'In our opinion it must be taken to be established law that, if trees encroach whether by branches or roots and cause damage, an action for nuisance will lie.'

1.79 The question of the scope of the duty in nuisance caused by things naturally on the land was next considered by the Court of Appeal in the case of *Leakey and Others v National Trust for Places of Historical Interest or Natural Beauty.*[2] This case concerned damage caused by the movement of a mound of earth from the defendants' land onto the plaintiffs' land. The defendants had done nothing to prevent the damage occurring, apparently in the belief that they owed no duty at law so to do. The Court of Appeal explained the duty as follows:

> 'The duty is a duty to do that which is reasonable in all the circumstances ... to prevent or minimise the known risk of damage or injury to one's neighbour or to his property ... there will fall to be considered the extent of the risk. What, so far as reasonably can be foreseen, are the chances that anything untoward will happen or that any damage will be caused? What is to be foreseen as to the possible extent of the damage if the risk becomes a reality?'

1.80 A similar situation arose in *Holbeck Hall Hotel Limited and Another v Scarborough Borough Council.*[3] As a result of a massive land slip the lawn and part of the claimant's hotel collapsed. The council owned land forming the undercliff below the hotel. The coast in the area was subject to marine erosion and the council knew that if appropriate remedial action was not taken the land slip would be likely to progress and at some indeterminate future time affect the claimant's land. What it could not foresee, however, was that the hazard was of such a magnitude that it would be likely to involve a large part of the grounds and the hotel itself. Relying on *Leakey,* the Court of Appeal rejected the council's submission that there was no duty to take positive steps to provide support for a neighbour's land. It was, however, clear that the council did not foresee a danger of anything like the magnitude that eventuated and it could not have appreciated the risk without further geological investigation by experts. In a case of non-feasance, where the defendant had done nothing to create the danger which had arisen by the operation of nature, the duty was a measured duty depending on factors including the ease and expense of abatement, the ability of the defendant to achieve it and the extent of the foreseen damage. Justice did not require that a defendant should be held liable for damage which, albeit of the same type, was

---

1   [1957] 2 All ER 305.
2   [1980] 1 QB 485.
3   [2000] QB 836.

vastly more extensive than that which was foreseen or could have been foreseen without extensive further geological investigation.

1.81 Although the position following *Leakey* might appear to be clear, it was still thought that liability for nuisance caused by the encroachment of tree roots, as laid down in *Davey v Harrow Corporation*,[1] did not require proof of foreseeability. The Court of Appeal in *Solloway v Hampshire County Council*[2] clarified the law by following the *Leakey* decision (see further Chapter 11). Foreseeability is an element which a plaintiff must establish in cases of nuisance involving damage caused by the encroachment of tree roots.

1.82 Reliance was placed on *Leakey* and the principle in *Holbeck Hall Hotel Limited* to support the claim in *Marcic v Thames Water Utilities Limited*.[3] The claimant's property suffered flooding resulting from the inability of public sewers to effectively drain the local area. The Court of Appeal held that Thames Water knew or should have known of the problem and that following the decision in *Leakey*, it should have taken such steps as were reasonable to prevent the discharge of surface and foul water on to the claimant's property. The House of Lords disagreed. The sewers were subject to an elaborate statutory scheme which was regulated by the Director General of Water Services. It was clear that the Water Industry Act 1991 did not enable individual householders to launch proceedings in respect of a failure to build sufficient sewers. To allow a claim in nuisance would be inconsistent with the statutory scheme.

1.82 The duty to do what is reasonable in the circumstances, expressed in *Leakey*, was followed in *Bybrook Barn Centre Ltd and Others v Kent County Council*.[4] A culvert built by the defendant many years previously had become inadequate because of the increased flow of water from upstream. This caused the claimants' property to flood. The Court of Appeal accepted that there was no nuisance, and indeed no foreseeable nuisance, when the culvert was built. The important question was whether the defendant could be said to owe a duty once it had become aware that flooding was occurring. The Court of Appeal traced the law through *Sedleigh-Denfield v O'Callaghan and Others*[5] and *Leakey*. They decided that a duty existed in such circumstances placing on the defendant:

'... a high obligation to see that the natural stream can continue to flow under the highway.'

The Court of Appeal said that the duty on the defendant was to do what was reasonable to avert the flooding, the question of reasonableness including the likely expenditure and the defendant's ability to raise the money. Because the court considered that Kent County Council would be able to pay the amount involved, the council was held to be liable.

---

1   [1957] 2 All ER 305.
2   (1981) 79 LGR 449.
3   [2003] 3 WLR 1603.
4   [2001] LGR 239.
5   [1940] 3 All ER 349 and see para **1.75**.

Trees falling on the highway

1.84 It is apparent that foreseeability and knowledge are essential components to establishing a cause of action where a tree falls on the highway causing damage or injury. In *Caminer v Northern and London Investment Trust*,[1] the defendant landowner was found not liable when his tree on land adjacent to a highway fell causing injury in circumstances where it had previously appeared sound and healthy. The plaintiff had not been able to prove that an inspection of the tree by an expert would have revealed that it was diseased and liable to fall: accordingly the necessary elements of foreseeability and knowledge were not present.[2]

Liability for nuisance caused by others

1.85 Where a person himself causes or creates a nuisance, liability will follow; but there are occasions where a nuisance occurs on the defendant's land which he did not cause or create.

1.86 In *Sedleigh-Denfield v O'Callaghan and Others*,[3] a ditch running through the defendant's land was culverted by the local authority without any permission being sought from the defendants and without their knowledge. No proper guard was put at the entrance to the culvert. Three years later the culvert became blocked, and the plaintiff's land was flooded. The defendants were found liable. Although they had no knowledge of the culvert, the person who cleaned the ditch twice a year on their behalf did and, therefore, the defendants had means of knowing about the culvert and the lack of an adequate guard. The House of Lords considered that the defendants had adopted the nuisance brought about by the culverting of the ditch. Lord Wright expressed the position as follows:

> 'The liability for a nuisance is not, at least in modern law, a strict or absolute liability. If the Defendant, by himself, or those for whom he is responsible, has created what constitutes a nuisance, and if it causes damage, the difficulty now being considered does not arise; but he may have taken over the nuisance, ready made as it were, when he acquired the property, or the nuisance may be due to a latent defect or to the act of a trespasser or stranger. Then he is not liable unless he continued or adopted the nuisance, or, more accurately, did not without undue delay remedy it when he became aware of it, or with ordinary, reasonable care should have become aware of it.'

The purchaser of a property

1.87 As the House of Lords set out in *Sedleigh-Denfield*, a purchaser of property on which a nuisance already exists will be liable for continuing or adopting the nuisance when he becomes aware of it or should with ordinary and reasonable care have become aware of it.

---

1   [1951] AC 88.
2   See also *Chapman v London Borough of Barking and Dagenham* [1998] CLY 4053, where the Court of Appeal confirmed the judge's decision against a highway authority in similar circumstances. See para **11.59**.
3   [1940] 3 All ER 349.

Independent contractor

1.88 Liability for a nuisance caused by an independent contractor will depend upon whether a person could or should reasonably have foreseen that a nuisance was likely to result from the operation which he asked the independent contractor to carry out on his behalf. This will, for example, arise in circumstances where a local authority appoints a contractor to carry out works of demolition or repair to a property which causes vibration damage to the claimant's property or creates noise.

Withdrawal of support

1.89 The owner of land has a right of support for his land in its natural state from his neighbour's land. On the other hand, there is no natural right of support for buildings. If, however, a neighbour has an easement of support for his building from the adjoining building, his neighbour must not pull down his building so as to remove the support from the neighbouring building.[1] It is submitted that this would normally be the case where there is a terrace of houses or where there are semi-detached buildings.

1.90 Similarly, where there is an easement of support, a building owner may be guilty of nuisance if he allows his property to fall into disrepair. In *Bradburn v Lindsay*,[2] the defendant allowed her property, which was one of two semi-detached houses, to fall into disrepair. The plaintiffs complained that the dry rot from which the defendant's property was suffering might come through the party wall. The defendant took no steps to repair her house which was eventually demolished by the local authority as a dangerous structure. The judge decided in favour of the plaintiffs on the basis that the defendant should reasonably have appreciated the dangers to the plaintiffs' property from the dry rot and from the lack of repair and that there were steps which could reasonably have been taken to prevent the damage occurring. Because the defendant had failed to take any reasonable steps, she was liable for the damage caused. The judge relied on the decision in *Leakey v National Trust for Places of Historical Interest or Natural Beauty*,[3] referred to above, and it would therefore appear that liability in nuisance can arise from the neglect of a building by the owner which causes damage to his neighbour's building rather than the previous understanding of the law that there had to be a positive act by the defendant withdrawing support from his neighbour's building.

1.91 In *Phipps v Pears*,[4] Lord Denning MR held that if, by pulling down one's house, this exposed the neighbouring house to the weather, there would be no liability. *Phipps* was a case where the two houses involved, although very close together, were separated by a small gap. The case decided that there is no easement requiring a neighbour to provide weather-proofing of an exposed wall when demolishing the neighbouring property. It should be noted that *Phipps* was distinguished by the Court of Appeal in *Rees and Another v Skerrett and Another*.[5] The defendant had demolished his house which shared a party wall with the claimants' house. The exposed wall suffered cracking and there was damp penetration. Because of the

---

1   *Dalton v Angus* (1981) 6 App Cas 740.
2   [1983] 2 All ER 408.
3   [1980] 1 All ER 17.
4   [1965] 1 QB 76.
5   [2001] 1 WLR 1541.

decision in *Phipps*, the claimants had to show that the defendant owed a common-law duty to weather-proof the exposed party wall on the basis that he knew, or ought to have known, of the risk of damage likely to result from the demolition works, if not accompanied by weather-proofing. The claimants also had to show that the damage suffered would have been prevented by work which, in all the circumstances, was reasonable. In *Phipps*, there had been no question of interference with support. Distinguishing that decision, the Court of Appeal held that in the light of *Leakey*, and *Holbeck Hall Hotel Ltd and Another v Scarborough Borough Council*,[1] it was appropriate to hold that a common-law duty of care to weather-proof the exposed wall existed in circumstances of the *Rees* case.[2]

Defences – coming to the nuisance and inevitable accident

1.92 It is no defence that the claimant came to the nuisance. Where the claimant builds an extension to his house near a tree, the defendant will still be liable if roots from that tree encroach and cause damage.

1.93 Something which cannot be prevented by the exercise of reasonable care can only be raised in a defence in a case of nuisance where liability in nuisance depends upon negligence. On rare occasions, it may be possible to plead act of God.

Statutory authority

1.94 If nuisance results from the performance of a statutory duty, there is no liability without negligence. If the nuisance arises from the performance of a statutory power then it is necessary to consider the terms of the statute conferring that power. The general law on this subject was summarised by Webster J in *Department of Transport v North West Water*:[3]

'1. In the absence of negligence, a body is not liable for a nuisance which is attributable to the exercise by it of a duty imposed on it by statute;

2. it is not liable in those circumstances even if by statute it is expressly made liable, or not exempted from liability, for nuisance;

3. in the absence of negligence, a body is not liable for a nuisance which is attributable to the exercise by it of a power conferred by statute if, by statute, it is neither expressly made liable, nor expressly exempted from liability, for nuisance;

4. a body is liable for a nuisance by it attributable to the exercise of a power conferred by statute even without negligence, if by statute it is expressly either made liable, or not exempted from liability for nuisance.'

Webster J's summary was approved by the House of Lords,[4] although they overruled Webster J on his interpretation of the particular statute involved.

---

1   [2000] QB 836.
2   Note that now s 2(2)(n) of the Party Wall etc Act 1996 requires a neighbour to weather-proof an exposed party wall when demolishing his own property. The facts in *Rees* pre-dated this Act.
3   [1983] 1 All ER 892.
4   [1983] 3 All ER 273.

The rule in *Rylands v Fletcher*[1]

1.95 This rule of law is often considered to stand on its own but is probably part of the law of nuisance. Water in a reservoir on the defendant's land flooded the plaintiff's mine through underground passages, the existence of which was not known to either party. The defendant was found liable. The rule was expressed by Blackburn J as follows:

> 'We think that the true rule of law is, that the person who for his own purposes brings on his land, and collects and keeps there anything likely to do mischief if it escapes must keep it in at his peril, and, if he does not do so, is prima facie answerable for all the damage which is the natural consequence of its escape.'

1.96 In the House of Lords, Lord Cairns agreed, but restricted the rule to circumstances in which the defendant has made a 'non-natural use' of the land.

1.97 For more than 100 years the rule has been interpreted as one of 'strict liability', without the need to show foreseeability. However, in the case of *Cambridge Water Co Ltd v Eastern Counties Leather Plc*,[2] the House of Lords confirmed that foreseeability was an essential element. Lord Goff said:

> '... it appears to me to be appropriate now to take the view that foreseeability of damage of the relevant type should be regarded as a prerequisite of liability in damages under the rule. Such a conclusion can, as I have already stated, be derived from Blackburn J's original statement of the law; but I can see no good reason why this prerequisite should not be recognised under the rule as it has been in the case of private nuisance ... it would moreover lead to a more coherent body of common law principles if the rule were to be regarded essentially as an extension of the law of nuisance to cases of isolated escapes from land, even though the rule as established is not limited to escapes which are in fact isolated.'

1.98 It seems clear that Lord Goff regarded the rule in *Rylands v Fletcher* as part of the law of nuisance and not a separate rule of law.

1.99 Until the decision in *Cambridge Water Company v Eastern Counties Leather Plc*, the courts had sought to restrict the rule by giving a narrow interpretation of what amounted to a 'non-natural use of land'. Indeed, Ian Kennedy J, at first instance, had found in favour of the defendants on the basis that the storage of substantial quantities of chemicals on industrial premises was not a non-natural use of land. In the House of Lords, Lord Goff was prepared to find that it was a non-natural use of land:

> 'Indeed I feel bound to say that the storage of substantial quantities of chemicals on industrial premises should be regarded as an almost classic case of non-natural use.'

1.100 Lord Goff felt that if strict liability was appropriate, this should be imposed by Parliament which could establish the scope of the liability identifying particular activities and laying down other criteria.

1.101 The continuing application of the rule in *Rylands v Fletcher* has been confirmed by the House of Lords in *Transco Plc v Stockport Metropolitan Borough Council*,[3] a case concerned with damage to the claimant's property caused by water

---

1   (1866) LR 1 Ex 265, affirmed in the House of Lords: (1886) LR 3 HL 330.
2   [1994] 2 AC 264; see also Chapter 7.
3   [2003] UKHL 61, [2003] 3 WLR 1467.

leaking from a water pipe owned by the defendant. The House of Lords confirmed that the rule in *Rylands v Fletcher* still survived in English law in spite of the fact that:

(a)   the rule in *Rylands v Fletcher* does not apply in Scotland;
(b)   the High Court of Australia has decided that *Rylands v Fletcher* should be absorbed by the principles of ordinary negligence, thus requiring fault;
(c)   Lord Goff, in *Cambridge Water Company*, considered that matters of strict liability should be imposed by Parliament.

MISFEASANCE IN PUBLIC OFFICE

1.102   This is a separate tort which can be committed by local authorities and their officers. It was briefly defined by Lord Browne-Wilkinson in *X (Minors) v Bedfordshire County Council*:[1]

'... misfeasance in public office ie the failure to exercise, or the exercise of, statutory powers either with the intention to injure the Plaintiff or in the knowledge that the conduct was unlawful.'

1.103   The tort of misfeasance in public office has been considered in detail by the House of Lords in *Three Rivers District Council and Others v Bank of England (No 3)*.[2] Lord Steyn set out certain requirements in his judgment as follows.

(1)   The defendant must be a public officer. A local authority can be sued.
(2)   The defendant must be exercising power as a public officer.
(3)   When dealing with the state of mind of the defendant, two types of conduct may give rise to misfeasance in public office as follows:
      (a)   targeted malice, namely conduct which is specifically intended to injure a person or persons. This involves bad faith in the sense of the exercise of public power for an improper or ulterior motive;
      (b)   the officer acts knowing that he has no power to do the act complained of and that it will probably injure the claimant. This involves bad faith in as much as the public officer does not have an honest belief that his act is lawful.

1.104   The Court of Appeal in *Cornelius v London Borough of Hackney*[3] has confirmed that the chief executive of a council and councillors are in a position of public office and abuse by them of this office could give rise to a claim for misfeasance for which the council could be vicariously liable.

1.105   There was argument before the House of Lords that recklessness on the part of the defendant was not enough to establish misfeasance in public office; however, their Lordships disagreed. Lord Steyn, dealing with para (3)(b) above, said:

'It can therefore now be regarded as settled law that an act performed in reckless indifference as to the outcome is sufficient to ground the tort in its second form.'

Lord Steyn then went on to confirm that the test of recklessness was subjective:

---

1   [1995] 3 All ER 353.
2   [2000] 2 WLR 1220.
3   [2002] EWCA Civ 1073, [2003] LGR 178.

'The plaintiff must prove that the public officer acted with a state of mind of reckless indifference to the illegality of his act.'

1.106 The *Three Rivers District Council* case was concerned with the liability, if any, of a bank to its depositors. The House of Lords therefore had to consider how far a claimant has to go in establishing proximity. They decided that bank depositors can sue even if their precise identities are not known to the bank. Lord Steyn continued:

'What can be said is that, of course, any plaintiff must have sufficient interest to found a legal standing to sue. Subject to this qualification, principle does not require introduction of proximity as a controlling mechanism in this corner of the law. The state of mind required to establish the tort, as already explained, as well as the special rule of remoteness hereafter discussed, keeps the tort well within reasonable bounds.'

1.107 Lord Steyn then went on to consider the question of remoteness. It was argued that a claimant should be entitled to recover all foreseeable loss on ordinary principles; however, Lord Steyn referred to the special nature of this tort and the strict requirements governing it. He continued as follows:

'This results in the rule that a plaintiff must establish not only that the defendant acted in the knowledge that the act was beyond his powers, but also in the knowledge that his act would probably injure the plaintiff or persons of a class of which the plaintiff was a member.'

In deciding against allowing the claimant to recover all foreseeable loss, Lord Steyn pointed out that recklessness was enough to establish the tort.[1]

1.108 The decision on proximity in the *Three Rivers District Council* case was considered by the Court of Appeal in *Akenzua and Another v Secretary of State for the Home Department and Another*.[2] The result of the alleged misfeasance was the murder of an individual whose personal representatives brought an action against the Home Office for misfeasance in having previously released the murderer from custody. The defendants argued that misfeasance is a tort of intention and that even where the case is not one of targeted malice the tortfeasor must still have intended harm to his victim. The Court of Appeal rejected this argument. Where the consequence of misfeasance in public office is alleged to have been personal injury or death, Sedley LJ said:

'What matters is not the predictability of his killing the deceased, but the predictability of killing someone. That is my understanding of the effect of the reasoning in *Three Rivers* ... [the murderer's] single known victim stands in the same situation as each of those claimants who, at the time of the alleged misfeasance in *Three Rivers* were only potential depositors (that is to say, she too was a potential victim).'

1.109 In *W v Essex County Council and Another*,[3] the Court of Appeal unanimously rejected a claim of misfeasance in public office. Stuart-Smith LJ said:[4]

'The tort ... can be committed in one of two ways, namely where a public officer has either:

---

1   In *Kuddus v Chief Constable of Leicestershire Constabulary* [2001] UKHL 29, [2001] 2 WLR 1789, the House of Lords refused to rule out a claim for exemplary damages in a claim for misfeasance in public office.
2   [2002] EWCA Civ 1470, (2002) 99(47) LSG 29.
3   [1998] 3 WLR 534.
4   Ibid at 551F.

(a)   performed or omitted to perform an act with the object of injuring the plaintiff (ie targeted malice) or

(b)   where he has performed an act which he knew he had no power to perform and which he knew would injure the plaintiff . . .

Both limbs require an invalid, unauthorised or unlawful act . . .'

1.110   Successful cases of misfeasance in public office are comparatively rare, no doubt because it is necessary to plead and prove 'a deliberate and dishonest wrongful abuse of the powers given to a public office' as set out in the *Three Rivers District Council* case.[1]

1   A claim for misfeasance in public office also failed before the Court of Appeal in *Lam v The Borough of Torbay* [1997] PIQR 488, a case where claims against environmental health officers and planning officers failed.

Chapter 2

THE HUMAN RIGHTS ACT 1998

INTRODUCTION

2.1   The Human Rights Act 1998 came into force on 2 October 2000. The Act incorporates the European Convention on Human Rights (ECHR) into UK law. The direct impact upon public authorities can therefore be summarised as follows.

(1)   The courts are obliged to take into account the ECHR in every case. This means that the courts will have to grapple with potential conflicts between the Convention and existing UK law.
(2)   It is unlawful for a public authority to act in a way which is incompatible with the ECHR (Human Rights Act 1998, s 6).

2.2   Section 6 applies to public bodies only. The implications are immediate and obvious. By way of example, it will be open to a member of the public to argue that his child has a right to education (Article 2 of the First Protocol). How far does this right extend? Does it extend to a right to 'good' education? Who sets the standards? What are the implications for the potential liability of a local authority for failing to provide adequate education?

2.3   This chapter focuses upon those areas where the liabilities of local authorities may be affected by the obligations imposed on them by the Human Rights Act 1998 (in this chapter, the Act). It is probable that the true impact of the Act will only become clear after a period of time when the courts in the UK, particularly the appellate courts, have had the opportunity of interpreting the provisions in the Act.

EUROPEAN CONVENTION ON HUMAN RIGHTS

2.4   The ECHR is concerned with preserving civil/political rights, securing:

'... to everyone within their jurisdiction the rights and freedoms defined in Section I of this Convention'.[1]

It is important to bear in mind that the ECHR is generally concerned with negative rights (not being tortured, not being detained without trial, etc) rather than positive rights (the right to social security payments, health service, housing, etc).[2] The rights are therefore defined in broad terms. The significance is that the rights can be interpreted by a court in any country either broadly or narrowly. The interpretation will in turn determine the potential impact.

---

1   ECHR, Art 1.
2   See L Clements 'The Human Rights Bill' [1998] JLGL Issue 1.

2.5   The rights which are incorporated by the Act are enshrined in 13 articles of the Primary Convention, and three additional articles in the First and Sixth Protocols. They can be summarised as follows:

(1)   *Convention Rights*

Article 2	The right to life
Article 3	Prohibition of torture, inhuman or degrading treatment or punishment
Article 4	Prohibition of slavery and forced labour
Article 5	The right to liberty and security of person
Article 6	The right to a fair and public hearing
Article 7	Applicability of the criminal law which is in application at the time of the events complained of
Article 8	The right to respect for private and family life
Article 9	Freedom of thought, conscience and religion
Article 10	Freedom of expression
Article 11	Freedom of peaceful assembly and association with others
Article 12	The right to marry and found a family
Article 14	The right not to be discriminated against on grounds of sex, race, colour, language, religion, political or other opinion

(2)   *The First Protocol*

Article 1	The right to every natural and legal person to the enjoyment of his possessions
Article 2	The right to education
Article 3	The right to free and fair elections

(3)   *The Sixth Protocol*

Articles 1 and 2	The right not to be subjected to the death penalty.

2.6   The Human Rights Act 1998 does not incorporate Article 13, which creates the right to an effective remedy before a national authority. The UK Government concluded that this was encompassed within Article 6 – the right to a fair and public hearing. A claim that there has been a breach of Article 13 can, nevertheless, be made by way of an application to the European Court of Human Rights.[1]

2.7   It should be noted that whilst some of the rights (Articles 2, 3, 4, 7, 12 and 14) are absolute rights, others (Articles 8, 9, 10 and 11) are qualified rights, where legitimate interference with a right is permissible in certain limited circumstances, namely if what is done:

(1)   has its basis in law;
(2)   is necessary in a democratic society, which means it must:
    (a)   fulfil a pressing social need,
    (b)   pursue a legitimate aim,
    (c)   be proportionate to the aims being pursued;
(3)   is related to the permissible aim set out in the relevant article, for example:
    (a)   the prevention of crime, *or*
    (b)   protection of public order or health.

---

1   See, eg, *Z and Others v United Kingdom* [2001] 2 FLR 612.

2.8   Articles 5 and 6 are limited rights, in that the Convention itself provides exceptions to the general right. It is not necessary to explore those exceptions here, save to note that they do exist and may need to be taken into account on a case by case basis.

HUMAN RIGHTS ACT 1998

2.9   The Act incorporates the ECHR into UK law, with the exception of Article 13. The key provisions are as follows.

–   Every court or tribunal in the UK must take account of the ECHR and decisions of the European Court of Human Rights (s 2).
–   Legislation must be read by the courts in a way which is compatible with the ECHR (s 3).
–   It is unlawful for a public authority to act in a way which is incompatible with the ECHR (s 6).
–   A court may award damages for breach of the Convention, but only if:
    (a)   it has the power to award damages in civil proceedings; and
    (b)   taking into account (i) other available relief and (ii) the consequences, the court feels an award is 'necessary to afford just satisfaction to the person in whose favour it is made' (s 8).

2.10   Section 7 gives a right to sue for breach of s 6 provided the claimant is a 'victim' of the unlawful act. The word 'victim' is defined by the Act: it must be someone who is directly affected by the act in question. Victims can include companies as well as individuals and may also be relatives of the victim where a complaint is made about his death. As a general principle, an organisation or interest group or trade union cannot bring a case unless it is itself a victim. However, there is nothing to stop it providing legal or other assistance to a victim.[1]

2.11   A 'public authority', as referred to in ss 6, 7 and 8, is defined as a court or tribunal (s 6(3)(a)) and any person 'certain of whose functions are functions of a public nature' (s 6(3)(b)). This term, of course, covers local authorities as well as medical authorities, health bodies and the police. The guidance[2] states that it also includes any person exercising a public function. A specific reference is made to Railtrack plc and it is concluded that such a quasi public body is covered under the Act, at least to the extent to which it is performing a public function. What amounts to a 'public function' in this context is likely to give rise to legal debate. For the purposes of this book, the argument is unlikely to arise save to the extent that public authorities may wish to pass on their liabilities to third parties.

2.12   Section 8 of the Act entitles a court which has found a public authority's actions to be in breach of Convention rights to grant such relief as it considers 'just and appropriate'. This will include, where appropriate, granting injunctive relief; however, the most common remedy will be damages. In deciding whether to award damages and/or the amount of the award, the courts are required to take into account

---

1   *A New Era of Rights and Responsibilities* Court Guidance for Public Authorities published by the Home Office.
2   Ibid.

the principles applied by the European Court of Human Rights. It is, perhaps, arguable that, at present, those principles are not altogether clear. However, the European Court awards damages for pecuniary loss (special damages), non-pecuniary loss (general damages), together with costs and expenses.[1]

2.13   On a practical level, three other key points should be noted.

(1)   Any aggrieved party can still apply to the European Court of Human Rights if they feel there has been a breach of the ECHR, notwithstanding any judgment in the UK courts.
(2)   A court has no power to revoke UK legislation, merely a power to declare that a particular statutory provision is incompatible with the ECHR (s 4 of the Act). If a Minister deems it appropriate, he can seek to amend legislation to resolve any incompatibility; s 11 of the Act provides a fast-track procedure for doing so.
(3)   The primary and secondary legislation must be interpreted, so far as is possible, in a manner which is compatible with the ECHR (s 3 of the Act). This is likely to give greater scope to judges to interpret legislation and marks a move away from attempts to determine the intention of Parliament giving greater power to the courts.

2.14   An example of the courts considering whether UK legislation is compatible with the ECHR is to be found in *Marcic v Thames Water Utilities Limited*.[2] The case concerned flooding of the claimant's property due to an inadequate sewerage system. The House of Lords rejected the claims in nuisance and under Article 8 of the ECHR because Parliament had provided a statutory scheme under which Thames Water operated the offending sewers. A balance had to be struck between customers of Thames Water whose properties were prone to sewer flooding, on the one hand, and all the other customers of the company whose properties were drained through their sewers, on the other. Only a minority of customers suffered sewer flooding, but the company's customers as a whole had to meet the cost of building more sewers. The House of Lords considered that the statutory scheme balanced the interests of all customers. Lord Nicholls said:

> 'The balance struck by the statutory scheme is to impose a general drainage obligation on a sewerage undertaker but to entrust enforcement of this obligation to an independent regulator who has regard to all the different interests involved. Decisions of the Director are of course subject to an appropriately penetrating degree of judicial review by the courts. In principle this scheme seems to me to strike a reasonable balance. Parliament acted well within its bounds as policy maker.'

2.15   Similarly, in *Arscott and others v The Coal Authority and Another*[3] the Court of Appeal decided that the long-established rule of law allowing a landowner to erect defences against floodwater, leaving it to others to protect themselves against that floodwater ('the common enemy'), did not offend Article 8 and Article 1 of the First Protocol. There was a balance to be struck between the demands of the general interst of the community and the requirement for the protection of the individual's rights. According to Tuckey LJ:

---

1   See paras **2.58–2.71**.
2   [2003] UKHL 66, [2003] 3 WLR 1603.
3   [2004] EWCA Civ 892, (unreported) 13 July 2004.

'In my judgment the common enemy rule subject as I have said to the possibility of exceptional instances not exemplified by the present case, meets this balance. This is a department of the law which (like so many: perhaps most) has always involved a painstaking search for a fair result between self and other. The quest of the ECHR is just the same. I see no reason to suppose that in this field the common law does not answer both.'

IMPLICATIONS: LIABILITY OF LOCAL AUTHORITIES

2.16 The effect of the Human Rights Act 1998 on local authorities and other public bodies is undoubtedly wide ranging. The Act affects them both directly (s 6) and indirectly (ss 1–3). It creates a subtle shift in thinking which is likely to take some time to become apparent. The impact will be seen on a case-by-case basis.

2.17 What, then, is the likely impact for those dealing specifically with the legal liability of local authorities? The following areas will be affected.

(1) Previous legal decisions surrounding the duty of care owed by local authorities and their officers, many of which are referred to in this book, will be open to challenge as being in contravention of the ECHR.

(2) Section 6 creates a fresh cause of action against public authorities, where they act in a manner which is incompatible with the Convention.

2.18 The duty of care owed by local authorities has been discussed in Chapter 1. It will be recalled that the third requirement to establish a duty of care is:

'... that the court considers it fair, just and reasonable that the law should impose a duty of a given scope upon one party, for the benefit of the other.'[1]

This enables courts to have regard to policy considerations when deciding whether a duty of care can be said to arise in a set of circumstances. Until recently,[2] it appeared that the courts' approach to questions of policy would have to change following the decision of the European Court of Human Rights in *Osman v United Kingdom*.[3] This case considered an earlier decision by the Court of Appeal which had concluded that, on grounds of public policy, the police do not owe a duty of care arising out of failures in the investigation of crime.[4] In considering arguments under Article 6, the right to a fair and public hearing, the majority judgment of the European Court of Human Rights stated:

'It would appear to the Court that in the instant case the Court of Appeal proceeded on the basis that the rule provided a water tight defence to the police and that it was impossible to prise open an immunity which the police enjoy from civil suit in respect of their acts and omissions in the investigation and suppression of crime.'

2.19 The judgment of the Court continued:

---

1   *Caparo Industries plc v Dickman* [1990] 2 AC 605 at 618.
2   See paras **2.23–2.30**: *Z and Others v United Kingdom* [2001] 2 FLR 612.
3   [1999] 1 FLR 193.
4   *Osman v Ferguson and Another* [1993] 4 All ER 344 and see *Hill v Chief Constable of West Yorkshire* [1989] AC 53.

'The Court would observe that the application of the rule in this manner without further enquiry into the existence of competing public interest considerations only serves to confer a blanket immunity on the police for their acts and omissions in the investigation and suppression of crime and amounts to an unjustifiable restriction on an applicant's right to have a determination of the merits of his or her claim against the police in deserving cases.'

2.20 The European Court of Human Rights was of the view that other factors should be taken into account, to include allegations that there was a catalogue of acts and omissions which amounted to grave negligence and that the harm sustained was of the most serious nature. As a result, the Court's view was that:

'... these are considerations which must be examined on the merits and not automatically excluded by the application of a rule which amounts to the grant of an immunity to the police. In the instant case, the court is not persuaded by the government's argument that the rule as interpreted by the domestic court did not provide an automatic immunity to the police.'

2.21 The Court therefore concluded:

'... the pursuit of these remedies could not be said to mitigate the loss of their right to take legal proceedings against the police in negligence and to argue the justice of their case ... they were entitled to have the police account for their actions and omissions in adversarial proceedings.'

2.22 The implications of the European Court of Human Rights' decision in *Osman* have been considered in Chapter 1.[1] In deciding questions of policy the Court of Appeal and House of Lords have, since *Osman*, shown a reluctance to strike out claims[2] for reasons of policy, namely the third limb laid down in *Caparo*, referred to above. The courts have taken the view that the question of policy, together with those questions of foreseeability and proximity, should be dealt with at trial after hearing evidence on the conflicting policy arguments.

2.23 A different approach now seems possible, however, following the decision of the European Court of Human Rights in *Z and Others v United Kingdom*.[3] This was the consideration by the European Court of Human Rights of the House of Lords' decision in *X (Minors) v Bedfordshire County Council*.[4] *X (Minors)* concerned allegations against local authority social services departments: first, against Bedfordshire County Council, that there had been negligence in failing to take into care a number of children, described as having suffered from neglect and abuse at the hands of their parents. In the second case, against London Borough of Newham, it was alleged that a child was wrongly taken into care as a result of alleged negligence in the identification of a possible abuser of that child. The House of Lords struck out both claims on the basis that, as a matter of public policy, the local authorities did not owe a duty of care when exercising a discretion in deciding whether to take children into care. The claimants made an application to the European Court of Human Rights alleging the following breaches:

---

1   See paras **1.28–1.30**.
2   See, eg, *Barrett v Enfield London Borough Council* [1999] 2 FLR 426, *W v Essex County Council* [1997] 2 FLR 535 and *L (A Child) v Reading Borough Council* [2001] 1 WLR 1575.
3   [2001] 2 FLR 612; see also *TP and KM v United Kingdom* [2001] 2 FLR 549.
4   [1995] 2 AC 633; see Chapters 1 and 3.

(1) Article 3 – prohibition of torture, inhuman or degrading treatment or punishment;
(2) Article 6 – the right to a fair and public hearing;
(3) Article 8 – the right to respect for private and family life;
(4) Article 13 – the right to effective remedy before a national authority.

2.24 The Government did not contest the earlier finding of the European Commission of Human Rights that the treatment suffered by the children in the Bedfordshire case had reached the level of severity prohibited by Article 3 and that the State had failed in its positive obligation under Article 3 to provide them with adequate protection against inhuman and degrading treatment. In the light of this, the Court held that no separate issue arose under Article 8. In the *London Borough of Newham* case the Court found a breach of Article 8 because of a failure to involve the mother in the decision-making process when taking her daughter into care.[1]

2.25 Significantly, however, the Court also held that there had been no violation of Article 6 and, in this regard, the Court seems to have altered its opinion as previously expressed in *Osman*.

2.26 The Court noted that Article 6 may be relied on by anyone who considers that an interference with the exercise of one of his civil rights is unlawful and complains that he has not had the possibility of submitting that claim to a tribunal meeting the requirements of Article 6. Having accepted this proposition, however, the Court explained the position further:

'The right is not however absolute. It may be subject to legitimate restrictions, for example, statutory limitation periods, security for costs orders ... Where the individual's access is limited either by operation of law or in fact, the Court will examine whether the limitation imposed impaired the essence of the right and in particular whether it pursued a legitimate aim and there was a reasonable relationship of proportionality between the means employed and the aims sought to be achieved. If the restriction is compatible with these principles, no violation of Article 6 will arise.'

2.27 It is important to note that the Court observed that the claimants had not been prevented in any practical manner from bringing their claims before the domestic courts and indeed noted that the case 'was litigated with vigour up to the House of Lords'. Unlike its decision in *Osman*, the Court did not consider that the House of Lords' decision that, as a matter of law, there was no duty of care owed by the local authority, could be characterised as either an exclusionary rule or an immunity which deprived the claimant of access to the court. The Court observed that:

'The House of Lords, after weighing in the balance the competing considerations of public policy, decided not to extend liability in negligence into a new area. In so doing, it circumscribed the range of liability under tort law.'

2.28 The Court noted that the House of Lords' decision ended the case, without the factual matters being determined on the evidence, but expressed the following view:

'However, if as a matter of law, there was no basis for the claim, the hearing of evidence would have been an expensive and time-consuming process which would not have provided the applicants with any remedy at its conclusion. There is no reason to consider

---

1   *TP and KM v United Kingdom* [2001] 2 FLR 549.

the striking out procedure which rules on the existence of sustainable causes of action as per se offending the principle of access to court.'

2.29 The Court did not consider that the House of Lords' decision amounted to an immunity in fact, or in practical effect, due to its alleged sweeping or blanket nature. It was concerned only with one aspect of the exercise of local authorities' powers and duties and could not be regarded as an arbitrary removal of the courts' jurisdiction to determine a whole range of civil claims:

'It is not enough to bring Article 6 into play that the non existence of a cause of action under domestic law may be described as having the same effect as an immunity, in the sense of not enabling the applicant to sue for a given category of harm.'

2.30 The Court accepted that the House of Lords had acknowledged that the public policy principle that wrongs should be remedied requires strong counter considerations to be overridden. However, it also accepted that they had weighed that principle against other public policy concerns in reaching the conclusion that it was not fair, just or reasonable to impose a duty of care on the local authority. In an important passage of its judgment the Court said:

'The Court considers that its reasoning in the *Osman* judgment was based on an understanding of the law of negligence ... which has to be reviewed in the light of the clarifications subsequently made by the domestic courts and notably the House of Lords. The court is satisfied that the law of negligence as developed in the domestic courts since the case of *Caparo* and as recently analysed in the case of *Barrett v Enfield LBC* includes the fair, just and reasonable criterion as an intrinsic element of the duty of care and that the ruling of law concerning that element in this case does not disclose the operation of an immunity. In the present case, the court is led to the conclusion that the inability of the applicants to sue the local authority flowed not from an immunity but from the applicable principles governing the substantive right of action in domestic law. There was no restriction on access to the court ...'

2.31 It is submitted that in *Z and Others v United Kingdom* the European Court of Human Rights has, in effect, stated that its earlier decision in *Osman v United Kingdom* was wrong. At the very least it would seem that domestic courts are now entitled to follow the decision in *Z and Others v United Kingdom* rather than the earlier *Osman* decision. A decision to strike out a claim on policy grounds will no longer be regarded as necessarily giving rise to a breach of Article 6. This has now been confirmed by the Court of Appeal in *JD and Others v East Berkshire Community Health NHS Trust and Others*.[1]

2.32 Having decided that there was no breach of Article 6, the European Court of Human Rights, however, decided that there had, in fact, been a breach of Article 13 – the right to effective remedy before a national authority. The Court expressed its views as follows:

'It is fundamental to the machinery of protection established by the Convention that the national systems themselves provide redress for breaches of its provisions ... in that context, Article 13, which requires an effective remedy in respect of violations of the Convention, takes on a crucial function. The applicants' complaints are essentially that they have not been afforded a remedy in the courts for the failure to ensure them the level of protection against abuse which they were entitled under Article 3 of the Convention.

---

1   [2003] EWCA Civ 1151, [2004] 2 QB 558.

The domestic courts referred to "the public policy consideration that has first claim on the loyalty of the law" as being that "wrongs should be remedied". As far as Convention wrongs are concerned, that principle is embodied in Article 13. It is under Article 13 that the applicants' right to a remedy should be examined, and if appropriate, vindicated.'

2.33 Although the Government argued that there had been a number of remedies available to the applicants which went some way towards providing effective redress, namely the payment of compensation from the Criminal Injuries Compensation Board, and the possibility of complaining to the local government ombudsman, nevertheless the Government accepted that in the particular circumstances of this case they were insufficient alone or cumulatively to satisfy the requirements of Article 13. The Criminal Injuries Compensation Board could only award compensation for criminal acts, not for the consequences of neglect, and, further, any recommendation by the ombudsman would not have been legally enforceable. Against this background the Court concluded that the applicants had not been afforded an effective remedy in respect of the breach of Article 3 and there had therefore been a violation of Article 13 of the ECHR.

2.34 Another example of the European Court of Human Rights finding a violation of Article 13, although rejecting claims alleging other breaches of the ECHR, is *DP & JC v United Kingdom*.[1] The applicants claimed that they had been sexually abused by their stepfather who admitted the offences some years later. On two occasions the applicants had told social workers that they were being assaulted; however, their mother denied the abuse and no action was taken by the social services department. They brought proceedings against the local authority for failing to protect them from the sexual abuse they had suffered as children, but these claims were struck out. Relying on *Z and Others v United Kingdom*, the European Court of Human Rights decided that there had been no violation of Article 6. Although the Court confirmed that Article 3 and Article 8 could apply to the claimant's allegations, nevertheless the facts indicated that there was no reason why the social services department should have suspected that sexual abuse was occurring in the applicants' family household and accordingly the local authority could not be regarded as having failed in any positive obligation to take effective steps to protect the applicants from abuse. Nevertheless the court upheld the applicants' complaint that there had been a violation of Article 13. The complaints had not been declared inadmissible as manifestly ill-founded and an effective domestic procedure of enquiry would have offered more prospect of establishing the facts. The applicants, at the relevant time, did not have available to them an appropriate means of obtaining a determination of their allegations that the local authority had failed to protect them from ill-treatment. Accordingly, even though there had been no violation of Articles 3 and 8, nevertheless there had been a violation of Article 13. Each applicant was awarded a small sum by way of compensation.

A fresh cause of action against public authorities

2.35 A public body can be sued for a breach of s 6 of the Human Rights Act 1998, and be held liable for damages. In reality, a breach of s 6 of the Act is likely to be added as a separate cause of action to a claim in negligence, but it is important to note that it is not strictly necessary for there to be an existing claim in negligence. In the course of

---

1   [2003] 1 FLR 50.

argument in *Z and Others v United Kingdom*,[1] the Government pointed out that in future, under the Human Rights Act 1998, victims of human rights breaches will be able to bring proceedings in courts empowered to award damages. Thus, looking at the decision in *X (Minors)*, it would now be possible for the claimants to sue the local authority under s 6 of the Act, arguing that it was in breach of Article 3. Similarly, in respect of the child taken into care in the *London Borough of Newham* case, that claimant would allege that the local authority had acted in breach of Article 8. Following the decision in *Z and Others v United Kingdom*, the domestic court would be entitled to strike out any claim in negligence; however, it would be entitled to award damages for a breach of s 6 of the Human Rights Act 1998.[2]

IMPLICATIONS: SPECIFIC MATTERS

The environment

2.36   In *Lopez Ostra v Spain*,[3] a neighbour was affected by noxious fumes, from a nearby site. The public authority had granted planning permission for the building of a factory on the site. The Spanish courts held that the use of the factory with planning permission was 'reasonable'. However, the neighbour appealed to the European Court of Human Rights on the grounds of a breach of Article 8 (the right to respect for private and family life). The applicants were successful.

2.37   The key point arising out of the *Lopez Ostra* case was that the public authority was the enforcing authority in respect of Spain's environmental regulations. The town council was found responsible because it failed to take steps to close down the plant or minimise the effect of the pollution. In effect, the courts were using the ECHR to encourage the public authority to exercise its powers pursuant to the legislation. This may have a direct impact in the UK, not only on local authorities' existing duties under the Environmental Protection Act 1990 etc, but also in connection with the duties under s 57 of the Environment Act 1995 (see Chapter 8).

2.38   A similar decision was given in *Guerra and Others v Italy*.[4] In that case, the population of an Italian village successfully complained that the local government had failed to provide them with essential information relevant to their well-being, health and homes. They were concerned about a nearby chemical factory, which was classified as high risk in terms of hazards to the environment and to the local population. Applications under Articles 2 and 10 were unsuccessful, but the applicants succeeded under Article 8.

2.39   These two decisions are noteworthy for three other reasons: first, because they appear to override the principle of reasonableness, which is a fundamental part of the UK law of nuisance (see Chapter 8); secondly, because in both cases the public

---

1   [2001] 2 FLR 612.
2   See also *JD and Others v East Berkshire Community Health NHS Trust and Others* [2003] EWCA Civ 1151, [2004] QB 558, where the Court of Appeal decided that a duty of care is owed to children when a local authority is deciding whether children should be taken into care. See also paras **2.48** and **3.42–3.45**.
3   (1995) 20 EHRR 277.
4   [1998] 4 BHRC 63.

authority was found liable even though it was not in fact causing the nuisance; and, thirdly, the court made an award of damages against the public authority in respect of the nuisance.[1]

2.40   Closer to hand, the decision of the European Court of Human Rights in *Powell and Rayner v United Kingdom*[2] should also be noted. The applicants lived near Heathrow Airport and the Court concluded that Article 8 (the right to respect for private and family life) could apply in relation to noise pollution. In fact, no breach of the ECHR was found as the Court decided that reasonable steps had been taken to abate the pollution and compensate residents for the disturbances. Regard should also be had to *Hatton and Others v United Kingdom*,[3] where the European Court of Human Rights decided that the Government had been in breach of Article 8 by failing to implement an adequate scheme to limit night-time aircraft movements at Heathrow Airport. The Court considered that the Government had failed to strike a fair balance between the UK's economic well-being, and the residents' effective enjoyment of their right to respect for their homes and their private and family lives.

2.41   Reference should also be made to the decision of the European Court of Human Rights, sitting as a Grand Chamber, in *Hatton v United Kingdom*.[4] The applicants lived near Heathrow Airport and claimed that the Government's policy on night flights at Heathrow violated their rights under Article 8. The Court overturned an earlier decision and decided that there was no breach of Article 8. The Court emphasised that governments are elected bodies and are aware of the local situation:

> 'The national authorities have direct democratic legitimation and are, as the court has held on many occasions, in principle better placed than an international court to evaluate local needs and conditions … In matters of general policy, on which opinions within a democratic society may reasonably differ widely, the role of the domestic policy maker should be given special weight.'

While the State is required to give due consideration to the particular interests of individuals, it must in principle be left to choose between different ways and means of meeting this obligation:

> 'The court's supervisory function being of a subsidiary nature, it is limited to reviewing whether or not the particular solution adopted can be regarded as striking a fair balance.'

The Court decided that in considering night-time aircraft movements at Heathrow, Parliament had struck a fair balance between the interests of individuals and the UK's economic well-being.

2.42   In *Dennis v Ministry of Defence*[5] Buckley J held that the noise created by aircraft flying from RAF Wittering was a breach of the claimant's rights under Article 8 and Article 1 of the First Protocol (the right to peaceful enjoyment of a person's possessions). He relied, however, upon the earlier decision of the European Court of Human Rights in *Hatton v United Kingdom*, now overturned as mentioned above, and the decision of the Court of Appeal in *Marcic v Thames Water Utlities*

---

1   See paras **2.62** and **2.65**.
2   (1990) 12 EHRR 355.
3   (2001) 11 BHRC 634.
4   (2003) 37 EHRR 611.
5   [2003] EWHC 793, [2003] EnvLR 34.

Ltd,[1] which was subsequently overturned by the House of Lords. It is therefore arguable that *Dennis* would be decided differently if it came before the courts now.

2.43 Local authorities and other public authorities have a clear regulatory role in this area, and in particular in relation to environmental health. The potential for a breach of s 6 is therefore real, and those involved in this area should be fully aware of their obligations. For example, an authority could incur a liability for failure to issue an enforcement notice against the creators of a statutory nuisance (breach of Article 8 (the right to respect for private and family life) or Article 5 (the right to liberty and security)).

The police and emergency services

2.44 The judgment of the European Court of Human Rights in *Osman v United Kingdom*[2] called into question the immunity apparently afforded to the police in the investigation and suppression of crime, established by the House of Lords in *Hill v Chief Constable of West Yorkshire*.[3] It seems, however, following *Z and Others v United Kingdom*,[4] that the European Court of Human Rights may now accept that the domestic courts are entitled to decide, as a matter of policy, that it is not 'fair, just and reasonable' to impose a duty of care on the police in the investigation and suppression of crime. The relevant question is to ask whether there has been a breach of any of the articles in the ECHR in respect of which a claim can now be made in the domestic courts under the Human Rights Act 1998.

2.45 An example of an article which might give rise to a claim under the Act is Article 5 (the right to liberty and security). A claim under Article 5 will be similar to a claim for false imprisonment. It is likely that, as with the current law surrounding false imprisonment, a police officer will be in breach of Article 5 unless he complies with the provisions of the Police Act 1976 and the Police and Criminal Evidence Act 1984. It is unlikely that a breach of Article 5, coupled with a breach of the tort of false imprisonment, will give rise to a separate entitlement to damages; however, a breach of Article 5 alone could give rise to a claim for damages under the Human Rights Act 1998.

2.46 Article 8 (the right to respect for private and family life) may give rise to claims under the Human Rights Act 1998 in relation to police powers of search and seizure, the undertaking of intimate samples, photographs and fingerprints. Surveillance, and the use of CCTV cameras, may also give rise to a breach of Article 8. The European Court of Human Rights has already held that surveillance must be 'in accordance with the law'.[5] Article 8 is, however, a qualified right and proceeding in accordance with the Police and Criminal Evidence Act 1984 could bring surveillance within the law.

Social services

2.47 As has already been seen in para **2.24**, the consideration whether to bring a child into care has been held to have given rise to breaches of Article 3 (freedom from

---

1   [2003] UKHL 66, [2003] 3 WLR 1603.
2   [1999] 1 FLR 193.
3   [1989] AC 53.
4   [2001] 2 FLR 612.
5   *Halford v United Kingdom* (1997) 24 EHRR 523.

torture, inhuman or degrading treatment or punishment) and Article 8 (the right to respect for private and family life), the latter arising out of London Borough of Newham's failure to show promptly a video of a 'disclosure interview' between child and social worker, which the court considered had deprived the mother of an adequate opportunity to involve herself in the decision-making process when her daughter was removed from her care.

2.48   The particular influence of the Human Rights Act 1998 in this area can be seen in *JD and Others v East Berkshire Community Health NHS Trust and Others*.[1] The case concerned children's allegations that they had been abused by their fathers. They were taken into care. Subsequently the accusations proved to be unfounded. The parents claimed damages for psychiatric harm alleged to have been caused by the false accusations. In one case a child also claimed damages. The Court of Appeal concluded that the decision in *X (Minors) v Bedfordshire County Council*[2] had been restricted by subsequent decisions (in particular *Barrett v London Borough of Enfield*[3]) to the core proposition that:

> 'Decisions by local authorities whether or not to take a child into care were not reviewable by a claim in negligence.'

On this basis the child's claim had been struck out correctly. However, the Court of Appeal went on to consider the impact of the Human Rights Act 1998. Although the events in question had taken place before the Act came into force, the Court of Appeal considered that it was appropriate to ask whether there was any justification for preserving the rule that no duty of care towards a child can arise out of a decision whether or not to take that child into care. Was it no longer fair, just and reasonable to impose such a duty given the fact that it was clear, following *Z and Others v United Kingdom*,[4] that there could be a breach of Article 3 and/or Article 8 of the European Convention on Human Rights and that the Act would now allow a child to bring a claim for breach of those articles? In the circumstances the Court of Appeal concluded that insofar as claims by children are concerned, the decision in *X (Minors) v Bedfordshire County Council* cannot survive the Human Rights Act 1998. The decision of the Court was given by Lord Phillips MR:

> 'In the context of suspected child abuse, breach of a duty of care in negligence will frequently also amount to a violation of article 3 or article 8. The difference, of course, is that those asserting that wrongful acts or omissions occurred before October 2000 will have no claim under the Human Rights Act. This cannot, however, constitute a valid reason of policy for preserving a limitation of the common law duty of care which is not otherwise justified. On the contrary, the absence of an alternative remedy for children who are victims of abuse before October 2000 militates in favour of the recognition of a common law duty of care once the public policy reasons against this have lost their force. It follows that it will no longer be legitimate to rule that, as a matter of law, no common law duty of care is owed to a child in relation to the investigation of suspected child abuse and the initiation and pursuit of care proceedings.'

2.49   Because of the scope of the duties of social services departments, it is foreseeable that the Human Rights Act 1998 will impact in a number of respects. In

---

1   [2003] EWCA Civ 1151, [2004] QB 558.
2   [1995] 3 All ER 353.
3   [1999] 3 WLR 79.
4   [2001] 2 FLR 612.

addition to Articles 3 and 8, it is submitted that Article 5 (the right to liberty and security), Article 9 (freedom of thought, conscience and religion) and Article 14 (prohibition of discrimination) are likely to come before the court in considering matters such as care proceedings; procedures for adoption; treatment in children's homes, old people's homes or hostels which might be considered degrading; and care for the disabled and mentally ill.

Education

2.50   The most immediate point of concern for those involved in education is, of course, the 'right to education', enshrined in Article 2 of the First Protocol, which provides:

> 'No person shall be denied the right to education. In the exercise of any functions which it assumes in relation to education and to teaching, the State shall respect the right of parents to ensure such education and teaching in conformity with their own religious and philosophical convictions.'

The Act, however, sets out an important reservation in relation to Article 2 of the First Protocol (Schedule 3, Part 2), in that Article 2 is accepted by the UK:

> '... only so far as it is compatible with the provision of efficient instruction and training, and the avoidance of unreasonable public expenditure.'

2.51   The inclusion of this reservation is likely to mean that the potential impact of the Act in relation to education may be less than was at first anticipated. Nonetheless, this does not mean that the Act can be ignored. There are three areas of significance:

(1)   the right not to be denied education;
(2)   the duty to respect the religious and philosophical convictions of parents;
(3)   the impact of other articles under the ECHR.

The right to education

2.52   The following points should be noted.

(1)   'Education' is defined as: '... the whole process whereby, in any society, adults endeavour to transmit their beliefs, culture and other values to the young, whereas teaching or instruction refers in particular to the transmission of knowledge and to intellectual development'.
(2)   Education does not extend to vocational training.
(3)   There is no requirement to educate children to any set minimum level or in any particular subjects.
(4)   The ECHR will not assess the quality of the education provided.
(5)   There is no guarantee of university education.
(6)   The State is free to establish selection criteria.
(7)   Importantly, the State may take into account 'the need and resources of the community and of individuals' but must not 'injure the substance of the right to education nor conflict with other rights enshrined in the Convention'.[1]

The right to education therefore encompasses:

---

1   *Belgian Linguistic Case (No 2)* (1968) 1 EHRR 252.

(a) the right of access to educational institutions existing at a given time – but the right is not absolute, which is likely to be relevant where children are excluded, suspended, or withdrawn from school;[1]
(b) the right to an effective education – although, as stated, there is no entitlement to a particular level of education. This should be contrasted with the obligation to provide 'suitable education' in domestic law irrespective of any argument about the lack of available finance.[2] This is also an area where domestic law provides a potential remedy for damages in common law negligence.[3]

State's duty to respect the religious and philosophical convictions of parents

2.53 Again, the impact of Article 2 of the First Protocol will largely depend upon whether it is interpreted narrowly or broadly. It has been interpreted as preventing the State/local authority from pursuing an 'aim of indoctrination'. The term 'philosophical' encompasses ideological and non-religious beliefs and attitudes, but not language preferences; the term 'religious' covers 'known religions', including Jehovah's Witnesses. Perhaps crucially, education in a manner which does not indoctrinate a particular religious or philosophical attitude is allowed. Teachers are allowed to express their opinion, save for moral or religious beliefs which may contravene Article 10 (freedom of expression).

2.54 The following Articles may also be of relevance:

– Article 3: prohibition of torture or inhuman or degrading treatment or punishment, in relation to bullying;
– Article 6: the right to a fair and public hearing, in relation to internal disciplinary matters as well as the disciplining of pupils;
– Article 9: freedom of thought, conscience and religion, in relation to the beliefs of both pupils and teachers;
– Article 10: freedom of expression, again applying to both pupils and teachers;
– Article 14: prohibition of discrimination.

Highways

2.55 It is arguable that the compulsory purchase of land for a new road would constitute an interference with the landowner's right and enjoyment under Article 1 of the First Protocol, although authorities would normally be able to validate their actions by paying appropriate compensation.[4]

Housing

2.56 The unreasonable eviction of gypsies may violate Article 8. A series of gypsy cases were declared admissible by the Commission on 4 March 1998.[5] Local authorities also face claims in respect of their role as landlords. In *Kroon v Netherlands*[6] the Court stated that the 'essential object' of Article 8 was:

---

1   *SP v United Kingdom* [1997] EHRLR 284.
2   *R v East Sussex County Council, ex parte Tandy* [1998] 2 WLR 884.
3   *Phelps v London Borough of Hillingdon* [2000] 3 WLR 776 – see Chapter 4.
4   L Clements 'The Human Rights Bill' [1998] JLGL Issue 1.
5   *Costa, Beard, Smith, Lee, Varey, Chapman* 10 BHRC 48.
6   (1994) A297-C, para 31.

'. . . To protect the individual against arbitrary action by the local authorities. There may in addition be positive obligations inherent in "effective" respect for family life . . .'

'Home' is generally defined as where one lives on a settled basis. It may include a place where one intends to live (*Gillow v United Kingdom*[1]) and business premises (*Niemietz v Germany*[2]). There is then a right to access and occupation and a right not to be expelled or evicted from such premises. The interests protected by 'home' include the peaceful enjoyment of residence (see, eg, *Arrondelle v United Kingdom*[3]). However, it is important to note that compliance with the statutory provisions – which are perceived as being strict in the UK – would normally protect a landlord from an action under Article 8. In three unreported cases, attempts to rely upon the ECHR in the context of possession proceedings failed.[4]

2.57 The Court of Appeal has now confirmed that there may be cases where a local authority, as the landlord of a dwelling house let for the purposes of social housing, can be in breach of Article 8. Nevertheless Article 8 does not impose some general and unqualified obligation on local authorities in relation to the condition of their housing. In *Lee v Leeds City Council*[5] the claimant took proceedings against the council complaining about condensation, mould and damp in her house. The claim for breach of the covenant implied under s 11 of the Landlord and Tenant Act 1985 failed because of the decision in *Quick v Taff Ely Borough Council*[6] and the Court of Appeal did not consider that the facts of the case revealed any breach of Article 8.

DAMAGES

Damages against central government

2.58 Damages may be awarded for a breach of EC law. In *R v Secretary of State for Transport, ex parte Factortame*,[7] the Court of Appeal concluded that the Government was in breach of Community law by creating certain provisions in the Merchant Shipping Act 1988, which discriminated against citizens of other Member States of the European Community. The Court of Appeal concluded that damages could be awarded against the State where the breach of Community law was sufficiently serious, which in this case it was.

Damages against public authorities

2.59 Section 8 of the Human Rights Act 1998 gives rights to the following remedies:

(1)   injunctive relief;

---

1   (1989) 11 EHRR 335.
2   (1993) 16 EHRR 97.
3   (1983) 5 EHRR 118.
4   See *Mayor and Burgesses of London Borough of Hounslow v Perea* (unreported) 11 March 1982, *Metropolitan Property Realizations v Cosgrove* (unreported) 27 January 1992, and *Mayor and Commonality and Citizens of London v Prince* (unreported) 6 July 1995.
5   [2001] EWCA Civ 06, [2002] 1 WLR 1488.
6   [1985] 3 WLR 981.
7   [1998] 3 CMLR 192.

(2) damages.

It is important to note that s 8(4) of the Act states as follows:

'In determining –

(a) whether to award damages, or
(b) the amount of an award,

the court must take into account the principles applied by the European Court of Human Rights in relation to the award of compensation under Article 41 of the Convention.'

2.60 Article 41 of the ECHR enables the European Court of Human Rights to allow compensation for 'pecuniary damage' (namely what is generally regarded as 'special damages' in the domestic courts) and 'non-pecuniary damage' (namely what the domestic courts regard as general damages). The European Court of Human Rights also awards compensation for costs and expenses.

Pecuniary damages

2.61 The most recent example is to be found in *Z and Others v United Kingdom*.[1] The claimants, who had been abused as children, claimed the cost of future treatment, loss of future earnings and handicap on the labour market. The European Court of Human Rights noted that the damages had been claimed on the basis of domestic case-law and scales of assessment. The Court then set out certain principles as follows:

'As regards the applicants' claims for pecuniary loss, the Court's case-law establishes that there must be a clear cause or connection between the damage claimed by the applicant and the violation of the Convention and that this may, in the appropriate case, include compensation in respect of loss of earnings ... A precise calculation of the sums necessary to make complete reparation in respect of the pecuniary losses suffered by the applicants may be prevented by the inherently uncertain character of the damage claimed from the violation.'

Having dealt with matters of principle, the Court allowed damages on the following basis:

	Future medical treatment		Future loss of earnings/handicap on labour market	
	Claimed (£)	Allowed (£)	Claimed (£)	Allowed (£)
Claimant Z	9,000	8,000	40,000	Nil
Claimant A	50,000	50,000	200,000	50,000
Claimant B	50,000	50,000	90,000	30,000
Claimant C	4,500	4,000	10,000	Nil

2.62 It will be noted from the above that the Court was more receptive to claims for medical expenses than to claims for loss of future earnings and future earnings prospects. This seems to reflect a reluctance on the part of the Court to award substantial sums by way of pecuniary damage. In *Lopez-Ostra v Spain*,[2] in a claim relating to distress caused by fumes and smells from a nearby factory and anxiety

---

1   [2001] 2 FLR 612.
2   (1994) 20 EHRR 277.

arising from a child's illness caused by toxic fumes and the inconvenience of moving, the Court awarded a global sum of £16,000 compared with a claim of just over £100,000.

2.63   In *Gaskin v United Kingdom*[1] the Court upheld the applicant's argument that his rights under Article 8 had been breached by the refusal of the local authority to disclose documents relating to his upbringing in care. The applicant sought £380,000 in loss of earnings, alleging that his employment prospects had been affected. The Court disagreed, saying there had been no causal link between the loss claimed and the violation, namely the non-disclosure of documents. Nevertheless the Court awarded £5,000 non-pecuniary damages.

2.64   In *Niemietz v Germany*[2] the applicant succeeded in his claim that his right to private life had been violated when a third party obtained access to his business premises and certain confidential information. However, the Court did not consider that the applicant had proved that he had suffered damage and felt that its finding of a violation constituted sufficient satisfaction.

2.65   The environmental cases referred to at paras **2.36–2.41** also led to awards of damages. In *Guerra v Italy*[3] each applicant was awarded about £3,000 for a breach of Article 8 on the grounds of the local government's failure to inform local inhabitants of the hazards of the chemical factory less than one mile away from the village.

Non-pecuniary damages

2.66   In *Z and Others v United Kingdom*, dealt with above, the claimants sought non-pecuniary damages in respect of physical and psychiatric damage. The European Court of Human Rights noted the scale of damages applied in the domestic courts, but did not regard these as decisive. At the end of the day the Court awarded each claimant the sum of £32,000 compared with claims varying from £25,000 up to £45,000. The Court did not feel able to distinguish between the children in this context.

2.67   One of the highest previous awards was made in *Z v Finland*.[4] Reference was made in a published legal judgment in a family law case to the applicant's full name, which led to the disclosure of her HIV status. This was held to be a breach of the applicant's Article 8 rights and she was awarded the equivalent of £22,000.

2.68   For a breach of Article 3, in *A v UK*[5] the claimant, who was beaten by his stepfather, was awarded £10,000 compensation for non-pecuniary damage.

2.69   In *TP and KM v United Kingdom*[6] the European Court of Human Rights awarded £10,000 to mother and child for a breach of Article 8. This is to be compared with the amounts claimed which varied between £15,000 and £35,000 for each claimant.

2.70   In summary, it is apparent that damages awarded by the European Court of Human Rights have been relatively low. In particular, it would seem that the Court has

---

1   [1990] 1 FLR 167.
2   (1993) 16 EHRR 97.
3   [1998] 4 BHRC 63.
4   (1998) 25 EHRR 371.
5   (1999) 27 EHRR 611.
6   [2001] 2 FLR 549.

made more modest awards in regard to future loss than might have been awarded by the domestic courts. Section 8(1) of the Human Rights Act 1998 gives the domestic courts a discretion to:

> '... grant such relief or remedy, or make such order, within its powers as it considers just and appropriate.'

At the same time, however, s 8(4) of the Act specifically requires the domestic courts to take into account the principles applied by the European Court of Human Rights in relation to the award of compensation. It remains to be seen what approach the domestic courts will take to the award of damages for breach of s 6 of the Act, but it is submitted that such awards should be relatively low if the domestic courts follow the approach adopted by the European Court of Human Rights.

2.71 An example of the courts' approach is *R (Bernard and Another) v Enfield London Borough Council.*[1] The court considered a claim against the council's social services department for delay in assessing the claimants' needs and accommodation. The court considered that there had been a breach of Article 8. When considering damages, although Sullivan J noted that awards by the European Court of Human Rights had been moderate, he considered that the award of damages should be no lower than tortious awards by English courts because otherwise it would diminish respect for the policy underlying the Act. In the absence of any comparative tortious awards, guidance was to be had from awards by the local government ombudsman for disruption, distress, worry and inconvenience suffered as a result of maladministration.

CONCLUSION

2.72 The ECHR is now enshrined in UK law. The domestic courts will have to become accustomed to deciding whether UK law is broadly compatible with the ECHR; furthermore, they will have to decide whether certain factual situations amount to a breach of the ECHR, which will involve considerations not altogether the same as those encountered under the common law. There is, in any event, no doubt that s 6 of the Human Rights Act 1998 makes it unlawful for local authorities to act in contravention of the ECHR in their day-to-day activities.

---

1   [2002] All ER (D) 383 (Oct).

Chapter 3

SOCIAL SERVICES

INTRODUCTION

3.1 Social workers are almost invariably employees of local authorities whose duties are derived from statute. Claims against social workers have largely been brought by or on behalf of children for whom local authorities have a statutory responsibility. This chapter is primarily concerned with such claims.

THE STATUTORY FRAMEWORK

3.2 In the mid-1940s, a new code of social legislation was brought into effect. Under the Children Act 1948, local authorities were required to take children under the age of 17 into care in appropriate circumstances. The child would remain in local authority care until attaining the age of majority, or for as long as was necessary for his or her welfare. Thereafter, numerous statutory provisions added to the powers and duties of local authorities in this context. In 1970, the Local Authority Social Services Act 1970 (the 1970 Act) attempted to unify social services departments. The Act remains the primary statutory code for the establishment and operation of local authority social services departments.

3.3 Various statutory provisions, such as the Children and Young Persons Act 1969 and the Child Care Act 1980, further defined the duties of local authorities. But it was not until the Children Act 1989 that there was brought into force a single public and private law code relating to children. A local authority has a general duty to safeguard and promote the welfare of children in its area and has greater control over the extent to which regard should be had to the wishes of the child, parents and relevant adults. The Children Act 1989 was accompanied by comprehensive guidance and regulations prepared by the Department of Health and issued under s 7 of the 1970 Act.

INQUIRIES

3.4 There have been a number of government inquiries of relevance. The Inquiry into Child Abuse in Cleveland 1987 resulted in the report *Working Together*. In 1992, Lord Clyde reported on the removal of children from Orkney; Lady Howe chaired an inquiry into the provision of residential care services in the public sector; and Andrew Kirkwood QC chaired the Leicestershire Inquiry relating to Frank Beck, which reported in 1993. In 1997 and 1998, Sir Ronald Waterhouse chaired the North Wales

Tribunal of Inquiry into suspected abuse at children's homes. The report, *Lost in Care*, was published in 2000.

3.5 There are currently a considerable number of police investigations ongoing into widespread sexual abuse in children's homes either directly run by local authorities or supervised by them. In addition to such investigations, there have, over the last 25 years, been a number of inquiries into particular failings of local authorities often resulting in death or serious injury where local authorities have either been ignorant of the child's predicament or have failed to take adequate steps to protect the welfare of a child.

CLAIMS

3.6 The basis for private law claims for damages against local authorities was first considered by the courts in this country at an appellate level in the case of *X (Minors) v Bedfordshire County Council; M (A Minor) and Another v Newham London Borough Council and Others.*[1]

3.7 Claims had been brought against social workers before *X (Minors)*. In *Surtees v Kingston-Upon-Thames Royal Borough Council,*[2] the plaintiff had been fostered out to a family when she was only 2 years old. Whilst there, her foot had been very badly scalded by hot water in circumstances that never became entirely clear. On an examination of local authority files, it became apparent that the foster-parents had expressed some disquiet about the continuing fostering of the child. There were, it was argued, all the signs of an unsuccessful fostering (as the judge at first instance found it to be). It was alleged that the social worker concerned should have taken the plaintiff away before the accident. She had failed to carry out the required number of visits as provided by the Boarding Out of Children Regulations 1955[3] (now replaced by the Foster Placement (Children) Regulations 1991[4]). It was alleged that the local authority was negligent and in breach of statutory duty. Leggatt J doubted that the 1955 Regulations could give rise to a duty of care but neither he nor the Court of Appeal considered that the circumstances warranted a finding of negligence against the local authority based upon common-law principles. The judges did not deal with the question of any general immunity for social workers.

3.8 Liability had been found against social workers. In the *Vicar of Writtle v Essex County Council,*[5] a youth on remand was placed in an open community home. The social worker concerned knew that the youth had the propensity to wander and light fires but did not tell the house parent. The youth escaped and set fire to a church. The court held there were no good policy reasons justifying the decision of the social worker not to pass on the relevant information and thus ordinary negligence principles applied.

---

1   [1995] 2 AC 633.
2   [1991] 2 FLR 559.
3   SI 1955/1377.
4   SI 1991/910.
5   (1979) 77 LGR 656.

3.9   Social workers in America have been held liable where their decisions have been regarded as operational rather than involving matters of policy. In *Johnson v The State of California*,[1] the State placed a youth with foster-parents and was liable for failing to warn them of his violent tendencies with the result that he assaulted the mother. This was considered an operational case. On the other hand, the maintenance by a State Government of 'open house' in a reformed school for young offenders from which an inmate escaped to burn down the plaintiff's property did not give rise to a claim since this was regarded as a policy matter.[2]

3.10   But until *X (Minors)*, the courts in this country had not considered, as a matter of principle, whether it was appropriate that social workers should be the target of claims for damages and, if so, whether there were limits to the circumstances in which they could be sued.

X (MINORS) V BEDFORDSHIRE COUNTY COUNCIL

3.11   The appeals to the House of Lords included two claims against the social services department of local authorities, Newham London Borough Council and Bedfordshire County Council.[3] Conjoined with these appeals were three claims against local education authorities.

3.12   In the *Newham* case, the plaintiff and her mother claimed damages against the council as a result of being separated from one another for a period of one year. The separation came about as a result of a local authority investigation into suspected sexual abuse. A psychiatrist with particular experience in the field and a specialist social worker conducted a diagnostic interview of the child and concluded that: (a) she had been sexually abused; and (b) the abuser was the mother's cohabitee. The mother failed to satisfy the social worker that she would be able to protect the child from further sexual abuse and thus the child was taken into care. Following wardship proceedings, they remained living apart until, on closer examination of some video evidence, it transpired that the social worker and the psychiatrist had wrongly identified the abuser as being the mother's cohabitee. The claim was brought against the local authority in negligence and breach of statutory duty.

3.13   In *X (Minors)*, five plaintiffs claimed damages for personal injury arising out of alleged breach of statutory duty and negligence during a 5-year period when they had been exposed to parental abuse and mistreatment. It was said that the council had failed to investigate the matter adequately or to institute care proceedings.

3.14   The Court of Appeal[4] had heard both the social services cases together and decided that the local authorities did not owe a duty of care at common law, nor was there a breach of statutory duty capable of giving rise to a private law claim for damages. The decision was by a majority and the Master of the Rolls (Sir Thomas

---

1   1968 447 P 2D 35 T.
2   *Dalebite v US* 1953 346 US 15.
3   *X (Minors) v Bedfordshire County Council; M (A Minor) and Another v Newham London Borough Council and Others* [1995] 2 AC 633.
4   [1995] 2 AC 648, CA.

Bingham) delivered a powerful dissenting judgment. The Court of Appeal gave leave to appeal to the House of Lords.

3.15 The House of Lords, unanimously, dismissed the appeals and held that the plaintiffs' claims failed. The decision involved a thorough review of the circumstances in which public authorities, generally, and social services departments and local education authorities, specifically, could be liable for private law claims for damages.

Breach of statutory duty

3.16 It was held that a breach of statutory duty did not give rise to any private law cause of action. The relevant statutes were all concerned with the establishment of a system to promote social welfare, where difficult decisions often had to be taken on the basis of inadequate and disputed facts. Exceptionally clear language was needed to indicate a parliamentary intention to create a private law remedy, and the actual words used were inconsistent with such an intention.[1] This approach was confirmed by the House of Lords in *Barrett v London Borough of Enfield*[2] and *W v Essex County Council*.[3]

Common law duties

3.17 Lord Browne-Wilkinson, who gave the main speech, discussed what he described as the 'General Approach' to the liabilities of public authorities. In his view, a common law duty *might* arise where there was no claim for breach of statutory duty. But where Parliament had given a local authority discretion, the first requirement was to show that a particular decision was outside the scope of that discretion altogether; otherwise a local authority could not be in breach of any duty of care.

3.18 If a decision fell outside a statutory discretion, it could give rise to common law liability. But if factors relevant to a decision included policy matters then the decision was not justiciable. Lord Browne-Wilkinson expressed approval of Lord Keith of Kinkel's comments in *Rowling v Takaro Properties*,[4] when he said of the policy/operational dichotomy:

> 'This distinction does not provide a touchstone of liability, but rather is expressive of the need to exclude altogether those cases in which the decision under attack is of such a kind that a question whether it has been made negligently is unsuitable for judicial resolution, of which notable examples are discretionary decisions on the allocation of scarce resources or the distribution of risks.'

3.19 Provided the alleged carelessness is justiciable the question of whether there is a common law duty of care falls to be considered in accordance with the principles laid down in *Caparo Industries Plc v Dickman*.[5] Was the damage to the plaintiff

---

1   *Cutler v Wandsworth Stadium Limited* [1949] AC 398, *Lonhro Limited v Shell Petroleum Co Limited (No 2)* [1982] AC 173 and *R v Deputy Governor of Parkhurst Prison, ex parte Hague* [1992] 1 AC 58.
2   [1999] 2 FLR 426.
3   [2000] 2 WLR 601.
4   [1988] AC 473.
5   [1990] 2 AC 605 at 617–618.

reasonably foreseeable? Was the relationship between the plaintiff and the defendant sufficiently proximate? Is it just and reasonable to impose a duty of care?

3.20 The social services claims came before the House of Lords by way of striking out proceedings. The House of Lords considered that it was at least arguable that there was the requisite foreseeability and proximity. It was further accepted for the purposes of the decision that at least some of the allegations were justiciable and thus the claim could not be struck out on these grounds. In the course of his speech, Lord Browne-Wilkinson considered whether or not the decisions came within the ambit of the local authority's statutory discretion. Dealing with the case against Bedfordshire County Council, he said:

> 'I strongly suspect that, if the case were to go to trial, it would eventually fail on this ground since, in essence, the complaint is that the local authority failed to take steps to remove the children from the care of their mother, i.e. negligently failed properly to exercise a discretion which Parliament has conferred on the local authority.'

On the face of it, the vast majority of decisions by social workers would seem to fall into this category.

3.21 Lord Browne-Wilkinson turned then to consider in accordance with *Caparo* principles where it was fair, just and reasonable to 'superimpose a common law duty of care on the local authority in relation to the performance of its statutory duties to protect children'.[1] In his view, there were strong reasons for concluding that it was not fair, just and reasonable to impose a duty of care. The reasons included:

(a) the system for protecting children at risk was multi-disciplinary and to impose liability on any one of the participant bodies would cut across the whole system;
(b) the task for local authorities in dealing with children is extraordinarily delicate;
(c) imposing liability might well cause local authorities to adopt a more cautious and defensive approach which might result in the postponement of the decision-making process and an increased workload in making investigation, diminishing the time available for dealing with other cases and other children;
(d) the relationship between the social worker and the child's parents is often one of conflict and the spectre of vexatious and costly litigation was a compelling reason why there should not be a legal duty;
(e) the existence of other remedies including the Ombudsman and the various statutory complaints procedures.

Lord Browne-Wilkinson also reminded himself that the *Caparo* decision had suggested that the court should proceed incrementally and by analogy with decided categories when deciding whether or not a duty of care should be held to exist. He considered that the administration of a statutory social welfare scheme should not result in the courts holding liable in negligence those who had been charged with protecting society from the wrongdoing of others.

---

1   *Caparo Industries Plc v Dickman* [1990] 2 AC 605 at 749F–G.

THE AUTHORITIES SINCE *X (MINORS)*

3.22 In *H v Norfolk County Council*[1] the plaintiff, who was then aged 22, had been taken into care at the age of 4 and placed with foster-parents until he was 14. He alleged that he had been sexually abused by his foster-parents. It was further alleged that the council had been negligent in failing to supervise his placement, to investigate reports of abuse and to remove him from foster care. The judge struck out the statement of claim as disclosing no cause of action. The Court of Appeal refused leave to appeal. An attempt was made to distinguish *X (Minors)* on the grounds that the policy considerations in placing and continuing a child in foster care were not the same as those that were relevant when the question was whether or not the child should be taken into care. Simon Brown LJ (with whose judgment Waite LJ agreed) rejected this argument although he recognised that the policy considerations were not precisely the same as in *X (Minors)*.

3.23 In *Barrett v London Borough of Enfield*[2] the plaintiff had been in the care of the local authority between the ages of 10 months and 18 years. During that time, he had been moved nine times in different foster placements. He alleged that he had developed a psychiatric illness as a result and this was due to the negligence of the local authority. The claim was struck out and the Court of Appeal dismissed the appeal from the judge's decision. The decision in *H v Norfolk County Council* was approved. As Lord Woolf MR said:

> 'The complaints which go to the heart of the plaintiff's claim are all ones which involve the type of decisions which an authority has to take in order to perform its statutory role in relation to children in its care. The decision whether or not to place a child for adoption, the decision as to whether to place a child with particular foster parents, the decision whether to remove the child from a foster parent, the decisions as to the child's relationship with his mother and sister, all involve the exercise of discretion in the performance of the differing statutory responsibilities of the local authority.'

The court said that the case could not be distinguished in principle from *X (Minors)*.

3.24 But in a passage in his judgment, which was probably *obiter*, the Master of the Rolls said:

> 'Social workers and other members of staff could, however, be negligent in an operational manner. They could, for example, be careless in looking after property belonging to the child or in reporting what they had observed for the purposes of the inter-disciplinary assessment of what action should be taken in relation to a child. They could also be negligent in failing to carry out instructions properly. If in implementing their decisions or the decisions of the authority a social worker was careless, I accept there would be a case for the defendant being vicariously liable if the necessary causation of injury or other damage could be established.'

3.25 *Barrett* then proceeded to the House of Lords,[3] which reversed the decision of the Court of Appeal. The House considered that *X (Minors)* could be distinguished on the basis that the public policy consideration militating against the imposition of liability when a local authority was deciding whether or not to take a child into care

---

1   [1997] 1 FLR 384.
2   [1997] 3 All ER 171.
3   [1999] 3 WLR 79.

did not have the same force once the child was already in local authority care. The court also considered that in all but the clearest cases it was important to see what facts were proved. Only then would it be apparent whether a claim was justiciable and whether it was fair, just and reasonable to impose a duty of care.

3.26 In referring to the passage from the Master of the Rolls' judgment set out in para **3.24** above, Lord Slynn observed: [1]

> 'Lord Woolf MR makes it clear that he does not suggest that a social services authority has a total immunity for whatever happens when it is acting or purporting to act pursuant to statutory powers or duties.'

Lord Slynn specifically approved Lord Woolf's suggestion that social workers 'could however be negligent in an operational manner'.

3.27 The House of Lords also sought to draw a distinction between the position of the parents and that of the local authority. Lord Hutton said: [2]

> 'My Lords, I agree that it would be wholly inappropriate that a child should be permitted to sue his parents for decisions made by them in respect of his upbringing which could be shown to be wrong, and I also agree with the observations of Sir Nicholas Browne-Wilkinson VC in *Surtees v Kingston-Upon-Thames Borough Council*: [3]
>
>> "I further agree with Stocker LJ that the Court should be wary in its approach to holding parents in breach of a duty of care owed to their children. It is accepted that the duty owed by Mr and Mrs H, as foster parents, to the plaintiff was exactly the same as that owed by the ordinary parent to his or her own children. There are very real public policy considerations to be taken into account if conflicts inherent in legal proceedings are to be brought into family relationships."
>
> But I do not agree, with great respect, that because the law should not permit a child to sue his parents, the law should not permit a child to sue a local authority which is under a duty by statute to take him into care and to make arrangements for his future. I consider that the comparison between a parent and a local authority is not an apt one in the present case because the local authority has to make decisions of a nature which a parent with whom a child is living in a normal family relationship does not have to make, *vis* whether the child should be placed for adoption or placed with foster parents, or whether a child should remain with foster parents or be placed in a residential home. I think it is erroneous to hold that because a child should not be permitted to sue his parents, he should not be permitted to sue a local authority in respect of decisions which a parent never has to take. Moreover, a local authority employs trained staff to make decisions and to advise it in respect of the future of a child within its care, and if it can be shown that decisions taken in respect of the child constitute, in the circumstances, a failure to take reasonable care, I do not think the local authority should be held to be free from liability on the ground that it is in the position of a parent to the child.'

3.28 The decision in *H v Norfolk County Council* must be considered of doubtful status in the light of *Barrett*, although Lord Hutton considered the case distinguishable. He said: [4]

---

1   [1999] 3 WLR 79 at 98C.
2   Ibid at 112D.
3   [1991] 2 FLR 559.
4   [1999] 3 WLR 79 at 114H.

'The circumstances of that case, involving allegations of sexual abuse by the foster father, were very different from the circumstances of the present case and, unlike the present defendant, the Council was able to rely strongly on the point that the system for the protection of children at risk was an inter-disciplinary one and that there would be difficulty in disentangling the respective roles of the various agencies concerned if there was to be liability. Therefore as, in my opinion, the case is clearly distinguishable I consider it unnecessary to express an opinion upon the correctness of the decision.'

3.29 In the light of *Barrett* it is not easy to advise a local authority whether as a matter of law any claim in negligence is likely to fall outside the apparent immunity provided by *X (Minors)*. What can be said with reasonable confidence is that since *Barrett* it seems unlikely that a local authority will be successful in striking out a claim but rather will have to wait until a trial before seeking to argue either non-justiciability or that it would not be fair, just and reasonable to impose a duty upon the local authority in the light of the particular facts of a case.

HUMAN RIGHTS ACT 1998

3.30 *Barrett* was decided before the Human Rights Act 1998 came into force. Lord Browne-Wilkinson, alone of the judges, considered the effect of the Human Rights Act 1998 and the decision in *Osman v The United Kingdom*.[1] In *Osman*, the European Court of Human Rights had to consider the position of the police in the light of *Hill v The Chief Constable of West Yorkshire*.[2] The Court of Appeal in *Osman*[3] had struck out the claim relying upon the apparent immunity given to the police in the course of their activities preventing and pursuing crime by *Hill*.

3.31 The European Court of Human Rights decided that there was a breach of Article 6(1) of the European Convention on Human Rights, which provides that:

'In the determination of his civil rights and obligations . . . everyone is entitled to a fair and public hearing . . .'

In considering the *Osman* decision, Lord Browne-Wilkinson said that he found it extremely difficult to understand. He suggested, somewhat gently, that the European Court may not have fully understood the way in which the English courts decide questions of duty of care. Referring to a passage in the *Osman* judgment in the European Court of Human Rights,[4] Lord Browne-Wilkinson said:

'This passage seems to treat the Osmans as having a right under English law to go to Court for a declaration that, apart from public policy preventing suits against the police, they would have had a claim in negligence against the police and further, that it was not fair, just and reasonable in the circumstances of that case to apply the "exclusionary rule", i.e. the rule excluding negligence actions against the police.

Having so defined the ambit of Article 6, the Strasbourg Court held that there was in the *Osman* case a breach of such a right of access to the English Court, such breach lying in the application of a blanket exclusionary rule which excludes all claims against the police for negligent failure to investigate or protect from crime. In the view of the Strasbourg

---

1   [1999] 1 FLR 193.
2   [1989] AC 53.
3   *Osman v Ferguson* [1993] 4 All ER 344.
4   [1999] 1 FLR 193 at paras 139–140.

Court, apparently, the applicability of such exclusionary rule has to be decided afresh in each individual case. If this is not done then it is impossible to determine whether the public interest in an efficient police force is or is not proportionate to the seriousness of the harm suffered by the plaintiff in the individual case.[1] On these grounds, the Strasbourg Court held that the English Court had breached Article 6 by striking out the claim made by the Osmans against the police without hearing any evidence by reference to which the proportionality of the rule in that particular case could be judged. The Court said that the police had been granted a "blanket immunity" which was disproportionate and therefore an unjustifiable restriction to the Osmans' right of access to the Court. The Osmans were entitled to have their case against the police determined in deserving cases.'[2]

Later in his judgment in *Barrett* Lord Browne-Wilkinson said:

'In view of the decision in the *Osman* case it is now difficult to foretell what would be the result in the present case if we were to uphold the striking out order. It seems to me that it is at least probable that the matter would be then taken to Strasbourg. That Court, applying its decision in the *Osman* case if it considers it to be correct, would say that we had deprived the plaintiff of his right to have the balance struck between the hardship suffered by him and the damage to be done to the public interest in the present case if an order were to be made against the defendant council. In the present very unsatisfactory state of affairs, and bearing in mind that under the Human Rights Act 1998 Article 6 will shortly become part of the English law, in such cases as these it is difficult to say that it is a clear and obvious case calling for striking out; ...'

Although the remainder of their Lordships did not overtly acknowledge the effect of the *Osman* case in their reasoning, it seems likely that the reluctance to strike out the claim in *Barrett* was influenced by these considerations.

3.32 The *Newham* case (considered as part of *X (Minors)*), was then being considered by the European Commission of Human Rights.[3] In its report, the European Commission decided that the House of Lords in *X (Minors)* had contravened both the mother and her child's human rights. By a majority of 17 to 2 the Commission considered that there had been a contravention of Article 8 of the Convention vis-à-vis the mother who had not been given an opportunity to participate in the decision-making procedures following the removal of her child. The Commission considered that there was a breach of Article 6 (fair trial) (by a majority of 10 to 9) as regards the child; but by a majority of 18 to 1 that there was no violation in respect of the mother. The Commission considered that there was a breach of Article 13 (by a majority of 18 to 1) as regards the mother in that she was provided with no effective remedy. The Commission considered by a majority of 10 to 9 that no separate issue arose in relation to the child as regards Article 13.

3.33 In *Z and Others v United Kingdom*,[4] the Commission considered the facts from *X (Minors)*. The report of the Commission was unanimous that there had been a breach of Article 3 of the children's rights in that the local authority had failed to take appropriate steps to protect the children from serious ill-treatment and neglect. No separate issue was considered to arise as regards Article 8 (the right to private and family life) but the Commission was unanimous that there had been a breach of

---

1   [1999] 1 FLR 193 at para 150.
2   Ibid, at paras 151 and 152.
3   *TP and KM v UK* (unreported) 10 September 1999, EComHR.
4   [2001] 2 FLR 612.

Article 6 in that the striking out of the children's claims constituted a disproportionate restriction of their right of access to court.

3.34 The *Newham* case thereafter proceeded to the European Court of Human Rights.[1] The Court decided that there had been a violation of Articles 8 and 13 but rejected the argument that there had been a violation of Article 6. The *X (Minors)* case was heard at the same time.[2] The Court found violations of Articles 3 and 13 but not of Article 6. In failing to find violations of Article 6, the Court was effectively modifying the impact of *Osman* which had seemed to suggest that a denial of a cause of action based on the fair, just and reasonable requirement would always amount to a violation of Article 6, particularly where the strike out procedure was adopted.

3.35 The courts in this country had already shown some reluctance to interpret *Osman* as preventing their deciding cases by a strike out. In *Jarvis v Hampshire*[3] the Court of Appeal considered that if a case was clear and obvious then a defendant is entitled to have a claim struck out. In the court's view, if Article 6 confers the right to a hearing at which competing public policy considerations affecting the existence of a cause of action are weighed then it could not see why the hearing which took place in *X (Minors)* (for example) would not suffice. This was also the approach of Tucker J in the case of *Kinsella v The Chief Constable of Nottinghamshire*,[4] where he struck out a claim against the police. In the course of the judgment Tucker J purported to weigh up the policy considerations and decided that the 'immunity' was proportionate, so as not to fall foul of the *Osman* decision. In *Palmer v Tees Health Authority*,[5] the Court of Appeal struck out a claim against a health authority notwithstanding the decision in *Osman* on the basis that *Osman* and *Barrett* did not preclude a court from holding as a matter of law that there was no proximity established on the pleaded facts. In *Palmer*, counsel for the defendant had submitted that *Osman* precluded the court from striking out on the fair, just and reasonable ground. It does not seem now that the concession was appropriately made.[6]

3.36 The position has been confirmed in *JD and Others v East Berkshire Community Health NHS Trust and Others*[7] where the Court of Appeal considered that there had been no violation of Article 6 when the lower court had struck out claims alleging negligence in and about the taking into care of children who, it was alleged, had suffered abuse at the hands of their parents.

W v ESSEX COUNTY COUNCIL

3.37 Most of the claims have been brought by children who were either in the care of the local authority or should have been. But in *W v Essex County Council*[8] the first two claimants were parents who together with their four minor children brought an

---

1   *TP and KM v United Kingdom* [2001] 2 FLR 549.
2   *Z and Others v United Kingdom* [2001] 2 FLR 612.
3   [2000] ELR 36; see also *S v Gloucestershire County Council* [2001] 2 WLR 909.
4   (1999) *The Times*, August 24.
5   [1999] PIQR 1.
6   See also, Lord Hoffmann 'Human Rights and The House of Lords' 62 MLR, March 1999.
7   [2003] EWCA Civ 1151, [2004] QB 558.
8   [2000] 2 WLR 601.

action against Essex County Council and a social worker employed by Essex. The claim arose out of the fostering with the children of G, then 15 years old, on the ground that the first and/or second defendant knew that G was an active sexual abuser. The parents had taken a course to qualify them to become full-time specialist adolescent carers and during their training it was alleged that they had informed those with whom they were dealing that they were not willing to accept any adolescent known or suspected to be a sexual abuser. They received oral assurances that this condition would be met. The parents signed a written specialist carer agreement. The foster-child sexually abused all the children and the plaintiffs brought claims in negligence, negligent mis-statement, misfeasance in public office and breach of contract. The judge at first instance dismissed all claims except those of the children in negligence. He distinguished *X (Minors)* on the grounds that the policy considerations were different where fostering was concerned. In particular, he did not consider that there would be a problem in disentangling the responsibility of the respective bodies' liability for reaching a decision. On the particular facts he considered that a social worker placing a child with foster-parents had a duty of care to provide the foster-parents with such information as a reasonable social worker would provide and that the local authority was vicariously liable for the conduct of its social worker in this respect. He considered that the children suffered a grievous wrong and that there was no policy reason for denying them a remedy on the facts of the case. But he struck out the parents' claims as unarguable.

3.38 The Court of Appeal (by a majority) dismissed the appeals and cross-appeals against the decision of the judge at first instance. Judge LJ felt able to distinguish the case from *X (Minors)*. He was unimpressed by the argument that the procedure was a multi-disciplinary one when the real question posed was 'is there any danger that the placement will adversely affect the family already living in the foster home?' In his view the question presupposed that the multi-disciplinary process had been completed. Nor did he think that the imposition of liability would place a great burden on local authorities. Rather, he considered it difficult to envisage how the disclosure of facts already known to the local authority would result in an inappropriate degree of caution in the decision-making process. He was also concerned that if local authorities could, with apparent immunity, make decisions which left actual or potential foster-parents uninformed about known risks, this would lead to a smaller number of potential foster-parents.

3.39 On the particular facts of *W*, Judge LJ considered that the local authority had assumed responsibility for the accuracy of the assurances they had given to the parents and there were at least arguably the necessary ingredients for a claim within *Hedley Byrne & Co Limited v Heller & Partners Limited*.[1] Mantell LJ agreed. Was the position of the parents, and the children, the same or different? Whatever public policy considerations might militate in favour of there being immunity from claims by children in care or potentially in care, these apparently did not preclude successful proceedings when the plaintiffs were foster-parents or where there are other children. Judge LJ made this observation despite the observations of Toulson LJ in *Lambert and Others v Dyer and South Glamorgan County Council*[2] who said:

---

1 [1964] AC 465.
2 (Unreported) 11 June 1997.

'It would be bizarre if a council's decision to put a child in an allegedly inappropriate placement could give rise to no action by the child for whose benefit the statute is primarily intended, but could give rise to such an action by a third party.'

Judge LJ was also undeterred in his conclusions by the fact that the plaintiffs in *X (Minors)* included the mother in the *Newham* case, whose claim had also struck out. He said:

'Immunities (whether partial or complete) and decisions based on public policy sometimes create anomalies, and decisions about where the appropriate line should be drawn tends to produce results in cases on one side or the other which can be analysed and described as "illogical" or "bizarre".'

3.40   The House of Lords considered the claim of the parents in *W* to be arguable, notwithstanding the unanimous dismissal of their claim on a striking out by the Court of Appeal. Their Lordships considered that whether or not the parents' claim was justiciable depended on an investigation of the full facts. It could not be said that the psychiatric injury the parents claimed was outside the range of psychiatric injury which the law recognised, nor could it be said that a person of reasonable fortitude would be bound to take in his stride being told of the sexual abuse of his young children when he had, albeit innocently, brought together the abuser and the abused. The House of Lords was influenced by the fact that the categorisation of primary and secondary victims of this type of negligence was still developing and it was not conclusively shown that the parents were prevented from being primary victims. In the course of their speeches, their Lordships seemed anxious not to strike out any but the most clear-cut case, although Lord Slynn, who gave the leading speech, said:

'I stress to the parents that I am not giving any indication either way as to the outcome of the case, but, win or lose, if they wish to pursue the claim they should not be barred from doing so.'

3.41   The question whether social workers, and police, owe a common-law duty of care when investigating allegations of child abuse committed by a parent, was considered in *L (A Child) v Reading Borough Council*.[1] A mother alleged that her child had been abused by the father. A social worker and woman police officer interviewed both child and father. The father was then arrested, but subsequently he was exonerated of the sexual abuse allegations. The Court of Appeal had little doubt that it was arguable that a duty of care was owed to the child. The position of the father was more difficult. He was interviewed as a suspect in a potential crime. The Court of Appeal accepted that there was no assumption of responsibility to him at that stage. The problem was that the social worker and woman police officer then misrepresented to their superiors what the child had said during the interview. Dealing with whether the father had an arguable case against the local authority and police, Otton LJ said:

'Although there was no evidence to support criminal proceedings, the WPC nevertheless came to the conclusion that the complaint by the mother was of sufficient substance that the child was at risk of further abuse from her father. It is arguable, in my judgment, that from then on there was a legal assumption of responsibility and a special relationship between the WPC and the social worker on the one hand, and the father on the other, and that a duty of care arose to take reasonable steps not to damage the father by their subsequent conduct.'

---

1   [2001] 1 WLR 1575.

The Court of Appeal then went on to hold that it was not prepared to decide on a striking out application that it was not fair, just and reasonable for the claim against the local authority and police to proceed. To some extent, the court seems to have been influenced by the European Court's decision in *Osman*.

3.42 The decision in *X (Minors)* has been further considered in *JD and Others v East Berkshire County Community Health NHS Trust and Others*.[1] The case was one of three appeals concerning allegations that children had been abused by their parents. The allegations were made by the professionals concerned for the welfare of the children. In each case a doctor was involved, and in one of the cases a local authority was also involved. The Court of Appeal had to consider whether it was appropriate to strike out claims by parents against the doctors and whether to strike out a claim by a child and her father against the local authority.

3.43 The authorities since *X (Minors)* led to the conclusion that it was only the 'core proposition' which remained, namely that the decision whether or not to take a child into care was not reviewable by the courts in a claim for damages alleging common law negligence. The Court of Appeal went on to consider the position, however, in the light of the Human Rights Act 1998. The court noted that similar issues will arise when considering, on the one hand, breach of any duty of care in negligence which might exist, and, on the other hand, violations of the European Convention on Human Rights. Lord Phillips MR said:

> 'In the context of suspected child abuse, breach of a duty of care in negligence will frequently also amount to a violation of article 3 or article 8. The difference, of course, is that those asserting that wrongful acts or omissions occurred before October 2000 will have no claim under the Human Rights Act. This cannot, however, constitute a valid reason of policy for preserving a limitation of the common law duty of care which is not otherwise justified. On the contrary, the absence of an alternative remedy for children who are victims of abuse before October 2000 militates in favour of the recognition of a common law duty of care once the public policy reasons against this have lost their force.'

The fact that the child did not have a remedy under the Human Rights Act 1998 before October 2000 was regarded as a clear policy reason why there should be no limitation of the common law duty of care. Thus it would seem that the children in *X (Minors)* would now be considered by the courts to have had a claim in negligence and, for events occurring after October 2000, a claim under the Human Rights Act 1998.

3.44 Considerable doubt can be expressed at the legitimacy of the Court of Appeal's decision.[2] The case is to be heard in 2005 by the House of Lords. The effect of the Court of Appeal's decision is to overrule essentially the decision of the house of Lords in *X (Minors)*, certainly as regards the investigation of sexual abuse of children.

3.45 The position of the parents in *JD and Others v East Berkshire Community Health NHS Trust and Others* was regarded as different. In the Court of Appeal's view, there will always be a potential conflict between the interests of the child and the parents. There were considered to be cogent public policy considerations for concluding that, where childcare decisions are being taken, there should be no duty of care owed to the parents.

---

1   [2003] EWCA Civ 1151, [2004] QB 558.
2   *Journal of Professional Negligence* (Tolley, 2004).

3.46   An example of the approach to human rights issues referred to by the Court of Appeal in *JD v East Berkshire* is to be found in *DP and JC v United Kingdom*.[1] The claimants alleged that they had been sexually abused by their stepfather. They reported the abuse to social workers; however, their mother denied that abuse was taking place and no action was taken by the social services department. Subsequently, the stepfather admitted the abuse. The European Court of Human Rights decided that there had been no violation of Article 3 of the European Convention on Human Rights (prohibiting inhuman or degrading treatment) because it had not been shown that the local authority knew about the sexual abuse and accordingly it could not be said to have failed in any positive obligation to take effective steps to protect the claimants from that abuse. Similarly, there was no violation of Article 8 (the right to respect for private and family life) for the same reason. There was, however, a breach of Article 13 (the right to effective remedy before a national authority) because the claims had been struck out by the English courts. The Court considered that an effective domestic procedure of enquiry would have offered more prospect of establishing the facts and throwing light on the conduct reasonably to be expected from the social services in a situation where the applicants had demonstrated long-term and serious problems which arguably might have called for additional efforts of investigation. As the Court of Appeal pointed out in *JD v East Berkshire*, the Human Rights Act 1998 has provided such a remedy since October 2000.

FOSTERING

3.47   Whatever limited immunity there may be for social workers in relation to children in care, does fostering fall outside the scope of this immunity? The decision in *W v Essex County Council*[2] appears to suggest that there may be public policy considerations which place fostering in a distinct category.

3.48   In *Beasley v Buckinghamshire County Council*,[3] the plaintiff acted as a paid foster-parent to a handicapped teenage boy who was placed with her by the defendant. She claimed to have suffered a back injury when trying to catch, lift, save or restrain him, and argued that she should have been provided with a hoist or other lifting equipment at an earlier stage. It was said that the defendant failed properly to assess the placement, and, had it done so, it would not have put such a heavy and disabled child with her, given her complete lack of experience in caring for a child with such disability. It was further argued that she should have been trained in lifting techniques and should have been warned of the risks to her which the work involved. The defendant sought to strike out her claim, arguing that it was ruled out by public policy, and placing reliance on *X (Minors)*.

3.49   The judge in *Beasley* refused to strike out the claim applying the principles in *Caparo Industries Plc v Dickman*.[4] He considered that the circumstances of the case were some considerable distance from *X (Minors)* and much closer to normal employment situations. The case concerned injury to a quasi-employee of the

---

1   [2003] 1 FLR 50.
2   [1998] 3 WLR 534.
3   [1997] PIQR 473.
4   [1990] 2 AC 605,

defendant sustained while helping to discharge its duty to a child in its care. There was little in the way of delicate discretionary decisions on the balancing of conflicting interests, in contrast to the situation in *X (Minors)*. It was arguable that the plaintiff's complaint concerned the 'practical manner' in which the defendant was proceeding, and this, as was held by Lord Browne-Wilkinson in *X (Minors)*, fell to be decided by applying the principles laid down in *Caparo*. It was at least arguable that the same considerations applied to a local authority vis-à-vis a paid foster-parent as applied to its duties to nurses in its employment to provide a safe system of work or suitable equipment.

3.50 The judge in *Beasley* was probably influenced by the fact that local authority employees charged with the care of the elderly and/or infirm in the community have often brought claims against local authorities. Injuries have been sustained by such employees, particularly to the back, where there has been inadequate assistance or equipment for lifting a heavy patient or the employee has received inadequate training in lifting techniques. There remains some difficulty in reconciling *Beasley*, *X (Minors)* and *H v Norfolk County Council*,[1] particularly where, in placing children in foster care, local authorities act pursuant to wide-ranging statutory powers, duties and discretions under the Children Act 1989, the Foster Placement (Children) Regulations 1991,[2] the Arrangements for Placement of Children (General) Regulations 1991[3] and *The Children Act Guidance*, Volume 3.

3.51 The nature of the relationship between the local authority and foster-parents was considered in *S v Walsall Metropolitan Borough Council*[4] where the question was whether foster-parents were the agents of the defendant council who had placed the child in care. Oliver LJ, with whose judgment Balcombe LJ agreed, reviewed the statutory provisions which were similar to those presently in force. He said that the statute and the regulations 'form a statutory code and they underline the fact that the whole of this area is covered by a complicated and detailed statutory scheme'. He added that 'the relationship between the child and the local authority, and indeed between the child and the foster-parents, is one which is regulated ... simply and solely by the provisions of the statutory scheme'.

3.52 The potential liability of local authorities in circumstances where a child suffers injury when in the care of foster-parents was considered by the Court of Appeal in *Surtees v Kingston Upon Thames Royal Borough Council*.[5] A 2-year-old child suffered a severely burnt foot while in the care of foster-parents. It was alleged against the local authority that social workers had failed adequately to vet the foster-parents before the placement. It was also alleged that they had failed to monitor the fostering. The trial judge, with whom the Court of Appeal agreed, rejected the allegation that the foster-parents had deliberately inflicted the injury on the child. Dealing therefore with an injury which occurred as the result of an accident, the Court of Appeal held first that there could be no liability on the part of the local authority in the absence of a finding of negligence on the part of the foster-parents. Continuing, Stocker LJ said:

---

1   [1997] 1 FLR 384.
2   SI 1991/910.
3   SI 1991/890.
4   [1985] 3 All ER 294.
5   [1991] 2 FLR 559.

'Against the local authority, it seems to me as a matter of causation that the claim is bound to fail unless the injuries were deliberately inflicted. The occurrence of accidental injury by negligence cannot, in my view, be affected by the number of visits paid to the foster parents or the claimant, nor can the circumstances in which he was boarded out unless urgent removal from the foster parents was required. Accidents by negligence are not prevented by these factors. This accident could have occurred precisely as it had had [the social worker] visited the house on the morning of its occurrence. As a matter of causation, any breach of any of the duties involved in the formulation of the case against the local authority could not have caused the occurrence of this accident once it is established that it was not deliberate.'

As has already been said,[1] the trial judge doubted that the Boarding Out of Children Regulations 1995[2] could give rise to a duty of care. The Court of Appeal decided the case without reaching any conclusion as to whether the Regulations afforded any civil cause of action to an injured person.

ADOPTION

3.53   Until the Court of Appeal decision in *A v Essex County Council*[3] it was unclear whether any claim could be brought against a local authority arising out of its role as an adoption agency. In that case, a couple brought a claim against Essex County Council on the grounds that they had been given inadequate information about the child before they proceeded with the adoption.

3.54   The judge at first instance held that Essex County Council was liable for not passing on 'all relevant information'. Nevertheless the council was only liable in respect of what happened during the placement period and not once the court had made the adoption order because the parents had decided to proceed with the adoption with knowledge of the child's difficulties during the placement period and any information which should have been passed to them by the council would not have added to this knowledge.

3.55   The Court of Appeal upheld the decision, albeit for different reasons. The court concluded that there is, in general, no duty of care owed by an adoption agency, or the staff whom it employs, towards prospective adopters, first because of the statutory framework of the adoption procedure, which is closely regulated with a view to ensuring best contemporary practice in a difficult and sensitive area and, secondly, because a balance has to be struck between the interests of all three parties to the adoption procedure, namely the prospective adopters, the birth parents and the child. The Court of Appeal did not rule out the possibility that a duty of care might be owed to the child, but did not have to decide this point.

3.56   An adoption agency is entitled, in accordance with its statutory obligations under the Adoption Act 1976, to decide what information should, or should not, be divulged to prospective adoptive parents. However, once it has decided what information to pass on to the prospective adopters, the adoption agency can be held to be negligent if that information is not, in fact, adequately conveyed to the prospective

---

1   See para **3.7**.
2   SI 1955/1377.
3   [2004] 1 WLR 1881.

adopters. In *A v Essex County Council* the Court of Appeal upheld the judge's decision against the council for this reason, namely that it had not passed on available medical evidence about the child which it had earlier decided the prospective adopters should see. The court agreed that on the evidence, the parents would not have proceeded with the placement had they received this information. Nevertheless the Court of Appeal also agreed with the judge that by the time of the adoption order, the claimants had enough information about the child to decide whether or not to go ahead with the adoption. Damages should therefore be limited to the period of the placement.

3.57 In New Zealand the courts have decided that no duty of care should be imposed on an adoption agency, whether in relation to adoptive parents or to the child.[1] It remains to be seen whether the courts here make the distinction between the position of the adoptive parents, on the one hand, and the child, on the other, as in *JD and Others v East Berkshire Community Health NHS Trust*.[2]

MISFEASANCE IN PUBLIC OFFICE

3.58 Lord Browne-Wilkinson in *X (Minors)*[3] acknowledged that local authorities could be liable for misfeasance in public office, 'ie the failure to exercise, or the exercise of, statutory powers either with the intention to injure the plaintiff or in the knowledge that the conduct is unlawful'. On the rather extreme (assumed) facts of *W v Essex County Council*, the Court of Appeal considered the scope of the tort insofar as it applied to social workers.

3.59 The Court of Appeal in *W* said that the tort could be committed in one of two ways, namely where a public officer has either:

(a) performed or omitted to perform an act with the object of injuring the plaintiff (ie where there was targeted malice); or
(b) where he has performed an act which he knew he had no power to perform and which he knew would probably injure the plaintiff.[4]

Both limbs require an invalid, unauthorised or unlawful act. The court was unable in *W* to identify any power that had been exceeded. In its view the social worker was acting pursuant to statutory powers conferred upon the council. The fact that while so acting he carelessly or even deliberately gave misleading information did not mean that he knowingly exceeded his powers.

---

1   *Attorney General v Prince and Gardner* [1998] 1 NZLR 262.
2   [2003] EWCA Civ 1151, [2004] QB 558.
3   [1995] 2 AC 633 at 731A.
4   *Three Rivers District Council v Bank of England* [2000] 2 WLR 1220 and see paras **1.103–1.107**.

NEGLIGENT MISSTATEMENT

3.60 There is some authority that a claim can lie in appropriate circumstances for a negligent misstatement even where there is otherwise immunity for a local authority in negligence.[1] In dealing with this point in *W* at first instance, Hooper J said:

'Mr Levy submits, in effect, that the principles in *X* have no application when considering liability for negligent misstatement. I do not accept that proposition for the reasons put forward by Mr Faulks. The consequences would be absurd. The child in care who asks the social worker: "Will the proposed foster-parent abuse me?" and is subsequently abused would succeed if the social worker made a negligent misstatement but would not succeed under the principles in *X*, *H* and *Barrett* if he had not asked the question or if the social worker had refused to answer. As Mr Faulks says: "There would be a premium on reticence". Furthermore, whereas before *Hedley Byrne* there was liability for acts and not statements, the situation would be reversed.'

3.61 In specifically approving this passage of Hooper J's judgment, Stuart-Smith LJ said:

'The giving of information or advice to the foster-parents is all part and parcel of the performance of their statutory powers and duties by the defendants.'

Judge LJ, on the other hand, found that on the facts of *W* the ingredients of a claim under *Hedley Byrne* were established. He felt able to distinguish the facts of *W* from *X (Minors)* where Lord Browne-Wilkinson had said:[2]

'Even if the advice tendered by the professionals to the local authority comes to the knowledge of the child or his parents they will not regulate their conduct in reliance upon the report. The effect of the report will be reflected in the way in which the local authority acts.'

In Judge LJ's view, on the facts of *W*, the advice tendered by the local authority was precisely reflected in the way the parents acted and physical injury had resulted. He also pointed out that the third *Caparo* requirement – that it must be fair, just and reasonable to impose a common-law duty of care – arguably only applied where the claim was for pure economic loss and not to claims for physical damage.

3.62 It is submitted that it is less than satisfactory for there to be different principles for establishing liability dependent upon whether complaints are made as to either the acts of a social worker or his words.

DIRECT/VICARIOUS LIABILITY

3.63 In *X (Minors)*, the House of Lords stressed that in some circumstances the distinction between direct and vicarious liability can be important.[3] It proved to be crucial in the education cases.[4] But in the social services cases the distinction is of less significance. Lord Browne-Wilkinson did not consider that the social workers in

---

1   *T v Surrey County Council* [1994] 4 All ER 577.
2   [1995] 2 AC 633 at 753B.
3   [1995] 2 AC 633 at 739G.
4   See Chapter 4.

X (Minors) came under any separate duty of care to the plaintiffs as distinct from the local authority itself. And he said:

'Even if, contrary to my view, the social workers and psychiatrist would otherwise have come under a duty of care to the plaintiffs, the same considerations which have led me to the view that there is no direct duty of care owed by the local authorities apply with at least equal force to the question whether it would be just and reasonable to impose such a duty of care on the individual social workers and the psychiatrist.'

OTHER REMEDIES

3.64   Whether or not a child has a claim for damages against a local authority there may be other remedies available. There is a statutory complaints procedure contained in s 76 of the Child Care Act 1980 and further procedures available under the Children Act 1989,[1] to allow grievances to be investigated, though not to recover compensation. In *X (Minors)*, it was also suggested that the local authorities Ombudsman would have power to investigate cases. Where a criminal offence has been committed, a child's injuries can give rise to a claim for compensation under the Criminal Injuries Compensation Scheme. In appropriate circumstances, it might be possible to obtain relief by judicial review.

NATURE OF THE DAMAGE

3.65   Damage suffered by the children in most of these claims was either physical or psychological or both. Where the injuries are physical in nature there can be no difficulty in establishing as a matter of law that a claim will lie. More difficulty exists when there is no physical injury. It was argued in *X (Minors)* that the nature of the plaintiff's illnesses was not the result of a 'sudden appreciation by sight or sound of a horrifying event, which violently agitates the mind'.[2] The House of Lords did not consider that such an argument was appropriate as a striking out application.

3.66   The Court of Appeal struck out the parents' claims in *W v Essex*[3] on the grounds that the shock must be sustained through the medium of the eye or the ear without direct contact. It did not include psychiatric illness caused by the accumulation over a period of time of more gradual attacks on the nervous system.[4] But the House of Lords in *W v Essex* did not feel able to strike out the parents' claims on this basis. It was stressed that the law was developing in this area. The removal of the 'shock' requirement is one of a number of changes in the law suggested by the Law Commission.[5]

---

1   See *X (Minors)* [1995] 2 AC 633 at 751A.
2   *Alcock v Chief Constable of South Yorkshire* [1992] 1 AC 310 at 410F.
3   See **3.37**.
4   *Alcock v Chief Constable of South Yorkshire* [1992] 1 AC 310 at 400E–401F, per Lord Ackner.
5   Law Commission Report No 249 *Liability for Psychiatric Illness*.

EMPLOYMENT

3.67　That the social services department owes a duty of care to its employees cannot seriously be in doubt. Indeed, such duties now extend beyond taking reasonable care to avoid causing physical injury. In *Walker v Northumberland County Council*[1] the plaintiff was a senior social worker. He suffered a nervous breakdown as a result of the stressful nature of his job. He took time off work but then returned. His employers had taken no steps to reduce his workload or otherwise organise his work to take into account his mental health. He suffered a second breakdown causing him to leave his job permanently. The trial judge held that the defendants were liable for his second breakdown in that they ought to have foreseen it in the light of the previous one. The law in relation to cases alleging that injury has been caused by stress at work has generally been clarified by the House of Lords in *Barber v Somerset County Council*.[2]

DISCOVERY/DISCLOSURE

3.68　In *Gaskin v Liverpool City Council*[3] the Court of Appeal refused discovery to a young man who was unhappy with his treatment whilst in care. Lord Denning MR said:

> 'I wonder how many more actions might follow by children who have been in care up and down the country. How many more of them would start blaming their misfortunes on the local authority in whose care they have been?'

Gaskin can no longer be considered good law. Local authority files will almost always be disclosable in that the public interest is more readily served by the open disclosure of such material than by refusing access – subject to appropriate safeguards such as anonymity of other children in care. Further, the European Court of Human Rights decided[4] that Gaskin's Article 8 rights had been infringed, in that the restriction of his access to the material was 'disproportionate'.

3.69　It might be said that information would be less freely provided if it was thought that the files would enable the sources to be identified. But the so-called 'candour' argument rarely meets with success since *D v NSPCC*.[5] In fact, there is now a statutory right to the relevant files pursuant to the Access to Personal Files Act 1987 and the Access to Personal Files (Social Services) Regulations 1989,[6] which contain only very limited exceptions to the right of access. These statutory rights exist in parallel with the right to pre-action disclosure in appropriate circumstances as provided by s 31 of the Supreme Court Act 1981 and the Civil Procedure (Modification of Enactments) Order 1998.[7]

1　[1995] 1 All ER 737 and see paras **6.89–6.91**.
2　[2004] 2 All ER 385.
3　[1980] 1 WLR 1549.
4　[1989] 12 EHRR 36, ECHR.
5　[1978] AC 171.
6　SI 1989/206.
7　SI 1998/2940.

ALLEGATIONS OF ABUSE IN CHILDREN'S HOMES

3.70   A substantial number of actions have been brought as a result of abuse suffered by children, particularly in the 1970s and 1980s. A series of claims arose following the Waterhouse enquiry, whose report, *Lost in Care*, was published in 2000. The first tranche of these cases was tried by Scott Baker J, in Chester.[1]

3.71   None of the claims involved consideration of the nature of the duty of care owed by local authorities. Liability had been admitted, leaving causation, limitation and damage in dispute. One significant point of principle emerged from the judgment. Most of the claimants (as will often be the case in this type of claim) had troubled upbringings, sometimes involving abuse, before coming to the relevant children's home. A number had subsequently taken large amounts of drugs, committed criminal offences and been physically or sexually abused elsewhere. The claimants argued that these other potential causation factors should be ignored when assessing the proper level of compensation on the basis that once it had been established that the defendant had negligently caused psychiatric damage to the claimants, the court should award damages on the basis that all such damage was attributable to the defendant.

3.72   The judge rejected this argument. He preferred the approach of the court in *Thompson v Smiths Ship Repairers Ltd*[2] and, more recently, in *Holtby v Brigham & Cowan (Hull) Ltd*,[3] which was to apportion damage between the various causative factors. Thus the defendant was only liable for that part of the damage which was found by the judge to be attributable to it.[4]

3.73   A similar approach was taken by Connell J in another series of cases in North Wales.[5] He also had to consider the effect of the House of Lords' decision in *Lister and Others v Hesley Hall Ltd*,[6] and which had widened the scope of vicarious liability to include liability for deliberate sexual assaults by care workers, thereby reversing the decision of the Court of Appeal in *Trotman v North Yorkshire County Council*.[7] The judge concluded that the employers were, in most cases, responsible in law for the physical and sexual abuse visited upon residents at the children's home.

Limitation

3.74   Arguments about limitation periods are common in these claims. Sometimes claimants may wait 20 years or more before commencing proceedings. In the *Flintshire* and *Bryn Alyn* cases the judges decided that all claimants had the necessary 'knowledge' more than 3 years before issuing proceedings, but disapplied the limitation period in the exercise of the court's discretion.[8]

---

1   *Various Claimants v Flintshire County Council* (unreported) 21 July 2000.
2   [1984] 1 QB 405.
3   [2000] 3 All ER 421.
4   Note also that in *Coxon v Flintshire County Council* (2001) *The Times*, February 13, the Court of Appeal refused to interfere with an award of damages to a sexually abused child which appeared to be higher than the Judicial Studies Board Guidelines.
5   *Various Claimants v Bryn Alyn Community Homes and Another* (unreported) 26 June 2001.
6   [2001] 2 WLR 1311.
7   [1999] LGR 584.
8   Limitation Act 1980, ss 11, 14, 33.

3.75 The Court of Appeal considered the proper approach to limitation periods in *KR and Others v Bryn Alyn (Holdings) Ltd (In Liquidation) and Another*.[1] The court took a different approach to the date of knowledge provisions in this type of case than the judge at first instance had done. Where an adult was seeking damages for childhood abuse the court had to consider whether it would reasonably occur to the claimant, given the circumstances of the abuse and his subsequent way of life, to bring a civil action for damages within 3 years of his majority. A claimant may only have acquired the necessary knowledge to start the limitation clock running following therapy with a psychiatrist.

3.76 As to the application of s 33 of the Limitation Act 1980, as a general rule the longer the delay after the occurrence of the abuse the less likely the court would be to disapply the normal limitation period, particularly where allegations were easy to make and often hard to refute.

3.77 Courts at first instance are encouraged, where possible, to decide limitation by way of preliminary issue. Quite what 'knowledge' a claimant must have is not clear from the judgments. It would seem that he or she must be able to make the link between the mental illness and the sexual or physical assaults, irrespective of any immediate physical effects of such assaults.[2] The Court of Appeal followed this approach in *H v N&T*.[3] The trial judge had approached the limitation issue on the basis that 'the injury in question' for the test of knowledge under s 14 of the Limitation Act 1980 was the initial abuse. In fact, as the Court of Appeal pointed out, the claim was for alleged post-traumatic stress disorder which may not have emerged until years later. Because the judge had addressed the wrong question, the case was sent back for further argument.

3.78 Where a claim is based on vicarious liability of an employer for the assaults of its employee, the appropriate limitation period is 6 years, non-extendable, rather than the extendable 3-year period.[4] A defendant cannot be deprived of an accrued time bar by subsequent legislation giving the court power to extend limitation periods.[5] It is ironic that in many cases abusers will be able to escape liability on the basis that the 6-year limitation period for claims of assault has expired.[6] Nevertheless, while the Court of Appeal confirmed the 6-year limitation period for assault in *C v D*,[7] nevertheless it allowed the claim for an alleged direct duty of care owed by the defendant to the claimant to continue.

3.79 Other issues which arise in these claims include:

(a)   the standard of care applying in the 1960s, 1970s and 1980s;
(b)   the duties of a 'placing' authority where a child is at a home which is run privately or by another local authority;

---

1   [2003] QB 1442.
2   See also *Hodges v Northampton County Council* (unreported) 29 April 2004.
3   (Unreported) 29 April 2004.
4   See *KR and Others v Bryn Alyn (Holdings) Ltd (In Liquidation) and another* [2003] QB 1442, particularly para [108].
5   *McDonnell v Congregation of Christian Brothers Trustees (formerly Irish Christian Brothers)* [2004] 1 All ER 641.
6   *Stubbings v Webb* [1993] 2 WLR 120; *Seymour v Williams* [1995] PIQR 470; *Limitation of Actions*, Law Com No 270.
7   (Unreported) 4 March 2004.

(c)   the insurance position where local authorities have not specifically insured against liability for sexual abuse and have failed to inform insurers of bad practices and thus an increased risk of abuse.

CONCLUSION

3.80   Claims against social workers have increased. Following the decision in *X (Minors)* it seemed that there was a defence to such claims, as a matter of law. However, *Barrett v London Borough of Enfield*[1] and *JD v East Berkshire Community Health NHS Trust*[2] have substantially qualified any such immunity. Inroads were also made by *W v Essex County Council*.[3] The effect of these cases and the coming into force of the Human Rights Act 1998 is that it will be very difficult to strike out claims, with the result that many are likely to proceed to trial. The law may then become clearer, although judges may focus on the facts of each case and thus on questions of breach rather than duty.

3.81   Meanwhile, there are certain principles which can, perhaps, be extracted from the case law:

(a)   there is no general immunity for social workers;
(b)   if an action is brought against a local authority based on the lawful exercise of a discretion, a claim may not be justiciable if there are 'policy' elements in the relevant decision-making process;
(c)   if a claim is brought based on 'operational' negligence, a duty of care will arise unless, on the particular facts, the public policy considerations identified in *X (Minors)* persuade a court that it would not be fair, just and reasonable to impose a duty;
(d)   there is more likely to be a duty of care owed to a child already in care;
(e)   any claimant will have to satisfy a court, on the facts, that there was a breach of duty, to be assessed on *Bolam*[4] principles.

---

1   [1997] 3 All ER 171.
2   [2003] EWCA Civ 1151, [2004] QB 558.
3   [2000] 2 WLR 601.
4   *Bolam v Friern Hospital Management Committee* [1957] 1 WLR 582.

Chapter 4

EDUCATION – THE LIABILITY OF TEACHERS AND LOCAL EDUCATION AUTHORITIES

THE NATURE OF THE DUTY

4.1 In *Van Oppen v Clerk to the Bedford Charity Trustees*,[1] a case involving a serious injury sustained by the plaintiff when playing a rugby match at school, it was accepted by both parties that the school, being *in loco parentis*, owed a general duty to the plaintiff and to all pupils to exercise all reasonable care for his and their safety both in the classroom and on the games field. The nature of the duty has been established for more than 100 years and is well understood in actions involving personal injury. Recent years have, however, seen cases establishing that the duty of care can extend to the quality of education received by certain pupils, for example those suffering from dyslexia, and possibly to cases of bullying, where the injury has been psychiatric or there has been a failure to ameliorate a congenital condition. This chapter will consider the traditional claims against schools and will then go on to deal with the newer areas of liability.

4.2 The duty owed by school teachers in supervising their pupils was expressed by Lord Esher MR in the case of *Williams v Eady*:[2]

'The school master is bound to take such care of his boys as a careful father would take of his boys.'

In *Eady* the plaintiff was injured when a fellow pupil was playing with a bottle containing phosphorus which exploded. The Court of Appeal did not interfere with the decision of the jury in favour of the plaintiff at the original trial because the bottle had been left in a conservatory. Had it been locked away, as a careful father would have ensured at home, it was unlikely that the boys would have found the bottle and there would have been no finding of negligence.

4.3 Although in *Ricketts v Erith Borough Council and Another*[3] Tucker J followed the principle set out in *Eady*, he added a further consideration to the test:

'The duty of the Defendants is that of a reasonably careful parent ... incidentally, in considering the facts of a case like this, one has to visualise a parent with a very large family, because 50 children playing about in a yard is, of course, a different thing from 4 or 5 children playing about together in a garden.'

---

1   [1989] 1 All ER 273.
2   (1893) 10 TLR 41.
3   [1943] 2 All ER 629.

In *Nicholson v Westmoreland County Council*,[1] Lord Denning MR agreed that the test was the position of a reasonably careful parent, but that it must be a reasonably careful parent looking after a family as large as 20.

4.4   The above cases set out the common law duty of care owed by teachers. Schools also face liability under the Occupiers' Liability Act 1957, and under various regulations laid down by the Department of Education.

4.5   This chapter will consider the way in which the courts have applied the above principles when dealing with particular facts. It is submitted that an analysis of the various cases shows the following:

(1)   a general reluctance on the part of the courts to impose liability for the actions of teachers alone, namely without a breach of duty by the school or education authority or in the absence of a specific danger;

(2)   a particular reluctance to impose liability for accidents occurring in the playground where supervision of pupils is likely to be more difficult;

(3)   a greater willingness on the part of the courts to impose liability on schools or local education authorities where accidents have resulted from the condition of the school premises.

The courts have been more willing to find a breach of the duty laid down in *Williams v Eady* where accidents have occurred in the classroom and gymnasium, where a teacher is expected to be present at all times, rather than in the playground, where it would seem that the courts accept that teachers cannot be expected to be present at all times. Finally, it may be possible to discern that the courts are imposing a higher standard of care now, when compared with cases decided more than 20 years ago.

ACCIDENTS IN THE CLASSROOM

4.6   In *Wray v Essex County Council*,[2] a schoolmaster asked a pupil to take an oil can to another room. The boy ran and, as it coincided with a change in classes, there were other boys in the corridor. Unfortunately the spout of the oil can struck the plaintiff in the eye. The Court of Appeal held that an oil can was not inherently dangerous, being an ordinary article of domestic use and not calculated to cause damage to anybody. The court compared this to the stick of phosphorus in *Williams v Eady* which had been held, without much hesitation, to be a dangerous article. It also referred to *Chilvers v London County Council*,[3] where a child was injured by the point of a lance which was part of a toy soldier and where, according to Bailhache J:

'The fact that the master had allowed a toy soldier to be in the room could not be treated as evidence of negligence or lack of proper supervision.'

In *Wray* the Court of Appeal held that the accident to the plaintiff was not foreseeable. Lord Wright MR said:

'It is necessary to consider whether there is something which the schoolmaster ought to have anticipated, something reasonably foreseeable and something, therefore, because it

---

1   (1962) *The Times*, October 24.
2   [1936] 3 All ER 97.
3   (1916) 80 JP 246.

is foreseeable, the master ought to have guarded against. I say "foreseeable" because the mere fact that he did not foresee a risk or particular contingency would not excuse him if it was something which he ought to have foreseen. But when I look at the facts of this case, it seems to me to be a misadventure which could not have been reasonably foreseen by anybody.'

4.7   In *Fryer v Salford Corporation*,[1] the Court of Appeal held the school (but not the teacher) liable for failing to place a guard around a stove which was being used during a cookery class. The plaintiff's apron caught fire and she suffered injuries. Although there was no evidence that other schools placed guards around stoves in the classroom, the Court of Appeal considered that the accident was foreseeable. Slesser LJ said:

> 'If the learned Judge had come to a contrary conclusion, upon a consideration of all the evidence, it may well have been that this Court would not have thought fit to disturb his finding, however, having heard all the evidence in this case . . . he came to the conclusion, on the balance of consideration, first, that this was a danger which ought reasonably to have been anticipated and, secondly, that it was a danger that could reasonably be guarded against.'

The judge had dismissed a claim in negligence against the teacher and there was no appeal against that finding. Arguably this case should be considered with those cases dealing with the condition of the school premises.[2] In *Ralph v London County Council*[3] a teacher allowed boys to play a game of chase indoors when a PE class could not be conducted outside due to bad weather. The plaintiff pushed his hand through a panel of a glass partition and was injured. Byrne J held the teacher liable for failing to foresee that such an accident might occur and failing to keep the boys away from the glass partition.

4.8   In *Camarthenshire County Council v Lewis*,[4] a 4-year-old boy ran out of the classroom and onto the road through an unlocked gate, causing a lorry to swerve, killing the driver. The House of Lords considered that there was no negligence on the part of the schoolteacher who had left the plaintiff and another child unattended for about 10 minutes while she bandaged another child who was injured. It did, however, hold that as the council had not been able to explain how the child got onto the road when he was in its care, the council was liable as it was foreseeable that an accident might occur if the child was alone in the street, and this was evidence of a failure to take reasonable care to prevent the child leaving the school.

4.9   In *Nicholson v Westmoreland County Council*,[5] a teacher in a small schoolroom with about twenty 5–11-year-olds had limited opportunity for a break and was therefore provided with a kettle with which to make a cup of tea. She poured a cup which she placed on top of a cupboard. She then turned to discipline a boy, and the plaintiff reached up and pulled the cup over, scalding herself. The Court of Appeal upheld the council's appeal, holding this had been a pure accident with no negligence on the teacher's part. It is possible that the decision would have been different had the

---

1   [1937] 1 All ER 617.
2   See, eg, *Lyes v Middlesex County Council* and *Reffell v Surrey County Council* at paras **4.37** and **4.38** below.
3   (1947) 111 JP 548.
4   [1955] 1 All ER 565.
5   (1962) *The Times*, October 24.

teacher moved away from the cupboard, but she was still within arm's reach of the cup and could not have anticipated that the plaintiff would come up behind her and pull the cup down.

4.10 In *Crouch v Essex County Council*,[1] the plaintiff was injured during a chemistry lesson when other pupils in the class squirted a chemical into the plaintiff's face. The judge was satisfied that the schoolmaster had given a warning to the pupils about the nature of the chemical and he was satisfied that there was no need to label the beaker from which the chemical was obtained. The plaintiff argued that the teacher had failed to maintain discipline in the class and that this had led to the accident, but Widgery J did not agree. He said:

> 'So really, in the last analysis, one has to ask oneself whether it was reasonably foreseeable to this master, approaching his duties as being equivalent to those of a careful and prudent parent, that on this occasion not only should some pupils have studiously ignored everything which was said to them in the earlier part of the period but also should have proceeded to his desk and then proceeded to squirt a wholly unidentified liquid at the Plaintiff's face. This conduct was little short of lunatic and was utterly irresponsible and I am quite sure, from the evidence I have heard, that the general atmosphere and standard of the class was not such as to make that kind of conduct foreseeable.'

4.11 Two contrasting decisions, possibly indicating a raising of the standard of care by the courts, are *Butt v Cambridgeshire County Council*[2] and *Black v Kent County Council*.[3] In both cases the plaintiff was stabbed in the eye by the point of a pair of scissors and in both cases this had happened by accident. In *Butt* the evidence of the teacher was that if she saw a child holding scissors and not cutting anything she would tell the child to put the scissors down. The Court of Appeal considered that the teacher was conducting her class properly and efficiently and that the system was in no way at fault. Salmon LJ said:

> 'I do not believe that any system of supervision or any degree of care on the part of the teacher can make it impossible for an accident of this kind to happen. It is a very remote possibility; unfortunately this remote possibility turned up on this occasion.'

4.12 On the other hand in *Black*, almost 15 years later, the class had been provided with a variety of scissors, some having blunt ends and some having only one end blunted. The judge had held that it was reasonably foreseeable that the use of sharp-pointed scissors as opposed to blunt-ended scissors involved greater risk of injury. The Court of Appeal upheld the decision and Sir John Donaldson MR said:

> 'If the Judge is right that there is an appreciably increased risk from the use of sharp scissors – which seems to me as a matter of common sense must be the case – then the staff ought to avoid that risk unless there is some countervailing reason for taking it. There would be a countervailing reason if there were a real need for sharp-ended scissors, and in those circumstances no doubt the staff would allow children to select sharp-ended scissors, pointing out to them the risks involved. But that was not this case ... I would agree with the Judge that the teachers in those circumstances were making an error of judgment which amounted to a breach of the duty of care which they owed the Plaintiff.'

---

1   (1966) 64 LGR 240.
2   (1969) 68 LGR 81.
3   (1983) 82 LGR 39.

It is noticeable that in *Black* the court was referred to a pamphlet from the Department of Education which recommended the use of scissors with rounded ends although the Court of Appeal considered that the pamphlet was saying no more than would have been clear already to the educational profession.

4.13   The above cases suggest a reluctance on the part of the courts to find teachers negligent when the only issue is one of supervision. In *Eady*, *Ralph* and *Black* there was liability because the plaintiff was injured by a dangerous item. In *Fryer* and *Lewis* liability was imposed on the school rather than the teacher. The case of *Black* perhaps shows a greater willingness to impose liability on teachers in the classroom. More particularly, where advice from the Department of Education is available, the courts will probably impose liability if there has been a failure to follow such guidance.

ACCIDENTS IN THE GYMNASIUM

4.14   The courts have been more willing to impose liability in cases concerning gymnasium accidents, probably because of the more obvious potential danger. In *Gibbs v Barking Corporation*[1] the Court of Appeal upheld the judge's finding of negligence on the part of a games instructor who failed to make sure that the plaintiff did not fall when completing a vault over a horse. In *Gillmore v London County Council*[2] the council was found liable where the plaintiff slipped on a highly polished floor. The duty of the council was to provide a floor which was reasonably safe in the circumstances, and this it had failed to do. On the other hand, in *Wright v Cheshire County Council*,[3] the Court of Appeal decided in favour of the teacher. A group of boys was vaulting over a 'buck'. Each boy, on completing his vault, had to wait at the receiving end of the buck to assist as necessary the next boy to come over. The school bell rang denoting the end of the class whereupon the boy at the receiving end of the buck ran off without waiting for the plaintiff to complete his vault. The teacher was a little distance away supervising activities of other boys in the class. The evidence before the court was that the teacher had followed ordinary and recognised practice. Singleton LJ said:

> 'I cannot see how it can be said that the Defendants were negligent if they adopted the well-recognised practice in a matter of this kind. The view of the Plaintiff's witnesses would seem to indicate the necessity of having four adult instructors in the gymnasium for a class of 40 boys. I cannot accept that. There may well be some risk in everything that one does or in every step that one takes, but in ordinary everyday affairs the test of what is reasonable care may well be answered by experience from which arises a practice adopted generally, and followed successfully over the years so far as the evidence in this case goes.'

The Court of Appeal also considered that it was not foreseeable that the boy would run off when the bell sounded.

4.15   In *Moore v Hampshire County Council*,[4] the plaintiff was disabled and as a result her mother had arranged with the school that her daughter should not do PE.

---

1   [1936] 1 All ER 115.
2   [1938] 4 All ER 331.
3   [1952] 2 All ER 789.
4   (1981) 80 LGR 481.

During a lesson the plaintiff told her teacher that she was allowed to do PE and the teacher did not check whether this was correct. Unfortunately the girl fell while attempting a handstand and injured herself. The Court of Appeal held the council liable. Lord Denning MR considered that the teacher should have checked whether the girl was now allowed to do PE and he also considered that the teacher should have kept a close watch on the plaintiff while she performed her handstand. He said:

> 'It seems to me that the standard of care to be exercised by school teachers in regard to the children is quite high. The parents entrust the children to the school – not only to give them instruction – but to take care of them when they are playing games and the like.'

Watkins LJ considered that there was a failure of supervision on the part of the teacher, but he also considered that the school owed a duty to comply with the mother's requirement. He said:

> 'When a parent of a child who suffers from a physical disability forbids participation by that child in school games and physical education the school, to whose attention that prohibition is made known, is under a duty to give effect to it until there is a relaxation of it from the quarter from which it emanated.'

It is noticeable that the court considered that the teacher and the school had failed to have regard to the earlier agreement reached with the plaintiff's mother that the child should not take part in PE lessons.

4.16   In *Jones v Hampshire County Council*,[1] the plaintiff fell from a vaulting table on which she had been performing somersaults, and suffered a broken arm. The Court of Appeal upheld the decision of the judge that the teacher had failed to exercise any judgement in establishing whether it was safe for the pupils to carry out the exercise. In particular, the court rejected the council's argument that when considering whether there had been a breach of the teacher's duty of care, it was relevant that the plaintiff was known to have attended extra classes in gymnastics outside school.

ACCIDENTS IN THE PLAYGROUND

4.17   A review of relevant cases indicates a reluctance on the part of the courts to impose liability for accidents in the playground. In *Langham v Governors of Wellingborough School and Fryer*,[2] a schoolboy was walking along a corridor when he was hit in the eye by a golf ball which had been struck by a boy in the playground. The golf ball had entered the corridor through an open door. In the Court of Appeal Scrutton LJ considered that there was no evidence justifying a finding of liability against the school because:

(1)   there was no evidence that the headmaster had not provided supervision; and
(2)   in any event there was no evidence that supervision, if provided, would have prevented the accident.

Scrutton LJ noted that the plaintiff's own evidence was to the effect that he had never known a golf ball to be hit with a stick in the playground before.

---

1   (Unreported) 20 March 1997.
2   (1932) 101 LJ KB 513.

4.18   In *Rawsthorne v Otley and Others*[1] the plaintiff was injured when he jumped onto a lorry which was delivering fuel in the playground. The headmaster's evidence was that he did not know that the lorry would arrive during break. He had left the boys unsupervised in the playground when the lorry had arrived. Hilbury J did not consider that the lorry was an allurement to a 14-year-old boy and then went on:

> 'As to control, what supervision or control ought a headmaster to have exercised over boys in a senior class in a playground in playtime? He saw them start to play; then he went in. In my view it is not the law and it never has been the law, that a schoolmaster should keep boys under supervision during every moment of their school lives. Having regard to the fact that the schoolmaster did not know that the lorry was there, I find that there is no negligence. It has been said that he knew it might have come. I still do not think that he should have stayed, lest such a possibility should have become the event. Should he have stopped its coming during playtime? I do not think that that is lack of supervision and it would necessitate extra supervision.'

4.19   In *Rich and Another v London County Council*[2] the infant plaintiff was injured by a piece of coke thrown at him by another boy. The Court of Appeal overturned the original decision where Slade J had considered that a careful parent would have removed the coke from his back yard or would have taken steps to prevent the boy having access to the coke. Singleton LJ considered that the judge's test imposed too high a burden on the education authority, which had to place the coke somewhere. It is noticeable, however, that the Court of Appeal relied on the lack of evidence of a similar previous incident and also on the express finding by Slade J that the supervision in the playground had been adequate. It is arguable, therefore, that had the level of supervision in *Rich* been the same as that in *Rawsthorne*, where the headmaster left the boys unsupervised in the playground, the Court of Appeal might have decided in favour of the plaintiff.

4.20   The cases of *Rawsthorne* and *Rich*, where there was no finding of liability, can be compared with *Martin v Middlesbrough Corporation*,[3] where the council was held liable. The 11-year-old plaintiff fell in the school playground during the lunchtime break and injured her hand on a piece of broken glass from a milk bottle. The court heard evidence that empty milk bottles were stacked in crates in a recess at the side of the entrance to the playground. Other milk bottles were also left standing loose on the ground alongside the stack of crates. The judge held that there was no negligence in the stacking of the milk crates and dismissed the plaintiff's claim. However, the Court of Appeal considered that there was evidence that arrangements for disposing of the empty milk bottles could have been improved and also considered that there was a lack of supervision. Willmer LJ said:

> 'In my Judgment, on the evidence, the risk of an accident such as this occurring was a reasonably foreseeable risk against which the Defendants could and should have guarded by making better arrangements for the disposal of empty milk bottles. I do not think that the arrangements which they in fact made were such as would commend themselves to any reasonable, prudent parent.'

The significant factor in the *Martin* case causing the Court of Appeal to find that there had been a breach of duty of care, may have been that it was known to the school that

---

1   [1937] 3 All ER 902.
2   [1953] 2 All ER 376.
3   (1965) 63 LGR 385.

potentially dangerous items, namely milk bottles, were on the school premises and that the school could have done more to keep the milk bottles in a safe place. This is to be compared with most playground cases which the courts have tended to approach on the basis that 'boys will be boys' and where only minute supervision would prevent the accident.

4.21 In *Ricketts v Erith Borough Council and Another*[1] a 6-year-old boy left the school playground through an unlocked gate, and went to a nearby shop where he purchased pieces of bamboo made up in the form of a bow and arrow. The boy returned to the playground and fired an arrow which struck the plaintiff in the eye. The court heard that although teachers went into the playground from time to time, the playground was unsupervised throughout the relevant period. Tucker J held in favour of the local authority and decided that the level of supervision in the playground was adequate in all the circumstances of the case:

> 'I find it impossible to hold that it was incumbent to have a teacher, even tender as were the years of these children and bearing in mind the locality of this school, continuously present in that yard, throughout the whole of this break; and nothing short of that would suffice. Unless that is their duty, nothing less is any good, because small children, or any child, can get up to mischief if the parents' or teacher's back is turned for a short period of time.'

4.22 Similarly, in *Nwabudike v Southwark London Borough Council*,[2] a primary school pupil was injured when he was struck by a car after running out of school during the lunch period. The claim was dismissed on the basis that the school had demonstrated that appropriate steps had been taken, there had been no recent accidents of this type, and there was little which a school could do in the face of a pupil's determination to surmount the safeguards which were in place. The claimant left the playground while it was busy and when there were six supervisors on duty. Judge Zucker QC said:

> 'I agree that a balance had to be struck between security and preventing a school being turned into a fortress. No school can ensure that accidents never happen. Whatever precautions are taken there is always a risk that they could, particularly if a child is determined to act in a way which breaks the rules designed to protect him or her. What is required of a school is that it takes reasonable and proper steps to ensure that its children are safe.'

4.23 *Nwabudike* should be compared with *Jenney (A Minor) v North Lincolnshire County Council*,[3] where the Court of Appeal found in favour of the claimant in similar circumstances. The claimant was an 8-year-old boy who was retarded. He left school, probably through an open gate, during the afternoon break. No one saw him leave the school. Unfortunately, about 1,000 metres from the school, on a major road, he was struck by a motor car and sustained serious injuries. Because the school could not explain how the claimant had got out of the school, the Court of Appeal followed the House of Lords' decision in *Carmarthenshire County Council v Lewis*[4] where their Lordships had held that if a child in a school's care is injured as a result of being where he should not be, namely unaccompanied, by a highway, then the onus is on the

---

1   [1943] 2 All ER 629.
2   [1997] ELR 35.
3   [2000] LGR 269.
4   [1955] 1 All ER 565 and see para **4.8**.

school to show how it was that the child came to be where he or she should not be, and to show that that state of affairs had come about through no fault of the school. Henry LJ said:

> 'The appellant accepts that *Carmarthenshire County Council v Lewis* places the initial evidentiary burden on them. The defendant cannot say how Ryan left the safety of the school unobserved. So then theirs is the even more testing task of showing that they had taken all reasonable precautions to prevent the escape of someone whose escape they could not explain.'

4.24 The claimant had been seen heading for the school gates on previous occasions. Furthermore, there was evidence that there had been a number of instances when pupils had, without authority, walked out of the school. There was evidence that one school gate could not be secured adequately. Although the school argued that to establish causation it would have to be proved that the claimant left the school through that gate, the Court of Appeal held that the principle of *res ipsa loquitur* applied. Because of the *Carmarthenshire* case the school had to show that all reasonable precautions had been taken to keep the child in, namely it had to disprove negligence. As the school had failed to discharge the evidential burden on it to show that the accident was not due to negligence on its part, the claimant succeeded in his claim. According to Henry LJ:

> 'Therefore the school failed to discharge the evidential burden on it to show that the accident was not due to negligence on its part ... as the evidential burden does not shift back to him [the plaintiff], he need not prove causation. By definition the plaintiff cannot prove how the accident happened, and so cannot put forward any set of facts as causing the accident. And the law does not require him to.'

4.25 In *Clarke v Monmouthshire County Council*,[1] the plaintiff was stabbed in the leg with a knife by another boy in the playground. Denning LJ (as he then was) considered that there was no reason why the teachers should have known that the boy had a knife and they were not negligent in failing to observe the knife. He also considered that the supervision in the playground had been adequate although the two prefects who would normally have been on duty were not present on this occasion. The master on duty passed through the yard twice during the break; Denning LJ said:

> 'The duty of a school does not extend to constant supervision of all the boys all the time; that is not practicable. Only reasonable supervision is required. I do not think that it can be said that the school was negligent in not having a master on duty all the time.'

As the incident had taken place in a fraction of a second, Denning LJ did not consider that the presence of prefects or of a master would have done anything to prevent the incident occurring.

4.26 In *Price v Caernarvonshire County Council*[2] the plaintiff was struck in the eye by a rounders bat which had slipped out of the hand of the boy batting. This was an unsupervised game of rounders in the playground where boys had first played with their hands, but on this occasion the boys had obtained a bat. The judge held that lack of supervision in the playground had resulted in the boy using a rounders bat, which was forbidden. However, the Court of Appeal overturned the decision and found in

---

1   (1954) 53 LGR 246.
2   (1960) *The Times*, February 11.

favour of the council on the basis that lack of supervision had not caused the accident. It was just as probable that the accident would have occurred in an open field with a group of boys playing an organised and supervised game. Accordingly unless rounders was to be treated as so dangerous as not to be allowed, the plaintiff's claim must fail.

4.27 The cases illustrate a reluctance on the part of the courts to impose liability for accidents in the playground, particularly where the level of supervision is in question. On the other hand, *Martin* shows that the courts may be more inclined to impose liability where something which is potentially dangerous, in that case milk bottles, is left unguarded, and it is submitted that even in *Rich* (the unfenced pile of coke) the Court of Appeal might have been prepared to find in favour of the plaintiff had not the judge made a firm finding that there had been adequate supervision.

ACCIDENTS BEFORE THE BEGINNING OF THE SCHOOL DAY

4.28 As in the playground cases, the courts have been reluctant to impose liability for accidents before the beginning of the school day, and the adequacy of supervision has been a relevant factor. In the case of *Ward v Hertfordshire County Council*,[1] the plaintiff, aged 8, tripped while running in the playground and struck his head against a flint wall. The Court of Appeal rejected an argument that the wall was dangerous and then considered the level of supervision which should have been provided in the playground before the start of school. The judge had held that there should have been supervision of the boys in the playground; however, Lord Denning MR did not agree:

> 'The headmaster said that the teachers took charge of the children from the moment they were due to be in school at 8.55 am until the time when they were let out. Before the school began the staff were indoors preparing for the day's work. They cannot be expected to be in the playground too.'

In any event, the Court of Appeal also considered that if there had been a teacher in the playground he would not have stopped the children running and would not have been able to prevent this accident occurring. A teacher could not stop children running around the playground in break or before school. On the other hand, Salmon LJ considered that the position might have been different had the accident occurred through some particularly dangerous activity which a teacher should have stopped:

> 'If this accident had been caused by the children fighting or indulging in some particularly dangerous game which a master should have stopped if he had been there, the fact that there was no supervision at the time might have afforded anyone who was injured in that way a good cause of action. It is not necessary to express any concluded view on that point. To my mind the fact that there was no master in the playground on this occasion is irrelevant, because even if a master had been there, I can see no reason why he should have prevented the children racing or playing as the infant plaintiff was doing at the time when he met with this unfortunate accident.'

4.29 The Court of Appeal has now, however, confirmed in *Kearn-Price v Kent County Council*[2] that schools do owe a duty of care to pupils in respect of accidents

---

1   [1970] 1 All ER 535.
2   [2002] EWCA Civ 1539, [2003] ELR 17.

occurring on school premises before the start of the school day. The claimant was in the school playground before the start of school when he was struck in the eye by a football and seriously injured. The use of leather footballs in the playground had been banned by the school. There had been at least one previous incident and pupils had been warned that the use of these footballs was contrary to school rules. Nevertheless the school had taken no further steps to enforce the ban. The Court of Appeal considered that the decision in *Ward* did not go so far as to say that a school owed no duty to supervise pupils on its premises before the start of the school day. The decision in *Ward* was really based on causation, namely that the presence of the staff in the playground would not have prevented the claimant from running into the wall. Dyson LJ expressed the duty as follows:

> 'In my judgment a school owes to all pupils who are lawfully on its premises the general duty to take such measures to care for their health and safety as are reasonable in all the circumstances. It is neither just nor reasonable to say that a school owes no duty of care at all to pupils who are at school before or after school hours . . . The real issue is the scope of the duty of care owed to pupils who are on school premises before and after school hours.'

However, the longer before the start of the school day that a pupil is injured, the more difficult it may be to show a breach of the duty to supervise. Further it may be unreasonable to expect constant supervision before the start of the school day. Dyson LJ continued:

> 'Moreover, it may be unreasonable to expect constant supervision during the pre-school period, but entirely reasonable to expect constant supervision during the break periods.'

4.30 Having decided that a duty of care existed, the Court of Appeal agreed with the judge that there had been a breach of that duty which included the taking of steps to enforce the ban on leather footballs and the carrying-out of spot checks before the start of the school day. These steps were required because the school knew that the ban on leather footballs was regularly flouted. It knew that leather footballs were dangerous and furthermore the carrying-out of spot checks before the start of the school day did not add a substantial burden to the teachers' duties. The Court of Appeal rejected the defendant's argument on causation. It considered that the judge had been entitled to conclude that the pupils would have complied with the ban on leather footballs if they had thought that it was being taken seriously by the school. Accordingly, the accident would not have occurred if the school had taken more rigorous steps to enforce the ban.

4.31 In *Mays v Essex County Council*[1] an 8-year-old boy received permanent brain damage as a result of a fall which occurred when he was sliding on ice in the playground before school began. The headmaster had issued a circular to all parents to discourage them from sending children to school too early, emphasising the dangers of dark mornings. Furthermore, the school did not feel it necessary to provide supervision in the playground before the start of school. The judge considered that sliding on ice was an innocent and healthy amusement and that there was no evidence of disorder amongst the children on this particular occasion. As sliding on ice was not a dangerous game the judge held that the school had no duty to prevent the children from playing on the ice and also that it had no duty to supervise the playground before school began unless the school had voluntarily adopted responsibility for children

---

1   (1975) *The Times*, October 11.

arriving at school early, which was not the case. Finally, the judge considered that there was no duty on the part of the school caretaker to spread salt on the playground when the ground was frosty.

ACCIDENTS OCCURRING AFTER SCHOOL

4.32 Again, the courts have shown a reluctance to impose liability for accidents occurring after school. In *Jeffrey v London County Council*[1] a 5-year-old boy climbed up a water pipe onto a roof of a lavatory from which he fell through a glass roof, sustaining fatal injuries. The court heard that it was the practice of the school to instruct the children aged 5 and upwards to remain in the playground until they were collected by a relative, and to report to a mistress if they were not collected within a short time. On the day of the accident, the mother of the deceased, who regularly called for him at the end of school hours, was late in arriving. McNair J considered that the instructions given by the school represented 'a responsible decision as to detailed supervision' and he dismissed the action. He did not regard the drain pipe as a particular allurement to children and therefore did not consider that the school should have done anything further to prevent the children climbing the drain pipe.

4.33 In *Good v Inner London Education Authority*,[2] the plaintiff, aged 6, was injured when he was struck in the eye by sand thrown at him by another pupil. The Court of Appeal had to consider a situation where at the end of the school day each class of infants was ushered through the classroom by the teacher as they left school. The plaintiff's classroom was on the ground floor and led directly to a play centre through an archway. The majority of children were collected by their parents who waited in the playground, but the remaining children would go out to play on fine days and on wet days would go to the play centre which opened at the end of the school day. A week or so before the accident a pile of sand and stones had been laid in the corner of the junior playground. This had been roped off. The headmistress had specifically warned the children in assembly not to go anywhere near the ropes. The day of the accident was wet and while the play centre staff were preparing to take in the children, the plaintiff and his companion escaped unnoticed into the corner of the playground where the sand and stones were situated. The judge had held in favour of the education authority on the basis that some obedience in children was to be expected or otherwise life would be impossible, that it would have been impracticable to fence off the sand and stones and that the accident must have been over in a moment. The Court of Appeal agreed with the judge and held that no one could reasonably have been expected to supervise the children every minute of the day. In particular, there was no breach of duty on the part of the authority in failing to supervise the whole of the journey from the infant school building to the play centre.

4.34 In *Wilson v Governors of Sacred Heart RC*,[3] the plaintiff, aged 9, was injured as he was walking towards the school gate at the end of the day and another boy, waving his coat in the air, struck the plaintiff in the eye. When considering the level of supervision, the Court of Appeal drew a distinction between lunchtime, when there

---

1   (1954) 52 LGR 521.
2   (1980) Fam Law 213.
3   [1998] 1 FLR 663.

might be over a 100 pupils in the playground for more than an hour, and the very short period during which pupils ran or walked from the school to the gates. The need for supervision at lunchtime was clear, but the Court of Appeal was not satisfied as to the need for supervision at the end of the school day and, as was pointed out by Mantell LJ, the confrontation between the two boys might just as well have taken place outside the school gates.

4.35   On the other hand, in *Barnes (An Infant) v Hampshire County Council*,[1] the plaintiff, a 5-year-old girl, was injured in a road accident outside the school having been, with the rest of her class, released from school about five minutes earlier than the normal end of the school day. The House of Lords was satisfied that, on the evidence presented to the court, had the child been released from school at the appointed time she would have been met by her mother. Accordingly, on the balance of probabilities, the premature release of the children by the school was a cause of the accident. Lord Pearson accepted that there was a risk that the accident would have occurred in any event, even had the children been released from school at the appropriate time, but considered that in all the circumstances this was not a great risk and that it was a risk which could be taken by the school in the circumstances. Nevertheless, by releasing the children 5 minutes earlier, the teacher had added an unnecessary risk. The school had a system which was known to the parents and, as Lord Pearson said:

> 'It was the duty of the school authority not to release the children before the closing time. Although a premature release would very seldom cause an accident, it foreseeably could, and in this case it did cause the accident to the appellant.'

In effect this was a case where there was something approaching an agreement between the school and the parents as to the time at which children would be released from school, and by breaching this agreement the school laid itself open to liability.

SAFETY OF PREMISES

4.36   It is clear that the Occupiers' Liability Act 1957 applies to schools. Under s 2(2) the duty is set out as follows:

> '... the common duty of care is a duty to take such care as in all the circumstances of the case is reasonable to see that the visitor will be reasonably safe in using the premises for the purposes for which he is invited or permitted to be there.'

4.37   The courts have been more inclined to make findings of liability in cases where the condition of the school premises has led to the injury to the pupil. For example, in *Lyes v Middlesex County Council*,[2] the plaintiff was injured when his hand slid off the woodwork of a changing room door and went through a glass panel in the door. Edmund Davies J held that the glass was too thin. Because the case was argued on the basis that the plaintiff would have to show negligence in order to establish liability, the judge dealt with this point and considered that the defendants should have realised that, given the additional hazards of school life compared with life at home, the glass in the changing room doors was too thin.

---

1   [1969] 3 All ER 746.
2   (1962) 61 LGR 443.

4.38 Similarly, in *Reffell v Surrey County Council*,[1] the council was held liable in circumstances where the plaintiff, a girl aged 12, put her hand through the glass panel of a door in the corridor. The case was decided under reg 51 of the Standards for School Premises Regulations 1959,[2] made under the Education Act 1944. Where relevant the regulation read:

> 'In all parts of the buildings in every school, the design, the construction and the properties of the material shall be such that the Health and Safety of the occupants shall be reasonably assured.'

Veale LJ considered that a private right of action for damages did arise out of the regulation and then went on to explain the duty as follows:

> 'I think that the duty to secure, that is the word in the section, that safety shall be reasonably assured (which are the words of the regulation) is an absolute duty and the test of breach or no breach is objective. Putting it another way, if safety is not reasonably assured in the premises in fact, then there is a breach.'

The judge was in no doubt that the glass in the door was too thin and went on to hold that not only was there a breach of reg 51, but that the council was negligent in having failed to renew the glass with thicker glass earlier.

4.39 There are, however, cases where the decision has been made in favour of the school. In *Gough v Upshire Primary School*,[3] an 8-year-old pupil fell from banisters at first floor level. He was either sitting on the banisters or had attempted to slide down them. The banisters had been in place since 1936 and complied with the relevant building regulations. The judge considered that the test was whether the school should reasonably have foreseen that a pupil might attempt to slide down the banisters and, assuming that it was foreseeable, whether the risk that a pupil might do so was such as to require preventative measures aimed at that risk. The judge concluded that the risk was foreseeable, but that this was not the only question. Responsible persons had either not considered that there was a risk, or had considered it insufficient to take preventative steps. Other risks in connection with using the stairway had been assessed and met. Although the risk of a child climbing onto the banisters was foreseeable, it was no more so than other risk which might befall children at school.

4.40 In *Barrie v Cardiff City Council*,[4] a 6-year-old girl tripped in the playground over a 15mm-high concrete fillet between paved and tarmacked areas. The site of the accident had been in the same condition for some time and there had been no previous accidents. The Court of Appeal considered that the question whether the danger might reasonably have been anticipated had to be considered on the basis of the use of the playground by children generally. Some children are more active than others and some are more prone to tripping. Some (like the claimant, who had brittle bone disease) were more likely to suffer serious injury if they tripped. There had been no previous related accidents and the location had been in the same condition for some time. It was not reasonable to expect the playground to be completely level. There was no evidence that the change in level presented any significant problems. The danger

1   [1964] 1 All ER 743.
2   SI 1959/890.
3   [2002] ELR 169.
4   [2001] EWCA Civ 703, [2002] ELR 1.

could not reasonably have been anticipated from the presence of the 15mm ridge and there was no breach of duty.

TRAVELLING TO AND FROM SCHOOL

4.41   Although the courts have shown a reluctance to impose liability on schools for supervision of pupils in the playground and indeed when arriving at or leaving school, nevertheless they have imposed liability, in certain circumstances, where pupils have been injured on, or alighting from, buses provided to take them to and from school. In *Shrimpton v Hertfordshire County Council,*[1] the plaintiff, a young girl, was travelling in a vehicle provided by the local education authority on her journey home from school. The plaintiff fell while getting out of the vehicle and was injured. The court heard that there was no conductor or other adult person to accompany the children on the vehicle. At first instance it was decided by the jury that the child had been injured by reason of the negligence of the driver of the vehicle, coupled with the fact that there was no conductor or adult person to accompany the vehicle. Loreburn LC, having recited that the jury had found that it was not a reasonable and proper way for the county council to convey children to school in this vehicle without a conductor or some adult person to take care of them, said:

> 'If the County Council did, through their representative, agree to provide a vehicle for this child, it was their duty to provide a reasonably safe motor conveyance, and in the opinion of the jury, they did not do so.'

4.42   In *Ellis v Sayers Confectioners Ltd and Others,*[2] the 8-year-old plaintiff was travelling home from a special school in a school bus provided by the local education authority. The children on the bus were in the care and under the charge of an employee of the authority in addition to the driver. The child was seen off the bus by the employee, who gave the child certain instructions. However, as the child crossed the road he was knocked over by a van coming in the opposite direction to the bus. The judge heard that the child was known to the employee of the education authority to be not very well trained or disciplined in crossing roads. He held that the employee had a duty towards the child, in the same way as that of a parent, to warn him more carefully or see that he did not go out into the opposite side of the road when a van was being driven fast in the other direction. The judge held the education authority liable, but apportioned liability on the basis of 20 per cent to the education authority and 80 per cent to the driver of the van which hit the child. In the Court of Appeal, Sellers LJ said:

> 'I think that in the circumstances Mrs McVey (the Education Authority's employee) had a duty of acting as a reasonable parent. One asks oneself whether she wholly fulfilled that duty. I do not think it is a case where she need feel any moral blame. It is one of those situations which arise where, along with her other duties, she may be excused for having erred to the extent which she did . . . but I cannot help feeling that the Judge was justified in taking the view that she ought to have ascertained (that the situation was safe) or at any rate given a little more definite instruction to the little boy to look before he crossed from the particular place.'

1   (1911) 104 LT 145.
2   (1963) 61 LGR 299.

It seems apparent that the Court of Appeal was reluctant to make a finding of liability against the education authority and that had the judge's apportionment of liability against the education authority been any higher than 20 per cent then it might have decided differently. In the circumstances, however, the Court of Appeal did not consider it appropriate to absolve the education authority from liability altogether.

4.43 However, in *Jacques v Oxfordshire County Council and Another*,[1] Waller J dismissed a claim against a local education authority where, apart from the bus driver, the only supervision had been provided by two prefects. The plaintiff, a 14-year-old boy, was injured when a pellet was flicked into his eye by another child travelling on the bus. The court heard evidence that there were 42 pupils on the bus and that although paper pellets had been flicked in the bus previously, such conduct was generally stopped by the prefects and on the whole the boys responded to control fairly well. The court considered what duty was owed by the local education authority in the circumstances and Waller J said:

> 'What is the duty of the local authority in these circumstances? They owe a duty to see that the bus is reasonably safe and that includes a duty to see that it is reasonably safe for the children who are going on the bus including the provision of supervision if it is necessary. I think that the standard which is to be adopted is that of the reasonable parent ... applying his mind to school life where there is a greater risk of skylarking, and it may be that it is a reasonable parent of a rather large family.'

Having found that the children on the bus had not been abnormally boisterous or undisciplined, Waller J held that there was no evidence that the local education authority was guilty of negligence.

INJURIES ON THE SPORTS FIELD

4.44 Before the case of *Condon v Basi*,[2] there appears to have been no decision in the English courts as to the standard of care governing the conduct of players in competitive sports generally. In *Condon*, Sir John Donaldson MR accepted the decision of the High Court of Australia in *Rootes v Shelton*,[3] where that court held that there is a general standard of care in the sense of *Donoghue v Stevenson*[4] that a player is under a duty to take all reasonable care taking account of the circumstances in which he is placed. Clearly, in a game of football, the circumstances are different from those applying when someone is merely walking in the countryside.

4.45 Although there do not appear to have been earlier reported cases involving injuries to school children on the sports field, nevertheless in *Van Oppen v Clerk to the Bedford Charity Trustees*,[5] a case involving serious injury to a 16-year-old school boy in the course of a rugby match at the school, it was accepted by both parties that Bedford School owed a general duty to the plaintiff, and to all pupils, to exercise reasonable care for his and their safety both in the classroom and on the games field. The plaintiff was injured while making a tackle. He alleged that the school had been

---

1   (1968) 66 LGR 440.
2   [1985] 2 All ER 453.
3   (1968) ALR 33.
4   [1932] AC 562.
5   [1989] 1 All ER 273.

negligent in failing to take reasonable care for his safety on the rugby field, by failing to coach or instruct him in proper tackling techniques. Boreham J held that the injury had been a 'tragic accident' and was not the fault of the school:

> 'I am satisfied that the Defendants, through the staff taking rugby, were well aware of the inherent risks in playing rugby football and the need for the application of correct techniques and the correction of the potentially dangerous errors and lapses. I am also satisfied that the standard of supervision was high, that the refereeing was vigilant and strict and that, as one of the Plaintiff's contemporaries put it, there was at the school an emphasis on discipline which meant playing the game correctly. There was therefore no substance in the allegations of negligence insofar as they relate to the playing of rugby football at Bedford School.'

4.46 The second allegation in *Van Oppen* involved the school's alleged failure to advise on the inherent risk of serious injury in playing rugby, the consequent need for personal accident insurance and the fact that the school had not arranged such insurance for the plaintiff. The court heard evidence about the availability of personal accident insurance and that the school had considered whether to take out such insurance or give advice to parents, but had decided not to do so.

Boreham J held that there was no duty on the school to take out personal accident insurance or advise parents so to do. He observed that there was no duty on a parent to insure his child and that it would be neither fair nor reasonable to place a wider duty on the school than was imposed on the parent:

> 'The school's duty is more limited than that of the parent. It relates to matters over which the school has control and to no other matters. What is a matter of choice or discretion for the parent is outside the ambit of the duty of the school. A duty is not established merely because a prudent headmaster or a prudent parent might think, in certain circumstances, it was desirable to have personal accident insurance. Schools are under a duty to protect their pupils from harm. This involves taking reasonable care to ensure, inter alia, that the school's activities are reasonably safe and well organised. The taking out of personal accident insurance could not justify relaxation of that duty and in particular would not justify allowing the boys to participate in any activity which, because of inherent dangers, should not be undertaken. No one has seriously suggested that rugby football is such an activity.'

4.47 *Van Oppen* went to the Court of Appeal,[1] but only in connection with the alleged failure to insure. The Court of Appeal agreed with Boreham J that it would be neither just nor reasonable to impose on the school a greater duty than that which rests on a parent. Furthermore, the plaintiff's allegation that the school assumed responsibility to give advice to parents on the insurance issue failed. Because there was no duty on the school to provide information, it necessarily followed that failure to provide such information could not in itself have resulted in the assumption by the school of a duty to advise.

4.48 The liability of a referee to the players in a rugby match was considered in *Smoldon v Whitworth and Another*.[2] Although this case did not involve a school, nevertheless the players were under 19 years of age and therefore the decision is relevant to games played at school. The plaintiff, aged 17 at the time, was seriously injured when a scrummage collapsed towards the end of what the court heard was a

1   [1989] 3 All ER 389.
2   [1997] PIQR 133, [1997] ELR 249.

strongly contested match. The court was satisfied that there had been a number of collapsed scrums during the game and the court was also satisfied that the referee had failed to apply the laws containing special provisions relating to players aged under 19 specifically in regard to the way in which scrummages should take place. The referee accepted that he owed a duty to the plaintiff. As a result the Court of Appeal did not have to consider whether it was just and reasonable to impose a duty, but simply had to decide on the extent of the duty owed. Bingham LCJ followed the decision in *Condon v Basi* and held that the second defendant:

> 'owed a duty to the Plaintiff to exercise such degree of care as was appropriate in all the circumstances.'

Because the referee had failed to apply the laws relating to scrummaging, and because there was evidence that the referee had received a warning from a touch judge earlier in the game that someone would be hurt if the referee did not do something about the scrummaging, the Court of Appeal held that the referee had been in breach of his duty of care.

4.49 The referee argued that the plaintiff had consented to the risk of injury by voluntarily playing as a member of the front row in the scrummage. The Court of Appeal, however, agreed with the judge's observation that although the plaintiff had consented to the risk of injury in the game of rugby, he could not be held to have consented to the referee's breach of duty:

> 'Given that the rules were framed for the protection of him and other players in the same position, he cannot possibly have been said to have consented to breach of duty on the part of the official whose duty it was to apply the rules and to ensure insofar as possible that they were observed.'

4.50 The Court of Appeal made it clear that it considered that the threshold for establishing liability against a referee is a high one and that it did not consider that there would be many claims brought against referees.

4.51 In *Smoldon* the existence of a duty of care was conceded by the referee in the context of a game involving players under the age of 19. The position of a referee of a rugby match has now been confirmed in *Vowles v Evans*.[1] The case involved allegations of negligence against the referee of an amateur rugby match. He allowed one team to use a substitute player in the front row of the scrum. He did not know that the substitute player was not trained for that position. Shortly before the end of the match, a front row forward (not the substitute) was injured. The Court of Appeal confirmed that a duty was owed by the referee to the players. The court referred to the inherently dangerous nature of rugby, that some of the rules are designed to limit these dangers, and that players are dependent for their safety on due enforcement of the rules. Where a referee undertakes to perform the role, it is fair, just and reasonable that the players should be entitled to rely on the referee to exercise reasonable care in so doing. On the facts, the referee was in breach of the duty because he should have satisfied himself that the substitute player was suitably trained to play in the front row before allowing him to do so. The Court of Appeal also refused to interfere with the judge's finding that the presence of the untrained player in the front row had caused the claimant's accident.

---

1   [2003] EWCA Civ 318, [2003] 1 WLR 1607.

4.52 Although neither *Smoldon* nor *Vowles* were cases involving school rugby matches, nevertheless both decisions are relevant to school and local education authorities. It must follow that teachers face potential liability if boys are injured during rugby matches which teachers are refereeing at school.

4.53 Before leaving the subject of rugby it should be noted that in the case of *Affutu-Nartoy v Clarke and Another*,[1] Hodgson J held that although a teacher could take part in a game of rugby to keep the game and the ball moving and to demonstrate the skills of the game, it was wrong and a breach of duty of care for that teacher to tackle and have physical contact with 15-year-old schoolboys taking part in the game.

LIABILITY FOR ACTIVITIES OUTSIDE SCHOOL

4.54 There are two circumstances in relation to activities outside school which might give rise to a duty of care.

School trips[2]

4.55 Although the existence of a duty of care to pupils on school trips was not seriously in doubt, the position has been confirmed in *Chittock v Woodbridge School*.[3] Three senior boys travelled on a school ski trip organised for the school's juniors. It was agreed by their parents that, once in the resort, the senior boys did not have to ski with the juniors and would therefore be unsupervised. The claimant, one of the senior boys, suffered a serious injury when he accidentally lost control whilst skiing on a piste which was well within his capability. On the day before the accident, the claimant, and another senior boy, were seen by the teachers to be skiing back to their hotel off-piste. They were admonished by the teacher in charge of the ski trip. It was suggested by the claimant, and accepted by the judge, that the teacher should have removed his ski pass, or made him ski with the junior boys. This would have prevented the accident.

4.56 The Court of Appeal confirmed that the teachers on the skiing trip owed a duty to the claimant. Auld LJ expressed it as a duty:

> 'To show the same care in relation to him as would have been exercised by a reasonably careful parent credited with experience of skiing and its hazards and of running school ski trips, but taking into account the claimant's known level of skiing competence and experience, the nature and condition of the particular resort, and the teacher's responsibilities for the school group as a whole.'

The duty was not a duty:

> 'To ensure his safety against injury from skiing mishaps such as those that might result from his own misjudgement or inadvertence when skiing unsupervised on-piste. It was a duty to take such steps as were in all the circumstances reasonable to see that he skied safely and otherwise behaved in a responsible manner.'

---

1   (1984) *The Times*, February 9.
2   It should be noted that the Department for Education and Skills has issued guidance about which schools should be aware, *Good Practice Guide for Health and Safety of Pupils on Educational Visits* (HASPEV).
3   [2002] EWCA Civ 915, [2002] ELR 735.

It was relevant to bear in mind that the claimant's parents had allowed him to ski unsupervised. The school had, however, implicitly accepted responsibility for general oversight of his skiing and other activities at the resort.

4.57 Dealing with breach of duty, the question was whether the off-piste skiing incident, the only relevant behaviour during the ski trip where the claimant had acted irresponsibly (there had been other minor incidents), was of such a nature that the teacher in charge of the trip should have stopped the claimant skiing or made him ski under supervision. Was the reprimand given by the teacher sufficient? The Court of Appeal held that there had been a number of options open to the teacher and that negligence is not established if a teacher:

> 'Chooses one which, exercising the *Bolam*[1] test, would be within a reasonable range of options for a reasonable teacher exercising that duty of care in the circumstances.'

The off-piste skiing incident had been the first infraction by the senior boys which was relevant to their conduct as skiers. Otherwise their skiing had been competent and sensible. The teacher had not acted unreasonably in giving them a reprimand and accepting their assurance that they would not ski off-piste again.

4.58 It is suggested that the scope of the duty might have been different if the case had concerned an accident to one of the junior boys. There was a duty to supervise the junior boys while they were skiing. If the teachers had seen one of the junior boys skiing off-piste then the court might have concluded that a reasonable teacher should have removed his ski pass. Nevertheless the claimant in *Chittock* also failed to satisfy the Court of Appeal that he would have established causation as the accident could still have occurred even if the claimant had been skiing under supervision. The same must be the case in respect of junior boys.

4.59 Is there a duty on the school to inspect the activity centre or resort before the journey takes place? Some guidance might be had from the case of *Brown v Nelson and Others*.[2] For several years, an approved school had sent small groups of pupils to a confidence course run by the Outward Bound Organisation. Each group of pupils was accompanied by a master who did not, however, inspect the site or the equipment. The plaintiff, a 16-year-old boy from the approved school, was performing an exercise suspended from a rope between two trees. He was injured when a rusty cable supporting the rope broke. The cable was not new when it had been brought to the campsite. It had been stored for some time and had been placed in position to replace a flawed cable four months before the accident. The claim against the camp warden succeeded under the Occupiers' Liability Act 1957. However, the judge dismissed the claim against the school on the basis that the school had discharged its general duty to take reasonable steps for the safety of those under their charge as it knew the premises, and knew that they were apparently safe and were staffed by competent and careful persons. The school was under no obligation to make an inspection. Nield J said:

> 'What duty did the school authority owe to the Plaintiff? They were not the occupiers of
> the site or of the apparatus. They had, in my view, a general duty to take reasonable steps
> for the safety of those under their charge and use such care as would be exercised by a
> reasonably careful parent. Counsel tell me that there is no authority covering the situation

---

1	*Bolam v Friern Hospital Management Committee* [1957] 1 WLR 582.
2	(1970) 69 LGR 20.

where a school makes use of someone else's equipment at premises other than the school premises. In my Judgment, where a school must take their pupils to other premises, they discharge their duty of care if they know the premises and if the premises are apparently safe, and if they know that the premises are staffed by competent and careful persons. They further discharge their duty if they permit their pupils there to use equipment which is apparently safe and is under the control of competent and careful persons who supervise the use of such equipment. They do not in such circumstances have an obligation themselves to make an inspection.'

Note also *Dickinson v Cornwall County Council*,[1] where the local authority successfully defeated a claim arising out of the murder of a 13-year-old schoolgirl in France. Someone had gained access to the hostel where the school children were staying. It was alleged that the hostel chosen by the local education authority had been insecure and that the choice was negligent. Steel J found for the local education authority on the basis that the hostel had been used previously, without incident, and was registered with the appropriate authorities. Further, the attack was not foreseeable.

Work experience

4.60   Where pupils are sent by schools or local education authorities to undertake work experience, it is submitted that the school or education authority must be under a duty to exercise reasonable care, but judged against the relevant circumstances. This would include reasonable care in the selection of the work place. *Brown v Nelson and Others* indicates how the school might discharge its duty of care. In any event, it is submitted that the employer should face a greater responsibility in circumstances where a pupil is injured on the employer's premises.

LIABILITY OF SCHOOLS FOR BULLYING

4.61   Until recently, there have been few decided cases concerning bullying in schools. The first case to be heard by the High Court in England was *Bradford-Smart v West Sussex County Council*,[2] which will be dealt with below. The following paragraphs deal briefly with the cases heard before *Bradford-Smart*.

4.62   In 1994, a claim for bullying was pursued in *Walker v Derbyshire County Council*,[3] a case which proceeded in the Nottingham County Court and which was reported widely in the newspapers, although it does not appear to have been otherwise reported. Miss Walker, who suffered from cerebral palsy, claimed that she was subjected to a year-long campaign of 'whispering, staring and unkind behaviour' from three girls who resented her presence in the school orchestra. She maintained that a particular teacher ignored her pleas for help and took no effective action to stop the bullying. The council denied breach of duty and also denied that the plaintiff was suffering from post-traumatic stress disorder. Although the judge seems to have accepted that the school owed a duty of care, he formed the view that there was no

---

1   (Unreported) 10 December 1999.
2   (2001) 3 LGLR 28.
3   (Unreported).

breach of duty, principally because even the evidence given by the witnesses for the plaintiff was of very slight complaints, with mentions of 'looks and atmosphere' only.

4.63   In a decision in the Court of Session in Edinburgh, *Scott v Lothian Regional Council*,[1] the court dismissed a claim of alleged bullying. Although it was alleged that the education authority had failed to implement a proper policy for dealing with bullying, this was not pursued at trial, where it was alleged that the guidance teachers at the school had failed to take all reasonable steps to ascertain whether bullying was continuing and to encourage the pursuer to report further incidences of the injury at the hands of her fellow pupils. Lord MacLean held that the test was whether the guidance teachers had been proved to be guilty of failure which no guidance teacher of ordinary skill would have been guilty when acting with ordinary care. The judge considered that the evidence did not support the allegation of negligence against the guidance teachers.

4.64   The judge in the *Bradford-Smart* case, Garland J, was referred to *Scott v Lothian Regional Council*. He was also referred to *Cotton v Trafford Borough Council*,[2] where the judge had dealt with the law as follows:

'There is no disagreement between Counsel as to the general principles. The duty of the school is to take reasonable care for the health and safety of its pupils. This duty is no greater than the duty which rests on the parents, just as with the parents, the duty is a high one.'

4.65   In *Bradford-Smart* the allegations concerned bullying both inside and outside school. The judge first had to decide whether the incidents described by the claimant amounted to bullying. He formed the view, guided by the expert evidence, that:

'Bullying is unprovoked, intended to hurt and persisted in over a period of time.'

4.66   Dealing with the general duty of care, the judge found no particular difficulty in accepting the claimant's argument that teachers owe a duty to their pupils to take reasonable care to prevent bullying occurring inside school. This followed from general principles and also from the judgment of Auld LJ in *Gower v London Borough of Bromley*,[3] when he said:

'The headteacher and teachers have a duty to take such care of pupils in their charge as a careful parent would have in like circumstances, including a duty to take positive steps to protect their wellbeing.'

4.67   The judge held that there had been no bullying inside school, and certainly no bullying about which the school could have been aware during the first 2 of the claimant's 3 years spent at the school. The judge accepted that there was evidence of bullying outside school during the third year. It was alleged that the school had a duty in relation to this bullying and, as a result, the judge had to decide:

(a)   whether the bullying outside school 'spilled over' into the school; if so,
(b)   whether the teachers had been in breach of any duty which they owed to the claimant; and

---

1   1999 Rep LR 15.
2   (Unreported decision in the Manchester County Court) 23 October 2000.
3   [1999] ELR 356.

(c)   whether the school owed any duty (and, if so, what duty) to the claimant in respect of the bullying which was taking place outside the school gates.

4.68   On the facts, the judge decided that the school, particularly through the claimant's class teacher, had acted reasonably in preventing the bullying outside the school from 'spilling over into the school'.

4.69   When *Bradford-Smart* came before the Court of Appeal the court agreed with the judge's finding that the bullying had not been allowed to spill over into school. The Court of Appeal then considered the extent to which a school owes a duty to its pupils outside the school gates. It considered that there might be a duty on a teacher to intervene if he saw a pupil being attacked outside the school gates. There is also a duty where pupils are outside school on a school trip. Nevertheless, the duty is limited, as explained by Judge LJ:

> 'But the school cannot owe a general duty to its pupils, or to anyone else, to police their activities once they have left its charge. That is principally the duty of parents and, where criminal offences are involved, the police. There is evidence … that some schools do patrol "areas of concern" outside school to prevent incidents after children have left. But we agree with the judge that this is a matter of discretion rather than duty.'

4.70   Although a duty of care exists in relation to bullying inside school, and to a limited extent, outside school, the duty is owed to all pupils in the school. Judge LJ pointed out:

> 'Like any parent, the school will often be faced in this, or in any other context, with the problem of balancing one child's interests with another. There will also be difficult questions of judgment as to how far the school should seek to step in where the parents or other agencies such as police and social services have not done so. Above all, an ineffective intervention may, in fact, make matters worse for the victim because she cannot be protected while she is out of school. It cannot be a breach of duty to fail to take steps which are unlikely to do much good.'

4.71   An example of the courts' approach to bullying cases in practice is *Faulkner v London Borough of Enfield and Another*.[1] The claimants made allegations about a number of incidents of bullying. They also alleged that the school had failed to have in place an appropriate anti-bullying policy and that there had been a failure to keep the parents fully informed. The judge found that there had been some instances of bullying, although not to the extent alleged by the claimants. In all the circumstances he considered that the school had dealt with the bullying properly and was not negligent. Moreover, some of the incidents were isolated assaults, not amounting to bullying, which could not have been prevented by the school. Although the judge considered that there is a duty on a school to keep parents informed about incidents involving their children, nevertheless it must be a matter of judgment for the school to decide at what stage parents should be informed. A school cannot be expected to advise parents of every incident involving their children. Finally, although the school's anti-bullying policy did not accord with government guidelines, this was not evidence of negligence if the school's policy was effective in practice.

---

1   [2003] ELR 426.

Bullying – Human Rights Act 1998

4.72   As with many areas affected by the Human Rights Act 1998, it is too early to say how far the Act will influence claims in respect of bullying. The relevant part of the European Convention on Human Rights (ECHR) is probably Article 3, which states:

> 'No one shall be subjected to torture or to inhuman or degrading treatment or punishment.'

There has been no decided case of the European Court of Human Rights whether a state is required to prevent inhuman or degrading treatment of a school child by other children, namely bullying. It is arguable that where bullying is proved to have taken place, and the local education authority has not taken adequate steps to prevent it, then Article 3 might give rise to a claim under the Human Rights Act 1998. However, it is not clear how far this would add to the law expressed by the court in *Bradford-Smart*.

FAILURE TO EDUCATE

4.73   Since 1994, a novel duty of care has been established by the courts in cases where it is argued that a school, or education authority, has failed to provide adequate education for children with special needs. Most of the decided cases to date have involved pupils with dyslexia.

4.74   Section 8(1) of the Education Act 1944 provides:

> 'It shall be the duty of every Local Education Authority to secure that there shall be available for their area sufficient schools ... [which] shall not be deemed to be sufficient unless they are sufficient in number, character and equipment to afford for all pupils opportunities for education offering such variety of instruction and training that may be desirable in view of their different ages, abilities and aptitudes ...'

Section 8(2) of the 1944 Act in its original form reads as follows:

> 'In fulfilling their duties under this section, a Local Education Authority shall, in particular, have regard ...
>
> (c)   to the need for securing that provision is made for pupils who suffer from any disability of mind or body by providing, either in special schools or otherwise, special educational treatment, that is to say, education by special methods appropriate to persons suffering from that disability ...'

4.75   The Education Act 1981 contains provision for the education of children with special educational needs. A duty is imposed on every local education authority to identify pupils with special educational needs. Thereafter the local education authority must make an assessment of a pupil's educational needs and then form a further opinion as to whether it should determine the special provision which should be made for that pupil. If it does so, the education authority must make a statement of the special needs and of the special provisions to be made for the pupil, and hence the pupil becomes 'statemented' under the 1981 Act. The result is that the education authority must provide funding for the special educational provision under the statement of special educational needs.

4.76   The question whether a local education authority owes a duty of care to children with special educational needs came before the Court of Appeal in *E (A Minor) v Dorset County Council and Other Appeals*.[1] The Court of Appeal heard three claims raising broadly similar allegations against local education authorities that they had failed to identify dyslexia and/or failed to provide proper teaching to take into account special needs. The claims had been struck out and the appeals were against those striking out orders.

4.77   The Court of Appeal held that none of the statutory provisions in question was intended to confer a private law right of action for damages for breach of statutory duty. The court refused, however, to strike out the claims in negligence.

4.78   The cases in *E (A Minor) v Dorset County Council* came before the House of Lords in *X (Minors) v Bedfordshire County Council*.[2] Their Lordships were in no doubt that a claim for breach of statutory duty could not succeed and they therefore agreed with the Court of Appeal that Parliament had not intended to confer a private right of action in either the Education Act 1944 or the Education Act 1981. As Lord Browne-Wilkinson emphasised:

> 'I have never previously come across a statutory procedure which provided for such close involvement of those who would be affected by a decision (the parents) in the making of that decision or which conferred more generous rights of appeal. To suggest that Parliament intended, in addition, to confer a right to sue for damages is impossible.'

4.79   On the other hand, their Lordships were not prepared to strike out claims alleging a duty of care owed directly by the local education authority to the children concerned. Lord Browne-Wilkinson considered that in this regard, the education authority was arguably offering a service (psychological advice) to the public. Although, in the absence of a statutory power or duty, the authority could not offer such a service, nevertheless once it had been decided to do so then his Lordship considered that the position was directly analogous with a health authority running a hospital. Lord Browne-Wilkinson could see no ground on which it could be said that the local education authority, in providing a psychology service, could not have come under a duty of care to a child, who, through his parents, took advantage of that service. In *Barrett v London Borough of Enfield*,[3] however, Lord Browne-Wilkinson accepted that these remarks had been based on a mistaken assumption and that the psychology service was established to advise the local authority.[4]

4.80   Similarly, the House of Lords was not prepared to strike out claims against educational psychologists and other members of staff where the local education authority would be vicariously liable for their acts or omissions. Lord Browne-Wilkinson viewed educational psychologists and teachers as being professionals who are bound both to possess special skills and to exercise them carefully. They were, in his view, under a duty to exercise the ordinary skill of a competent psychologist or teacher and their liability was subject to the test laid down in *Bolam v Friern Hospital Management Committee*.[5]

---

1   [1994] 4 All ER 640.
2   [1995] 3 All ER 353, and see Chapters 1 and 3.
3   [1999] 2 FLR 426.
4   But see *Phelps v London Borough of Hillingdon* at para **4.83**.
5   [1957] 2 All ER 118.

Phelps v London Borough of Hillingdon

4.81   The issues raised in the above paragraphs have been considered both in the Court of Appeal and in the House of Lords in the case of *Phelps v London Borough of Hillingdon*.[1] The claimant had been identified as having educational problems at junior school. This information was passed to the secondary school when the claimant joined that school. During her first term at secondary school the claimant was seen by an educational psychologist employed by the defendant, which was the local education authority. Although the educational psychologist identified that the claimant was seriously under-functioning in reading and spelling, she considered that the claimant had no specific weaknesses. She lacked confidence, and there was an emotional basis to her difficulties. In the light of subsequent analysis, and on hearing expert evidence in the case, the judge formed the view that the educational psychologist had been negligent in failing to identify the claimant as being dyslexic. The judge also rejected the defendant's arguments on causation. Garland J said:

> 'I accept that the techniques of teaching dyslexics have moved on during the last ten years, but I find that had the plaintiff been diagnosed, she would have been specifically taught as a dyslexic ... in addition both she and her parents would have had the advantage of knowing what her difficulty was and what might have been done to mitigate it. What the extent of such progress would have been is a matter of speculation.'

4.82   In the Court of Appeal the local education authority was successful. First, the Court of Appeal categorised claims of this nature as economic loss. Stuart-Smith LJ said:

> 'Dyslexia is not itself an injury and I do not see how failure to ameliorate or mitigate its effects can be an injury.'

In order to succeed, therefore, the claimant had to establish that the educational psychologist had assumed or undertaken personal responsibility towards the claimant and in the court's view that was not the case. The Court of Appeal noted that Garland J had acknowledged that 'what the level of progress would have been is a matter of speculation' and therefore held that the claimant had failed to establish that any breach of duty by the educational psychologist had caused the claimant loss. The Court of Appeal also criticised the basis on which the judge had awarded damages to the claimant. Stuart-Smith LJ said:

> '... it is far from clear how the Judge reached his figures for future loss of earnings and general damages or what factors he took into account. It is difficult to resist the conclusion that he simply plucked a figure out of the air. One cannot blame him; in my view the task was virtually impossible.'

4.83   *Phelps v London Borough of Hillingdon* came before the House of Lords with appeals in three other cases raising similar issues which were heard together.[2] The tribunal of seven Law Lords overruled the Court of Appeal in *Phelps* and, at the same time, refused to strike out the similar claims brought in the other cases.

4.84   The issues in the cases which were involved in the appeal before the House of Lords were broadly similar. The allegations were as follows.

---

1   [1999] 1 WLR 500, CA; [2000] 3 WLR 776, HL.
2   *Anderton v Clwyd County Council, Jarvis v Hampshire County Council* and *Gower v London Borough of Bromley*.

Phelps

A failure to diagnose dyslexia, as a result of which the claimant did not receive appropriate education.

Jarvis

A failure to diagnose dyslexia. The claimant was identified as suffering from specific learning difficulties and the education authority considered that he would benefit from attendance at a school catering for children with moderate learning difficulties.

Gower

The claimant suffered from duchenne muscular dystrophy involving progressive muscle wasting. He was provided with a statement of special educational needs which emphasised the need for him to have access to a computer and to be trained in its use. Although he was transferred to a school which had facilities for children with special disabilities, he claimed that there was a failure to provide him with proper computer technology and suitable training to enable him to communicate and to cope educationally and socially.

House of Lords' decision

4.85   The House of Lords overruled the Court of Appeal's decision in *Phelps* and, at the same time, decided that the cases of *Jarvis* and *Gower* should not be struck out and should proceed.

4.86   First, the House of Lords decided that an educational psychologist can owe a duty of care to a child even though he or she has been involved in pursuance of the performance of the local authority's statutory duties. It must still be shown that the educational psychologist is acting in relation to a particular child in a situation where the law recognises a duty of care. The position was explained by Lord Slynn as follows:

> 'Where an educational psychologist is specifically called in to advise in relation to the assessment and future provision for a specific child, and it is clear that the parents acting for the child and the teachers will follow that advice, prima facie a duty of care arises.'

4.87   Turning to teachers, Lord Slynn agreed with Lord Browne-Wilkinson in *X (Minors)* when he said that a head teacher owes a duty of care to exercise reasonable skill in relation to a child's educational needs. It is also clear that the House of Lords approved the judgment of Auld LJ in *Gower v London Borough of Bromley* when he held that:

> 'A head teacher and teachers have a duty to take such care of pupils in their charge as a careful parent would have in like circumstances, including a duty to take positive steps to protect their wellbeing.'

This is the well-established duty referred to in paras **4.1–4.3**, but Auld LJ went further, when saying:

> 'A head teacher and teachers have a duty to exercise the reasonable skills of their calling in teaching and otherwise responding to the educational needs of their pupils.'

4.88 More particularly, it is important to note that Lord Nicholls, in *Phelps*, extended the duty of care beyond simply those pupils with special educational needs, to children generally. He said:

> 'It cannot be that a teacher owes a duty of care only to children with special educational needs. The law would be in an extraordinary state if, in carrying out their teaching responsibilities, teachers owed duties to some of their pupils but not others. So the question which arises, and cannot be shirked, is whether teachers owe duties of care to *all* their pupils in respect of the way they discharge their teaching responsibilities ... I can see no escape from the conclusion that teachers do, indeed, owe such duties.'

4.89 The standard of care to be expected of educational psychologists and teachers was expressed by the House of Lords in *Phelps* to be that laid down by the court in *Bolam v Friern Hospital Management Committee*,[1] a case involving the negligence of a doctor, where, inter alia, McNair J said:

> 'A doctor is not guilty of negligence if he has acted in accordance with a practice accepted as proper by a responsible body of medical men skilled in that particular art ... putting it the other way round, a doctor is not negligent, if he is acting in accordance with such a practice, merely because there is a body of opinion that takes contrary views.'

Dealing with the *Bolam* test, Lord Clyde in *Phelps* pointed to the difficulties in establishing negligence:

> 'In the field of educational matters there may well exist distinct, but respectable opinions upon matters of method and practice, and it may be difficult to substantiate a case of fault against the background of a variety of professional practices. In cases of a failure to diagnose a particular disability from which a child may be suffering there may well be considerable difficulties in the making of the diagnosis which may render proof of negligence hazardous.'

Lord Nicholls was at pains to point out that their Lordships were not 'opening the door' to claims based on poor-quality teaching. He said:

> 'It is one thing for the law to provide a remedy in damages when there is manifest incompetence or negligence comprising specific, identifiable mistakes. It would be an altogether different matter to countenance claims of a more general nature, to the effect that the child did not receive an adequate education at the school, or that a particular teacher failed to teach properly.'

Lord Slynn made a similar comment:

> 'The difficulties of the tasks involved and of the circumstances under which people have to work in this area must also be borne fully in mind. The professionalism, dedication and standards of those engaged in the provision of educational services are such that cases of liability for negligence will be exceptional.'

So far, the courts have adopted the restrictive approach forecast by Lord Nicholls, at least, when considering claims for negligence by teachers.[2]

Personal injury or economic loss

4.90 The categorisation of these claims is relevant when considering the issue of limitation. The Court of Appeal, in *Phelps*, had categorised these claims as being

---

1   [1957] 2 All ER 118.
2   See paras 4.102–4.107.

claims for economic loss. The House of Lords appeared, at first sight, to leave the question unresolved. Lord Slynn said that psychological injury could constitute damage for the purposes of a claim in negligence and:

'So ... can a failure to diagnose a congenital condition and to take appropriate action as a result of which failure a child's level of achievement is reduced, which leads to loss of employment and wages.'

When Lord Slynn came to deal with the appeal in *Anderton v Clywd County Council*,[1] which was concerned with the court's power to order pre-action disclosure of documents under the rules of court which then applied, he said:

'A failure to diagnose a congenital condition and to take appropriate action as a result of which a child's level of achievement is reduced (which leads to loss of employment and wages) may constitute damage for the purpose of a claim. Accordingly, I consider that Garland J in the *Phelps* case was right ... that a failure to mitigate the adverse consequences of a congenital defect is capable of being "personal injuries to a person" within the meaning of the rules.'

4.91   The question was considered by the Court of Appeal in *Robinson v St Helens Metropolitan Borough Council*[2] when Sir Murray Stuart-Smith (who, in the Court of Appeal, had decided that these were economic loss claims in *Phelps*) adopted what Lord Slynn had said and concluded as follows:

'Dyslexia ... may itself be an "impairment of a person's mental condition". It is not of course caused by the defendant; but negligent failure to ameliorate the consequences of dyslexia by appropriate teaching may be said to continue the injury, in the same way that the negligent failure to cure or ameliorate a congenital physical condition so that it continues, could give rise to an action for personal injuries.'

4.92   The matter has now been considered again by the House of Lords in *Adams v Bracknell Forest Borough Council*,[3] where their Lordships confirmed that the claims should be categorised as claims for personal injury. Lord Hoffmann noted that the award of general damages in *Phelps* could only be justified on the basis that the claim was for a personal injury consisting in the lack of ability to read and write. Actions for negligence against local educational authorities for educational neglect are a new development and, to a certain extent, Lord Hoffmann felt that an expedient approach was required. Dyslexia is a congenital condition whose cause is unclear. At the end of the day it was appropriate to categorise these as claims for personal injury:

'It seems to me that Evans LJ (in *E (a Minor) v. Dorset County Council*) was quite right to draw an analogy with negligent failure to treat a physical injury which the defendant did not itself cause. It would be drawing too fine a distinction to say that the neglect caused no injury because nothing could be done to repair the congenital damage in the brain circuitry and the other parts of the brain which would have to be trained to compensate had never been injured. What matters is whether one has improved one's ability to read and write. Treating the inability to do so as an untreated injury originally proceeding from other causes produces a sensible practical result.'

---

1   [1999] ELR 1.
2   [2003] PIQR 9.
3   [2004] UKHL 29, [2004] 3 WLR 89.

Lord Scott considered that the deprivation of the benefit of literacy did not fit comfortably within the concept of a 'personal injury'; however, he was prepared to accept that the matter had been decided in *Phelps* and *Anderton*.

What is the relevant limitation period?

4.93 Since these are actions for personal injury, the ordinary limitation period is governed by s 11(4) of the Limitation Act 1980 and is therefore 3 years from:

(a)   the date on which the cause of action accrued; or
(b)   the date of knowledge (if later) of the person injured.

Since such claims are inevitably brought by or on behalf of children, the ordinary limitation period will expire 3 years after the date of majority, namely on the individual's twenty-first birthday.

4.94 The date of knowledge under s 11(4)(b) is defined in s 14(1) of the Limitation Act 1980 as being the date on which the claimant first had knowledge of the following facts:

(a)   that the injury in question was significant;
(b)   that the injury was attributable in whole or in part to the act or omission which is alleged to constitute negligence; and
(c)   the identity of the defendant.

Knowledge means 'actual knowledge'. However, the Limitation Act also provides that a claimant can be held to have 'constructive knowledge'. Section 14(3) of the Limitation Act 1980 says:

> 'For the purposes of this section a person's knowledge includes knowledge which he might reasonably have been expected to acquire:
> (a)   from facts observable or ascertainable by him; or
> (b)   from facts ascertainable by him with the help of medical or other appropriate expert advice which it is reasonable for him to seek;
> But a person shall not be fixed under this sub-section with knowledge of a fact ascertainable only with the help of expert advice so long as he has taken all reasonable steps to obtain (and, where appropriate, to act on) that advice.'

Actual knowledge – Limitation Act 1980, s 14(1)

4.95 Actual knowledge arose in *Rowe v Kingston Upon Hull City Council*.[1] The claimant issued a writ in 1998, about 3 years after he reached his majority. The claimant argued that before the decision in *Phelps v London Borough of Hillingdon*, which was decided at first instance in September 1997, a reasonable person would not have regarded the failure to mitigate the adverse effects of dyslexia as an injury for the purposes of the Limitation Act 1980. In fact, the claimant knew that he was dyslexic before his eighteenth birthday. The Court of Appeal rejected the claimant's argument, Keene LJ said:

> 'The mere fact that a person may not realise that he has a good claim in law until a particular decision of the courts clarifies the situation provides no justification for

---

1   [2003] EWCA Civ 1281, [2003] ELR 771.

interpreting the 1980 Act in other than the normal way. A claimant can always bring a claim to establish for the first time that he has a good cause of action. He is not prevented from obtaining access to the courts. Moreover ... to interpret section 14(1) of the Act so that the three year period runs from the date when the law first recognised such a claim by means of a judicial decision, would bring into existence a host of stale claims, some of which could be twenty, thirty or more years old, and so give rise to great unfairness to the defendants ... In my judgment, the three year period in this case must have commenced when the claimant reached his majority, because he already had the requisite knowledge before that date.'[1]

4.96 The question of actual knowledge also arose in *Meherali v Hampshire County Council*.[2] The claimant commenced proceedings in 1998, about 18 months after expiry of the ordinary limitation period. The claimant alleged that he did not have knowledge for the purposes of s 14(1) of the Limitation Act 1980 until he received a report from an educational psychologist in 1997. In fact there was evidence that it was known to the claimant and his parents, from the age of 10, that he was considered to have learning difficulties. There was a diagnosis of dyslexia when the claimant was 14. The court decided that the educational psychologist's report which was obtained in 1997 did not bring to light any fact of which the claimant was previously unaware. Accordingly, the claimant had sufficient knowledge under s 14(1) of the Limitation Act 1980 by the time he reached his majority, and therefore the claim was statute barred.

Constructive knowledge – Limitation Act 1980, s 14(3)

4.97 The House of Lords has now considered constructive knowledge in the context of failure to educate cases in *Adams v Bracknell Forest Borough Council*.[3] The claimant attended schools for which the defendant was responsible between 1981 and 1988. He alleged that the schools had failed to assess the educational difficulties which he was experiencing and had failed to provide him with appropriate treatment. It was later diagnosed that he was suffering from dyslexia. The claimant reached his majority in March 1990 and his action was commenced more than 12 years later. The claimant alleged that his date of knowledge, as defined in s 14(1) of the Limitation Act 1980, had accrued less than 3 years before the commencement of proceedings. He said that he was not aware that he might be suffering from dyslexia until he attended a salsa party when he spoke to someone who, by chance, was an educational psychologist who told him that she thought that he might be dyslexic.

4.98 The House of Lords confirmed that the test for constructive knowledge is essentially objective. 'Knowledge which the claimant might have been expected to acquire' is a reference to knowledge which a person in the situation of the claimant, namely an adult who knows that he has literacy problems, could reasonably be expected to acquire. According to Lord Hoffmann:

> 'In my opinion, section 14(3) requires one to assume that a person who is aware that he has suffered a personal injury, serious enough to be something about which he would go and see a solicitor if he knew he had a claim, will be sufficiently curious about the causes of the injury to seek whatever expert advice is appropriate.'

---

1   The Court of Appeal also rejected an argument for breach of Article 6 of the ECHR.
2   [2002] EWHC 2655 (QB), [2003] ELR 338.
3   [2004] UKHL 29, [2004] 3 WLR 89.

And he went on:

> 'There is no reason why the normal expectation that a person suffering from significant injury will be curious about his origins should not also apply to dyslexics.'

4.99   Lord Hoffmann agreed that if the injury itself would reasonably inhibit the claimant from seeking advice, then it was a factor to be taken into account. However, he found it difficult to understand why a person suffering from untreated dyslexia could not reasonably be expected to reveal the source of his difficulties to his medical adviser.

Discretion under Limitation Act 1980, s 33

4.100   Section 33 gives the court discretion to disapply the provisions of the Limitation Act 1980 if it considers that it would be equitable for the action to proceed. Section 33 requires the court to balance the prejudice which would be suffered by the claimant if the provisions of the Act were to apply, against the prejudice suffered by the defendant if the action were to proceed. In the context of 'failure to educate' cases, the Court of Appeal dealt with the exercise of discretion in *Robinson v St Helens Metropolitan Borough Council*.[1] The court noted that the onus is on the claimant to establish that it would be equitable to allow the claim to proceed. It also noted the stale nature of some education claims and that contesting such claims diverted resources from the education authority. The Court of Appeal concluded that courts should be slow to exercise their discretion. Sir Murray Stuart-Smith said:

> 'The likely amount of an award is an important factor to consider, especially if, as is usual in these cases, they are likely to take a considerable time to try. A claim that the claimant's dyslexia was not diagnosed or treated many years before at school, brought long after the expiry of the limitation period, extended as it is until after the claimant's majority, will inevitably place the defendants in great difficulty in contesting it, especially in the absence of relevant witnesses and documents. The contesting of such a claim would be both expensive and likely to divert precious resources. Courts should be slow in such cases to find that the balance of prejudice is in favour of the claimant.'

4.101   In *Adams v Bracknell Forest Borough Council* the House of Lords agreed with the Court of Appeal in *Robinson*. It saw no reason to exercise the court's discretion in favour of the claimant, particlarly where, in the event of success, any award was likely to be relatively modest.

Courts' approach to *Phelps v London Borough of Hillingdon*

Claims against teachers
4.102   The first example of the difficulty in bringing such claims is *Christmas v Hampshire County Council*.[2] This was one of the three cases which came before the Court of Appeal and House of Lords as *E (A Minor) v Dorset County Council* and *X (Minors) v Bedfordshire County Council*. Between 1978 and 1984 the claimant attended a primary school maintained by the defendant, the local education authority. The claimant showed signs of severe behavioural problems and learning difficulties, especially in learning to read. The headmaster told the claimant's parents that the

---

1   [2002] EWCA Civ 1099, [2003] PIQR P128.
2   [1998] ELR 1.

claimant did not have any specific learning difficulties. Later the headmaster referred the claimant to an advisory service run by the defendant for an assessment of the claimant's learning difficulties. The advisory service reported that the claimant had no serious handicaps, and that his problem was mainly a question of a good deal of regular practice. The claimant completed his primary education in 1985 and his parents then sent him to a private school. His difficulties persisted and in 1988 the defendant carried out an assessment of the claimant's special educational needs under s 5 of the Education Act 1981. As a result, a final statement of special educational needs was drawn up which concluded that the claimant was significantly under-achieving in literacy and especially in terms of his spelling skills and accuracy, which might be regarded as a severe specific learning difficulty. Special educational provision was recommended and was provided by the defendant from January 1989.

4.103 The claimant alleged that the headmaster had been negligent in failing to refer him for formal assessment of his special educational needs or to an educational psychologist. The claimant also alleged that the advisory service had been negligent in failing to ascertain that the claimant had a specific learning difficulty, and in failing to diagnose dyslexia. The court noted that an educational psychologist, employed by the private secondary school, had highlighted the claimant's lack of application. This, together with the fact that the private school did not devise any new teaching approach, was evidence which the judge considered he was entitled to take into account in finding that nothing very obvious had been missed previously by the primary school.

4.104 As far as the advisory teaching service was concerned, the judge considered that whatever was done was ineffective, but this did not mean that the attention which the claimant had received from the advisory teachers was necessarily sub-standard. In particular, the judge noted that the private secondary school did not appear to have been any more successful with the claimant, even though it claimed to be specialist school. Commenting on the lack of evidence available to him, Ian Kennedy J said:

> 'Unless there is evidence to point towards some failure on their part [the advisory teachers] I cannot think that it is right to assume that they were at fault. It is not every problem that can be resolved, even if statistically the great majority can be ameliorated or overcome. It is here that what happened at [the private secondary school] has its relevance ... Once there his problems continued, even worsened. If I conclude that the defendant council's advisory teachers failed the plaintiff, it must, on the evidence that I have heard, follow that [the private secondary school] in its turn failed him. While it is perfectly possible that a series of teachers and schools missed what was, at this time, a fairly well-known difficulty, the improbability of that explanation increases with each opportunity for a review.'

The judge therefore held that neither the primary school, its headmaster, nor the council's advisory teaching service had been negligent.

4.105 The approach in *Christmas* was followed by the judge in *Hansen v Isle of Wight Council*.[1] The claimant made allegations against a school which she had attended for about 2 years. She had already been diagnosed as dyslexic before joining the school. Tests indicated that during her 2 years at the school, the claimant's reading age only advanced by one year and 5 months, while her spelling age had actually

---

1   (Unreported) 23 February 2001.

regressed by about 3 months. The claimant alleged that the school had failed to deliver the appropriate teaching services required to overcome her innate disability caused by her dyslexia. Wright J pointed out that the apparent failure to make progress at school was not enough to establish a breach of duty:

> 'Indeed, in the circumstances of this particular case, I do not consider that those facts, standing alone, even amount to prima facie evidence of such a failure. If I may be forgiven for stating the obvious, dyslexia is a congenital defect, the effects of which require great efforts in both the subject and the remedial workers to overcome its effects, which is capable of creating, and does create in its victims very considerable emotional and psychological distress and, in my judgment, the degree of competence shown by teachers and others in seeking to ameliorate the effects of such a disability is not to be judged by the degree of success achieved. I gratefully adopt the observation of Ian Kennedy J in *Christmas v Hampshire County Council* to the effect that the fact that whatever was done to remedy the state of dyslexia was ineffective, or at best not very effective, does not enable the court to reason back from that that the attention that the pupil had received was necessarily substandard.'

4.106   Again in *Hansen* it was submitted that the school had failed to comply with the recommendations of the code of practice on the identification and assessment of special educational needs, issued by the Department of Education under the Education Act 1993. The judge rejected the submission that the code represented a minimum standard with which all schools must comply if they were to be regarded as acting competently. The code was more in the nature of guidance and represented 'best practice' in the field of remedial education.

4.107   The relevance of the availability of a range of options when considering the *Bolam* test was illustrated in *Smith v London Borough of Havering*.[1] The claimant was seen by the council's educational psychologists in 1987 and 1988. He was provided with educational support at his primary school. At secondary school he was given withdrawal lessons by the school's special educational needs department and he was also given lessons by the council's specialist teaching service. Like many such children, the claimant did not enjoy being withdrawn from ordinary classes. By January 1990 it was concluded that the claimant would benefit from a classroom assistant who could only be provided by resources from the council. This would require the making of a statement of special educational needs. The claimant alleged that the statementing procedure should have taken place much earlier. There had been at least two options open to the council. The court had to consider whether the decision to provide the claimant with lessons from the council's specialist teaching service before going through the statementing procedure was 'outside the bounds of reasonable responses to the claimant's individual position'. Mr David Foskett QC, sitting as a deputy High Court judge, said:

> 'I can accept that following blindly one path, irrespective of the needs of the individual, could not be justified. However, I do not think that that is what the defendant did in this case. Raphael House [the specialist teaching service] was one of at least two possible options, the other being statementing, and it was the choice made at this time ... The judgment was made that he should receive the additional one hour per week on a one-to-one basis at Raphael House. It has not been demonstrated that such a judgment fell below the acceptable standards of the day.'

---

1   (Unreported) 18 March 2004.

Claims alleging negligence by educational psychologists

4.108 In *Phelps v London Borough of Hillingdon*,[1] the educational psychologist failed to diagnose the claimant's dyslexia. The psychologist was held by the judge to have been negligent, a view with which the House of Lords agreed, on the following basis:

(1) She limited her testing of the claimant to WISC Test and should have used the Bangor Test in addition.[2]

(2) She assumed that the claimant's lack of progress was due to emotional difficulties and failed to make adequate or further enquiries as to the cause of the claimant's difficulties.

(3) The claimant's difficulties in reading and writing were such that her exceptionally high degree of specific learning difficulty was unlikely to have been caused by emotional difficulties alone.

4.109 The educational psychologist was also held to have been negligent in *Clarke v Devon County Council*.[3] The claimant was already receiving support from his school's special educational needs team and from the council's learning support team. The claimant made no real progress and the position was reviewed by an educational psychologist who then prepared a report as part of the council's procedure for making a statement of special educational needs for the claimant. It was alleged that in preparing the report the educational psychologist had been negligent because the report directed the council towards deciding that the claimant should be educated in a mainstream school without giving the option of education in a specialist school. The council argued that the claimant's parents had rejected the option of a specialist school and that this was why its educational psychologist had written her report in the way which she had. The judge held that it was not appropriate for an educational psychologist to be influenced by the views of parents. It was a matter for the council, as local education authority, to take into account any views which the parents might express. The educational psychologist's duty was to make a recommendation which was in the claimant's reasonable interest.

4.110 In *DN v London Borough of Greenwich*[4] the issue again concerned a report prepared by the council's educational psychologist when the council was considering which secondary school the claimant should attend. The claimant already had a statement of special educational needs. Relying on its educational psychologist's report, the council decided that the claimant should attend a school which specialised in children with emotional and behavioural difficulties. The Court of Appeal held that the judge had been entitled to find that the educational psychologist had been negligent in his assessment of the claimant and that, without this negligence, the claimant would have been placed in a much more appropriate school. The fact that the claimant was later diagnosed as suffering from Asperger's Syndrome, the failure to diagnose which could not be criticised at the time, did not affect the position.

---

1   [2000] 3 WLR 776.
2   These are standard diagnostic tests carried out by educational psychologists.
3   (Unreported) 25 July 2003.
4   [2004] EWCA Civ 1659, (unreported) 8 December 2004.

Claims against local education authorities direct and their officers

4.111   The House of Lords in *X (Minors) v Bedfordshire County Council*,[1] held that a local education authority owed no common-law duty of care in the exercise of the powers and discretions relating to children with special educational needs specifically conferred on it by the Education Act 1981. There was therefore no direct duty of care. However, in *Phelps v London Borough of Hillingdon*,[2] the House of Lords did not rule out the possibility of a direct claim. Lord Slynn considered that if a local authority exercised its discretion pursuant to a policy which it had lawfully adopted, then a direct claim would be unlikely, but he did not rule out such a claim and gave the following example:

> 'If, however, it then, for example appoints to carry out the duties in regard to children with special educational needs, a psychologist or other professionals who at the outset transparently are neither qualified nor competent to carry out the duties, the position is different. That may be an unlikely scenario, but if it happens, I do not see why as a matter of principle a claim at common law in negligence should never be possible.'

Both *X (Minors)* and *Phelps* were decided on the basis of the existence of a vicarious liability on the part of the local education authority.

4.112   The existence of a direct duty of care on a local education authority was considered in *Keating v London Borough of Bromley*.[3] This was one of the cases heard by the House of Lords as part of the appeal in *X (Minors)*. In the circumstances the judge accepted that the claimant was precluded from arguing that a direct duty of care existed because the point had been decided against him in *X (Minors)*. At the same time, however, the judge accepted the defendant's submission that had the question come before the courts at the time of the claimant's education, namely some time earlier, the court would, at that stage, have held that it was not fair, just and reasonable to say that there was a direct duty of care on local education authorities. According to Stanley Burnton J:

> 'Furthermore, apart from the binding effect of the decision of the House of Lords in this case, it seems to me that that decision is the best evidence of what the courts would have held if the existence of a direct duty of care had been litigated at a time near to the events in question in this case. I accept (the defendant's) submission that there has been a relevant change in the perception of the requirement of fairness, justice and reasonableness. For that reason too, I should hold that no direct duty of care was owed by the defendant.'

4.113   The existence of a direct duty of care was again considered in *Carty v London Borough of Croydon*.[4] The claimant submitted that a direct duty of care could arise if there had been a 'systemic failure', namely a complete failure of the defendant's educational service in its dealings with the claimant. On the facts, Gibbs J did not consider that there had been such a failure. However, he doubted the existence of a direct duty:

> 'But in any event, I find a conceptual difficulty with the notion of a separate duty of care owed by an authority independently of the acts or omissions of its servants or agents. In the absence of some catastrophic event over which the authority can exercise no control

---

1   [1995] 3 All ER 353.
2   [2000] 3 WLR 776.
3   [2003] EWHC 1070, [2003] ELR 590.
4   [2004] EWHC 228 (QB), [2004] ELR 226.

(such as the complete withdrawal of funding, or widespread physical damage to its resources), it is very difficult to see circumstances in which a systemic failure can be anything other than the product of individual or collective failure on the part of the authority's servants or agents. Thus the need for a separate "direct" duty is by no means clear.'

Gibbs J preferred to deal with the case on the basis of vicarious liability. It therefore seems that while the House of Lords has left open the question whether a direct duty of care on the part of a local education authority exists, nevertheless most, if not all cases will proceed on the basis of vicarious liability.

4.114 Whether a duty of care is owed by an education officer for whom the local education authority is vicariously liable was considered in *Carty v London Borough of Croydon*. The claimant alleged that for a period of 5 years he was placed in a school which catered for children with emotional and behavioural difficulties while he should have been placed in a school which catered better for his moderate learning difficulties. The claimant alleged negligence on the part of the council's education officer for the delay in placing him in a more suitable school. Dealing first with the existence of a duty of care, Gibbs J referred to the judgment of Lord Slynn in *Phelps* when he said:

'It is long and well-established, now elementary, that persons exercising a particular skill or profession may owe a duty of care in the performance to people who it can be foreseen will be injured if due skill and care are not exercised, and if injury or damage can be shown to have been caused by the lack of care. Such duty does not depend on the existence of any contractual relationship between the person causing and the person suffering the damage. A doctor, an accountant and an engineer are plainly such a person. So in my view is an educational psychologist or psychiatrist and a teacher including a teacher in a specialised area, such as a teacher concerned with children having special educational needs. So may be an education officer performing the functions of a local education authority in regard to children with special educational needs.'

Gibbs J held that Lord Slynn was definitely including an education officer within the category of persons who could owe such a duty if the facts of the individual case justified that conclusion:

'It seems to me that the passage taken as a whole means that, where an officer, exercising a particular skill or profession, is taking decisions whose consequences could foreseeably damage a child if due care and skill is not exercised, he has a duty of care towards that child. It seems to me that the word "may" is used to indicate that not all the actions of an officer will give rise to such a duty, but only those in relation to which all the conditions required for the existence of such a duty are proved.'

4.115 Having decided that there was no reason in principle why a local education officer should not be under a duty of care towards children affected by his decisions, Gibbs J emphasised that such a duty could not apply to all decisions taken by education officers:

'Plainly an officer's decisions are taken against a particular policy background, and are subject to a number of restraints, such as the availability of resources. It would be wrong to use a private law negligence action as a device to attack a particular policy, or to characterise as negligent an officer who made a decision which, whilst not ideal, was reasonable in the light of available resources. But in my judgment, decisions by an officer which, after due allowance for the policy background and other constraints, fall outside the scope of acceptability in the eyes of any reasonable body of education opinion are actionable in negligence ...'

The claimant alleged that the education officer had not ensured that the statutory scheme of assessment and statementing had been complied with. Gibbs J did not consider that this could give rise to a claim in negligence:

'How far can such non-compliance assist the claimant to prove negligence, given that non-compliance is not in itself actionable? ... I do not accept that such failure in itself gives rise to actionable negligence at the suit of the child for whom the statutory scheme is supposed to operate. If it were to do so, the result would indeed be to introduce an action for breach of statutory duty by the back door.'

4.116   Having considered the facts of the case, Gibbs J held that there had been no negligence on the part of the education officer. Although the claimant might have been better placed at a different school, the options open to the council had been limited. The education officer had taken advice from the educational psychologist, who had confirmed that the claimant should not be returned to mainstream schooling. Furthermore there was no evidence that the claimant's placement at school was breaking down. Steps were taken to try to find an alternative suitable placement. Looking at all the evidence Gibbs J did not consider that it revealed a case of negligence. He commented:

'In my judgment it would have been irresponsible simply to move the claimant without identifying a suitable alternative.'

Approach to causation

4.117   As has been seen, the House of Lords in *Phelps* considered that causation was a difficult issue. It is a matter which will depend upon the facts of each case. Having considered the facts of the case in *Phelps*, Lord Slynn considered that Garland J had been entitled to accept that:

'The adverse consequences of the plaintiff's dyslexia could have been mitigated by early diagnosis and appropriate treatment or educational provision.'

4.118   Similarly, Henriques J found in favour of the claimant on causation in *Liennard v Slough Borough Council*,[1] although otherwise finding in favour of the defendant:

'I am not prepared to say that if intervention had taken place that the claimant would not have been materially assisted between say 1988 and the date it was first appreciated that he had a problem in 1996. Whilst I find that his educational attainment may well have been greater and his employability thus enhanced, I find great difficulty in envisaging the claimant in any kind of regular employment, but I am not disposed to say that there is no chance or indeed that the chances are so low that I can dismiss them as fanciful.'

4.119   In *Smith v London Borough of Havering*,[2] Mr David Foskett QC, sitting as a deputy High Court judge, doubted whether the claimant would have been taught differently if he had received a statement of special educational needs earlier, as was the claimant's case. Nevertheless, he was prepared to accept that if taught differently,

---

1   (Unreported) 15 March 2002.
2   (Unreported) 18 March 2004.

the claimant would have made some progress with his literacy skills which would probably have had some impact on his self-esteem.

4.120 The Court of Appeal considered causation in *DN v London Borough of Greenwich*.[1] It decided that, without negligence on the part of the educational psychologist, the claimant would have been placed in a much more appropriate school. Dealing with the approach to causation, Brooke LJ said:

> 'The nature of the analysis is then to assess what, on the balance of probabilities, would have been the extent of the better outcome if he had had much more suitable schooling within that scenario.'

The Court of Appeal held that the judge had been wrong to decide that, on the evidence, the educational psychologist's negligence had caused the claimant to lose the opportunity to improve his social skills and gain some educational opportunities. In view of the evidence, and as the law stands at present, Brooke LJ explained the position as follows:

> 'If, on the present evidence the claimant has not, on the balance of probabilities proved that if [the educational psychologist] had not been negligent, he would have had an outcome so much substantially better that he would have been capable of earning his own living ... then it would be a revolutionary step to hold that he should nevertheless be compensated for the loss of the chance that the outcome would have been more satisfactory.'

4.121 The Court of Appeal looked at the House of Lords' approach to causation in *Phelps* (above) where it felt that their Lordships appeared to have realised that they were 'travelling on uncharted seas'. It adopted the same approach as that shown in *Phelps* but emphasised that any award of damages should be limited. Brooke LJ described the approach which the judge would have to adopt as follows:

> 'He will need to remember that DN's brain has at all material times been quite severely damaged, and all that the experts could really say on the balance of probabilities was that the outcome would have been better (or different) if his education had been different. That apart, their language was the language of uncertainty.'

Damages

4.122 In *Phelps v London Borough of Hillingdon* the House of Lords observed that the quantification of claims of this nature was likely to be difficult. It adopted the approach of the trial judge. Lord Slynn said:

> 'Although I agree that there is room for much debate as to quantum in this type of case, no better approach in this case has been suggested than that adopted by the learned judge. I would not interfere with his assessment of the damages.'

The judge, Garland J, had awarded the claimant £12,500 by way of general damages, together with £25,000 representing the lost opportunity for more remunerative employment, following the decision in *Blamire v South Cumbria Health Authority*.[2] Finally, he awarded approximately £6,500 to represent the cost of past and future tuition fees incurred by the claimant to ameliorate her dyslexia.

---

1   [2004] EWCA Civ 1659, (unreported) 8 December 2004.
2   [1993] PIQR 1.

4.123 Since *Phelps* the courts have followed the approach of Garland J when quantifying claims of this nature. Courts have so far refused to award damages representing past and future loss of earnings. In *Liennard v Slough Borough Council*,[1] which was decided in favour of the defendant, Henriques J said that he would have awarded £15,000 for general damages together with £20,000 to represent lost opportunity. In *Smith v London Borough of Havering*,[2] Mr David Foskett QC, sitting as a deputy High Court judge, although again deciding the case in favour of the defendant, said that he would have awarded £7,500 general damages together with £10,000 to represent a slower start on the earnings ladder.

Failure to educate and the Human Rights Act 1998

4.124 Article 2 of the First Protocol to the European Convention on Human Rights provides, inter alia, as follows:

> 'No person shall be denied the right to education ...'

It is here that the Human Rights Act 1998 might become relevant; but guidance to date indicates that the European Court of Human Rights has not analysed the quality of education offered, beyond considering whether or not there was effective education. In *SP v United Kingdom*,[3] it was argued that teachers had failed to take account of a child's special educational needs. The local education authority had refused to make a statement of educational needs when the child was aged 5, following which the child was removed from the State sector and placed, by his parents, in an independent school. The European Commission of Human Rights[4] decided that, as the child's problems had worsened over a period of time, it was not possible to conclude that it would have been right to statement him as having special educational needs at 5 years old; and, accordingly, there was no violation of the Convention in spite of the mother's claim that her son had not derived a positive benefit from his education.

4.125 It should also be noted that under the Human Rights Act 1998 the government has entered a reservation to Article 2 of the First Protocol, which it accepts:

> 'Only insofar as it is compatible with the provision of efficient instruction and training, and the avoidance of unreasonable public expenditure.'

It remains to be seen how far the courts will seek to impose liability on teachers for failing to discharge their teaching responsibilities to their pupils following the House of Lords' decision in *Phelps*. It is submitted that the *Phelps* decision, at present, provides sufficient scope for courts to make findings of liability against teachers. The Human Rights Act 1998 probably adds little to this area of the law.

---

1 (Unreported) 15 March 2002.
2 (Unreported) 18 March 2004.
3 [1997] EHRLR 284.
4 The Commission conducted an initial screening function until its abolition by the Eleventh Protocol to the Convention, in November 1998.

Chapter 5

HOUSING AND OCCUPIER'S LIABILITY

INTRODUCTION

5.1 This chapter is concerned with the liabilities of local authorities, as owners or occupiers of property, to third parties who suffer damage either to person or to property. Liability can arise, first, out of the local authority's position as landlord, and, secondly, as owner or occupier of buildings. Of course, local authorities own or occupy a variety of buildings such as schools and swimming pools where accidents can occur. It is proposed to deal first with the local authority's position as landlord.

LIABILITIES OF LOCAL AUTHORITIES AS LANDLORDS

5.2 The starting point when considering the duties owed by landlords is the lease or tenancy agreement. However, Parliament has from time to time passed statutes under which certain non-excludable obligations are to be implied as terms in the lease or tenancy agreement. [1]

Common law position

5.3 The limited nature of the duty owed by a landlord at common law can be seen in the case of *Cavalier v Pope*, [2] where the house was in a dangerous state of dilapidation when it was let and, in particular, the flooring of the kitchen was dangerous. The tenant drew this to the attention of the landlord's agent and threatened to leave, but agreed to remain when the landlord promised to effect repairs. However, no repairs were carried out and the tenant's wife fell through the kitchen floor, injuring herself. Dealing with the wife's claim against the landlord, Lord Atkinson said:

> '. . . it is well-established that no duty is, at law, cast upon a landlord not to let a house in a dangerous or dilapidated condition, and further, that if he does let it while in such a condition, he is not thereby rendered liable in damages for injuries which may be sustained by the tenant, his (the tenant's) servants, guests, customers, or others invited by him to enter the premises by reason of this defective condition.'

The action by the tenant's wife against the landlord therefore failed. [3]

---

1   See paras **5.17** and **5.18**.
2   [1906] AC 428, HL(E).
3   The tenant did recover damages, but these were awarded under the contract to repair and not under the tenancy agreement.

5.4 *Cavalier v Pope* was followed in *Travers v Gloucester Corporation and Others*, [1] where Lewis J held that there was no legal duty incumbent on the corporation as the builders, owners or landlords of the house towards the tenant's lodger who died in the bathroom of the house as a result of the defective and dangerous installation of a hot water geyser. This was in spite of the fact that the defect had been brought to the attention of the corporation.

5.5 *Cavalier v Pope* remains good law as can be seen from the case of *McNerny v Lambeth London Borough Council*. [2] In this case the plaintiff's flat had been built in the late 1940s with solid walls and metal windows in accordance with the standard of the times. The plaintiff, who moved into the flat in 1982, complained of condensation which began about a year later. The Court of Appeal confirmed that there was no liability because there was no evidence of negligence when the property was built. That left the local authority as bare landlord and, as such, *Cavalier v Pope* was binding authority in its favour. The court considered that it was a matter for Parliament to change the law if it was felt to give rise to any anomaly.

Position of landlord who has designed or built the premises

5.6 The courts have felt able to distinguish *Cavalier v Pope* in circumstances where the landlord designed or built the property and there is evidence of negligence in the design or construction. The first case which so distinguished *Cavalier v Pope* was *Rimmer v Liverpool City Council*, [3] a case in which the court's view of the decision in *Cavalier v Pope* can perhaps be seen in the comment of Stephenson LJ that:

> '*Cavalier v Pope* must be kept in close confinement.'

5.7 In *Rimmer* the local authority had designed and built a block of 24 flats, each flat having as part of an internal wall a glass panel 3mm thick directly opposite the lounge door. At the start of his weekly tenancy, about 18 months before the accident, the plaintiff complained to the authority that the glass panel was a danger to his 5-year-old son because it was too thin. He was told that it was a standard fitting and that nothing could be done about it. The tenant tripped over, put out his left hand thereby breaking the glass panel and sustaining severe injuries to his hand and wrist. Although a claim was pleaded under the Defective Premises Act 1972 (see para **5.51**) it was common ground that the plaintiff's claim could succeed only at common law and in this regard the Court of Appeal had to give careful consideration to the decision in *Cavalier v Pope* (a decision of the House of Lords and therefore binding on the court).

5.8 In the end the Court of Appeal distinguished *Cavalier v Pope* on the basis that there the landlord had not designed or built the property, while in *Rimmer* the local authority had both designed and built the block of flats. Stephenson LJ found support in the House of Lords' decision in *Anns v Merton London Borough Council*, [4] when he held as follows:

> 'the landowner, who designs or builds a house or flat, is no more immune from personal responsibility for faults of construction than a building contractor, or from personal responsibility for faults of design than an architect, simply because he has disposed of his

---

1   [1947] 1 KB 71.
2   (1988) 21 HLR 188.
3   [1985] QB 1.
4   [1978] AC 728.

house or flat by selling or letting it. The Council ... designed and, ... built, the Plaintiff's flat with its dangerous glass panel. They owed him, not as tenant but, like his wife or his child, as a person who might reasonably be expected to be affected by the provision of the glass panel in the flat, a duty to take such care as was reasonable in all the circumstances to see that he was reasonably safe from personal injury caused by the glass panel. They knew the thickness of the glass, and on the Judge's finding they ought to have known, placed where it was, it was dangerous to the occupants of the flat.'

5.9 The Court of Appeal was also conscious of another difficulty: namely that the plaintiff himself had considered the glass to be dangerous and thereby knew of the defect before suffering his accident. The Court of Appeal held, however, that it was neither reasonable nor practical for the plaintiff to leave the flat or to alter the glass panel and that therefore the local authority continued to owe him a duty under the principle in *Donoghue v Stevenson*.[1]

5.10 Any doubt as to the point raised in the previous paragraph seems to have been removed by the Court of Appeal in *Targett v Torfaen Borough Council*.[2] As in *Rimmer*, the plaintiff was the tenant of a council house which had been designed and built by the council. Access to the house was down two flights of stone steps. There was no handrail for the lower steps and no lighting in the immediate vicinity of the steps. Before moving into the house the plaintiff had complained to the council about the lack of lighting, but nothing was done. The plaintiff fell down the steps and was injured. The claims for breach of statutory duty were abandoned at trial and as a result, again like *Rimmer*, the case proceeded on the basis of the common law duty of care owed by the local authority.

5.11 The Court of Appeal refused to accept the council's submission that the absence of the handrail did not render the steps faulty and that the absence of proper illumination did not amount to a defect of manufacture or construction. On this basis, the court could not distinguish the facts of the case from *Rimmer*. The council, however, argued that it should not be under a duty of care following the House of Lords' decision in *Murphy v Brentwood*,[3] which had overruled *Anns v Merton London Borough Council* on which the court had relied on *Rimmer*. The council submitted that as the plaintiff was well aware of the conditions prevailing and the potential danger by reason of the absence of the handrail and adequate lighting, there was no duty owed. Russell LJ, however, noted that *Rimmer* had not been referred to by the House of Lords in *Murphy* and accordingly took the view that the House of Lords in *Murphy* had not overruled *Rimmer* by implication or otherwise. Furthermore, Leggatt LJ followed the approach adopted by Stevenson LJ in *Rimmer* and held that it was not reasonable to expect the plaintiff to remove or avoid the danger and that the local authority owed a duty of care to the tenant (and presumably to his family and visitors).

Interpretation of covenant for quiet enjoyment

5.12 The case of *Southwark London Borough Council v Tanner; Baxter v Camden London Borough Council*[4] involved the House of Lords hearing appeals in two

---

1 [1932] AC 562.
2 [1992] 3 All ER 27.
3 [1990] 2 All ER 908.
4 [1999] 3 WLR 939.

similar cases which had been decided differently in the Court of Appeal. In the *Southwark* case, the tenants occupied flats in a block which had been built in 1919. It was accepted that, by modern standards, the flats had inadequate sound insulation. The tenants complained that they could hear the normal day-to-day activities of their neighbours. In *Baxter*, the council had converted a three-storey Victorian house into three flats divided horizontally. The tenant took a tenancy of the middle flat. She was disturbed by the noise of domestic activity from the adjacent flats. In both cases the tenants sued the councils for breach of the covenant of quiet enjoyment under the tenancy agreements. In *Baxter* the tenant also claimed that the council was liable in nuisance.

5.13 The Court of Appeal, in the *Southwark* case, held in favour of the council on the basis that a covenant of quiet enjoyment did not amount to an obligation to alter or improve demised premises. In *Baxter*, however, the Court of Appeal held that a landlord was potentially liable for a breach of covenant of quiet enjoyment where the contemplated use for which the landlord let the demised premises was one which interfered with the reasonable enjoyment of another adjoining flat.

5.14 The matter came before the House of Lords because the Court of Appeal's decisions in the *Southwark* case and *Baxter* were in conflict. The House of Lords resolved this conflict by deciding that the Court of Appeal's decision in *Baxter* was wrong. It decided that in a tenancy agreement the term 'quiet enjoyment' means that the landlord covenants that he will not substantially interfere with the tenant's lawful possession of the premises. Each tenant took the property:

> 'Not only in the physical condition in which [she] found it, but also subject to the uses which the parties must have contemplated would be made of the parts retained by the landlord.'

The tenants knew that there would be other tenants in the neighbouring flats. A covenant of quiet enjoyment, according to their Lordships, does not require a landlord to do positive acts of repair or improvement which he would not otherwise be required to do under the normal landlord's covenant to keep the demised premises in repair. Parliament had, on several occasions, considered a landlord's responsibility to his tenants in regard to sub-standard housing. It was Parliament's view that there was no present need to require landlords to upgrade demised premises so that soundproofing accords with current standards. In Lord Hoffmann's view, the tenants were seeking to impose on the landlord councils an obligation to improve the demised premises after the tenancies had been entered into: that required the courts to go beyond anything which Parliament had said and was something which the House of Lords was not able to do.

5.15 Their Lordships then considered whether the councils might be liable in nuisance. They decided that there was no such liability because the essence of a nuisance is the doing of something on neighbouring land which constitutes an unreasonable interference with the claimant's land. Simply using a domestic flat for normal domestic purposes in a normal and reasonable way did not constitute a nuisance. Lord Hoffmann said:

> 'The normal domestic use of a residential flat could not possibly be a nuisance to the neighbours.'

5.16   Further consideration may have to be given to the House of Lords' decision to take into account the implications of the Human Rights Act 1998. Article 8 of the European Convention on Human Rights imposes a positive obligation to provide rights for individuals in relation to a person's private and family life and his home. This might require positive actions by a local authority. Thus a tenant might be in a position to sue a local authority if, for example, it failed to bring proceedings against a noisy tenant who was committing a nuisance. This would presumably require an analysis of the local authority's statutory powers to prevent a nuisance.

Landlord and Tenant Act 1985

5.17   Parliament has imposed terms to be implied in certain tenancies.[1] Section 8 of the Landlord and Tenant Act 1985 applies to tenancies with a very low rent and implies terms as to fitness for human habitation as follows:

'(1)   In a contract to which this section applies for the letting of a house for human habitation there is implied, notwithstanding any stipulation to the contrary:
   (a)   a condition that the house is fit for human habitation at the commencement of the tenancy; and
   (b)   an undertaking that the house will be kept by the landlord fit for human habitation during the tenancy.'

It seems unlikely that this section can be relied upon save in a few cases because of the low rent limits.[2]

5.18   The section which is relied upon more often is s 11 of the Landlord and Tenant Act 1985[3] which applies to a lease of a dwelling house granted on or after 24 October 1961 for a term of less than 7 years. Subsection (1) states that:

'(1)   There is implied a covenant by the lessor:
   (a)   to keep in repair the structure and exterior of the dwelling house (including drains, gutters and external pipes),
   (b)   to keep in repair and proper working order the installations in the dwelling house for the supply of water, gas and electricity and for sanitation (including basins, sinks, baths and sanitary conveniences, but not other fixtures, fittings and appliances for the making use of the supply of water, gas or electricity), and
   (c)   to keep in repair and proper working order the installations in the dwelling house for space heating and heating water.'

Notice required for liability under Landlord and Tenant Act 1985, s 11

5.19   It should be noted that for the landlord to be liable under s 11, he must have had notice of the defect to be remedied. This follows from *Morgan v Liverpool Corporation*,[4] where a tenant's claim for personal injury under a statutory requirement under the Housing Act 1925 to keep the house 'in all respects reasonably fit for human habitation' failed because the landlord had no notice of the defect. The Court of Appeal considered that this rule applied whether or not the landlord had a

---

1   See by way of previous examples the Housing Act 1957 and the Housing Act 1961.
2   In *Quick v Taff Ely Borough Council* [1986] 1 QB 809, Lawton LJ expressed surprise at the low rent limits under a similar provision in the Housing Act 1957.
3   Formerly the Housing Act 1961, s 32.
4   [1926] 2 KB 131.

right of access (either under the lease or by statute) to inspect the state of repair of the house. Although the Court of Appeal expressed the view that the rule was not absolute, nevertheless it would seem to be of general application.

5.20 An example of a case where the court held that the local authority had notice of the defect is *Sheldon v West Bromwich Corporation*.[1] The council, in the course of investigating complaints, became aware that the water tank in the plaintiff's council house, which had been installed some 30–40 years previously, was discoloured. It was not, however, 'weeping'. The council failed to repair the tank and it later burst, damaging the plaintiff's property. In an action against the council for failure to observe its implied covenant under s 32(1) of the Housing Act 1961 to keep the supply of water in repair, the county court judge dismissed the action on the grounds that in the absence of 'weeping' there was no immediate need for repair. However, on appeal, the council was held liable on the basis that the period of discoloration was sufficient, on being notified to the council, to show an immediate need for repair.

5.21 *Sheldon v West Bromwich Corporation* was relied upon by the plaintiff in *Murray v Birmingham City Council*.[2] The plaintiff was tenant of a house which had been built in 1908. Between 1976 and 1982 there had been six incidents of disrepair to the roof, all of which the council had dealt with sooner or later. During this period, there had been little damage to property inside the premises as a result of the problems with the roof. The plaintiff alleged that the roof was defective because of the absence of proper maintenance or repair and that the council was obliged to renew it rather than continuing to carry out piecemeal repairs. The Court of Appeal did not accept the submission that simply because of the six incidents of disrepair, it necessarily followed that the roof was incapable of repair by any other means than replacement. This was a matter to be decided on the available evidence in each particular case and Slade LJ said:

> 'I accept that in any case, where a landlord, or a tenant for that matter, is under an obligation to keep in repair an old roof, a stage may come where the only practicable way of performing that covenant is to replace the roof altogether. The difficulty, to my mind insuperable difficulty, with which the Plaintiff finds himself faced on this present appeal is that there is no evidence to support the submission that that stage had ever been reached.'

The court did not regard *Sheldon* as offering any help because in that case the court did not purport to decide whether the only way of complying with the covenant to repair in question was by replacing the tank. That point had been left open.

5.22 The position under s 11 of the Landlord and Tenant Act 1985 should be compared with that under s 4 of the Defective Premises Act 1972. In *Sykes v Harry and Another*,[3] the Court of Appeal considered a case where the claimant had been found unconscious and suffering from carbon monoxide poisoning. It was admitted at trial that this had been caused by emissions from the gas fire in the claimant's property due to various defects which would have been found and rectified had the fire ever been serviced. The judge held that the landlord was not liable under s 11 of the 1985 Act because of lack of knowledge of the actual defect. Furthermore, the judge did not

---

1   (1973) 25 P & CR 360, CA.
2   (1988) 20 HLR 39.
3   [2001] 3 WLR 62.

consider that s 4 of the 1972 Act gave a tenant any greater protection than that which existed between him and his landlord by virtue of the lease. Upholding the appeal, and deciding in favour of the tenant, the Court of Appeal held that the duty of reasonable care owed under s 4 of the 1972 Act was not dependent on the constraints imposed in the field of contractual liability between landlord and tenant. Under s 4(1) of the 1972 Act, a tenant merely had to show a failure on the part of the landlord to take such care as was reasonable in the circumstances to see that the tenant was reasonably safe from personal injury. By failing to repair or maintain the gas fire over a substantial period prior to the date of the claimant's injury, and in the light of the landlord's knowledge that the claimant was not having the fire serviced, the landlord was in breach of his duty under s 4 of the 1972 Act.

What is the structure and exterior of the dwelling house?

5.23 Although it might be considered a straightforward matter to understand what is meant by the 'structure and exterior of the dwelling house', the question has come before the courts in a number of cases. In *Liverpool City Council v Irwin and Another*, [1] the House of Lords was concerned with a 15-storey tower block and had to consider whether the council was under a duty to maintain the common parts of the building of which it retained control, including lifts, staircases, rubbish chutes and passages. There was no formal lease or tenancy agreement, although there was a 'conditions of tenancy' document issued by the council. The House of Lords considered that this was a case where it was entitled to imply terms into the contract so as to establish what the parties had intended, as they had themselves not fully stated the terms of the contract. On this basis the House of Lords was in no doubt that there must be implied easements for the tenants and their licensees to use the stairs, a right in the nature of an easement to use the lifts and an easement to use the rubbish chutes. The mere grant of an easement does not carry with it any obligation to maintain, but Lord Wilberforce considered that the nature of the building was important and, contrasting the case with one where responsibility for maintenance of a staircase giving access to an upper floor flat in a house might rest with the tenant, he went on:

> '... but there is a difference between that case and the case where there is an essential means of access, retained in the landlord's occupation, to units in a building of multi-occupation, for unless the obligation to maintain is, in a defined manner, placed upon the tenants, individually or collectively, the nature of the contract, and the circumstances, require that it be placed on the landlord.'

Lord Wilberforce then went on to consider the standard imposed on the landlord and said:

> 'The standard must surely not exceed what is necessary having regard to the circumstances. To imply an absolute obligation to repair would go beyond what is a necessary legal incident and would indeed be unreasonable. An obligation to take reasonable care to keep in reasonable repair and useability is what fits the requirements of the case.' [2]

---

1   [1977] AC 239.
2   Although insofar as it is relevant, this case was not decided under the Housing Act 1961; nevertheless it is relevant to the meaning of 'structure and exterior of the dwelling house'. See also Landlord and Tenant Act 1985, s 11(1)(a).

5.24 Other cases have been concerned with pathways or steps giving access to the demised premises. In *Brown v Liverpool Corporation*,[1] a small dwelling house was let by the corporation to the plaintiff. Access to the house from the road was through a gate, down four shallow steps and across a path comprising three flagstones about 7 feet in length. The steps and the path were demised with the house. The steps were in a state of disrepair and the plaintiff fell and suffered injury. The question which came before the Court of Appeal was whether the steps and path were an integral part of the building to which the covenants to repair implied by s 32 of the Housing Act 1961 applied. Danckwerts LJ held that they formed part of the exterior of the dwelling house. He said:

> 'They are attached in that manner to the house for the purpose of access to this dwelling house, and they are part of the dwelling house which is necessary for the purpose of anybody who wishes to live in the dwelling house enjoying that privilege. If they have no means of access of some sort they could not get there, and these are simply the means of access. The steps are an outside structure, and therefore, it seems to me that they are plainly part of the building, and therefore, the covenant implied by section 32 of the Act of 1961 fits and applies to the obligations of the landlords in this case.'

5.25 It is apparent that the Court of Appeal found it difficult to come to this decision. It is worth noting that it commented on the behaviour of the council which had promised to effect repairs on numerous occasions, but failed so to do, and the court clearly formed an adverse view of the council's conduct.

5.26 A similar case came before the Court of Appeal in *Hopwood v Cannock Chase District Council*.[2] The case again concerned access to and from the demised premises. The ordinary means of access to the house was from the front of the house, although there was a way out from the back door through a yard. The plaintiff came out of the house by the back door, but tripped over the edge of one of the paving slabs in the yard, there being a difference in height of 1½ inches. Again the question for consideration by the Court of Appeal was whether the paving slabs were part of the 'structure or exterior' of the house under s 32 of the Housing Act 1961. Cairns LJ considered *Brown v Liverpool Corporation*, which he distinguished on the basis that there was only one means of access from the house in the *Brown* case. Here, Cairns LJ doubted whether the yard could be regarded as a means of access and then considering the judgment under appeal he went on:

> 'I should be prepared to go still further and say that, treating it as Danckwerts LJ did, as a matter of law and construction of the section,[3] in my view the section cannot be extended beyond what was held in Brown's case to include a yard of this kind.'

What amounts to a failure to 'keep in repair?'

5.27 For liability 'to keep in repair the structure and exterior of the dwelling house' there must exist a physical condition requiring the repair of the structure or exterior of the dwelling house. In *Quick v Taff Ely Borough Council*,[4] the plaintiff was the tenant of a council house that suffered very severe condensation because of inadequate window lintels, the provision of single-glazed metal frame windows and inadequate

---

1   [1969] 3 All ER 1345.
2   [1975] 1 All ER 796.
3   Housing Act 1961, s 32.
4   [1986] 1 QB 809.

heating. As a result of severe condensation throughout the house, decorations, woodwork, furnishings, bedding and clothes rotted, and living conditions were appalling. The Court of Appeal rejected the plaintiff's argument that anything defective or inherently inefficient for living in or ineffective to provide the conditions of ordinary habitation was in disrepair, as this ran contrary to authorities such as *Ravenseft Properties Ltd v Davstone (Holdings) Ltd.*[1] Importantly, Dillon LJ noted that:

> 'The fact that a landlord is a local authority, which is discharging a social purpose in providing housing for people who cannot afford it, does not make the burden of the covenant greater on that landlord than it would be on any other landlord. The construction of the covenant must be the same whether it is implied as a local authority's covenant in a tenancy of a council house or is expressly included as a tenant's or landlord's covenant in a private lease.'

5.28 In *Quick* the liability under the implied covenant was to keep the structure and exterior of the house in repair – not the decorations. The condensation came about from the effect of the warm atmosphere in the rooms on the cold surfaces of the walls and windows, but there was no evidence at all of physical damage to the walls or to the windows. Although there was physical damage in parts of the wood surrounds of some of the windows caused by rot, and the Court of Appeal considered that the plaintiff was entitled to an award of damages in respect of this, nevertheless dealing with the case as a whole Dillon LJ said:

> 'In my Judgment, the key factor in the present case is that disrepair is related to the physical condition of whatever has to be repaired, and not to questions of lack of amenity or inefficiency ... where decorative repair is in question one must look for damage to the decorations but where, as here, the obligation is merely to keep the structure and exterior of the house in repair, the covenant will only come into operation where there has been damage to the structure and exterior which requires to be made good. If there is such damage caused by an unsuspected inherent defect, then it may be necessary to cure the defect, and thus to some extent improve, without wholly renewing, the property as the only practical way of making good the damage to the subject matter of the repairing covenant. That, as I read the case, was the basis of the decision in *Ravenseft*.'

5.29 In *Staves & Staves v Leeds City Council*[2] the Court of Appeal dealt with a case where the tenants complained about dampness which the defendants attributed to condensation. Further complaints were made and about 3 years later the defendants carried out works to the property and cured the dampness. The plaintiffs claimed damages for breach of the defendants' covenant to repair implied by s 11 of the Landlord and Tenant Act 1985 and were awarded special damages representing the cost of clothes damaged by the dampness and £5,000 general damages. The Court of Appeal upheld the decision and refused to accept the defendants' argument that because there were only certain areas where the plaster had perished there had been no failure to keep the structure of the property in repair. Furthermore, the court pointed to a letter from the defendants saying that the plasterwork in one bedroom was so saturated that it would require complete renewal. Lloyd LJ said:

> 'the test in these cases is to be found in the judgment of Dillon LJ in *Quick v Taff Ely Borough Council*. Again I would only repeat one sentence:

---

1   [1980] QB 12.
2   (1991) 23 HLR 107.

"But in my judgment, the key factor in the present case is that disrepair is related to the physical condition of whatever has to be repaired."

Here, by January 1985, the physical condition of the plaster, due to saturation, was such that it required to be renewed. We need not enquire how much of the plaster was "damaged". If the plaster required to be renewed as a result of saturation, then it seems to me that, as a matter of ordinary language, what was done was a repair. Once it was conceded, as it was, that the plaster was part of the structure, it follows that there was a breach of the condition implied by s 11(1)(a) of the Landlord and Tenant Act 1985 and the Plaintiffs were entitled to succeed.'

5.30   The decision in *Quick* and s 11 of the Landlord and Tenant Act 1985 were considered by the Court of Appeal in *Lee v Leeds City Council*.[1] The claimant sought an order requiring the council to remedy condensation, mould and damp in her house. Relying on *Quick*, the council denied that it was liable to remedy interior damp, condensation and mould unless caused by the structure and exterior of the property being out of repair. The Court of Appeal agreed with the council's argument. The claimant also submitted that the condition of her property was sufficiently serious to give rise to a breach of Article 8 of the European Convention on Human Rights (the right to respect for private and family life). The Court of Appeal decided that Article 8, and therefore s 6 of the Human Rights Act 1998, did not impose some general and unqualified obligation on local authorities in relation to the condition of their housing. While the Court of Appeal did not rule out the possibility that a local authority, as the landlord of a dwelling house which was unfit for human habitation, might be in breach of Article 8, nevertheless no breaches had been shown in the present case.

5.31   Condensation was again the issue, albeit in the context of the particular tenancy agreement rather than the Landlord and Tenant Act 1985, in *Welsh v Greenwich London Borough Council*.[2] Mould began appearing in the claimant's flat, which was caused by condensation, particularly by the windows, underneath the carpet and on chattels. Clause 2.1 of the tenancy agreement contained a requirement upon the council to 'maintain the dwelling in good condition and repair'. The council appealed against the judge's finding for the claimant and submitted that 'in good condition' meant good structural condition and that the judge had been wrong to hold the council liable for failing to remedy the condensation which damaged the decorations and chattels in the flat, but caused no damage to the structure of the dwelling and which arose as a result of a design defect.

5.32   The Court of Appeal held that the reference to 'good condition' was intended to make a significant addition to what was meant by the word 'repair'. Having done so, the Court of Appeal held that the context of clause 2.1 of the tenancy agreement did not restrict the term 'good condition' to good structural condition and, therefore, according to Robert Walker LJ:

'Where there is severe black spot mould growth generally within the flat . . . that cannot, in my judgment, be regarded as merely a matter of amenity disassociated from the physical condition of the flat, even if there was, as counsel agreed, no damage to the structure . . . In my judgment the judge was right to conclude that, by failing to provide thermal insulation or dry lining for external walls, Greenwich allowed excessive condensation and severe black spot mould to continue, and so failed to maintain the flat in good condition.'

---

1   [2001] EWCA Civ 06, [2002] 1 WLR 1488.
2   (2001) 33 HLR 40.

5.33   It is to be noted that in *Staves*, counsel for the defendants conceded that the plaster was part of the structure and this enabled there to be a finding of liability against the defendants. Whether such concession was correct is called into doubt by *Irvine v Moran*,[1] where there was more general analysis of s 11 of the Landlord and Tenant Act 1985 and s 32 of the Housing Act 1961. Mr Recorder Thayne Forbes QC had to decide as a preliminary issue what items fell within the landlord's implied covenants under s 32 of the Housing Act 1961. He considered that the equivalent of what is now s 11(1)(a) should be construed so that the word 'structure' means 'the structure of the dwelling house' as distinct from 'the exterior of the dwelling house'. He then went on:

> 'I have come to the view that the structure of the dwelling house consists of those elements of the overall dwelling house which give it its essential appearance, stability and shape. The expression does not extend to the many and various ways in which the dwelling house will be fitted out, equipped, decorated and generally made to be habitable.'

The judge then went on to conclude that a separate garage and separate gates do not ordinarily form part of the dwelling house. He considered other items and continued:

> 'It seems to me that internal wall plaster is more in the nature of a decorative finish and is not part of the essential material elements which go to make up the structure of the dwelling house. I therefore hold that internal wall plaster and, for the same reason, the door furniture do not form part of the structure of the dwelling house, bearing in mind I have held that those words mean something less than the overall construction.'

Finally, the judge concluded that the windows did form part of the structure of the dwelling house.[2] He made it clear that there was room for a different conclusion depending on the precise facts; however, this case would appear to be helpful in considering the extent of the obligation under s 11 of the Landlord and Tenant Act 1985.

5.34   The question whether work undertaken to prevent the occurrence of deterioration in the future, of a kind which has already occurred in the past, is capable of amounting to a 'repair' for the purpose of the implied covenant in s 11 of the Landlord and Tenant Act 1985 came before the Court of Appeal in *McDougall v Easington District Council*.[3] A number of defects had emerged in the house, which the plaintiffs occupied as tenants of the defendant authority, principally relating to the ingress of rainwater. The plaintiffs moved out of the premises to enable the defendant to carry out work designed to remedy the defects. When the plaintiffs moved back into the premises they discovered that the premises needed redecorating to restore them to their previous internal condition. The defendant refused to pay more than the sum of £50 which had been promised before the plaintiffs moved out and accordingly the plaintiffs claimed damages for the costs of decorating the house. The Court of Appeal decided that repair works of a preventive nature could amount to a repair for the purpose of the implied covenant in s 11 of the Landlord and Tenant Act 1985. Mustill LJ pointed out that in *Ravenseft Properties Limited v Davstone (Holdings) Limited*[4] the removal of the whole of the stone cladding on the face of a building, and its

---

1   [1991] 1 EGLR 261.
2   However, not the glazing where there had been a concession by counsel that this fell outside s 32 of the Housing Act 1961.
3   (1989) 21 HLR 310.
4   [1980] QB 12.

replacement by new cladding which incorporated expansion joints not previously there, in order to prevent further dangerous falls of stone, was capable of amounting to repair. In deciding whether preventive measures could amount to repair Mustill LJ said:

> 'in my opinion three different tests may be discerned, which may be applied separately or concurrently as the circumstances of the individual case may demand, but all to be approached in the light of the nature and age of the premises, their condition when the tenant went into occupation, and the other express terms of the tenancy:
>
> (i)   whether the alterations went to the whole or substantially the whole of the structure or only to a subsidiary part;
> (ii) whether the effect of the alterations was to produce a building of a wholly different character than that which had been let;
> (iii) what was the cost of the works in relation to the previous value of the building, and what was their effect on the value and lifespan of the building.'

In this case, Mustill LJ considered that when the work had been completed the house was different and had a substantially longer life. In the circumstances, he considered that in this particular case the works in question had not been repairs for the purposes of the implied covenant under s 11 of the Landlord and Tenant Act 1985. Had the Court of Appeal decided otherwise the tenants would have been entitled to the cost of making good any consequential damage to decorations.

5.35   In *McAuley v Bristol City Council*[1] the Court of Appeal agreed with the concession by counsel for the plaintiff that the statutory obligation imposed by s 32 of the Housing Act 1961 was limited to the extent established by decisions such as *Hopwood v Cannock Chase District Council*[2] and would not extend to a garden step because the step was not part of the exterior of the dwelling house.

5.36   The question of access to the demised premises again came before the Court of Appeal in *King v South Northamptonshire District Council*.[3] The plaintiff, who had been the weekly tenant of a council house for more than 20 years and had used a wheelchair for the previous 5 years, had to use a footpath from the rear access as her principal means of access to the premises. The Court of Appeal had to consider whether it was an implied term of the tenancy or a term implied by s 11 of the Landlord and Tenant Act 1985, that the council would repair the path. Mann LJ held that although it is a question of fact and degree as to what is included in the exterior of a dwelling house for the purposes of s 11 of the Landlord and Tenant Act 1985, he could not conclude that the footpath in this case could be part of the exterior of the demised premises:

> 'The lease of number 69 is a lease to which the section applies, but I for my part do not see how the path running between numbers 72 and 73 could be said to be the exterior of number 69. No doubt, as decisions such as *Hopwood v Cannock Chase District Council* show, it is a question of fact and degree as to what is included in the exterior of the dwelling house. However, in my Judgment, it would be an extravagant and unsupportable conclusion to say that the path was as a matter of fact and degree part of the exterior of number 69.'

---

1   [1991] 3 WLR 968.
2   [1975] 1 WLR 373.
3   [1992] 1 EGLR 53.

5.37 In fact, Mann LJ did decide the case in favour of the plaintiff, but rather (as in *Liverpool City Council v Irwin*) he considered that it was right to imply a term 'to maintain' into the unwritten tenancy agreement. He said:

> 'In my Judgment, it is important, in resolving the dispute between the Appellants and the Respondent, to bear in mind the layout of this estate and of the terraces within it. The houses within the terrace were designed with front and rear access. The rear access was plainly for the removal of refuse and the delivery of coal and the like, uses to which this rear access was in fact put. The houses could not be enjoyed or function in accord with their design without the rear access. In that circumstance, I, for my part, find no difficulty in concluding that the implication of an obligation to maintain the rear access is a necessary one to fulfil the purpose of the demise. The demise is of a dwelling house, which is designed to function as such with the mechanism of rear service. In my judgment, the demise of a house which is designed to function in that way is not efficacious unless the rear surface is adequately maintained.'

Landlord must have reasonable time to carry out repairs

5.38 It has been seen[1] that the implied obligation to keep the structure and exterior of the premises in repair under s 11 of the Landlord and Tenant Act 1985 arises only once the landlord has had notice of the disrepair. In addition, *Morris v Liverpool City Council*[2] confirms that the obligation is to carry out the repair within a reasonable time and that the onus is on the tenant to prove unreasonable delay. Following a fire in the block where the plaintiff's flat was situated, the fire brigade broke down the door which was then boarded up by the defendants by means of thin plywood. The plaintiff, who had been away from the flat, discovered the position and telephoned the defendants asking them to mend the door but nothing was done and a few days later the flat was burgled. The Court of Appeal held that the plaintiff had not established unreasonable delay on the part of the defendants. Although the court considered that by calling further evidence the plaintiff might have been able to establish unreasonable delay, Slade LJ observed:

> 'However, it seems to me that, if it had been explored, the reasonableness or otherwise of the delay would have depended upon evidence as to a number of imponderable matters such as the difficulty or otherwise for the Council in obtaining the proper size and quality of door and frame and also on what the Judge referred to as the Council's 'work load'. Furthermore, in assessing the reasonableness or otherwise of the period, it seems to me that the Court might have been entitled to take into account that the Plaintiff was not living in the flat at the time and that the Council had already taken at least some steps in an effort temporarily to secure the property.'

Buildings containing more than one leasehold property

5.39 For tenancy agreements entered into after 14 January 1989, under s 11(1A) of the Landlord and Tenant Act 1985[3] the landlord's obligation to keep in repair the structure and exterior of the demised premises is extended to any part of the structure and exterior of the building in which the lessor has an estate or interest and to any installation for water, gas, electricity, sanitation and heating which, directly or indirectly, serves the dwelling house and which is owned by the lessor or under his

---

1   At para **5.19**: *Morgan v Liverpool Corporation*.
2   (1988) 20 HLR 498.
3   Inserted by s 116 of Housing Act 1988.

control. There is, however, a defence under s 11(3A) of the 1985 Act if the landlord can show that, despite reasonable endeavours, he has been unable to obtain right of access to carry out the necessary works or repairs.

5.40   In *Passley v Wandsworth London Borough Council*[1] the plaintiff's flat was flooded when, following a cold spell, the pipes in the roof thawed and burst. Substantial damage had occurred before the plaintiff became aware of the problem as he had been away from the flat. There was no evidence that the pipes had been in disrepair before the onset of the frost and the council argued that it was not liable for the damage caused as it had not had notice of the defect. In the Court of Appeal Sir John Balcombe referred to *British Telecom Plc v Sun Life Assurance Society Plc*,[2] when Nourse LJ said:

> 'The general rule is that a covenant to keep premises in repair obliges the covenantor to keep them in repair at all times, so that there is a breach of the obligation immediately a defect occurs. There is an exception where the obligation is the landlord's and the defect occurs in the demised premises themselves, in which case he is in breach of his obligation only when he has information about the existence of the defect such as would put a reasonable landlord on enquiry as to whether works of repair are needed and he has failed to carry out the necessary works with reasonable expedition thereafter.'

In dealing with the case before him involving frozen pipes (and referring to an earlier case[3] where liability had been established when an external downpipe had been blocked by the body of a pigeon) he went on:

> 'It does seem to me that if the blocking of a pipe by a dead pigeon is not wholly outside the landlord's control, neither can be the bursting of a pipe due to freezing weather which caused the disrepair, followed by a thaw which permitted the water which had frozen to escape to cause the damage. Severe weather in this country is not so uncommon an occurrence that it cannot be foreseen and suitable precautions taken. In the circumstances, I am satisfied that we are bound by the rule set out in British Telecom ...'

The Court of Appeal therefore found in favour of the tenant.

Liability for breach of repairing covenant after order for possession

5.41   The question in *Rogers v Lambeth Borough Council*[4] concerned the council's liability for disrepair of demised premises during what was described as the 'limbo period' where the council had obtained, but not yet enforced, a possession order. The claimant fell into arrears with the rent and the council obtained a possession order in 1992, which was suspended provided the claimant punctually paid the arrears by instalments in addition to the current rent. She again fell into arrears, but remained in occupation. In 1996 the claimant started proceedings against the council for breach of the express repairing obligations under the tenancy agreement. Thereafter, in 1997, the claimant applied for the 1992 possession order to be discharged and then, in April 1998, made an agreement with the council to pay off the rent arrears, this agreement being silent on both the pending claim and the pending application to discharge the possession order. At trial, the council denied liability for breach of the express repairing obligations on the basis that following the possession order the claimant had

1   (1998) 30 HLR 165.
2   [1995] 3 WLR 622.
3   *Bishop v Consolidated London Properties Ltd* (1933) 148 LT 407.
4   [2000] LGR 191.

ceased to be a tenant and was not entitled to enforce the repairing covenant. The judge discharged the 1992 possession order and gave damages for breach of the repairing covenants.

5.42 The Court of Appeal held that the claimant's secure tenancy ended on the date when she failed to comply with the terms of the suspended possession order. She became a 'tolerated trespasser'. During the 'limbo period' the claimant could not enforce the repairing covenant against the council as there was no tenancy in existence. The council could have applied to the court in 1996 to strike out her claim, but did not do so; nor did it enforce the possession order. Instead, it made an agreement with the claimant in April 1998 tolerating her continued occupation of the premises. The Court of Appeal decided three key questions as follows.

(1) Without a court order, the old secure tenancy was not revived by the agreement in April 1998.
(2) The judge was entitled to exercise his discretion when he discharged the 1992 possession order.
(3) By discharging the 1992 possession order, the council's repairing obligations were retrospectively revived and accordingly the council was correctly held liable for damages for breach of the repairing covenant.

Statutory nuisance

5.43   As cases such as *Quick v Taff Ely Borough Council* (see para **5.27**) have shown, tenants may find it difficult to establish a breach of the implied covenant under s 11 of the Landlord and Tenant Act 1985 when the complaint is one of condensation. Circumstances which might not give rise to a breach of the implied covenant under s 11 might nevertheless amount to a statutory nuisance under Part III of the Environmental Protection Act 1990. Section 79(1)(a) of the 1990 Act states that a statutory nuisance exists where premises 'are in such a state as to be prejudicial to health or a nuisance'. Proceedings under the 1990 Act may be brought in the magistrates' court, where the defendant can be required to carry out works to abate the nuisance. In clear and simple cases magistrates can make a compensation order. This procedure was considered by the Court of Appeal in *Davenport v Walsall Metropolitan Borough Council*.[1] The magistrates' court's right to make a compensation order was accepted, but the Court of Appeal refused to interfere with the magistrate's refusal to make a compensation order in this particular case because the damages were not easily quantifiable, required a considerable amount of evidence, and were accordingly not within the magistrate's discretion. Similarly, in deciding whether premises are prejudicial to health within the meaning of s 79(1)(a) of the Environmental Protection Act 1990 the Court of Appeal in *Cunningham v Birmingham City Council*[2] confirmed that an objective test should be applied. The tenant had argued that because her child was autistic, the size and layout of the kitchen in her property was dangerous; however, the court, applying an objective test, disagreed. Pill LJ said:

> 'The extent of obligations upon Local Authorities would be enormous if they had to meet the reasonable, but individual health requirements of prospective occupiers. I agree that

---

1   (1996) 28 HLR 754.
2   (1998) 30 HLR 158.

the question is one of statutory construction. In my judgment the test to be applied . . . is an objective test.'

Note also that in *Issa v Hackney London Borough Council*[1] the Court of Appeal held that Part III of the Public Health Act 1936, which contained provisions allowing tenants to apply to the magistrates' court for the abatement of a statutory nuisance, did not create a civil cause of action for damages. It is submitted that the position under the Environmental Protection Act 1990 would be the same.

Damages

5.44   A detailed study of quantum is outside the scope of this work. However, the principles for measuring damages payable to a tenant for breach of a repairing covenant were laid down by the Court of Appeal in *Calabar Properties Ltd v Stitcher*.[2] The plaintiff had acquired the lease of a flat in a block of flats with the intention of living there permanently with her husband. The lease contained a repairing covenant by the landlords requiring them to maintain the external parts of the block in good repair. After about a year the tenant complained to the landlords that rainwater was penetrating into the flat and causing damage to the decorations, but the landlord failed to carry out any external repairs to the flat. Having remained in the flat for 5 years, the tenant and her husband moved out when it became uninhabitable and they were forced to rent alternative accommodation. When the landlords sued the tenant for charges due from her under the lease she counterclaimed for damages for breach of the landlord's covenant to repair. The Court of Appeal considered that any assessment of a tenant's damages for breach of a landlord's repairing covenant should start with the fundamental principle that they are:

'So far as is possible by means of a monetary award, to place the Plaintiff in the position which he would have occupied if he had not suffered the wrong complained of, be that wrong a tort or breach of contract. I take that statement from the judgment of Donaldson LJ in *Dodd Properties (Kent) v Canterbury City Council*[3].'

Applying the above principle, and also noting that the landlords had had no intention of carrying out the repairs, Griffiths LJ said:

'In these circumstances the tenant had two options that were reasonably open to her: either of selling the flat and moving elsewhere or alternatively of moving into temporary accommodation and bringing an action against the landlords to force them to carry out the repairs and then returning to the flat after the repairs were done.

If a tenant chooses the first option then the measure of damages would indeed be the difference in the price he received for the flat in its damaged condition and that which it would have fetched in the open market if the landlord had observed his repairing covenant. If, however, the tenant does not wish to sell the flat but to continue to live in it after the landlord has carried out the necessary structural repairs it is wholly artificial to award him damages on the basis of loss in market value because, once the landlord has carried out the repairs and any consequential redecoration of the interior is completed, there will be no loss in market value. The tenant should be awarded the cost to which he was put in taking alternative accommodation, the cost of redecorating, and some award for all the unpleasantness of living in the flat as it deteriorated and until it became

---

1   [1997] 1 All ER 994.
2   [1983] 3 All ER 759.
3   [1980] 1 All ER 928.

uninhabitable. These three heads of damage will, so far as money can, compensate the tenant for the landlord's breach.'[1]

5.45 The valuation of general damages was considered in *Lubren v London Borough of Lambeth*[2] when the Court of Appeal agreed with an award of damages of £800 per year between 1979 and 1984 for defects which resulted in a tenant having to leave the property while repairs were carried out.

5.46 In *Brent London Borough Council v Carmel (sued as Murphy)*[3] the Court of Appeal, when dismissing the council's application for leave to appeal, saw no prospect of a successful appeal against an award of damages which included general damages calculated at approximately £2,750 per annum. Although the Court of Appeal was referred to its own decision in *Chiodi v De Marney*,[4] where it had been indicated that £1,500 per annum for damages in cases of disrepair was the top of the bracket at that time, the court apparently saw no reason to interfere with the award of £2,750 per annum made in 1994.

5.47 The assessment of damages for breach of a repairing covenant has further been considered by the Court of Appeal in *Wallace v Manchester City Council*.[5] The court followed the fundamental principle referred to in *Calabar Properties Limited v Stitcher* and then made the following points:

(1) The assessment of damage inevitably involves a comparison of the property as it was for the period when the landlord was in breach of his obligation with that it would have been if the obligation had been performed.

(2) For periods when the tenant remains in occupation of the property notwithstanding the breach of obligation to repair, the loss to him requiring compensation is the loss of comfort and convenience which results in living in a property which is not in the state of repair it ought to have been in if the landlord had performed his obligation.

(3) If the tenant does not remain in occupation but, being entitled to do so, is forced by the landlord's failure to repair, to sell or sub-let the property, he can recover for the diminution of the price or recoverable rent occasioned by the landlord's failure to perform his covenant to repair.

The case in question concerned an award of damages under (2) above. The Court of Appeal considered that the sum to be awarded might be ascertained in a number of different ways, including but not limited to a notional deduction in the rent. Some judges might prefer to use that method alone, some might prefer a global award for discomfort and inconvenience and others might prefer a mixture of the two.

The Court of Appeal heard that there was an 'unofficial tariff' for damages in cases of this nature whereby courts awarded damages ranging between £1,000 and £2,750 for each year the property is considered to be in disrepair. In *Wallace* the Court of Appeal refused to interfere with an award of damages of £3,500 in favour of the tenant over a period of 3 years.

---

1 In this particular case the court was unable to make an award for the cost of alternative accommodation because the plaintiff had failed to plead such a claim.
2 (1988) 20 HLR 165.
3 (1996) 28 HLR 203.
4 (1988) 21 HLR 6.
5 (1998) 30 HLR 1111.

Local authority not liable for tenant's torts

5.48   In *Hussain and Another v Lancaster City Council*,[1] the Court of Appeal struck out a claim in which it was alleged that the plaintiffs had been harassed by tenants of the council, that the council had taken no steps to stop the harassment and that this amounted to a nuisance. The Court of Appeal considered that the claim fell outside the scope of the tort of nuisance because the matter complained of did not involve the tenant's use of the tenant's land. Furthermore, the court considered that *Smith v Scott*,[2] a case in which it was held that a landlord does not owe a duty to his neighbour to use care in selecting his tenants, was decisive authority in favour of the council. There was also a claim in negligence alleging that the council had failed to exercise its powers under the Housing and Highway Acts. However, the Court of Appeal considered that this claim failed as a result of *Stovin v Wise*[3] and *X (Minors) v Bedfordshire County Council*.[4]

5.49   *Hussain* was considered by the Court of Appeal in *Lippiatt and Another v South Gloucestershire County Council*.[5] The claimants' complaint was that damage was caused to their land by the acts of travellers who were being allowed to occupy land owned by the council. They were not the council's tenants and were trespassers, although possibly they were licensees of the council. The Court of Appeal distinguished *Hussain* on the basis that the conduct of the tenants in that case was not in any sense linked to, nor did it emanate from, the homes where they lived. In *Lippiatt*, the allegation was that the travellers had been allowed to congregate on the council's land and that they had used it as a base for the unlawful activities of which the claimants, as neighbours, complained. The Court of Appeal refused to strike out the claim, holding that it was at least arguable that the facts could give rise to a liability in nuisance.

Implications of the Human Rights Act 1998

5.50   Article 8 of the European Convention on Human Rights (ECHR) reads as follows:

> '1. Everyone has the right to respect for his private and family life, his home and his correspondence.
>
> 2. There shall be no interference by a public authority with the exercise of this right except such as is in accordance with the law and is necessary in a democratic society in the interests of national security, public safety or the economic wellbeing of the country, for the prevention of disorder or crime, for the protection of health or morals, or for the protection of the rights and freedoms of others.'

Furthermore, Article 1 of the First Protocol to the ECHR reads:

> 'Every natural or legal person is entitled to the peaceful enjoyment of his possessions. No one shall be deprived of his possession except in the public interest and subject to the conditions provided for by law ...'

---

1   (1998) 96 LGR 663.
2   [1973] 1 Ch 314.
3   [1996] AC 923. See Chapter 1.
4   [1995] 2 AC 633. See Chapter 1.
5   [1999] 4 All ER 149, and see para **1.75**.

It is submitted that in dealing with claims for breach of covenant and disrepair, courts will be called upon to consider whether the Human Rights Act 1998 provides tenants with legal rights over and above those described in the preceding paragraphs. For example, it is possible that the Act might provide opportunities for tenants who cannot rely upon s 8 of the Landlord and Tenant Act 1985 (see para **5.17**) and in cases where a statutory nuisance cannot be established (see para **5.43**).

Defective Premises Act 1972

5.51 It must be appreciated that whether considering covenants contained in a lease or tenancy agreement, or those implied by statute, while they can be relied upon by the tenant if he has a claim for personal injury arising out of breach of covenant by the landlord, such breach will not give rise to any liability as far as the tenant's family or visitors are concerned. The lease or tenancy agreement is a contract between the landlord and tenant alone. The first attempt to change this was s 4 of the Occupiers' Liability Act 1957, which said that where, under a tenancy, the landlord was under an obligation for the maintenance or repair of the premises, the landlord should owe to all persons lawfully on the premises the same duty in respect of dangers arising from default in carrying out that obligation as if the landlord were an occupier of the premises and the visitors were there by his invitation or permission. Section 4 applied whether or not the landlord's obligations arose from express covenants in the lease or from the statutory obligations. It should also be noted that s 4 applied only to the demised premises and that where a landlord retained part in his own occupation, for example staircases or lifts, he would be liable under the general provisions of the Occupiers' Liability Act 1957 as occupier.

5.52 Section 4 of the Occupiers' Liability Act 1957 was repealed and replaced by s 4 of the Defective Premises Act 1972, the first part of which reads as follows:

'(1) Where premises are let under a tenancy which puts on the landlord an obligation to the tenant for the maintenance or repair of the premises, the landlord owes to all persons who might reasonably be expected to be affected by defects in the state of the premises a duty to take such care as is reasonable in all the circumstances to see that they are reasonably safe from personal injury or from damage to their property caused by a relevant defect.

(2) The said duty is owed if the landlord knows (whether as a result of being notified by the tenant or otherwise) or if he ought in all the circumstances to have known of the relevant defect.'

Section 4 of the Defective Premises Act 1972 extends the previous obligation under s 4 of the Occupiers' Liability Act 1957. It is to be noted that the duty of care is owed if the landlord knows or ought to have known of the defect. It applies not only to the tenant's family and visitors, but to other persons who might reasonably be expected to be affected, including trespassers, neighbours, passers by and even the tenant himself.

5.53 Whether the landlord has notice of the defect was considered by the Court of Appeal in *Sykes v Harry and Another*.[1] The claimant sought damages against his former landlord for carbon monoxide poisoning caused by emissions from a gas fire which would not have occurred had the fire been serviced. Although the landlord had known of the lack of servicing, he had not known about the actual defects. The Court

---

1   [2001] 3 WLR 62.

of Appeal decided that while under s 11 of the Housing Act 1985 the tenant must establish that the landlord had notice of the actual defect giving rise to the injury, the position in this case was different. Under s 4(1) of the Defective Premises Act 1972 a tenant simply has to show a failure on the part of the landlord to 'take such care as is reasonable in all the circumstances' to see that the tenant is reasonably safe from personal injury. The landlord's failure to repair or maintain the gas fire over a substantial period prior to the date of the claimant's injury, coupled with knowledge that the claimant was not having the gas fire serviced, was sufficient notice under s 4(1) of the Defective Premises Act 1972.

5.54   Section 4 of the Defective Premises Act 1972 imposes a duty on the landlord for failure to carry out 'maintenance or repair' of the premises. The Court of Appeal in *Lee v Leeds City Council*[1] pointed out that Parliament had not imposed on the landlord a duty to remedy defects in any more general sense. Accordingly, because the condensation, mould and damp was not a defect arising from want of repair, it could not be a defect covered by s 4 of the Defective Premises Act 1972.

5.55   In *McAuley v Bristol City Council* (see para **5.35**) the plaintiff fell and broke her ankle while standing on a step forming part of the garden path. Her claim under s 32 of the Housing Act 1961 failed because that section did not extend to a defect in the garden, but her action under s 4(4) of the Defective Premises Act 1972 succeeded. In the Court of Appeal, Ralph Gibson LJ dealt with the two subsections of s 4 of the Act set out above and then went on to consider s 4(4) which extends the basis of liability by treating the landlord as being under an obligation to repair when in fact, under the lease or tenancy agreement, he is not. The extension of liability is not general but is made when the landlord is given a right to enter 'to carry out any description of maintenance or repair'. The landlord, when he is given that right, is to be treated as if he were under an obligation to the tenant 'for that description of maintenance or repair' (not all and any description of maintenance or repair).

5.56   The Court of Appeal then had to decide whether the court below had been correct to find that a right to repair the garden was to be implied into the tenancy agreement. Having reviewed *Liverpool City Council v Irwin and Another* (see para **5.23**) Ralph Gibson LJ went on:

> 'After some hesitation, I have reached the conclusion that the necessary reservation should be implied in restricted terms. The defect in the step exposed the tenants and visitors to the premises to the risk of injury . . . the Council had expressly reserved the right to enter "for any purpose for which from time to time entry may be required" if I have correctly construed the term, and the agreement did not expressly identify those purposes. If there should be a defect in the garden which exposed the tenants and lawful visitors to the premises to significant risk of injury, then I think that, to give business efficacy to the agreement, a right should be implied in the Council to carry out repairs for the removal of that risk of injury. A reasonable tenant could not sensibly object to such a right. If the Council became aware of a dangerous defect in the steps of a steep garden, as in this case, and asked the tenant for access to repair it, in the interest of all persons who might be expected to be affected by the defect, the Court could, in my Judgment, properly require the tenant to allow such access upon the basis of an implied right in the Council to do the work.'

---

1   [2001] EWCA Civ 06, [2002] 1 WLR 1488.

5.57   The duty under s 4 of the Defective Premises Act 1972 is one of reasonable care and it is therefore not an absolute duty. This is illustrated by the case of *Issitt v London Borough of Tower Hamlets*.[1] A 2-year-old boy fell from a bathroom window because of a defective catch. Shortly after they occupied the property, the boy's parents pointed out the defective nature of the catch to the defendant local authority. This happened about 5 or 6 weeks before the accident and no repairs had been carried out. The Court of Appeal considered that it was not reasonably foreseeable that the defective catch on the bathroom window would constitute a danger to a 2-year-old child. It also considered that the parents' own duty to children could not be ignored. Griffiths LJ said:

> 'In my view Defendants in this position are entitled, as one of the factors that they must weigh up when considering their duty, to take into account the fact that parents do – and certainly ought to – keep an eye on very little children.'

5.58   A similar case, but decided simply in negligence, is *Stevens v County of Blaenau Gwent*.[2] A 2-year-old child fell from the window of a first-floor flat let by the council. Some time previously another young child of the family had been found sitting on the windowsill. The mother had requested a lock for the window. The council said that it would look into this, but later said that there was a council policy that locks could not be fitted to windows because of fire regulations. After the accident the council fitted a safety catch which only allowed the window to open a short distance. The claimant alleged that the council was negligent. It had been alerted to the problem and should not have relied on the blanket policy against locks on windows, but should have looked into the fitting of a safety lock. The Court of Appeal disagreed. First, there was no evidence of disrepair. Dealing with the council's policy, Potter LJ said:

> '... the council was entitled to take a view that its policy, arrived at on the basis of a balance of risk, should be applied, in the absence of evidence that its application presented exceptional risk to the safety of the family.'

In refusing the request for a lock, the council was entitled to assume that the family would move furniture to make it more difficult for the children to reach the window. The fact that the council fitted a safety lock after the accident:

> 'does not in my view demonstrate that they were under any duty or assumed any responsibility to do so prior to the accident.'

5.59   The Defective Premises Act 1972 was pleaded in *Rimmer v Liverpool City Council* (see para **5.6**), but was abandoned and, as has been mentioned in para **5.7**, the claim succeeded on the basis of the common law duty of care. Commenting, albeit obiter, on s 4 of the Defective Premises Act 1972, Stephenson LJ said:

> 'The duty it imposes on a landlord is only a duty to take reasonable care to see that the premises let are reasonably safe from personal injury (or from damage to property) caused by a failure to carry out an obligation to maintain or repair the premises (Section 4(3)) and there was no such failure here. There was apparently no such obligation, and certainly no want of repair.'

---

1   (Unreported) 6 December 1983.
2   [2004] EWCA 715, [2004] All ER (D) 116 (June).

It will be recalled that the problem in *Rimmer* was the existence of a thin panel of glass which had been put in place when the property was erected. Again, presumably for similar reasons, the claim for breach of statutory duty under s 4 of the Defective Premises Act 1972 was abandoned in *Targett v Torfaen Borough Council* (see para **5.10**).

Duties to homeless persons

5.60 Part II of the Housing Act 1985 imposes upon local authorities a duty of a public law nature to provide accommodation for homeless persons in certain circumstances as well as other similar duties in connection with the performance of that function.

5.61 The case of *O'Rourke v Camden London Borough Council*[1] was concerned with the issue as to whether an individual has a private law cause of action for damages arising out of the alleged breach of those statutory duties. The House of Lords firmly rejected the argument that there should be or was such a private law of duty. As Lord Hoffmann put it in the leading judgment:

'The concept of a duty in private law which arises only when it has been acknowledged to exist is anomalous. It means that a housing authority which accepts that it has a duty to house the applicant but does so inadequately will be liable in damages, but an authority which perversely refuses to accept that it has any such duty will not. This seems to me wrong. Of course a private law relationship may arise from the implementation of the housing authority's duty. The applicant may become the authority's tenant or licensee and so brought into a contractual relationship. But there seems to me no need to interpose a statutory duty actionable in tort merely to bridge the gap between the acknowledgment of the duty and its implementation.'

OCCUPIER'S LIABILITY

5.62 Like any other person or organisation, a local authority will have duties as occupier both at common law, and under the Occupiers Liability Act 1957 in the case of duties owed to visitors, or under the Occupiers Liability Act 1984 in the case of duties owed to trespassers.

5.63 Section 2 of the Occupiers' Liability Act 1957 reads:

'(1) An occupier of premises owes the same duty, the "common duty of care", to all his visitors, except insofar as he is free to and does extend, restrict, modify or exclude his duty to any visitor or visitors by agreement or otherwise.

(2) The common duty of care is a duty to take such care as in all the circumstances of the case is reasonable to see that the visitor will be reasonably safe in using the premises for the purposes for which he is invited or permitted by the occupier to be there.'

Meaning of occupier

5.64 The Act does not define the word 'occupier'; however, this was considered by the House of Lords in *Wheat v E Lacon & Co Limited*,[2] where Lord Pearson said:

1   [1997] 3 All ER 23.
2   [1966] AC 552.

'The foundation of occupier's liability is occupational control, ie, control associated with and arising from presence in and use of or activity in the premises.'

In the same case Lord Denning said:

'In order to be an "occupier" it is not necessary for the person to have entire control over the premises. He need not have exclusive occupation. Suffice it that he has some degree of control. He may share the control with others. Two or more may be "occupiers". And whenever this happens, each is under a duty to use care towards persons coming lawfully onto the premises, dependent upon his degree of control.'

In *Bailey v Armes and Another*[1] the Court of Appeal held that for an occupier to be liable he had to exercise a degree of control over the premises sufficient to put him under a duty of care to those who came onto the premises.

5.65 In *Wheat v E Lacon & Co Limited*, the plaintiff was suing as a result of the death of her husband who fell down stairs at an inn owned by the defendant company. The deceased was a lodger with a couple who managed the inn on behalf of the defendant. The House of Lords concluded that the defendant company was an 'occupier' for the purposes of the Occupiers' Liability Act 1957 and that it owed a duty to the deceased. On the facts, however, the House of Lords decided in favour of the defendant. The plaintiff was descending a staircase in darkness, as the light bulb at the top of the stairs was missing. Furthermore, the handrail did not extend alongside the bottom two steps. There was no evidence as to how precisely the accident had happened and although the House of Lords concluded that it was foreseeable that a visitor might use the staircase when unlit, nevertheless it did not consider that the staircase was dangerous for someone taking proper care for his own safety if he could not see the floor.

5.66 A case with more specific application to local authorities when considering the meaning of 'occupier' is *Harris v Birkenhead Corporation and Another*.[2] The local authority made a compulsory purchase order for slum clearance of an area containing the second defendant's house which happened to be in good condition. The local authority served a notice to treat on the second defendant and a notice of entry under the Housing Act 1957. The house remained occupied for about 6 months. When, however, the occupant left she did not inform the local authority of her departure. As was unfortunately normal in the area, the empty house was vandalised and fell into a derelict condition. The local authority had a practice of bricking up such properties but did not do so on this occasion. A 4½-year-old child wandered into the derelict house through an open and unsecured door, climbed to the second floor and fell to the street below through a window, suffering serious injury. The Court of Appeal held that the local authority was the legal occupier of the house at the time of the accident because the effect of the notice of entry and the statutory authority on which it was based was that the local authority was asserting its right to control the property and it was in consequence of such assertion that the property had become empty. Megaw LJ said:

'By that Notice of Entry the Corporation was asserting its right to control this property after the expiry of 14 days. And it was asserting the right to exercise that control at any time thereafter when it saw fit. In my judgment, such an assertion of a right of control,

1   [1999] EGCS 21.
2   [1976] 1 All ER 341.

even though it has not been followed by an actual or symbolic, or a "deemed", taking of possession, is sufficient, at any rate when, as here happened, the property ceases to be physically occupied by any other person, to make the person who has that immediate right of control the occupier for these purposes. I do not see why it should be suggested that as between the Corporation and the Second Defendant there should be any duty owed to the Corporation, after the Notice of Entry, to give the Corporation notice that they were leaving the house – leaving it to the Corporation who had, and had asserted, the right to enter and control it.'

5.67 A highway authority does not occupy a footpath on land owned by another although it has a statutory duty to maintain it under s 41 of the Highways Act 1980.[1] The owner of land over which a public right of way passes, however, is under no liability towards members of the public for negligent nonfeasance. This was confirmed in *McGeown v Northern Ireland Housing Executive*,[2] when the House of Lords approved the earlier decision in *Gautret v Egerton*.[3] Lord Keith said:

'... the rule in *Gautret v Egerton* is deeply entrenched in the law. Further, the rule is in my opinion undoubtedly a sound and reasonable one. Rights of way pass over many different types of terrain, and it would place an impossible burden upon landowners if they not only had to submit to the passage over them of anyone who might choose to exercise them but were also under a duty to maintain them in a safe condition.'

Lord Keith went on to confirm that persons using a right of way are neither the licensees nor invitees of the landowner nor his visitors under the Occupiers' Liability Act 1957.

5.68 In the same case, Lord Keith compared a public right of way on the one hand with a pathway which had been adopted by the highway authority. The highway authority had no responsibility for maintenance of the right of way; however, areas adjoining the terrace where the plaintiff lived had been so adopted and in particular the strip of ground immediately adjoining the terrace which the plaintiff had to cross to go to or from her house. Lord Keith went on:

'if the Plaintiff was licensee of the Defendants upon the pathway where she fell she was equally their licensee upon that strip of ground. The circumstance that the Highway Authority is responsible under public law for its maintenance cannot logically make any difference to the position. The Defendants would still owe a personal duty to the Plaintiff to maintain the pathway in a reasonably safe condition, and be liable to her if she suffered injury owing to the area not being in such condition. That unreasonable result can be avoided if it is held that dedication as a public highway puts an end to any duty which might otherwise be owed by the housing executive.'

5.69 While agreeing with Lord Keith's decision in the case, Lord Browne-Wilkinson was reluctant to go so far as to say that the owner of the land over which a public right of way passed owed no duty of care to an invitee as opposed to a licensee. He stated that until the footpath became a public right of way, the defendants did formerly owe a duty of care as they had laid out the footpaths as a means of access to the dwellings on the estate.[4] He pointed out the possible drawback in the decision if,

---

1   *Whiting v Hillingdon London Borough Council* (1970) 68 LGR 437. Highways liabilities are dealt with in Chapter 7.
2   [1994] 3 All ER 53.
3   (1867) LR 2 CP 371.
4   See, eg, *Fairman v Perpetual Investment Building Society* [1923] AC 74.

for example, passages in a modern shopping centre should by long public use become public rights of way. He expressed the position as follows:

'In the present case, I can see no escape from the logic of Lord Keith's conclusion that, after the presumed dedication of the pathway as a public right of way, the housing executive ceased to owe any duty of care to the Plaintiff. The Plaintiff would, at best, be the licensee of the housing executive. Once the public right of way came into existence, those seeking access to the dwellings on the estate did not need any licence from the housing executive; they could go there as of right. Nor could the housing executive exclude anyone from the pathway. It would be an abuse of language to describe a person who is entitled to be on land without permission and who could not be excluded by the occupier of that land as being a "licensee" of that occupier. Therefore the Plaintiff was not a visitor to whom the duty of care was owed.

But it does not necessarily follow that the existence of a public right of way is incompatible with the owner of the soil owing a duty of care to an invitee, as opposed to a licensee. In the case of an invitee there is no logical inconsistency between the Plaintiff's right to be on the premises in exercise of the right of way and his actual presence there in response to the express or implied invitation of the occupier. It is the invitation which gives rise to the occupier's duty of care to an invitee. I do not understand your Lordships to be deciding that it is impossible to be an invitee (and therefore a visitor) on land over which there is a public right of way. I wish expressly to reserve my view on that point.'

5.70 In *Gulliksen v Pembrokeshire County Council*,[1] the Court of Appeal decided that a footpath built as part of a housing estate had been dedicated as a highway at common law from the date of construction, following the decision of Lord Diplock in *Suffolk County Council v Mason*:[2]

'At common law a highway is a way over which all members of public have the right to pass and re-pass without hindrance.'

The Court of Appeal in *Gulliksen* also explained the circumstances in which such a footpath could become a 'highway maintainable at public expense' under the Highways Act 1980.[3]

5.71 In *Peskett v Portsmouth City Council*,[4] the local authority occupied an office building together with footpaths which intersected, creating a right-angled turn. The respondent, who worked in the building, used the footpath frequently. She, like many people, used to cut across a grassed area between the corner of the footpaths. The grass and soil had worn away, creating a 'trip' between the path and the adjacent ground. Although it was accepted that the footpaths themselves were perfectly safe, and there had been no previous complaints, nevertheless the Court of Appeal considered that the judge had been entitled to find that the heavy usage of the footpath, the council's knowledge that people habitually cut the corner and the relative ease with which the danger could be averted, had entitled the judge to find in favour of the claimant (with a finding of 50 per cent contributory negligence). Each such case depended upon its facts.

1 [2002] EWCA Civ 968, [2003] QB 123.
2 [1979] AC 705.
3 See para **7.4**.
4 (Unreported) 25 June 2002.

5.72 *Peskett* should be contrasted with *Beaton v Devon County Council*.[1] The claimant was injured while cycling through a disused railway tunnel near Bideford which formed part of a cycle track. She stopped and placed her foot in a 6-inch-deep gulley running between the cycle track and the side of the tunnel. As a result she fell and suffered a serious injury. At trial the judge held the council liable on the basis that the accident was foreseeable. The Court of Appeal considered that the judge's approach to the nature of the council's duty was greater than the 'common duty of care' imposed by the Occupiers' Liability Act 1957. The duty is one to take reasonable care of and for visitors. It is not an obligation to insure against accidents.

5.73 A landlord who has given up possession will not normally be an 'occupier' for the purposes of the Occupiers' Liability Act 1957, but he will, of course, remain occupier of the common parts.[2]

Extent of the common duty of care

5.74 A detailed analysis of the circumstances in which occupiers have been held liable under the Occupiers' Liability Act 1957 is outside the scope of this work. However, it is worthwhile considering two contrasting cases which have considered liability under the Act in conjunction with ever-changing codes of practice. In the first case, *Ward v The Ritz Hotel (London) Ltd*,[3] the plaintiff was severely injured when he fell backwards over a low balustrade on the balcony in the hotel restaurant. When the hotel had been constructed in about 1905 the top of the balustrade had been at a height of about 3 feet 3½ inches above the floor. In about 1976, the floor of the balcony had been resurfaced, raising the floor level by about 4 inches, resulting in the balustrade being less than 3 feet above floor level. In 1976, the British Standards Institution's recommended standard for the height of any balustrade was 3 feet 6 inches. By a majority the Court of Appeal decided in favour of the plaintiff. Dealing with the approach to be adopted to the recommendations of the British Standards Institution, McCowan LJ said:

> 'The right approach, it seems to me, is to consider the position in 1976 when the floor tiling was laid. It should have been apparent to the Defendants at that time that the balustrading was in the result being significantly lowered. They either knew or ought to have known the result would plainly be in breach of the British Standard. They must have been aware that visitors were likely to stand in the position that the Plaintiff was standing at the time of his fall ... in those circumstances, the Defendants should have reasonably foreseen that unless they raised the height of the balustrade, sooner or later such a person might topple over it.'

Lloyd LJ, in a dissenting judgment, considered that the views of the British Standards Institution were no more than a recommendation and it was a matter for the judge to decide how much weight such recommendation deserved in the particular circumstances of the case.

5.75 In the second case, *Green v Building Scene Ltd and Another*,[4] the plaintiff was injured when she fell down a short stairway in the defendant's shop premises. She

---

1   [2002] EWCA Civ 1675, (2003) 100(1) LSG 26.
2   *Fairman v Perpetual Investment Building Society* [1923] AC 74.
3   [1992] PIQR 315.
4   [1994] PIQR 259.

alleged that there was no central handrail on the stairway, contrary to the requirements of the Building Regulations 1976[1] and the recommendations in the Code of Practice issued by the British Standards Institution. The Court of Appeal considered that non-compliance with the Building Regulations and British Standards did not create liability and it also considered that the absence of a central handrail was not causative of the accident. Commenting on the *Ward* case Ralph Gibson LJ said:

> 'Now, so to decide in this case is not, in my judgment, to debase or ignore the relevance of the British Standards requirements as stated in this Court in the Ritz case. The ignoring of the requirements there created a dangerous trap for the visitor. This stairway, in my judgment, did not create a trap for anyone.'

5.76 Because local authorities own a variety of buildings including, for example, schools and swimming pools, they are exposed to numerous situations where claims from visitors to those premises can arise. An example of this is the case of *Fowles v Bedfordshire County Council*.[2] The plaintiff, a student, regularly attended a youth centre catering for young people aged 16–25, where the facilities included an activities room where he engaged in gymnastics. A trainee youth worker at the centre had shown the plaintiff how to do a full somersault, performed by running along foam mats and somersaulting so as to land upright in the centre of a crash mat. On the day in question, the plaintiff attended the centre with a friend, and decided to do some gymnastics. They lined up some mats, but unfortunately placed the crash mat too close to the wall. While performing a forward somersault, the plaintiff over-rotated and hit the wall on the way down sustaining serious personal injuries. The council was held liable (albeit that the plaintiff was held two-thirds to blame for the accident) because of the absence of supervision and the failure to warn the plaintiff of the risks involved. Millett LJ said:

> 'Anyone who assumes the task of teaching the forward somersault is under a duty not only to teach the technique involved in the exercise and to explain the dangers associated with its performance, but to teach the steps which must be taken to prepare for it, including the laying of the crash mat, and to explain the dangers of performing the exercise in an inappropriate environment. It matters not how obvious a danger may be; it should be pointed out.'

Whether this claim fell strictly under the Occupiers' Liability Act 1957 was, in fact, left open by the Court of Appeal, which preferred to approach the case on the basis of the common law duty of care.

5.77 In *O'Shea v Royal Borough of Kingston-Upon-Thames*,[3] the council was held liable to the plaintiff (albeit with a finding of 50 per cent contributory negligence) in circumstances where he was injured while diving into a swimming pool which was too shallow for that purpose. The Court of Appeal held that the council had been negligent in failing to erect a sign prohibiting diving at the pool. Dealing with the duty owed by the defendant, Neill LJ said:

> 'Kingston was not under a duty to act as an insurer, nor was it necessary for it to make the premises so safe that users could not injure themselves even though they acted with complete disregard for their own safety. The duty owed to Mr O'Shea was a duty to take

1   SI 1976/1676.
2   [1995] PIQR 380.
3   [1995] PIQR 208.

such care as in all the circumstances of the case was reasonable to see that he would be reasonably safe in using the pool.'

5.78 *O'Shea* should be compared with *Ratcliffe v McConnell and Another.*[1] The claimant, a 19-year-old student, climbed over a locked gate at night and dived into the defendants' open-air swimming pool, hitting his head and suffering severe injuries. A notice at the pool said that it was closed, but there was no notice prohibiting diving. The trial judge held the defendants liable in spite of the claimant's evidence that he knew that the pool was closed for the winter, knew it was dangerous to dive into water of unknown depth and that the water level was low. The Court of Appeal allowed the appeal. Although a duty under s 1 of the Occupiers' Liability Act 1984 is owed to a trespasser, the nature and extent of what it is reasonable to expect of the occupier varies greatly depending upon the age of the trespasser. Stuart-Smith LJ said:

'... the nature of and extent of what is reasonable to expect of the occupier varies greatly depending on whether the trespasser is very young or very old and so may not appreciate the nature of the danger which is or ought to be apparent to an adult.'

Here, however, it was obvious to any adult, and to most children old enough to have learnt to dive, that if someone dived into a pool they might hit their head on the bottom if there was insufficient water. There was no hidden danger or trap and the defendants were under no duty to warn the claimant against it. Stuart-Smith LJ went on:

'[Counsel for the claimant] sought to portray the danger here as a hidden one or something in the nature of a trap. In my judgment it was nothing of the sort. Even if the defendants knew or had reasonable grounds to believe that students might defy the prohibition on the use of the pool and climb over the not insignificant barrier of the wall or gate, it does not seem to me that they were under any duty to warn the plaintiff against diving into too shallow water, a risk of which any adult would be aware and which the plaintiff, as one would expect, admitted that he was aware. Had there been some hidden obstruction in the form of an extraneous object in the pool or a dangerous spike, of which the defendants were aware, the position might have been different. Though even so I am doubtful whether the defendants needed to do more than they did, namely to prohibit use of the pool except during certain permitted hours in the Summer. Even in the case of a lawful visitor there is no duty to warn of a danger that is apparent.'

5.79 The question of foreseeability came before the Court of Appeal in *Berryman v London Borough of Hounslow.*[2] The plaintiff lived on the fifth floor of a block of flats and was the defendant's tenant. Under the tenancy agreement, the council owed the plaintiff a contractual duty to keep the lifts in the building in good working order. Returning to the block of flats with five bags of shopping, and carrying her baby, the plaintiff found that the lifts were out of order. She carried the bags of shopping upstairs one at a time, taking her baby with her on each trip. As a result she suffered a slipped disc. The case was, in fact, decided in contract, namely the terms of the tenancy agreement. However, dealing with the claim under the Occupiers' Liability Act 1957, Stuart-Smith LJ said:

'I cannot see that the fact that there was no lift operating in the building, if that be the case, so that the visitor has to walk up the stairs can be regarded as a breach of the common duty of care. There was no defect in the stairs and I cannot see that it is reasonably foreseeable that a visitor will suffer personal injury from having to walk up rather than going by lift.'

---

1   [1999] 1 WLR 670.
2   [1997] PIQR 83.

5.80 In fact, the claim was decided on the basis of the contractual obligation under the tenancy agreement whereby the defendant was under an obligation to keep the lifts in reasonable repair. The Court of Appeal considered that this was arguably a wider duty than the tortious obligation under the Occupiers' Liability Act 1957, but nevertheless found in favour of the defendant on the basis that there had to be a real danger or a serious possibility of harm of the sort the plaintiff had actually suffered so as to satisfy the test of foreseeability. Henry LJ said:

> '... it is not unlikely that someone discommoded by the fact that the lift is not operational will walk upstairs. Walking upstairs is marginally more dangerous than walking on the flat. But the fact that going upstairs might make you marginally more likely to stumble does not, in my judgment, make any injury arising from such a stumble a foreseeable consequence of the breach of contract to keep the lift in working order such as would satisfy the test as set out in *the Heron II.*
>
> I say that because stairs are an ordinary feature of life and in my judgment there is no more than a bare possibility of extra or added risk of injury in going up the stairs. To ascend four floors in a modern block is not an inordinate number of stairs although it is certainly longer than most would choose to do laden.'

5.81 Another case decided on foreseeability is *Jolley v Sutton London Borough Council.*[1] The claimant, aged 14, suffered serious injury when a boat, which had been left lying on a grass verge adjacent to a block of council flats, fell onto him. Although the boat looked sound, it was in fact rotten. The council accepted that it had been negligent in leaving the boat where it was and that it should have been removed. The claimant and his friend decided to try to repair the boat. They worked on it for about 6 weeks, using a car jack belonging to the claimant's father to prop the boat. Unfortunately, while the claimant was beneath the boat, it fell, causing him severe injury. It was common ground that the council owed the claimant, as a visitor, a common duty of care under the Occupiers' Liability Act 1957, where s 2(2)(a) makes specific reference to children as follows:

> 'An occupier must be prepared for children to be less careful than adults.'

The argument for the council, which had succeeded in the Court of Appeal, was that the accident was not of a type or kind which was reasonably foreseeable. The House of Lords allowed the claimant's appeal. Lord Steyn considered that the Court of Appeal had been wrong to reverse the judge's finding that an accident was foreseeable:

> '... to a young teenage boy with the strength and ability to raise the boat and prop it up.'

5.82 Lord Hoffmann seems to have gone further. Rejecting the argument that, apart from its rotten planking, the boat was simply a heavy object like any other, he stated that the rotten condition of the boat:

> '... had a significance beyond the particular danger it created. It proclaimed the boat and its trailer as abandoned, *res nullius*, there for the taking, to make of them whatever use the rich fantasy life of children might suggest.'

Lord Hoffmann further suggested that where children were involved, a very broad description of 'kind of injury' was permissible because the ingenuity of children finding unexpected ways of doing mischief to themselves and others should never be underestimated. Thus, once it was foreseeable that children might:

---

1   [2000] 1 WLR 1082.

'... meddle with the boat at the risk of some physical injury ...'

and the actual injury fell within that broad description, that was enough to establish liability.

5.83 The House of Lords has now made clear, however, that even where foreseeability can be established, it is not necessarily enough to establish the existence of a duty of care. In *Tomlinson v Congleton Borough Council*,[1] the claimant suffered a serious injury when he ran onto a beach surrounding a lake in Brereton Heath Country Park and then dived into the water, striking his head hard on the sandy bottom. The council knew that people swam in the lake and viewed this as unacceptable. Notice boards warning against swimming in the lake had been erected. The council formed the view that warning notices were having little effect and decided to deter swimmers by planting reeds and making the beach less attractive. Because of limited resources, the work had not been carried out before the claimant's accident.

5.84 The case proceeded on the basis that the claimant was a trespasser and, accordingly, the Occupiers' Liability Act 1984 applied. Section 1(1)(a) of the Act imposes a duty on the occupier in respect of risks of injury:

'By reason of any danger due to the state of the premises or to things done or omitted to be done on them.'

On the facts of the case the claimant could not establish that the risk was due to the 'state of the premises'. Furthermore, the House of Lords considered that the claimant could not establish that the risk of injury was due to 'things done or omitted to be done' on the premises. Lord Hoffmann said:

'In my opinion "things done or omitted to be done" means activities or the lack of precautions which cause risk, like allowing speedboats among the swimmers. It is a mere circularity to say that a failure to stop people getting into the water was an omission which gave rise to a duty to take steps to stop people from getting into the water.'

5.85 In the light of the above the House of Lords considered that there was no risk of a kind which gave rise to a duty under either the 1984 or 1957 Occupiers' Liability Acts. However, it went on to consider whether, if this were wrong, the conditions for a duty under the 1984 Act existed. The first two such conditions:

(a) knowledge or foresight of the danger; and
(b) knowledge or foresight of the presence of the trespasser

presented little difficulty. The council knew that people swam from the beach around the lake.

5.86 The House of Lords then considered the third condition:

(c) 'Is the risk one against which, in all the circumstances of the case, the occupier may reasonably be expected to offer the other some protection?'

The Court of Appeal had found in favour of the claimant on the basis that there was a foreseeable risk of serious injury. The House of Lords considered that this was not sufficient to enable the claimant to succeed. Even if the claimant had been a lawful

---

1	[2003] UKHL 47, [2003] 3 WLR 705.

visitor under the Occupiers' Liability Act 1957, Lord Hoffmann was of the opinion that:

'... the question of what amounts to "such care as in all the circumstances of the case is reasonable" depends upon assessing, as in the case of common law negligence, not only the likelihood that someone may be injured and the seriousness of the injury which may occur, but also the social value of the activity which gives rise to the risk and the cost of preventative measures. These factors have to be balanced against each other.'

5.87   The House of Lords distinguished its earlier decision in *Jolley* because in that case there was no social value to the council in leaving a derelict boat lying about. Lord Hoffmann confirmed that the social value of the activity had to be taken into account when establishing the existence of a duty of care under either the 1957 or 1984 Act:

'This is the kind of balance which has to be struck even in a situation in which it is clearly fair, just and reasonable that there should in principle be a duty of care or in which Parliament, as in the 1957 Act, has decreed that there should be. And it may lead to the conclusion that even though injury is foreseeable ... it is still in all the circumstances reasonable to do nothing about it.'

5.88   As well as bringing social value into the equation, the House of Lords also considered that it was appropriate to ask whether the council should be entitled to allow people of full capacity to decide whether to take the risk involved. Lord Hoffmann expressed the following view:

'I think it will be extremely rare for an occupier of land to be under a duty to prevent people from taking risks which are inherent in the activities they freely choose to undertake upon the land. If people want to climb mountains, go hang-gliding or swim or dive in ponds or lakes that is their affair. Of course the land owner may for his own reasons wish to prohibit such activities. He may think that they are a danger or inconvenience to himself or others. Or he may take a paternalistic view and prefer people not to undertake risky activities on his land. He is entitled to impose such conditions, as the council did by prohibiting swimming, but the law does not require him to do so.'

Lord Hoffmann considered that it was wrong that the majority of people should be prohibited from enjoying leisure activities on a beach:

'in order to comply with what is thought to be a legal duty to safeguard irresponsible visitors against dangers which are perfectly obvious. The fact that such people take no notice of warnings cannot create a duty to take other steps to protect them.'

5.89   Although *Tomlinson* proceeded under the Occupiers' Liability Act 1984, the House of Lords considered whether there was any practical difference, on the facts of the case, between this Act and the Occupiers' Liability Act 1957. The starting point is that Parliament has made it clear that in the case of a lawful visitor under the 1957 Act, one starts from the assumption that there is a duty owed, whereas in the case of a trespasser under the 1984 Act, one starts from the assumption that there is no duty owed. The House of Lords accepted that there is some degree of risk in swimming and diving; however, taking into account the social value of the activity and the fact that people should be allowed to decide for themselves whether to take a risk, even if the Occupiers' Liability Act 1957 had applied, the duty under that Act would not have required the council to take any steps to prevent the claimant from diving, or warning him against dangers which were perfectly obvious.

5.90 The general approach of the House of Lords is probably best illustrated by the views of Lord Scott:

> '[The claimant] was simply sporting about in the water with his friends, giving free rein to his exuberance. And why not? And why should the council be discouraged by the law of tort from providing facilities to young men and young women to enjoy themselves in this way? Of course there is some risk of accidents arising out of the joie de vivre of the young. But that is no reason for imposing a grey and dull safety regime on everyone.'

5.91 The Court of Appeal followed *Tomlinson* in *Rhind v Astbury Water Park Limited and Another*,[1] a case similar on its facts to those in *Tomlinson*. The claimant, trying to retrieve a football, did a running dive into the shallow water of the defendants' lake and hit his head on a fibreglass container. Following *Tomlinson*, the case proceeded on the basis that the claimant was a trespasser and that any duty of care owed to him had to be under the provisions of the Occupiers' Liability Act 1984. The Court of Appeal accepted that because the injury was due to the presence of the fibreglass container the injury was the result of the 'state of the premises' and, accordingly, unlike in *Tomlinson*, the claimant satisfied the provisions of s 1(1)(a) of the Occupiers' Liability Act 1984. Nevertheless, the claim failed because a subsequent inspection from the surface of the water had failed to locate the fibreglass container. It was only when a diver was employed that the container was found. Therefore the defendants had no knowledge of the existence of the container and the claimant could not establish that they had knowledge of the danger for the purposes of s 1(3)(a) of the Act. It was not reasonable to expect the defendants to make underwater inspections of the lake.

5.92 Another case following the approach of the House of Lords in *Tomlinson* is *Simmonds v Isle of Wight Council*.[2] A 5-year-old boy attended his primary school sports day with his mother. Having taken part in activities in the morning, and enjoyed a picnic lunch with his mother, it was intended that he watch the rest of the sports with his teachers. Unfortunately the boy was attracted by some swings from which he fell and injured himself. Gross J did not consider that the school was under any duty to 'immobilise' the swings. The question was not what the school might have done in retrospect, but whether there was a duty to immobilise the swings at the time. The judge did not consider that there was such a duty:

> 'I would not expect a prudent parent organising a sporting event on such a field to have immobilised the swings, any more than if there had been a tree on the field, the school or a prudent parent would have been duty bound to rope that off too.'

The judge accepted that a decision was a case on its own facts which might not merit an appeal. However, he justified the appeal against the original decision in favour of the claimant as follows:

> ' ... there is, however, a danger with decisions such as this. The upshot would not be that swings are fenced off, it is far more likely that sports days and other simple pleasurable sporting events would not be held if word got round that a school could be liable in a case such as this. Such events would become uninsurable or only insurable at prohibitive cost. A warning against such an approach is trenchantly contained in the recent decision of the House of Lords in *Tomlinson v Congleton Borough Council*.'

---

1   [2004] EWCA Civ 756, [2004] All ER (D) 129 (Jun).
2   [2003] All ER (D) 156 (Sep).

Independent contractors

5.93 An occupier will not normally be liable for the negligence of his independent contractors. Section 2(4)(b) of the Occupiers' Liability Act 1957 provides:

> 'where damage is caused to a visitor by danger due to the faulty execution of any work of construction, maintenance or repair by an independent contractor employed by the occupier, the occupier is not to be treated without more as answerable for the danger if in all the circumstances he had acted reasonably in entrusting the work to an independent contractor but had taken steps (if any) as he reasonably ought in order to satisfy himself that the contractor was competent and that the work had been properly done.'

5.94 Accordingly, an occupier will be liable only when he has an independent liability of his own, such as in failing to select a competent contractor or where he chooses to supervise the contractor and then fails to ensure that the contractor performs its tasks competently.

5.95 The reasonable steps to be taken by an occupier to satisfy himself as to the competence of his independent contractor have been considered by the Court of Appeal in three cases in the context of insurance. In *Gwilliam v West Hertfordshire Hospitals NHS Trust and Others*[1] the claimant was injured at a fair organised by the Trust when using play equipment provided by its contractors. The Trust had been told by the contractors that they had public liability insurance. Unfortunately it transpired that this insurance had expired a few days before the fair. In *Bottomley v Todmorden Cricket Club*[2] the cricket club arranged contractors to provide a fireworks display on its land. The claimant, who was helping the contractors with their show, was injured. The contractors had no public liability insurance, but, in any event, the cricket club had not checked the insurance position. In *Naylor (trading as Mainstreet) v Payling*[3] the respondent was injured when being ejected by a doorman at the appellants' nightclub. The doorman was an independent contractor who had no public liability insurance.

5.96 In *Naylor* the Court of Appeal considered the following questions:

(a) Does the duty to take reasonable care to ensure the competence of an independent contractor include a duty to see that the contractor has public liability insurance?

(b) Is there a freestanding duty to ensure that the independent contractor has such insurance?

(c) Is there, in fact, any duty on an occupier to ensure that his independent contractor has public liability insurance?

In *Gwilliam* and *Bottomley* the Court of Appeal held that the question of insurance was relevant to the competence of the contractor, although there was by no means a unanimous approach by the judge. On the facts of both cases, the claimant in *Gwilliam* failed because the Trust had received assurances from the contractor that public liability insurance was in place, while in *Bottomley*, the failure of the cricket club to make the same enquiry about insurance was a failure to take reasonable steps to ensure

---

1   [2002] EWCA Civ 1041, [2003] QB 443.
2   [2003] EWCA Civ 1575, [2004] PIQR P18.
3   (Unreported) 7 May 2004.

that the contractors were incompetent. Accordingly, the claimant in *Bottomley* succeeded.

5.97 In *Naylor* the Court of Appeal felt able to distinguish the earlier decisions in *Gwilliam* and *Bottomley* and gave further guidance. They said, first, that there can be no freestanding duty on an occupier to ensure that the independent contractor has public liability insurance. Moreover, unless required by statute, there is no duty on an occupier to have public liability insurance. It would be illogical, therefore, to impose an obligation on an occupier to ensure that his contractor is covered by such insurance. *Gwilliam* and *Bottomley* could be distinguished because the contractors, in both case, were carrying out one-off operations. Latham LJ thought that a check on the insurance position might have a bearing on the assessment of whether the contractor was competent. Neuberger LJ pointed out that the law recognises two situations. First, an employer is not liable for the torts of his contractors provided reasonable care is taken in the selection of that contractor. In the second case, an employer cannot avoid liability where that liability is non-delegable, or where the task is unlawful, extra hazardous or carried out on a public highway. He then continued:

> 'to invent a third and intermediate category, where the task is hazardous, but not extra hazardous, and where the employer can delegate, but only if he satisfies himself that the independent contractor is insured or otherwise good for a claim, seems to me to be unnecessary and to introduce an undesirable degree or rigidity into the field'.

Restricting liability

5.98 An occupier can seek to restrict, modify or exclude his duty to any visitor under s 2(1) of the Occupiers' Liability Act 1957. However, the freedom so to do is limited by the Unfair Contract Terms Act 1977.

5.99 Regardless of any possible contractual provisions which might change the position in negligence, the courts will always have the power to apportion liability as between joint wrongdoers. Section 2(1) of the Civil Liability (Contribution) Act 1978 provides that apportionment of liability:

> '. . . shall be such that may be found by the Court to be just and equitable having regard to the extent of that person's responsibility for the damage in question.'

5.100 Similarly, by the Law Reform (Contributory Negligence) Act 1945, a plaintiff's damages can be reduced to reflect the plaintiff's own contributory negligence.[1]

---

1   See, eg, *Fowles v Bedfordshire County Council* [1995] PIQR 380 and *O'Shea v Royal Borough of Kingston-upon-Thames* [1995] PIQR 208, discussed above.

Chapter 6

EMPLOYER'S LIABILITY

INTRODUCTION

6.1   Chapter 1 set out the fundamental principles of the law of negligence, in particular the three-stage approach to liability taken by the House of Lords in *Caparo Industries Plc v Dickman*,[1] the requirements for liability being:

(1)   foreseeability of damage;
(2)   a relationship of proximity between the parties; and
(3)   that it is just and reasonable that the law should impose a duty in the circumstances of the case.

The relationship of employer and employee is one instance in which these three criteria will be met and a duty of care will arise. Indeed, it is one of the relationships in which the law recognises a duty to take positive steps to prevent harm, rather than merely a duty not to cause harm.[2]

6.2   Essentially, the local authority owes the same duty of care to its employees as all other employers. At common law the employer's duty is to take reasonable care for the safety of the employee. It is classically broken down into the following duties:

(1)   to provide the employee with a safe place of work, including safe access to that place of work;
(2)   to provide him or her with a proper system of work (including, if necessary, proper supervision);
(3)   to provide him or her with plant, machinery or equipment adequate for the task; and
(4)   to provide him or her with competent fellow-employees.[3]

6.3   Each of these elements is continuously refined on a case-by-case basis, and there are many instances in which the duties overlap: the duty to provide a safe system of work may, for example, involve the provision of both adequate equipment and competent staff.

6.4   The employer's duty is owed to each employee individually.[4] It is said to be personal to the employer, and therefore non-delegable, and is owed even if the

---

1   [1990] 2 AC 605.
2   See, eg, *Stovin v Wise* [1996] AC 923 at 930, per Lord Nicholls, dissenting, but not on this point.
3   See, eg, *Wilsons and Clyde Coal Company Limited v English* [1938] AC 57. Each of these duties will be considered in turn from para **6.49** onwards.
4   *Paris v Stepney Borough Council* [1951] AC 367. See paras **6.26–6.28**.

employee is working under the supervision of another party or on another party's premises.[1]

6.5 The local authority employer's common law duties are supplemented by duties imposed by primary and secondary legislation. A good deal of such legislation responds to European directives on health and safety at work. Breach of most of these statutory duties will give rise to a civil liability for damages.[2] The content of duties imposed by statute is relevant when assessing how a reasonable employer should conduct his or her business. The existence of a statutory duty may, therefore, in appropriate circumstances be used as a guide in a claim brought in negligence.[3] A reasonable employer may be taken to be aware of the obligations which Parliament has imposed for the protection of employees, and should take appropriate steps to comply with those obligations. Further, if Parliament has identified that a particular activity carries a risk to health or safety against which an employer should guard, it cannot be said that the danger is not reasonably foreseeable by a prudent employer.

6.6 Furthermore, where injury is caused by a defect in equipment provided by the employer for the purposes of its business the local authority employer will be liable to the employee for that defect even if the fault for it lies elsewhere.[4]

6.7 The duty in its various forms is owed to the 'employee'. This term may be applied to persons outside the traditional employment (master and servant) relationship. The employer may therefore be held to owe its duties as employer to a worker who is for tax purposes self-employed, particularly if it has remained responsible for safety in the circumstances of the operation under scrutiny.[5]

6.8 Provided the requirements for liability are satisfied (duty, breach and foreseeable damage) the local authority employer will be liable for all recognised forms of injury: physical injury (including work-related upper limb disorders and vibration white finger), industrial disease, occupational deafness and psychiatric damage (including psychiatric damage caused by stress in the workplace if it meets the other conditions for liability).[6]

6.9 As in any other employment situation, the employee may himself be negligent or in breach of a statutory duty and the principles relating to contributory negligence and the maxim *volenti non fit injuria* then come into play. It must be noted, however, that the defence of *volenti non fit injuria* has very limited application in employers' liability cases.

---

1   *McDermid v Nash Dredging and Reclamation Company Limited* [1987] AC 906. See paras **6.28–6.33**.

2   This is not universally the case. See, eg s 47 of the Health and Safety at Work etc Act 1974 which excludes a right of action in civil proceedings for failure to comply with duties imposed by ss 2–7 of that Act, and reg 22 of the Management of Health and Safety at Work Regulations 1999, SI 1999/3242, which excludes civil liability for breach of most of those Regulations. Whereas, therefore, the default position is the breach of duty posed by health and safety regulations and will be actionable in civil claims (see s 47(2) of the Health and Safety at Work etc Act 1974), each set of regulations needs to be considered individually.

3   See *Franklin v Gramophone Co. Ltd* [1948] 1 KB 542.

4   Employers' Liability (Defective Equipment) Act 1969. See para **6.83**.

5   See *Lane v Shire Roofing Co* [1995] IRLR 493, [1995] PIQR 417. This issue is considered at paras **6.12–6.24**.

6   *Walker v Northumberland County Council* [1995] IRLR 35, *Sutherland v Hatton* [2002] ICR 613 and *Barber v Somerset County Council* [2004] 1 WLR 1089.

6.10   Local authorities do in some respects differ from other employers. Along with other government undertakings or bodies charged by the State with some of its functions they are considered for the purposes of European Community law as emanations of the State, [1] with consequences for the breadth of claims that may lie against them for breaches of statutory duty. [2] On the other hand, local authorities are exempted from the statutory requirement imposed upon employers carrying on business in Great Britain by the Employers' Liability (Compulsory Insurance) Act 1969 to maintain insurance against liability for bodily injury or disease sustained by employees arising out of and in the course of their employment in Great Britain. [3]

6.11   This chapter will consider first the meaning of the term 'employee' in the context of the duties owed in the workplace. It will then describe some important characteristics of the common-law duty before looking briefly at the significant impact of Europe in the field of health and safety at work. It will then look at each of the aspects of the duty in turn, both at common law and by way of statutory duties. The local authority being just one category of employer, it will be appreciated that the principles are derived from the law of employers' liability generally; many of the examples given will of necessity be taken from that law, rather than from the sphere of the local authority employer in particular.

WHEN WILL THE LOCAL AUTHORITY BE SEEN AS THE EMPLOYER (TO WHOM IS THE DUTY OWED)?

6.12   The question as to whether the employer's duties (either at common law or its statutory duties) are owed to a particular individual can be a complex one (it may be a pertinent one where the local authority has contracted some of its functions). There is no difficulty with full-time employees (where there is probably a contract of employment) but the relationship may be more casual, either in terms of time (the time it takes for the worker to complete a particular project, for example) or of the particular arrangements between the parties (the worker might work from home, in his own time).

6.13   What is clear is that the court will not be persuaded by the label the parties themselves put on the relationship; it will look behind any such label and investigate the reality. [4] It may also disregard the parties' stated intentions or preferences, as it did in *Davis v New England College of Arundel*, [5] where the respondent college was held to be employer of a teacher who had specifically requested to be treated as self-employed as a freelance lecturer and the respondent had treated him as such for its own financial reasons.

6.14   The traditional distinctions drawn are between employees and independent contractors, or between a contract of service as against one for services, the duties being owed in the former situation but not in the latter. A number of tests have been

---

1   *Fratelli Constanzo v Commune di Milano* [1990] 3 CMLR 239 and *Marshall v Southampton and South West Hampshire Area Health Authority* [1986] ICR 335.
2   See para **6.36**.
3   Employers' Liability (Compulsory Insurance) Act 1969, s 3.
4   See *Ferguson v Dawson & Partners (Contractors) Ltd* [1987] 1 WLR 1213.
5   [1977] ICR 6.

applied (and to a greater or lesser extent remain valid). Under the control test, for example, if the employer directed both what work was to be done and how it was to be done the worker is an employee rather than an independent contractor.[1]

6.15   In *Ferguson v Dawson*,[2] on the other hand, the Court of Appeal carried out a more detailed investigation of the terms (including terms it was itself prepared to imply) of the contractual relationship, finding that a labour-only sub-contractor was in reality the defendant's employee where his site agent could dismiss the workmen, move them from site to site, tell them what to do and how to do it and where the defendant provided any tools required and employed the men on an hourly basis, the money paid to them being described as a wage.

6.16   In *Park v Wilsons and Clyde Coal Co Ltd*,[3] four criteria were put forward: the master's power of selection; the payment of wages; the master's right to control the method of doing the work; and the master's right of suspension or dismissal. In *Bank voor Handel en Schleepvaart v Slatford*,[4] Denning LJ stated that the concept of employment for these purposes depended not on the submission to orders but whether or not the worker was 'part and parcel of the organisation'.

6.17   In *Ready Mixed Concrete (South East) Ltd v Minister for Pensions and National Insurance*,[5] three criteria were identified for determining the existence of a contract of service: the servant agreeing that in consideration of a wage or other remuneration he would provide his own work and skill in the performance of some service for his master; the servant agreeing that in performance of that service he would be subject to the other's control in a degree sufficient to make that other master; and the other provisions of the contract being consistent with the relationship being a contract of service.

6.18   In other cases, the independent contractor has been characterised as a worker carrying on his own business, during the course of which he undertakes to do a particular piece of work.[6]

6.19   A review of these principles was carried out by the Court of Appeal in *Lane v The Shire Roofing Company (Oxford) Ltd*,[7] where the plaintiff building contractor, a roofer in his own right, had agreed to attend to a roof on behalf of the defendant for an all-in fee. At first instance the judge found him to be an independent contractor.

6.20   Giving the judgment of the Court of Appeal, Henry LJ stated:

'We were taken to the standard authorities on this matter: *Ready Mixed Concrete (South East) Ltd v Minister of Pensions and National Security* [1968] 2 QB 497; *Market Investigations Ltd v Minister for Social Security* [1969] 2 QB 173; and *Ferguson v Dawson* [1976] 1 WLR 1213, to name the principal ones. Two general remarks should be made. The overall employment background is very different today (and was, though less so, in 1986) than it had been at the time when those cases were decided. First, for a variety

---

1   See, eg, *Performing Right Society Ltd v Mitchell and Booker (Palais de Danse) Ltd* [1924] 1 KB
      762.
2   [1987] 1 WLR 1213.
3   1928 SC 121 at 159.
4   [1953] 1 QB 248 at 295.
5   [1968] 2 QB 497.
6   See, eg, *Market Investigations Ltd v Minister for Social Security* [1969] 2 QB 173.
7   [1995] PIQR 417.

of reasons, there are more self-employed and fewer in employment. There is greater flexibility in employment, with more temporary and shared employment. Secondly, there are perceived advantages for both workman and employer in the relationship between them being that of independent contractor. From the workman's point of view, being self-employed brings him into a more benevolent and less prompt taxation regime. From the employer's point of view, the protection of employee's rights contained in the employment protection legislation of the 1970s brought certain perceived disincentives to the employer to take on full-time long-term employees. So, even in 1986 there were reasons on both sides to avoid the employee label.'

6.21 Remarking that, despite these perceived mutual benefits, there were good reasons of policy in the area of safety at work to ensure that a proper categorisation of the employee and the independent contractor was made, the principles to be applied were as follows:

(1) the control test, namely:
    (a) who lays down what is to be done and the way in which it is to be done;
    (b) who provides (ie hires and fires) the team by which it is done; and
    (c) who provides the plant and machinery;
(2) in the case of skilled employees, with discretion to decide how the work should be done, the question needed to be expanded so as to ask whose business was being carried out, that of the injured worker or that of his employer; and
(3) both these questions needed to be asked in the context of the further issue: who was responsible for the overall safety of the men doing the work.

6.22 At first instance the judge had founded his decision that the worker was an independent contractor on the following factors: the plaintiff had his own genuine roofing business and was a specialist roofer; he had the benefit of form 714 certificates so was paid gross and paid his own tax; he was capable of working without supervision and was expected to do so; and there was no provision for further work or dismissal. Henry LJ characterised these matters as equally applicable to a short-term single-job contract of employment. He therefore went on to ask the question 'whose business was it?' and found that the question had to be that it was the defendant's business. The plaintiff was not therefore an independent contractor.

6.23 This case represents a significant move towards a more liberal interpretation of the term 'employee' and has widened the class of worker to whom the employer's duty is owed.[1]

6.24 It was followed by the Court of Appeal in *Young v Charles Church (Southern) Limited*.[2] The employment status of labourers who were self-employed for purposes of tax and National Insurance was in issue. Hobhouse LJ said:

'The point has been considered by the Privy Council in *Lee v Chung* [1990] ICR 409 and by the Court of Appeal in *Lane v Shire Roofing* [1995] 24 IRLR 493. The answer to the question what duties are owed by one party to the other is to be decided by looking at the facts of the case and evaluating the relevant features of the relationship and not by simply

---

1 Although possibly not for the purposes of the Employers' Liability (Defective Equipment) Act 1969, s 1(3) of which states that '*employee* means a person who is employed by another person under a contract of service or apprenticeship and is so employed for the purpose of a business carried on by that person, and *employer* shall be construed accordingly'.
2 (1998) 39 BMLR 146.

attaching a label nor by looking solely at the tax and National Insurance position. In each of those cases relevant duties were held to be owed by the employer or quasi-employer to the workmen. The same applies to the present case.'

NATURE OF THE DUTY

6.25   Two aspects require consideration. The employer's duty is:

(1)   personal to each individual employee; and
(2)   non-delegable.

So far as the former is concerned, a good illustration is provided by *Paris v Stepney Borough Council*[1] where the plaintiff, employed by the defendant local authority as a garage hand, had only one good eye. During the course of his employment he sustained injury to that eye and alleged that, while it may not have been necessary for the majority of garage hands, the defendant had been under a duty to provide him with goggles to protect his remaining good eye. The defendant's case was that there was no such duty, as the risk of an accident occurring was the same for workers with both eyes intact as it was for this worker and that the severity of the injury in the event of any accident which did take place was irrelevant to the determination of the existence or scope of the duty.

6.26   This proposition was rejected by the House of Lords. Lord Simmonds (actually dissenting on the facts) said:[2]

'The issue, my Lords, is narrowed down and I will say at once that I do not dissent from the view that an employer owes a particular duty to each of his employees. His liability in tort arises from his failure to take reasonable care in regard to the particular employee and it is clear that, if so, all the circumstances relevant to that employee must be taken into consideration. I see no valid reason for excluding as irrelevant the gravity of the damage which the employee will suffer if an accident occurs ...'

6.27   Lord MacDermott said:[3]

'... the duty of the employer to take reasonable care for the safety of his workmen is directed ... to their welfare and for that reason, if for no other, must be related to both the risk and degree of injury. If that is so and if, as was very properly conceded, the duty is that owed to the individual and not to a class, it seems to me to follow that the known circumstance that a particular workman is likely to suffer a graver injury than his fellows from the happening of a given event is one which must be taken into consideration in assessing the nature of the employer's obligation to that workman.'

6.28   With regard to the duty being non-delegable, the plaintiff in *McDermid v Nash Dredging & Reclamation Co Ltd*,[4] employed as a deckhand by the defendant, had been sent to work on board a tug owned by a Dutch company under the control of a Dutch captain employed by that company. One of the plaintiff's tasks was to untie the ropes mooring the tug to a dredger. The system devised by the captain was for the

---

1   [1951] AC 367.
2   Ibid at 375.
3   Ibid at 389.
4   [1987] AC 906. See also *Wilsons & Clyde Coal Co Ltd v English* [1938] AC 57 and *Morris v Breaveglen Limited* [1993] ICR 766.

plaintiff to give a double knock on the wheel house when he had untied the ropes and it was safe to move off.

6.29 The plaintiff was injured when the captain moved off before he had untied one of the ropes. The House of Lords held that the defendant was under a duty to provide the plaintiff, its employee, with a safe system of work, both in its design and its operation, and that it remained under a duty to ensure that the system was properly performed. While it had delegated performance of the duty to the captain it remained liable for any breach of the duty. The duty was therefore personal, and non-delegable.

6.30 In his speech, Lord Brandon of Oakbrook said:[1]

'A statement of the relevant principle of law can be divided into three parts. First, an employer owes to his employee a duty to exercise reasonable care to ensure that the system of work provided for him is a safe one. Secondly, the provision of a safe system of work has two aspects: (a) the devising of such a system and (b) the operation of it. Thirdly, the duty concerned has been described alternatively as either personal or non-delegable. The meaning of these expressions is not self-evident and needs explaining. The essential characteristic of the duty is that, if it is not performed, it is no defence for the employer to show that he delegated its performance to a person, whether his servant or not his servant, whom he has reasonably believed to be competent to perform it. Despite such delegation the employer is liable for the non-performance of the duty.'

6.31 It should not be thought, however, that an employer will necessarily be liable for *every* injury caused to an employee during the course of employment by the default of the third party. In particular, at common law there is no more than a duty to take reasonable care that premises (other than premises of the employer) at which the employee has to work are safe. The courts have recognised that an employer may well have limited or no control over such premises.[2]

6.32 In *Wilson v Tyneside*,[3] Pearce LJ said this:

'Now it is true that in *Wilsons & Clyde Coal Co Ltd v English*, Lord Wright divided up the duty of a master into three main headings, for convenience of definition or argument; but all three are ultimately only manifestations of the same duty of the master to take reasonable care so to carry out his operations as not to subject those employed by him to unnecessary risk. Whether the servant is working on the premises of the master or those of a stranger, that duty is still, as it seems to me, the same; but as a matter of common sense its performance and discharge will probably be vastly different in the two cases. The master's own premises are under his control: if they are dangerously in need of repair he can and must rectify the fault at once if he is to escape the censure of negligence. But if a master sends his plumber to mend a leak in a respectable private house, no one could hold him negligent for not visiting the house himself to see if the carpet in the hall creates a trap. Between these extremes are countless possible examples in which the court may have to decide the question of fact: Did the master take reasonable care so to carry out his operations as not to subject those employed by him to unnecessary risk?'

6.33 This is of some importance to local authorities whose employees have often to carry out their duties in and around the premises of others. It must be said, however,

---

1   [1987] AC 906 at 919.
2   *Wilson v Tyneside Window Cleaning Co* [1958] 2 QB 110, *Cook v Square D Limited* [1992] ICR 262.
3   [1958] 2 QB 110 at 121–122.

that the dividing line between the *McDermid* type of case and *Wilson v Tyneside* type of case is not always easy to discern.

6.34 One general principle which must be kept in mind arises from the decision in *Withers v Perry Chain Co Ltd.*[1] The plaintiff suffered from dermatitis, but returned to work even though it was known both to the plaintiff and to her employer that continuation of her work would lead to a small risk of exacerbation of the condition. When the condition did indeed deteriorate, the plaintiff brought a claim. The Court of Appeal allowed the appeal by the employer on the basis that it would be an unwarranted restriction on individual freedom if an employer were effectively required to dismiss an employee in order to obviate a slight risk of injury.

6.35 That principle was reconsidered in *Coxall v Goodyear GB Limited.*[2] The Court of Appeal stated that the principle in *Withers* survived, but its application depended on the facts of the particular case. In particular where the risk was of serious harm, an employer might not be entitled to allow an employee to continue.

THE EUROPEAN DIMENSION

6.36 For these purposes, the impact of Europe on health and safety legislation in this country lies principally in the group of Directives produced in 1989 and 1990 with a view to implementation within the domestic law of each Member State. These were the Framework Directive 89/391 and the six consequent Directives:

(1) the Workplace (the First) Directive 89/654;
(2) the Work Equipment (the Second) Directive 89/655;
(3) the Personal Protective Equipment (the Third) Directive 89/656;
(4) the Manual Handling of Heavy Loads (the Fourth) Directive 90/269;
(5) the Display Screen Equipment (the Fifth) Directive 90/270; and
(6) the Carcinogens (the Sixth) Directive 90/394.

6.37 These Directives were implemented (or largely implemented) in the UK by a number of different regulations, mostly passed to take effect from 1 January 1993. Those regulations have been subject to amendment or replacement in the years since then. The current regulations which can be derived, at least in part, from the Directives are: the Management of Health and Safety at Work Regulations 1999;[3] the Provision and Use of Work Equipment Regulations 1998;[4] the Workplace (Health, Safety and Welfare) Regulations 1992;[5] the Personal Protective Equipment at Work Regulations 1992;[6] the Manual Handling Operations Regulations 1992;[7] the Health and Safety (Display Screen Equipment) Regulations 1992;[8] the Control of Substances Hazardous to Health Regulations 2002;[9] and the Control of Asbestos at Work Regulations

---

1   [1961] 1 WLR 1314.
2   [2002] EWCA Civ 1010, [2003] 1 WLR 536.
3   SI 1999/3242.
4   SI 1998/2307.
5   SI 1992/3004.
6   SI 1992/2966.
7   SI 1992/2793.
8   SI 1992/2792.
9   SI 2002/2677.

2002.[1] A number of these regulations are supplemented by approved codes of practice.

6.38   In the field of construction work, there have also been regulations to implement Council Directive 92/57/EEC. They are the Construction (Design and Management) Regulations 1994[2] and the Construction (Health, Safety and Welfare) Regulations 1996.[3] The former came into force on 31 March 1995, the latter on 2 September 1996.

6.39   The relevant Directives can be used as a guide to the interpretation of the Regulations which purport to implement them.

6.40   Where the relevant Regulations have succeeded in implementing the provisions of the corresponding Directive there is no requirement to look beyond the Regulations. If a Regulation fails properly to implement a Directive,[4] however, a claimant may have recourse to the Directive itself in a claim against a local authority. A local authority, along with other government undertakings or bodies charged by the State with some of its functions, are considered for the purposes of European Community law as emanations of the State (see *Fratelli Constanzo v Commune di Milano*[5] and *Marshall v Southampton and South West Area Health Authority*)[6] and Directives may be directly enforced against emanations of the State where the Regulations fail to implement it.

6.41   There are various ways in which the Regulations set out above are said to fail to implement the corresponding Directives. Perhaps the most common is the regular limitation in the Regulations of the employer's duty by the words 'so far as reasonably practicable' or equivalent, when no such words of limitation appear in the Directives. It is sometimes said that the words constitute a derogation from the Directive and that the duties in the Directive should be treated as absolute. The position is not, however, straightforward.

6.42   'Reasonably practicable' is a phrase which has appeared in domestic health and safety legislation for many decades. Its meaning was considered by the Court of Appeal in *Edwards v National Coal Board*,[7] where Asquith LJ said:[8]

> ' "Reasonably practicable" is a narrower term than "physically possible" and seems to me to imply that a computation must be made by the owner, in which the quantum of risk is placed on one scale and the sacrifice involved in the measures necessary for averting the risk (whether in money, time or trouble) is placed in the other; and that if it be shown that there is a gross disproportion between them – the risk being insignificant in relation to the sacrifice – the Defendants discharge the onus on them.'

---

1   SI 2002/2675.
2   SI 1994/3140.
3   SI 1996/1592.
4   A detailed analysis of these is provided in Redgrave *Health and Safety* 3rd edn (Butterworths, 1998).
5   [1990] 3 CMLR 239.
6   [1986] ICR 335.
7   [1949] 1 KB 704.
8   Ibid at 712.

6.43   Whilst the duty is limited by the words 'reasonably practicable', the burden on an employer to prove that everything reasonably practicable has been done is a heavy one.[1] The balance is tilted in favour of the employee.

6.44   The English Courts have not yet definitely answered the question whether the words 'so far as reasonably practical' are consistent with the obligations required by the Directive. In any event, there cannot be any simple answers since each case will turn on the particular wording of the Directive and Regulations in question. So far, however, claims based on an alleged failure to implement the Directive have not succeeded:

(1)   In the Scottish case of *McTighe v East and Midlothian NHS Trust*,[2] the Outer House of the Court of Session rejected the argument that reg 5 of the Provision and Use of Work Equipment Regulations 1992 did not fully comply with the relevant Directive since it required suitability to be judged by reference to what was reasonably foreseeable. That was rejected and the judge held that the Directive did not require the imposition of an absolute guarantee of protection.

(2)   In *Sussex Ambulance NHS Trust v King*,[3] the Court of Appeal held that there was no discrepancy between the relevant parts of the Manual Handling Operations Regulations 1992 and the Directive which they sought to implement.

(3)   In *Stark v Post Office*[4] the Court of Appeal accepted that the Directive under which the Provision and Use of Work Equipment Regulations 1992 were made did not require the English Regulations to impose an absolute obligation in respect of the maintenance of work equipment but held that in that respect Parliament had gone beyond the requirements of the Directive (as it was indeed entitled to do).

6.45   There are further general factors which might possibly suggest that some limitation on the employers' responsibilities under the Directives is acceptable:

(1)   The framework Directive states that liability may be excluded where the injury is due to 'exceptional events, the consequences of which could not have been avoided despite the exercise for due care'. Accidents occurring despite an employer doing all that was reasonably practicable to prevent them will often be 'exceptional'. Further, the concept of 'reasonably practicable' does not seem on the face of it to impose a lower obligation than 'all due care'.

(2)   Most health and safety Directives are made under what is now Article 137 of the EC Treaty. Article 137 authorises measures encouraging improvements for the health and safety of workers and aiming for the harmonisation of conditions in the Member States while maintaining improvements made. It also includes the following:

'. . . such Directives [ie health and safety Directives] shall avoid imposing administrative, financial and legal constraints in a way which would hold back the creation and development of small and medium-sized undertakings.'

---

1   The burden is on the employer: *Nimmo v Alexander Cowan* [1968] AC 107.
2   [1998] Rep LR 21.
3   [2002] EWCA Civ 953.
4   [2000] ICR 1013.

A Directive made under a specific provision of the EC Treaty will be ultra vires unless it conforms to the purpose and scope of the enabling power, and so a Directive will be interpreted wherever possible as conforming. Imposing widespread absolute obligations to protect health and safety, which might be very expensive or indeed impossible to implement, could be a constraint of the kind disallowed by Article 137.

(3) Community obligations are subject to a principle of proportionality. The means employed to achieve a given aim must be no more than those necessary for the achievement of the aim. This is a general principle of European law, developed by the European Court of Justice but now to be found in Article 3b of the EC Treaty. It might be argued that measures not reasonably practicable are not proportionate to the ends to be achieved, and that it would be wrong to interpret the Directives as requiring such measures.

6.46 There is a further European dimension to the law of employers' liability provided by the Transfer of Undertakings (Protection of Employment) Regulations 1981 (TUPE)[1] made pursuant to the Acquired Rights Directive.[2] TUPE is concerned with protecting the acquired employment rights of a worker when the ownership of the employing undertaking is transferred. It raises many difficult points which are outside the scope of this book. There are, however, two points raised by TUPE which fall squarely within the book's scope. They are of particular relevance to local authorities given the large-scale transfer of contracts of employment inherent in the contracting-out of council services.

6.47 The first point is that the right of a claimant in respect of a personal injuries claim arising out of his employment is transferred along with the business. If an employee is injured in the course of his employment with the transferor, and the business of the transferor is transferred to the transferee before legal proceedings are commenced, the employee must sue the transferee. This was decided in *Martin v Lancashire County Council*.[3] Peter Gibson LJ said:

> '... one notes the width of the language used in para. (a) of Regulation 5(2): "all the transferor's rights, powers, duties and liabilities under or in connection with" the contract of employment. The rights etc. are not limited to those under the contract but include those "in connection with" the contract. That prepositional phrase is far wider and it does not suggest that the rights etc. need be contractual. That is supported by para. (b) of Regulation 5(2). It is not just what is done by the transferor in respect of the contract that is deemed to have been done by the transferee but also anything done by the transferor in respect of the employee. That does not suggest that it is limited to what will result in contractual rights and liabilities.'

The words 'in connection with the contract of employment' were held sufficiently broad to encompass the liability of an employer in negligence or breach of statutory duty as well as in contract.

6.48 The second point is that the benefit of the employer's liability insurance policy held by the transferor passes to the transferee on transfer.[4] This was held to be

---

1   SI 1981/1794.
2   Council Directive 77/187/EEC.
3   [2000] 3 All ER 544.
4   *Martin v Lancashire County Council* [2000] 3 All ER 544.

consistent with the purpose of the Directive and of TUPE, namely to safeguard the rights of the employee on transfer. Not to hold that the rights under the policy passed on transfer could significantly jeopardise the position of the employee. If the contract of employment had remained with the transferor, the employee would have had the certainty of enforcing any judgment which he obtained against the employer because the employer was obliged by law to have insurance against such liability.[1] Even if the employer therefore became insolvent, the employee could enforce judgment directly against the insurer.[2] On transfer, the right to sue the transferor is lost. At that stage, the only right of action which the employee has in respect of his personal injuries claim is against the transferee. It is most unlikely, however, that the transferee would have insurance covering liability arising out of events before the date of transfer. Unless the rights under the transferor's employer's liability policy passed to the transferee, therefore, the employee would be deprived of the near certainty of being able to enforce his judgment which is provided by compulsory employers' liability insurance. The Court of Appeal held that such an outcome should be avoided, if possible, consistently with the words of TUPE and held that the words of TUPE when construed purposively were sufficiently wide to encompass such a transfer of rights under the policy of insurance.

DUTIES OWED

Place of work

6.49 At common law, the place of work encompasses the whole range of workplaces, including both those workplaces of which the employer is the occupier and those of which it is not. With regard to the latter the employer may need to carry out an inspection of the site of the work so as to satisfy itself that it is safe, provide the employee with any necessary warnings and ensure that any dangers are ameliorated by any necessary protective clothing or by any equipment. The limits of the duty have been dealt with above.

6.50 The requirement for a safe place of work extends to the means of access to the place of work. This is illustrated by those cases where the employee trips or slips on a dangerous substance in a hallway or falls from a ladder or a scaffold premises on the way to his place of work.

6.51 The duty is not absolute. It is a duty to take reasonable care to ensure that the place of work is safe. In *Houghton v Hackney Borough Council*,[3] for example, the claimant rent collector's place of work was seen as reasonably safe from assault by third parties where his office was within calling distance of a porter's post. Furthermore, the employer will not be liable where the danger in question is in reality a part of the employment and is as such incapable of remedy. In *Dixon v London Fire*

1　Employers' Liability (Compulsory Insurance) Act 1969. In fact, local authorities are exempted from this Act. That particular exemption, however, does not change the logic of the Court of Appeal's reasoning.

2　Pursuant to the Third Parties (Rights Against Insurers) Act 1930.

3　[1961] CLY 5929.

and Civil Defence Authority,[1] the plaintiff was injured slipping on water which had leaked onto the floor of a fire station from a fire appliance.

6.52   In *Andrews v Initial Cleaning Services Limited,*[2] a cleaner used a storeroom in the premises of the third party. Both her employer and the third party had sufficient control over the room to be occupiers for the purposes of the Occupiers' Liability Act 1957. Both employer and third party were liable to the claimant. The employer, however, bore 75 per cent of the responsibility on account of the special obligations inherent in the relationship of employment.

6.53   The protection in relation to the place of work afforded to employees by the duty imposed on the employer at common law (a duty to take reasonable care) has been greatly strengthened by the large number of statutory duties relating to the workplace where the duties are frequently absolute (it is of course common for both causes of action to be pleaded). Early examples were the duties imposed by the Factories Act 1961 (applicable to the local authority in at least some of its activities, given the wide definition of the term 'factory'[3]) and more obviously the Offices, Shops and Railway Premises Act 1963.

6.54   Both of these statutes have been largely repealed by (amongst others) the cluster of Regulations passed in 1992 to implement the European Directives of 1989 and 1990.[4]

6.55   With some exclusions[5] the Workplace (Health, Safety and Welfare) Regulations 1992 apply to every workplace and every employer. They lay down obligations in relation to maintenance of the workplace and its equipment, ventilation, temperature, lighting, cleanliness and waste materials, workstations and seating, and floors and traffic routes. For the most part these duties are absolute (the requirement to maintain the workplace and its equipment in an efficient state, efficient working order and in good repair, for example, and to provide ventilation and lighting), although some involve limited elements of reasonable practicability (in particular the duty to take effective measures to prevent persons falling a distance likely to cause personal injury or being struck by a falling object).

6.56   The Workplace (Health, Safety and Welfare) Regulations 1992 have been considered by the Court of Appeal. In *Furness v Midland Bank plc,*[6] the claimant was employed in a bank. She slipped on a very small amount of water on the stairs. There was no known previous history of water being there and no one was able to say how it got there on that particular occasion. Under reg 12(3) the employer was obliged so far

---

1   (1993) 157 LG Rev 1001, CA.
2   [2000] ICR 166.
3   For example, the cleaning or washing or the break up or demolition of any article and the storage of gas in gasholders of not less than 140 cubic metres: see s 175(1), (2) and (9).
4   In the case of the Factories Act 1961, largely by the Workplace (Health, Safety and Welfare) Regulations 1992, with effect from 1 January 1993, other than the case of a workplace which is not a new workplace started after 31 December 1992, when the repeal is effective from 1 January 1996, but also by the Provision and Use of Work Equipment Regulations 1992 as from 1 January 1997; in the case of the Offices, Shops and Railway Premises Act 1963, by the Management of Health and Safety at Work Regulations 1992 and the Workplace (Health, Safety and Welfare) Regulations 1992.
5   See SI 1992/3004, reg 3.
6   (Unreported) 10 November 2000, CA.

as reasonably practicable to keep the floor free from substances 'which might cause a person to slip'. The trial judge held that the only way to ensure that the stairs remained free from such substances would be to post someone on guard and that such an action would be wholly disproportionate to the very small risk and therefore not within the bounds of reasonable practicability. The Court of Appeal upheld the trial judge adding that an instruction to staff to keep an eye out for spillages would have been futile, particularly given the lack of any history of such spillages.

6.57　In *Robinson v Midland Bank plc*,[1] on the other hand, the claimant fell over a moveable stool used for gaining access to high shelves. She had passed by the site of the accident shortly before. She returned carrying files which obstructed her view. The stool had in the meantime been moved by another employee. The claimant did not see it and fell over it. Regulation 12(3) was again in issue. The judge dismissed the claim, holding that such a stool had by its very function to be moved from place to place and that the claimant should have kept a lookout. The Court of Appeal, however, allowed the claimant's appeal (and made no reduction for contributory negligence), holding that it was well within the bounds of reasonable practicability for the stool to be kept out of the path of the claimant or at least for a warning to be given if it had to be left in a position where it was a potential hazard.

6.58　The Health and Safety (Display Screen Equipment) Regulations 1992 provide protection to the employed and self-employed ('operators' and 'users') who habitually use display screen equipment as part of their normal work. The central duty imposed upon the employer is to perform an analysis of workstations used for the purposes of his undertaking for the purpose of assessing the health and safety risks of that use with a view to reducing those risks to the lowest extent reasonably practicable.[2] The Schedule to the Regulations provides detailed requirements to be satisfied in relation to each workstation, for example a stable image on the screen, the avoidance of reflective glare, a tiltable keyboard and an adjustable chair (to identify but a few).

6.59　So far as the local authority's involvement in building operations or works of engineering construction is concerned it will be subject to the Construction (Health, Safety and Welfare) Regulations 1996. These Regulations impose a large number of duties in respect of dangers likely to arise in the construction workplace and state (at reg 5) that every place of work 'shall, so far as reasonably practicable, be made and kept safe'. The Regulations impose duties on an employer but also on any person 'who controls the way in which any construction work is carried out'.[3] The Court in *McCook v Lobo*[4] held that whether a person has sufficient control is a question of fact in every case. Theoretical control (eg a contractual power to stop work) or general control over the site is not enough. To trigger a duty under the Regulations, there must be some degree of practical control over the manner of working.

6.60　The requirement for a risk assessment is also an important obligation under the Control of Substances Hazardous to Health Regulations 2002.[5] The central obligation is contained in reg 7(1):

1　(Unreported) 27 October 2000, CA.
2　See reg 2.
3　See reg 4(2).
4　[2002] EWCA Civ 1760, [2003] ICR 89.
5　See reg 6.

'Every employer shall ensure that the exposure of his employees to substances hazardous to health is either prevented or, where this is not reasonably practicable, adequately controlled.'

In *Dugmore v Swansea NHS Trust*,[1] the Court of Appeal held that both the primary duty of preventing exposure and the secondary duty of adequate control (where prevention is not reasonably practicable) were effectively absolute. Hale LJ said:

'"Adequately" is defined in regulation 7 without any reference to reasonableness or the foreseeability of risk: it is a purely practical matter depending upon the nature of the substance and the nature and degree of the exposure and nothing else.'[2]

6.61 Similar stringent requirements are imposed on employers by the Control of Asbestos at Work Regulations 2002.

6.62 Treatment of the problems of causation which arise in employers' liability claims is outside the scope of this chapter. However, this may be a convenient place to refer to the basic rules of causation, and one important recent exception in the case of asbestos exposure. For an action to succeed, the negligence or breach of statutory duty proved must be causative of the injury suffered. It need not be the only cause, or even a major one. It is enough that it made a material contribution to the injury in the sense of a more than minimal contribution.[3] Usually, it is a minimum requirement for the proof of causation that but for the breach the injury would not have happened. The 'but for' test is in general a necessary but not a sufficient condition for establishing liability. Causes which pass the 'but for' test may be viewed by the courts as being too far removed from the injury to be regarded as a legally effective cause. They may be too far removed in time or space to be regarded as effective, or there may be too many intervening events.

6.63 In the case of *Fairchild v Glenhaven Funeral Services Ltd*[4] the House of Lords formulated an exception to the above principles necessary to achieve justice in particular circumstances. Where an employee has worked for more than one employer, and has been negligently exposed to asbestos by each employer, it may not be possible (on the current state of scientific knowledge) to prove that the asbestos-related illness which subsequently arises was caused by the employee's

---

1 [2002] EWCA Civ 1689, [2003] ICR 574. The Court of Appeal was considering earlier versions of the Regulations, but with no material difference in the words.

2 See para [25] of judgment. Note that for the Regulations certain higher risk substances are identified and given what is called a maximum exposure limit, and certain lower risk substances are identified and given what is called an occupational exposure standard. These are substances which may be inhaled. For substances given a maximum exposure limit, control will be regarded as adequate only 'if the level of exposure is reduced so far as is reasonably practicable and in any case below the maximum exposure limit': reg 7(7). For substances given an occupational exposure standard, 'control of exposure shall . . . only be treated as being adequate if – (a) that occupational exposure standard is not exceeded; or (b) where that occupational exposure standard is exceeded, the employer identifies the reasons for the standard being exceeded and takes appropriate action to remedy the situation as soon as reasonably practicable': reg 7(8). The decision in *Dugmore* might therefore lead to the curious result that the law gives a higher degree of protection in relation to substances not classified as hazardous in one of the two classes above than in relation to substances which are. A further oddity is that both reg 7(7) and 7(8) are stated to be 'without prejudice to the generality of paragraph (1)' of reg 7. If that is so, and *Dugmore* correctly states the duty, then the system of classification may be largely redundant.

3 *Bonnington Castings v Wardlaw* [1956] AC 613.

4 [2002] UKHL 22, [2003] 1 AC 32.

work for one employer rather than another. In those circumstances, it is enough for a claimant to prove that the exposure in any one employment materially increased the risk of the disease. Note that the disease under consideration was mesothelioma, which is triggered by the presence of one or more of the many fibres which will be present in the lungs of a worker with long-term asbestos exposure. Once it occurs, the disease is not made worse by the presence of the other fibres in the lungs. Different considerations may apply in the case of asbestosis. Greater exposure to asbestos will lead to worse asbestosis. It is therefore possible to apportion between various employments, and an employer may seek a reduction in damages to reflect the fact that the symptoms suffered were in part caused by the claimant's work for another employer.[1]

System of work

6.64   At common law the duty to provide a safe system of work will apply to all work situations and the permutations are limitless: training, instruction on the requirements of a particular task, the method adopted, the provision of sufficient numbers of workmen for the task, the availability of assistance and proper planning, supervision or co-ordination may all be involved.

6.65   The following are illustrations of how the duty may operate:

(1)   The duty to warn the employee of any specific risk arising out of the employment itself was discussed in *Colclough v Staffordshire County Council*[2] where a social worker employed in the defendant's elderly care team, usually involved in assessing patients' needs, was called out to an elderly man's home and found him in a very distressed state halfway out of his bed. Out of concern that he might hurt himself the plaintiff and a neighbour attempted to lift him back into bed. He weighed 15 stone and the plaintiff sustained a lumbar strain. The defendant denied liability on the basis that it was not part of the plaintiff's duties to undertake any lifting tasks and averred that she ought to have summoned help from the emergency services.

It was held that it was foreseeable that the plaintiff would be confronted with emergency situations such as this one and that, although on these facts there was no duty to provide a training course, the defendant was under a duty to warn her of the dangers of lifting. The plaintiff succeeded without any deduction from damages for contributory negligence.

Of great relevance to the local authority, which employs a large number of clerical staff, this duty applies equally in employments of a repetitive nature carrying a risk of work-related upper limb disorder. In *Peppall v Thorn Consumers Electronics Ltd*,[3] it was held that there is a duty on an employer to warn of such a risk before the employment begins so that the employee can either decide not to do the work at all or will know that any early manifestation of the problem in question can be reported to the employer and preventative steps can be taken. The warning must therefore include an explanation as to why it must be reported.

---

1   See *Holtby v Brigham & Cowan (Hull) Ltd* [2000] ICR 1086.
2   [1994] CLY 2283.
3   Woolf J (unreported) 20 December 1985.

(2) The duty to provide proper training or instruction. In *Barcock v Brighton Corporation*[1] the defendant employer simply provided the plaintiff with a copy of the regulations which laid down the procedure to be followed when tests were to be carried out on a switchboard so as to render the tests safe. It was held that the duty to provide a safe system of work was not satisfied by simply requiring the employee to read and adhere to the instructions.

(3) The duty to ensure that the prescribed system is complied with. In *Pape v Cumbria County Council*,[2] for example, it was held that a reasonable employer, knowing that sustained exposure to cleaning agents meant a risk of dermatitis or eczema and appreciating that the risk was not so well known to employees, would take steps to ensure that the gloves were supplied with a warning, including explaining to the employee the danger involved and the reasons for the need to wear the gloves.

(4) The duty to provide reasonable protection against violence from third parties. In *Houghton v Hackney Borough Council*,[3] the defendant's rent collector was assaulted in his office. In this case it was held sufficient to have a porter within calling distance. This principle applies to schools. In *Marvier v Dorset County Council*[4] the plaintiff was a supervisory assistant at a local authority secondary school who was assaulted in the playground during a lunch break by a pupil who had a history of disruptive and violent behaviour. She had challenged him about not wearing school uniform in order to enforce an instruction from a senior member of staff that any pupil not wearing school uniform was to be asked to leave. The judge found that the headmaster ought to have warned the plaintiff that the pupil was violent and should not be approached and instructed her that, rather than challenging him herself, she ought to have sought assistance from other members of staff.

6.66 The standard of care will need to be examined in each factual situation. The employer, for example, must have regard to any specific characteristics of the individual employee, and so what is required to discharge the duty to one employee may not suffice to discharge it in relation to another. An illustration of this principle is provided by *Paris v Stepney Borough Council*[5] which has been discussed in some detail above.[6]

6.67 As with the place of work, the employer's common law duty to provide a safe system of work is not absolute. It may, for example, be satisfied without the provision of equipment. In *Brodie v Kent County Council*,[7] carers working at an old people's home and who suffered from back problems were told to stay away from work until their doctor passed them fit to return. The plaintiff did not consult her doctor about her return and hurt her back during the course of lifting an elderly resident from the floor. The Court of Appeal held that the system was safe, and that there was no duty to secure the use of lifting equipment. Each case will of course depend upon its own

---

1   [1949] 1 KB 339.
2   [1992] ICR 132.
3   See para **6.51**.
4   [1997] CLY 3849.
5   [1951] AC 367.
6   See paras **6.25–6.27**.
7   (Unreported) 14 February 1986, CA.

facts, but a similar analysis will be required in relation to accidents at work injuring firemen, social workers and all the other members of the local authority workforce.

6.68   So far as statutory duties are concerned, there is much overlap here with the requirements relating to a safe place of work – see, for example, the need for risk assessments under the Control of Substances Hazardous to Health (Amendment) Regulations 1988 and the Control of Asbestos at Work (Amendment) Regulations 1992 – as there is with the requirement for safe equipment (as to which see paras **6.74–6.85**).

6.69   Of particular significance here, however, are the Manual Handling Operations Regulations 1992, implemented in relation to all employments with effect from 1 January 1993 (there is no extension here for workplaces in existence on 31 December 1992).

6.70   Manual handling operations are defined as any transporting or supporting of a load, including lifting the load, putting it down, pushing, pulling, carrying or moving it by hand or bodily force. A load includes a person or an animal.[1] The Regulations will therefore apply across the whole range of local authority activities and services – clerical (manhandling heavy files), caring (lifting the elderly and the sick), emergency (carrying equipment and transporting the injured) and manual (collection of rubbish and laying paving stones).

6.71   Essentially every employer is required, so far as reasonably practicable, to avoid the need for its employees to undertake any manual handling operations at work. When considering whether or not an activity carries with it a risk of injury, the courts have said that the risk must be 'real'[2] (in the sense of being more than de minimis), or 'no more than a foreseeable possibility; it need not be a probability'.[3] Although the Regulations do not say that the risk must be foreseeable, the question must be judged from the point of view of the employer before the accident rather than with the benefit of hindsight. It seems likely and reasonable that the courts will approach the question in a similar way to the manner in which they have approached the question of whether or not a danger is foreseeable, that is to say whether the risk was 'a mere possibility which would never have occurred to the mind of a reasonable man'.[4] Where it is not reasonably practicable to avoid the need for such operations, the employer must make an assessment of all those operations, take appropriate steps to reduce the risk of injury and take appropriate steps to provide employees undertaking manual handling operations with at least general indications as to the weight of the load to be handled and the heaviest side of any load whose centre of gravity is not central.

6.72   The assessment must be carried out with regard to a number of factors listed and questions asked in Sch 1 to the Regulations. The factors are the tasks, the loads, the working environment and the capacity of the individual, together with any other factors, and a number of questions should be asked in relation to each. The assessment is a discoverable document.

---

1   See reg 2.
2   *Hawkes v London Borough of Southwark* (unreported) 20 February 1998, CA.
3   *Cullen v North Lanarkshire Council* 1998 SC 451 at 455.
4   *Fardon v Harcourt-Rivington* (1932) 146 LP 391 at 392, per Lord Dunedin.

6.73   The courts have considered when it will and will not be reasonably practicable to avoid the need for an employee to engage in manual handling which involves a risk of injury. In *Hawkes v London Borough of Southwark*,[1] the claimant was injured whilst carrying a door up some stairs. It would in theory have been possible to use some mechanical lifting device but the reality was that such a device was not reasonably practicable. The Court of Appeal, however, held that it would have been reasonably practicable to engage a second worker to assist the claimant in carrying the door.

Equipment

6.74   The term 'equipment' may be given a wider meaning than might at first be anticipated. In *Knowles v Liverpool County Council*[2] a defective flagstone which broke and which injured a council employee who was employed to lay flagstones was held to be equipment provided to him by his employer (for the purposes of the Employers' Liability (Defective Equipment) Act 1969, as to which see below). Both the Court of Appeal and the House of Lords rejected the defendant council's argument that a distinction had to be drawn between plant, on the one hand, and materials produced by plant, on the other, and that a flagstone fell into the latter category.

6.75   Lord Jauncey of Tullichettle, with whom all of their Lordships agreed, said:[3]

' ... I have no hesitation in concluding that the word "equipment" in section 1(1)(a) is habile to cover the flagstone in this appeal. In the first place, the requirement of the subsection is that the equipment is provided "for the purposes of the employer's business" and not merely for the use of the employee. Thus a piece of defective equipment which causes injury to a workman would fall within the ambit of the subsection even although the workman was neither required to use nor had in fact used it. Whatever the meaning of "equipment" this would go further than the circumstances in *Davie's* case [1959] AC 604 where the defective tool had been provided to the workman for the purposes of his job. In this case, the flagstone had undoubtedly been provided by the appellants for the purposes of their business of repairing and relaying the pavement. In the second place, there can be no logical reason why Parliament having recognised the difficulties facing workmen ... should have removed those difficulties in part rather than in whole. Indeed, partial removal, as contended for by the appellants, could produce bizarre results. To give one example which I put in argument to counsel, a pump manufacturer buys in tools required for assembling pumps as well as some components including the bolts for holding together the two parts of the housing. Workman A is tightening a bolt which shears and injures his eye. Workman B is tightening a similar bolt but his spanner snaps causing him similar injury. If the appellants are right, workman B could proceed under section 1(1) of the Act but workman A would have no remedy thereunder. My Lords, I cannot believe that Parliament intended the Act to produce results such as these. In my view, the only reasonable conclusion is that Parliament intended the Act to provide a remedy in the situations where an employer has provided for the purposes of his business an article which was defective and caused injury to a workman but where he was for the reasons set out in *Davie* not in breach of a common law duty of care owed to that workman.'

6.76   At common law the duty is to take reasonable care to select the right equipment for the task and to provide and maintain that equipment. In order to discharge the duty

1   (Unreported) 20 February 1998, CA.
2   [1993] 1 WLR 1428.
3   Ibid at 1433.

the employer will probably have to carry out regular inspections and carry out repairs and maintenance as and when required.

6.77   A variety of statutory duties (some of which have already been referred to) supplement the employer's obligation to provide a safe system of work. The most important are those implementing the European Directives discussed above.[1]

6.78   The Manual Handling Operations Regulations 1992 require an employer to avoid the need for employees to undertake manual handling tasks at work involving a risk of injury. Where it is not reasonably practicable to avoid such manual handling, the duty is to assess the risks and reduce them to the lowest level reasonably practicable.[2] In *Koonjul v Thameslink Healthcare Services*,[3] the Court of Appeal accepted that the risk of injury against which the employer had to guard need only be a modest one, no more than a foreseeable possibility. In *Palmer v Marks & Spencer*,[4] the Court of Appeal indicated that in considering whether there was a risk, the court should look at the position from the point of view of the employer considering it before the accident (so without benefit of hindsight). A very slight possibility of a serious injury might be enough to constitute a risk which should be taken into account, whereas a somewhat larger possibility of a more trivial injury might be acceptable. Other factors relevant would include the classes of people who might be expected to carry out the activity or use the place in question.

6.79   Training is one method of reducing the risk to the lowest level reasonably practicable. If training has not been provided, it is easy enough to find a breach, but difficult to know whether that breach has caused the accident. In *Warner v Huntingdonshire District Council*,[5] the failure to train a dustman was not causative of the injury since it had not been shown that the training would have made any practical difference to the way he went about his work. In *O'Neill v DSG Retail*,[6] the Court of Appeal approached the matter differently. A worker carrying a microwave was called to by someone. Instinctively, he turned around and injured his back. He had not been trained not to turn around. The judge rejected the claim, holding that it could not be said that training would have removed the instinct to turn in answer to a call. The Court of Appeal found this to be a conclusion which was not open to the judge, and allowed the appeal. The training would, in its view, have prevented the claimant turning around.

6.80   The Provision and Use of Work Equipment Regulations 1998 are the chief Regulations relating to the supply of suitable and properly maintained work equipment. They repealed and replaced a large number of older regulations relating to specific pieces of equipment. The 1992 version of these Regulations was considered by the Court of Appeal in *Stark v Post Office*.[7] Regulation 6(1) was in issue. It states: 'every employer shall ensure that work equipment is maintained in an efficient state,

---

1   See paras **6.36–6.45**.
2   See reg 4.
3   [2000] PIQR 123.
4   [2001] EWCA Civ 1528. The word 'risk' was in this case used in reference to the Workplace (Health, Safety and Welfare) Regulations 1992, but the considerations are equally valid to the Manual Handling Operations Regulations 1992.
5   [2002] EWCA Civ 791.
6   [2002] EWCA Civ 1139, [2003] ICR 223.
7   [2000] ICR 1013.

in efficient working order and in good repair'.[1] The claimant was injured when the bicycle which he had been given by his employer for purposes of his work stopped suddenly because part of the front brake broke in two and lodged in the front wheel. The accident was not foreseeable in the sense that an inspection of the bicycle immediately before the accident would not have revealed the defect. The Court of Appeal held that there was nonetheless liability under reg 6(1) since it imposed on the employer an absolute obligation to provide work equipment which was in good working order. The situation is, it seems, to be judged immediately before the accident rather than at the time the work equipment was first supplied. The Court of Appeal accepted that the Directive pursuant to which the Regulations were made did not require any such absolute obligation. It held, however, that the Directive laid down minimum standards and that Parliament was entitled to go beyond those.

6.81 Personal safety equipment is regulated by the Personal Protective Equipment at Work Regulations 1992, which require an employer to 'ensure that suitable personal protective equipment is provided' to employees who may be exposed to risks, except where the risk is adequately controlled by other means.[2] The protective equipment supplied must be properly maintained.[3] The scope of the duty to maintain was considered by the House of Lords in *Fytche v Wincanton Logistics*.[4] A driver was given steel-capped safety boots to protect against injury from heavy objects. One boot developed a small hole, which led to frostbite. By a majority, the House held that there was no breach of the duty to maintain equipment in good repair, because the defect was irrelevant to the functioning of the boots for the safety purposes for which they were supplied.

6.82 Similarly, the statutory regulation of the local authority's employer's activities in the building/construction industry extends to both the workplace and its equipment. In addition to the provisions relating to the workplace itself (scaffolds and ladders), the Construction (Health and Welfare) Regulations 1966[5] include reference to securing the safety of the workplace by means of safety nets and belts.[6] The Construction (General Provisions) Regulations 1961[7] impose duties with respect to the fencing of machinery. The Construction (Lifting Operations) Regulations 1961[8] provide a detailed code for the safety (including construction, maintenance, inspection and stability) of all lifting appliances and related structures. The Construction (Health, Safety and Welfare) Regulations 1996[9] specifically provide (by reg 27) that 'all plant and equipment used for the purpose of carrying out construction work shall, so far as reasonably practicable, be safe and without risks to health and shall be of good construction, of suitable and sound materials and of sufficient strength and suitability for the purpose for which it is used or provided'.

1 The equivalent provision is found at reg 5(1) of the 1998 Regulations.
2 See reg 4.
3 See reg 7.
4 [2004] UKHL 31, [2004] ICR 975.
5 SI 1966/95.
6 See reg 38.
7 SI 1961/1580.
8 SI 1961/1881.
9 SI 1996/1592.

6.83   Finally, additional protection in relation to defects in equipment is afforded to the employee by the Employers' Liability (Defective Equipment) Act 1969 (reference to which has been made above in relation to the meaning of the word 'equipment'), where the business in relation to which the equipment is provided expressly includes the activities carried on by public bodies.[1] This Act was passed as a result of the decision of the House of Lords in *Davie v New Merton Board Mills Ltd*,[2] where a workman was injured when using a defective tool supplied to him by his employer. The tool had been manufactured negligently by reputable manufacturers and no reasonable inspection by the employers would have revealed the defect. The action failed on the basis that the employer had discharged its duty to provide safe equipment to the employee by purchasing the tool from a reputable manufacturer.

6.84   In an action arising out of a defect in equipment (which expressly includes plant and machinery, vehicle, aircraft and clothing)[3] provided to the employer for use by the employee, the employer is not now able to say that the defect was caused by the negligence of another (the manufacturer, for example, or the supplier). Section 1 of the Act reads:

> '(1) Where after the commencement of this Act:
> (a) an employee suffers personal injury in the course of his employment in consequence of a defect in equipment provided by his employer for the purposes of the employer's business; and
> (b) the defect is attributable wholly or partly to the fault of a third party (whether identified or not),
> the injury shall be deemed to be also attributable to negligence on the part of the employer ... .'

6.85   In circumstances in which the Provision and Use of Work Equipment Regulations 1998 apply, as will appear from the above, the 1969 Act is unlikely to have relevance. Even without the Act, an employer could not defeat a claim under those Regulations by alleging that the work equipment had been produced by a third party. Further, as has been seen, the obligation to provide efficient work equipment under the Regulations is an absolute one.

Competent fellow employees

6.86   This duty overlaps with the duties to provide proper supervision and instruction which arise as part of a safe system of work. In its pure form its importance has to some extent declined (since the abolition of the doctrine of common employment). It does, however, retain significance in limited areas, the following of which may be important to the local authority employer:

(1)   the employer may be liable for injury to one employee arising out of bullying of that employee by another or others;[4]
(2)   similarly, the employer may be liable for injury to one employee resulting from practical jokes played by another. In *Hudson v Ridge Manufacturing Co Ltd*,[5] over a long period of time one of the defendant's employees had amused himself

---

1   See s 1(3).
2   [1959] AC 604.
3   See s 1(3).
4   *Veness v Dyston, Bell & Co* [1965] CLY 2691.
5   [1957] 2 QB 348.

by tripping up his fellows. He had been reprimanded on many occasions and the foreman had warned him that one day he would injure someone, but no other steps had been taken. The employer was found liable to the plaintiff for failing to prevent this behaviour in its employee;

(3) screening – many employments are now the subject of screening procedures, either in terms of health or suitability (qualifications, perhaps, or honesty). Liability is likely to result in the event of negligent screening leading to an unsuitable appointment. The most obvious example would be an asthmatic being employed to work with noxious substances and suffering an exacerbation of his condition.

6.87 In order to discharge its duties the employer must take reasonable steps to prevent the conduct in question. This may mean formal reprimands and, if such reprimands are ignored, dismissal.[1]

6.88 Again, the duty is not absolute and the analysis must be one of fact and degree. It is important to note that in *Hudson v Ridge Manufacturing* the judge stressed that this employee was not only incompetent but actually presented a danger to his colleagues and that a long time (some years) had elapsed between the behaviour coming to the notice of the employer and the particular instance of the behaviour which caused injury. The injury was therefore foreseeable.

6.89 One area in which the competence of fellow employees is of growing significance is in the field of claims arising from stress at work.[2] The phrase 'stress claim' can be misleading. In this context, stress is what causes the injury; it is not itself the injury. A claimant who could show no more than stress would fall foul of the rule that, where the damage is psychiatric alone, a claimant must be able to prove that he has suffered from a medically recognised psychiatric illness. A claimant who could prove no more than that he had suffered stress, in the sense of distress and anxiety, would fail. On the other hand, an employee able to prove such a recognised psychiatric illness would be treated by the courts as a primary rather than a secondary victim. That is to say, it would be sufficient to prove illness caused by breach of duty, and would not be necessary to meet the further preconditions which the courts have laid down for secondary victims.[3] This is an area of particular interest to local autohrities, since many local authority employees carry out difficult and demanding jobs. In *Walker v Northumberland County Council*,[4] Colman J said:

'Where it was reasonably foreseeable to an employer that an employee might suffer a nervous breakdown because of the stress and pressures of his workload, the employer was under a duty of care, as part of the duty to provide a safe system of work, not to cause the employee psychiatric damage by reason of the volume or character of the work which the employer was required to perform.'

---

1 *Hudson v Ridge Manufacturing Co Ltd* [1957] 2 QB 348 at 351–352, per Streatfield J, referring to the need to remove the source of the danger.
2 This could equally be dealt with under the heading of system of work.
3 Ie close ties of love and affection with the victim, presence at the traumatic event or its immediate aftermath, and where the injury was caused by direct perception. See *Alcock v Chief Constable of South Yorkshire Police* [1992] 1 AC 310, *Page v Smith* [1996] AC 155, *Frost v Chief Constable of South Yorkshire Police* [1999] 2 AC 455.
4 [1995] 1 All ER 737.

6.90　*Walker* did not, as has sometimes been suggested, enunciate any new principle of law. The case did represent the first successful claim in an English court in respect of psychiatric damage arising from stress at work. The judge, however, simply applied accepted legal principles to a novel factual matrix.[1] The House of Lords has made reference to *Walker* with no suggestion that it was incorrectly decided.[2]

6.91　Nonetheless, although cases of psychiatric injury caused by stress at work are decided on the general principles of negligence, the courts have recognised that they present different problems to the more usual type of employers' liability personal injury case: how is an employer to assess whether a person is at risk of psychiatric illness, particularly while respecting the employee's privacy? Even if there is a perceived risk of psychiatric illness, how is an employer to know that it is because of work stresses? Will intervention be welcomed or regarded as impertinent?

6.92　The Court of Appeal considered a number of stress at work cases, reported together as *Sutherland v Hatton*,[3] and gave some general guidance for the courts. Given the importance to local authority employers, it is worth setting out the summary at para 43 in full:

> '(1) There are no special control mechanisms applying to claims for psychiatric (or physical) illness or injury arising from the stress of doing the work the employee is required to do. The ordinary principles of employer's liability apply.
>
> (2) The threshold question is whether this kind of harm to this particular employee was reasonably foreseeable this has two components (a) an injury to health (as distinct from occupational stress) which (b) is attributable to stress at work (as distinct from other factors).
>
> (3) Foreseeability depends upon what the employer knows (or ought reasonably to know) about the individual employee. Because of the nature of mental disorder, it is harder to foresee than physical injury, but may be easier to foresee in a known individual than in the population at large. An employer is usually entitled to assume that the employee can withstand the normal pressures of the job unless he knows of some particular problem or vulnerability.
>
> (4) The test is the same whatever the employment: there are no occupations which should be regarded as intrinsically dangerous to mental health.
>
> (5) Factors likely to be relevant in answering the threshold question include: (a) the nature and extent of the work done by the employee. Is the workload much more than is normal for the particular job? Is the work particularly intellectually or emotionally demanding for this employee? Are demands being made of this employee unreasonable when compared with the demands made of others in the same or comparable jobs? Or are there signs that others doing this job are suffering harmful levels of stress? Is there an abnormal level of sickness or absenteeism in the same job or the same department? (b) Signs from the employee of impending harm to health ... Has he a particular problem or vulnerability? Has he already suffered from illness attributable to stress at work? Have there recently been frequent or prolonged absences which are uncharacteristic of him? Is there reason to think that these are attributable to stress at work, for example because of complaints or warnings from him or others?
>
> (6) The employer is generally entitled to take what he is told by his employee at face value, unless he has good reason to think to the contrary. He does not generally have to

---

1　Similar principles had been accepted in a previous unsuccessful claim: *Petch v Commissioners of Customs & Excise* [1993] ICR 789.

2　*Frost v Chief Constable of South Yorkshire Police* [1999] 2 AC 455.

3　[2002] EWCA Civ 76, [2002] ICR 613.

make searching inquiries of the employee or seek permission to make further inquiries of his medical advisers.

(7) To trigger a duty to take steps, the indications of impending harm to health arising from stress at work must be plain enough for any reasonable employer to realise that he should do something about it.

(8) The employer is only in breach of duty if he has failed to take the steps which are reasonable in the circumstances, bearing in mind the magnitude of the risk of harm occurring, the gravity of the harm which may occur, the costs and practicability of preventing it, and the justifications for running the risk.

(9) The size and scope of the employer's operation, its resources and the demands it faces are relevant in deciding what is reasonable; these include the interests of other employees and the need to treat them fairly, for example, in any redistribution of duties.

(10) An employer can only reasonably be expected to take steps which are likely to do some good: the court is likely to need expert evidence on this.

(11) An employer who offers a confidential advice service, with referral to appropriate counselling or treatment services, is unlikely to be found in breach of duty.

(12) If the only reasonable and effective step would have been to dismiss or demote the employee, the employer will not be in breach of duty in allowing a willing employee to continue in the job.

(13) In all cases, therefore, it is necessary to identify the steps which the employer both could and should have taken before finding him in breach of his duty of care.

(14) The claimant must show that that breach of duty has caused or materially contributed to the harm suffered. It is not enough to show that occupational stress has caused the harm.

(15) Where the harm suffered has more than one cause, the employer should only pay for that proportion of the harm suffered which is attributable to his wrongdoing, unless the harm is truly indivisible. It is for the defendant to raise the question of apportionment.

(16) The assessment of damages will take account of any pre-existing disorder or vulnerability and of the chance that the claimant would have succumbed to a stress related disorder in any event.

6.93 One of the *Sutherland* group of cases went on appeal to the House of Lords: *Barber v Somerset County Council*.[1] The claimant had succeeded at trial, but the decision was overturned by the Court of Appeal. The House of Lords was concerned with the narrow point of whether the Court of Appeal was entitled to interfere with the conclusions of the judge, and held that it was not. Lord Walker[2] called the general exposition and commentary by the Court of Appeal 'a valuable contribution to this area of the law'. In relation to how to treat information received on the mental well-being of an employee, he did, however, say[3] that the best statement of general principle was to be found in the often-quoted words of Swanwick J in *Stokes v Guest, Keen & Nettlefold*:[4]

'the overall test is still the conduct of the reasonable and prudent employer, taking positive thought for the safety of his workers in the light of what he knows or ought to know; where there is a recognised and general practice which has been followed for a substantial period in similar circumstances without mishap, he is entitled to follow it, unless in the light of common sense or newer knowledge it is clearly bad; but, where there is developing knowledge, he must keep reasonably abreast of it and not be too slow to apply it; and where he has in fact greater than average knowledge of the risks, he may be

---

1   [2004] UKHL 13, [2004] 1 WLR 1089.
2   Ibid at [63].
3   Ibid at [65].
4   [1968] 1 WLR 1776 at 1783.

thereby obliged to take more than the average or standard precautions. He must weigh up the risk in terms of the likelihood of injury occurring and the potential consequences if it does; and he must balance against this the probable effectiveness of the precautions that can be taken to meet it and the expense and inconvenience they involve. If he is found to have fallen below the standard to be properly expected of a reasonable and prudent employer in these respects, he is negligent.'

6.94 It is clear from *Sutherland* and *Barber* that foreseeability will generally be crucial when considering cases of psychiatric injury caused by stress at work. An example is *Pratley v Surrey County Council*.[1] The claimant, a council social worker, complained to her supervisor about her workload and that she feared for her health in the future if nothing was done to reduce her workload. The supervisor promised to introduce a new system of working which would reduce her workload. On the claimant's return from holiday, which had immediately followed her conversation with her supervisor, the claimant saw that the new system had not been introduced. She immediately suffered a breakdown and never returned to work. The Court of Appeal decided in favour of the council. What the employer, through the supervisor, foresaw, was the risk of illness through the continuing workload at some time in the future. The council could not foresee the claimant's immediate collapse. According to Buxton LJ, the failure to introduce the new system as promised was potentially negligent if persisted in for the longer term:

'but since the immediate collapse was neither foreseen, nor foreseeable, the failure to make immediate provision to prevent it could not be a relevant act of negligence.'

6.95 *Pratley* can be contrasted with *Young v Post Office*[2] where the Court of Appeal considered that psychiatric illness was foreseeable. The claimant had suffered a breakdown. He returned to work with a promise that his workload would be limited, and indeed that he could stop work and go home if he could not cope. The claimant found the workload too much on his return, but did not complain. He then suffered another breakdown. The Court of Appeal considered that the second breakdown was foreseeable. The court also rejected an argument that the claimant had contributed to his injury by not complaining to his employer.

6.96 Where an employee claims for psychiatric injury caused by disciplinary procedures and/or the termination of employment, difficult issues arise. The rule in *Addis v Gramophone Co Ltd*[3] is usually stated as being that damages for wrongful dismissal cannot include compensation for the manner of dismissal, for injured feelings and so forth. At that time, the contract of employment was treated much as any other contract. A dismissed employee might be entitled to compensation for the contractual period of notice, but could have no other claim either for the fact or manner of the dismissal. By means of employment protection legislation (at present chiefly contained in the Employment Rights Act 1996), Parliament has intervened to give a right to compensation for the manner of dismissal if it is unfair. In *Johnson v Unisys Ltd*,[4] the House of Lords had to consider whether a claimant who was rendered psychiatrically ill by the circumstances and manner of his dismissal had a right to compensation. The allegations were effectively that the employer had

---

1   (Unreported) 25 July 2003.
2   (Unreported) 30 April 2002.
3   [1909] AC 488.
4   [2001] 2 WLR 1076.

dismissed the claimant on the basis of ill-defined allegations which were never properly put to the claimant and against which he had no right to defend himself. Among other complaints was a failure to implement the proper disciplinary procedure. The claimant brought a claim for unfair dismissal in the employment tribunal and won. He now sought to claim some £400,000 for the psychiatric damage which had been caused to him, basing the claim chiefly on breach of the implied obligation of trust and confidence. His claim was dismissed by the House of Lords. The Court of Appeal had similarly dismissed the claim. It had based its decision on the rule in *Addis*. The House of Lords, however, took a different route, indicating that it would probably not have felt constrained by *Addis*. The majority of their Lordships held[1] that the crucial factor was that Parliament had legislated in this field, to fill a perceived gap in the common law. As Lord Hoffmann said:[2]

> 'Part X of the Employment Rights Act 1996 therefore gives a remedy for exactly the conduct of which Mr Johnson complains. But Parliament has restricted that remedy to a maximum of £11,000, whereas Mr Johnson wants to claim a good deal more. The question is whether the courts should develop the common law to give a parallel remedy which is not subject to any such limit. My Lords, I do not think it is a proper exercise of the judicial function of the House to take such a step.'

Parliament is able to balance the competing needs and interests, and had, among other ways of achieving the appropriate balance, imposed a cap on the compensation payable.[3]

6.97 As was anticipated, it has not proved easy to define the precise scope of the rule in *Johnson*. In *Eastwood v Magnox Electric plc*,[4] the House of Lords considered two cases on a strike out basis. The first was brought by two employees who claimed to have suffered stress-related illnesses caused by an alleged campaign of harassment on the part of their employer before they were dismissed. After dismissal, both employees brought and settled unfair dismissal claims. The second case was a claim by a teacher suspended and dismissed for inappropriate behaviour towards a female pupil. He brought and succeeded on an unfair dismissal claim. In the claim before their Lordships, he claimed damages for failures in the investigation procedures which he said led to stress-related illness. The House of Lords refused to strike out either claim, stating that on the assumed facts they did not fall foul of the rule in *Johnson*. Lord Nicholls stated:[5]

> 'Identifying the boundary of the "*Johnson* exclusion area", as it has been called, is comparatively straightforward. The statutory code provides remedies for infringement of the statutory right not to be *dismissed* unfairly. An employee's remedy for unfair dismissal, whether actual or constructive, is the remedy provided by statute. If before his dismissal, whether actual or constructive, an employee has acquired a cause of action at law, for breach of contract or otherwise, that cause of action remains unimpaired by his

---

1 The speeches were unanimously against the claimant. Lord Steyn, however, dissented on the issue of principle as to whether a cause of action might lie on facts of the kind alleged. He dismissed the claim on the basis that it had no reasonable prospects of succeeding in showing that his illness was caused by the manner of his dismissal rather than by the fact of his dismissal.
2 [2001] 2 WLR 1076 at [56]–[57].
3 Presently £50,000. Less when Mr Johnson made his claim.
4 [2004] UKHL 39, [2004] 3 WLR 322.
5 Ibid at [27].

subsequent unfair dismissal and the statutory rights flowing therefrom. By definition, in law such a cause of action exists independently of the dismissal.'

6.98   The House of Lords has now openly acknowledged that *Johnson* does not provide a satisfactory resolution to the difficulties arising from the overlap between unfair dismissal claims and employers' liability claims. Lord Nicholls pointed out:[1]

> 'It goes without saying that an interrelation between the common law and statute having these awkward and unfortunate consequences is not satisfactory. The difficulties arise principally because of the cap on the amount of compensatory awards for unfair dismissal. Although the cap was raised substantially in 1998, at times tribunals are still precluded from awarding full compensation for a dismissed employee's financial loss. So, understandably, employees and their legal advisers are seeking to side-step the statutory limit by identifying elements in the events preceding dismissal, but leading up to dismissal, which can be used as pegs on which to hang a common law claim for breach of an employer's implied contractual obligation to act fairly. This situation merits urgent attention by the Government and the legislature.'

Lord Steyn particularly pointed out that part of the chain of reasoning in *Johnson* was the view that damages for the distress caused by the manner of dismissal could be awarded in an unfair dismissal claim, and that this view had now been shown to be wrong by the decision of the House in *Dunnachie v Kingston upon Hull City Council*.[2]

6.99   The Disability Discrimination Act 1995 falls largely outside the scope of this chapter. In appropriate cases, however, a claimant would be able to use that Act to seek compensation avoiding difficult issues as to whether injury to feelings alone could be compensated,[3] and perhaps some of the difficulties outlined above.

6.100   As well as the stresses inherent in a particular job (which were considered above), bullying, harassment, or physical abuse by fellow employees or others may cause psychiatric or physical illness. An employer may be liable for such injury by one of two routes.

(1)   The employer may be directly responsible. An employer has a duty to create workplace systems which tend to prevent such conduct arising, and deal with it effectively if it does, so that no employee has to suffer such conduct at the hands of his fellow employees. It is no defence under this head for the employer to say that the person in question was acting outside the scope of his employment. The House of Lords considered such a case, which reached it on an application to strike out, in *Waters v Commissioner of Police of the Metropolis*.[4] The claimant was a police officer who alleged that a fellow officer sexually assaulted her while off duty. After she complained to superiors at work about the incident, she was allegedly subjected to ostracism, harassment and victimisation. She sued the Commissioner for failing to prevent such conduct. The House of Lords refused

---

1   Ibid at [33].

2   [2004] UKHL 36, [2004] 3 WLR 310.

3   Section 25(2) states expressly that they can.

4   [2000] 1 WLR 1607. While the Commissioner is not strictly an employer, and police officers are not strictly employees, the obligations owed were treated as indistinguishable for the purposes of the appeal.

to strike out the claim.[1] The duty of the employer also extends to assessing the risk of injury to employees from members of the public, for example by way of assaults, and to taking appropriate steps to minimise the risks.[2] This is an area of particular concern to local authorities, whose employees may have to deal with particularly difficult members of the public in particularly difficult circumstances.

(2) The employer may be vicariously liable for the acts or omissions of its employees. Vicarious liability was recently defined as follows: 'Vicarious liability is legal responsibility imposed on an employer, although he is himself free from blame, for a tort committed by his employee in the course of his employment'.[3] The circumstances in which such liability will be imposed by the courts finds its classic statement in *Salmond on Torts*:

'A master is not responsible for a wrongful act done by his servant unless it is done in the course of his employment. It is deemed to be so done if it is either (a) a wrongful act authorised by the master or (b) a wrongful and unauthorised mode of doing some act authorised by the master.'[4]

6.101 Where the acts of the employee amount to bullying, harassment or physical abuse, application of this dictum has often made it difficult to show that the act complained of was done in the course of employment. Recently, however, the House of Lords has tilted the balance strongly towards protection of the victim of the wrongdoing. In *Lister v Hesley Hall Ltd*,[5] the defendant was sued by a number of claimants who had been pupils at a school owned and managed by the defendant. They had suffered sexual abuse at the hands of the warden, who was responsible for the day-to-day running of the school and the maintenance of discipline. The House held that the employer was vicariously liable for these acts. Lord Steyn delivered the leading speech. He deprecated an overly analytical approach to the question of what fell within or without the course of employment. He approved of previous decisions in which the courts had advocated taking a broad view of the job which the tortfeasor was engaged to do, such as the approach of Scarman LJ in *Rose v Plenty*.[6] If approached in that way, Lord Steyn said:[7]

'it becomes possible to consider the question of vicarious liability on the basis that the employer undertook to care for the boys through the services of the warden and that there is a very close connection between the torts of the warden and his employment. After all, they were committed in the time and on the premises of the employers while the warden was also busy caring for the children.'

---

1 The issue which took most of their Lordships' time was that of a claimed police immunity, which would not be relevant to claims against local authorities.
2 See, eg, *Keys v Shoefayre Ltd* [1978] IRLR 476 and *Charlton v Forrest Printing Ink Co Ltd* [1980] IRLR 331.
3 *Lister v Hesley Hall Ltd* [2001] UKHL 22, [2002] 1 AC 215, at [14], per Lord Steyn.
4 First edition (1907) at p 83 and repeated in subsequent editions.
5 [2001] UKHL 22, [2002] 1 AC 215.
6 [1976] 1 WLR 141 at 147–148. There, a milkman brought a boy with him to help with his round in the face of a prohibition by his employer. Nonetheless, the carrying of the boy was in the course of employment, being a mode (albeit prohibited) of carrying out the job for which he was engaged.
7 [2001] UKHL 22, [2002] 1 AC 215 at [20].

Their Lordships pointed out that it was perhaps unfortunate that what *Salmond on Torts* went on to say on the subject after the passage cited above was not better known:

> 'A master ... is liable even for acts which he has not authorised, provided they are so connected with acts which he has authorised, that they may rightly be regarded as modes – although improper modes – of doing them.'

This decision will make it much more difficult for employers when faced with bullying and harassment claims to defend them on the grounds that the employees so behaving went outside the course of their employment.

6.102 Where the harassment is of a racial or sexual kind, and is committed in the course of employment, the employer will be liable unless he had done all that was reasonably practicable to prevent it.[1] Where an employee suffers from harassment of a racial or sexual kind, it is not necessary to prove psychiatric illness. Injury to feelings will suffice.[2]

6.103 Where long working hours contribute to the stress which causes psychiatric illness, a claimant may be able to rely on the Working Time Regulations 1998.[3] The Regulations, inter alia, and subject to agreement to exclude, require an average of no more than 48 hours work per week, limit the amount of night work which can be done, require rest periods of 11 hours in any 24 hours and a rest of 24 hours every 7 days. The European Court of Justice has held that working time is a health and safety issue, rather than simply a social issue.[4]

CONCLUSION

6.104 In most respects the local authority stands in no different a position to any other employer in terms of the duties – both at common law and by statute or statutory regulation – it owes to its employees. From the point of view of the protection given to employees these duties have been significantly enhanced by the intervention of the European Union, principally in terms of Directives implemented in the UK in the form of the series of regulations passed from 1992 onwards. To the extent that the Directives have not been implemented the local authority is one employer which is also vulnerable to actions pursuant to the provisions of the Directives themselves.

6.105 Unlike the common law duty to take reasonable care, many of these statutory duties are absolute. The introduction of these duties has combined with the courts' willingness to interpret the law widely (in particular the meaning of the words 'employee' and 'equipment') to create a health and safety environment which has moved a considerable way in favour of protecting the employee and calls for greater vigilance on the part of the employer. Nowhere can this be more so than for the local authority employer, which is involved in the workplace in almost all of its many aspects.

---

1   Sex Discrimination Act 1975, s 41; Race Relations Act 1976, s 32.
2   Sex Discrimination Act 1975, ss 65–66; Race Relations Act 1976, ss 56–57.
3   SI 1998/1833, implementing Council Directive 93/104/EC, and amended by the Working Time Regulations 1999, SI 1999/3372.
4   *United Kingdom v European Commission* [1997] ICR 443.

Chapter 7

HIGHWAYS

INTRODUCTION

7.1   Claims against local authorities in their capacity as highway authority are by far the most prevalent in terms of liability claims overall. Figures produced by insurers showed that the cost of highways claims rose from £12.7m in 1982 to £41.5m in 1990.[1] Claims range from the trivial (such as chipped windscreens and punctured tyres) through to commonplace pavement 'tripping' accidents, and claims of the utmost severity involving paraplegia, brain damage and fatality.

WHAT IS A HIGHWAY?

7.2   At common law, a highway has been defined as follows:[2]

'A highway is a way over which there exists a public right of passage, that is to say, a right for all of Her Majesty's subjects at all seasons of the year freely and at their wills to pass and repass without let or hindrance.'

7.3   The statutory definition of 'highway' is unhelpful.[3] However, for the purposes of highways law the important definition is found in s 36 of the Highways Act 1980 which defines 'a highway maintainable at the public expense'.

Section 36(1) states that unless some event has occurred which changes the situation, then all highways which were maintainable at public expense under the former Highways Act 1959 continue to be such highways. Section 36(2) then specifies five types of highway which for the purposes of the Act are 'highways maintainable at the public expense' as follows:

'(a)   a highway constructed by a highway authority, otherwise than on behalf of some other person who is not a highway authority;

(b)   a highway constructed by a council within their own area under Part II of the Housing Act 1985, other than one in respect of which the local highway authority are satisfied that it has not been properly constructed, and a highway constructed by a council outside their own area under the said Part V, being, in the later case, a highway the liability to maintain which is, by virtue of the said Part II, vested in the council who are the local highway authority for the area in which the highway is situated;

(c)   a highway that is a trunk road or a special road;

---

1   See *Report on Highways Liability Claims – The Issues* (Kindred Associations, 1998).
2   Per Willis J in *ex parte Lewis* (1888) 21 QBD 191 at 197.
3   Highways Act 1980, s 328.

(d)   a highway, being a footpath or bridleway, created in consequence of a public path creation order or a public path diversion order or in consequence of an order made by the Minister of Transport or the Secretary of State under section 247 of the Town and Country Planning Act 1990 or by a competent authority under section 257 of the Act, or dedicated in pursuance of a public path creation agreement;

(e)   a highway being a footpath or bridleway, created in consequence of a rail crossing diversion order, or of an order made under section 14 or 16 of the Harbours Act 1964, or of an order made under section 1 or 3 of the Transport and Works Act 1992.'

7.4   The questions, 'what is a highway' and 'when is a highway maintainable at the public expense' were considered in *Gulliksen v Pembrokeshire County Council*.[1] The claimant tripped over a manhole on a footpath running through a housing estate which had been built by the council's predecessors. The Court of Appeal considered that the footpath had been dedicated from the start as a highway in the common law sense described by Lord Diplock in *Suffolk County Council v Mason*:[2]

'At common law a highway is a way over which all members of the public have the right to pass and re-pass without hindrance.'

Furthermore, the footpath was 'a highway maintainable at the public expense' because of the following:

(1)   It was a highway constructed by the council of a borough or urban district within its own area under Part V of the Housing Act 1957.

(2)   A highway so constructed was maintainable at public expense under s 38(2)(c) of the Highways Act 1959.

(3)   Under s 36(1) of the Highways Act 1980 highways which were maintainable at the public expenses for the purposes of the Highways Act 1959 continue to be so maintainable.

7.5   Every county council, metropolitan district council and London borough is required under s 36(6) and (7) to keep a correct and up-to-date list of the streets within its area which are highways maintainable at the public's expense and these lists may be inspected by any person free of charge at all reasonable hours.

7.6   Sections 37, 38 and 40 of the Highways Act 1980 contain detailed provisions for the adoption of highways by a highway authority so as to become highways maintainable at the public expense, in particular either by notice served upon the highway authority by the highway owner[3] or by agreement.[4] There is also provision at s 228 of the Highways Act 1980 for a highway authority to give notice of intention to adopt a highway as being a highway maintainable at the public expense in the case of improvement works carried out to a private road.

7.7   ·A highway authority will normally own only the freehold of those highways which have been constructed by it, typically motorways, new bypasses and major road improvement schemes when, for example, roads might have been realigned. In these situations there will normally have been a compulsory purchase of the land on which the new highway is located. Otherwise for the vast majority of highways, the highway

1   [2003] QB 123.
2   [1979] AC 705.
3   Highways Act 1980, s 37.
4   Ibid, s 38.

authority does not own the highway, and its ownership still vests in the adjoining landowner. The only caveat to this is that by virtue of s 263 of the Highways Act 1980, the surface of the highway will vest in the highway authority. This does not, however, affect the land beneath the surface.

7.8 In *Rance v Essex County Council*,[1] the plaintiff was driving along an unclassified road along which contractor's lorries had regularly driven off the metalled carriageway onto grass verges thus causing ruts to develop in the verges immediately adjacent to the carriageway. The plaintiff, in passing a lorry travelling in the opposite direction, steered to her nearside where the wheels of her car became caught in a rut. As a result of steering to extricate her car from the rut, the plaintiff hit a tree and sustained injury. It appears to have been accepted by both parties and by the Court of Appeal that the verge formed part of the highway even though the outer edge of the metalled surface of the road was delineated by a white line.

7.9 Responsibility for scouring and cleansing a roadside ditch will normally be that of the adjoining landowner,[2] unless the ditch is owned by the highway authority. However, in *Thoburn v Northumberland County Council*[3] the Court of Appeal found the highway authority liable for an accident caused by flooding of a road by water from an adjacent ditch on land owned by the neighbouring farmer.

7.10 Whether a retaining wall is part of the highway will be a question of fact in each case.[4] However, what is clear from all the cases is that the deciding factor so far as the duties of the highway authority are concerned is that if a defect or need for maintenance at the edge of the highway is rendering the highway itself dangerous, then pursuant to s 41 there is a duty on the highway authority to repair or maintain. This was made clear in *Sandgate Urban District Council v Kent County Council*,[5] where in the case dealing with the maintenance of a sea wall, Lord Halsbury said:[6]

> 'I have no hesitation in saying that, assuming a thing to be necessary for the preservation of the road, and assuming that the local authority is under obligation to keep up the road, the law of England is that you shall keep up that road by whatever means are appropriate and necessary to do it.'

7.11 Similarly, in *Reigate Corporation v Surrey County Council*,[7] a case involving the maintenance of the walls and roof of a tunnel through which a highway passed, it was held that regardless of the question of the ownership of the walls and roof, the responsibility for their maintenance rested with the highway authority, in circumstances where a failure to maintain and repair would in turn have brought about an obstruction and disrepair of the highway. Thus, the courts expect the highway authority to take such reasonable steps within the area or curtilage of the highway to ensure that the highway itself is reasonably safe for those who would normally use it. This is a result of the overriding duty imposed upon the highway authority by s 41. In some situations, another party, perhaps the adjoining landowner, may also have responsibility. Where a lack of repair or want of maintenance by a neighbouring

---

1 (Unreported) 21 February 1997.
2 *Attorney General v Waring* (1899) 63 JP 789.
3 (1999) 1 LGLR 819. See also para **7.48**.
4 *R v Lordsmere (Inhabitants)* (1886) 54 LT 766.
5 (1898) 79 LT 425.
6 Ibid at 427.
7 [1928] Ch 359.

landowner or *a fortiori* positive action by such a landowner has caused a problem on the highway (eg flooding), then it can be argued that the landowner should bear the majority of the liability upon the basis that the highway authority is liable only as a result of s 41 of the Highways Act 1980 (see para **7.23**) because it has failed to 'police' those matters which were the primary cause of the problem.

WHO IS THE HIGHWAY AUTHORITY?

7.12   The definition of 'highway authority' is to be found in s 1 of the Highways Act 1980, as amended by subsequent legislation. The Minister is the highway authority for the following:

(1)   trunk roads;
(2)   any special roads provided by him;
(3)   any highways not being trunk roads for which it is provided by any enactment that he is the highway authority;
(4)   any highway transferred to him; and
(5)   any other highway constructed by him unless by any other enactment the highway is transferred to the local highway authority.[1]

In England, 'The Minister' is the Secretary of State for Transport. In Wales, the functions of the Secretary of State for Wales have been transferred to the Welsh Assembly.[2]

7.13   The definition of 'trunk roads' in the Highways Act 1980 is decidedly unhelpful.[3] However, the effect is that the definition follows that in the now repealed s 1 of the Trunk Roads Act 1936, namely a carriageway highway forming part of the national system of routes for through traffic. 'Local highway authority' is defined as 'a highway authority other than the Minister'.[4]

7.14   As far as other roads are concerned, the highway authority is the county council, unitary authority, or metropolitan district.[5] In Wales, the highway authority is the county council or county borough council.[6]

7.15   In the Greater London area, the highway authority is the London borough council or, in the case of the City of London, the common council.[7] In addition, s 154 of the Greater London Authority Act 1999 established a body corporate known as Transport for London, whose function is to facilitate the discharge by the Greater London Authority of its general transport duty and the implementation of transport strategy. The Act empowered the Secretary of State to designate 'GLA roads'.[8] It also empowers the Greater London Authority to direct that any road, except a trunk

---

1   Highways Act 1980, s 1(1).
2   Government of Wales Act 1998, s 22 brought into force by the Government of Wales Act 1998 (Commencement No 2) Order 1998, SI 1998/2789.
3   Highways Act 1980, s 10(1).
4   Ibid, s 329.
5   Ibid, s 1(2), as amended by s 8 of the Local Government Act 1985 and ss 17–23 of the Local Government Act 1992.
6   Highways Act 1980, s 1(3A) as inserted by s 22(1) of the Local Government (Wales) Act 1994.
7   Highways Act 1980, s 10(1).
8   Ibid, s 14A(1) as inserted by s 260 of the Greater London Authority Act 1999.

road, can be designated a GLA road or cease to be so designated.[1] It seems that GLA roads are likely to be the primary and 'red route' networks. Transport for London is the highway authority for all GLA roads.[2]

7.16 Although the above sets out the statutory definition of 'highway authority', the actual responsibility for the maintenance of highways does not necessarily rest there. Sections 4–6 of the Highways Act 1980 contain a detailed statutory framework for agreements between the Minister and the local highway authority concerning the carrying-out of their respective highway responsibilities. Typically, the Minister will delegate to the local highway authority the responsibility for the maintenance of those highways for which the Minister is highway authority within that local highway authority's area.

7.17 It should be emphasised that such an agreement does not affect the statutory definition of who is the highway authority in each case, but essentially is a contractual arrangement sanctioned by statute for administrative and operational convenience. Each agreement will deal with the financial aspects of such an arrangement, and importantly for these purposes will also deal with liabilities and indemnities against claims. Furthermore, by s 8 of the Highways Act 1980 neighbouring local highway authorities may enter into agreements with each other in relation to the construction, reconstruction, alteration, improvement or maintenance of a highway for which any party to the agreement is the highway authority.[3] Typically, a local highway authority will enter into such an agreement with its neighbouring authority either where there is a specific improvement or reconstruction project on a section of highway at or around the authority's boundary or in connection with routine maintenance of such a highway. Common sense dictates that such agreements should be sanctioned by statute for operational reasons. However, again this is essentially a contractual arrangement and the agreement between authorities must be considered in detail as regards the financial arrangements and liabilities or indemnities.

7.18 The agreements referred to above are usually referred to as 'agency agreements'. Such agreements are also authorised by s 42 of the Highways Act 1980 whereby a district council may undertake the maintenance of any highway within its district which is a highway maintainable at the public expense.[4] These will be agreements between the highway authority and the district council. The highway authority will reimburse the district council for the expenses incurred in connection with carrying out highways maintenance functions.[5] It should, however, again be emphasised that the identity of the highway authority remains the same and the duty to maintain the highway under s 41 of the Highways Act 1980 remains with the highway authority. The highway authority is essentially delegating by contract certain, or all, of its functions in this regard to the district council. The terms of each agreement must be considered in detail with particular regard to liabilities and indemnities as well as insurance arrangements. Although the district council will normally indemnify the highway authority for all liability claims of a highway nature, and the highway authority may seek to pass liability for such claims to the district council under the

---

1   Highways Act 1980, s 14B(1) as inserted by s 261 of the Greater London Authority Act 1999.
2   Ibid, s 1(2A) as inserted by s 259 of the Greater London Authority Act 1999.
3   Ibid, s 8(1).
4   Ibid, s 42(1).
5   Ibid, s 42(3).

terms of such indemnity, nevertheless it is wrong for the district council to be sued as highway authority.

7.19 The historical insurance arrangements of the vast majority of the local authorities in England and Wales have meant that there has been little (if any) litigation upon the interpretation of agency agreements. However, it is submitted that the more innovative wording being used in the modern form of such agreements, as well as the different insurance arrangements which may now exist between county councils and district councils, will mean that there is scope for argument in this regard.

7.20 A much closer analysis must now be made of the precise wording of such agreements in the circumstances of any given case. A not uncommon arrangement is for the district council to be responsible for all routine highway maintenance, but for the county council to maintain responsibility for strategic matters such as accident statistical analysis and skid resistance tests, and for decisions upon and funding for capital projects and non-routine maintenance expenditure. It is submitted that, in this situation, where there is legal liability for a highways accident caused by something which under the agency agreement remains the responsibility of the county council, then it is the county council which should bear the responsibility for that claim and not the district council, notwithstanding the terms of any agreement under s 42. This is because any indemnity clause will be effective only in favour of a party's own negligence if it is absolutely specific and clear in this regard.[1] It is most unlikely that an indemnity clause in a s 42 agency agreement would satisfy this requirement.

7.21 The only situation where a highway authority is able to absolve itself of its highways responsibilities is under a highways agreement pursuant to ss 1–5 of the New Roads and Street Works Act 1991. The scheme of this part of the Act is for the creation of new forms of toll roads. The highway authority may enter into agreements with third parties under which the third party agrees to undertake special obligations with regard to design, construction, maintenance operation or improvement of the special road. Whilst such an agreement is in force the highway authority will not be liable for anything done or omitted to be done in connection with those specified highway functions.

7.22 Section 43 of the Highways Act 1980 enables parish councils and community councils to undertake the maintenance of highways within their area, and at s 44 there is a similar provision for others to enter into a highways maintenance agreement with the highway authority. However, both provisions specify that the legal responsibility for the maintenance of the highway remains with the highway authority.[2]

THE STATUTORY DUTY

7.23 The statutory duty to maintain the highway is contained at s 41(1) of the Highways Act 1980 as follows:

'The authority who are for the time being the Highway Authority for a highway maintainable at the public expense are under a duty ... to maintain the highway.'

---

1 See *Smith v South Wales Switchgear* [1978] 1 All ER 18 and *Alderslade v Hendon Laundry Limited* [1945] 1 All ER 244.
2 Highways Act 1980, ss 43(3) and 44.

7.24 The term 'maintenance' includes 'repair' and the words 'maintain' and 'maintainable' are to be construed accordingly.[1] For there to be a breach of s 41 of the Highways Act 1980, there must have been a failure to maintain or a failure to repair. In turn this requires a consideration of what constitutes 'lack of repair'.

7.25 It is essential, when considering the statutory duty imposed on the highway authority, to consider at the same time the statutory defence provided by s 58 of the Act. This will be dealt with more fully later. However, in most, if not all of the cases which are mentioned in the following paragraphs, the statutory duty under s 41 of the Act and the statutory defence provided by s 58 have both been considered by the courts at the same time.

7.26 Sections 41 and 58 of the Highways Act 1980 re-enact the provisions of s 1 of the Highways (Miscellaneous Provisions) Act 1961 which came into force on 4 August 1964. Cases which predate the Highways Act 1980 interpret and explain identical or equivalent provisions in the previous legislation.

7.27 In *Burnside v Emerson*,[2] Lord Diplock explained the duty to maintain the highway as follows:

> 'The duty ... is ... not merely to keep a highway in such a state of repair as it is at any particular time, but to put it in such good repair as renders it reasonably passable for the ordinary traffic of the neighbourhood at all seasons of the year without danger caused by its physical condition.'

7.28 In *Rider v Rider*,[3] it was held that the highway authority's duty is reasonably to maintain and repair the highway so that it is free of danger to all users who use the highway in the way normally to be expected of them. The plaintiff was a passenger in a car which collided with a vehicle coming in the opposite direction. The accident happened on a road which had originally been a country lane, but had become increasingly used to avoid traffic jams on other roads. The judge held that the cause of the accident was the disrepair of the edge of the road which was uneven and led onto grass or mud verges. The Court of Appeal agreed with the judge that the condition of the lane was foreseeably dangerous to reasonable drivers. In the course of his judgment, however, Sachs LJ said:

> 'It is in my Judgment clear that the Corporation's statutory duty under Section 44 of the 1959 Act is reasonably to maintain and repair the highway so that it is free of danger to all users who use that highway in the way normally to be expected of them – taking account, of course, of the traffic reasonably to be expected on the particular highway. Motorists who thus use the highway, and to whom a duty is owed, are not to be expected by the authority all to be model drivers. ... the Highway Authority must provide not merely for model drivers, but for the normal run of drivers to be found on their highways, and that includes those who make the mistakes which experience and common sense teach us are likely to occur.'

Sachs LJ went on to emphasise that mere unevenness, undulations and minor potholes would not normally constitute a danger and also that the normal run of drivers did not include the drunk or the reckless.

---

1   Highways Act 1980, s 329(1).
2   [1968] 1 WLR 1490.
3   [1973] QB 505, [1973] 1 All ER 294.

7.29　The Court of Appeal considered that whether part of a highway is a danger for traffic is a question of fact to be decided by the judge in each particular case. Lawton LJ said:

'In most cases proof that there were bumps or small holes in a road, or slight unevenness in flagstones on a pavement, will not amount to proof of a danger for traffic through failure to maintain. But it does not follow that such conditions can never be a danger for traffic. A stretch of uneven paving outside a factory probably would not be a danger for traffic; but a similar stretch outside an old people's home, and much used by the inmates to the knowledge of the Highway Authority might be.'

7.30　The House of Lords adopted Lord Diplock's test in *Goodes v East Sussex County Council*[1] when it held that the duty to maintain did not include a duty to keep the highway free from ice and snow. The duty was concerned with dangers caused by the 'physical condition' of the highway.[2]

7.31　A similar approach was adopted by the Court of Appeal in *Thompson v Hampshire County Council*.[3] The claimant was walking along a path in a grass verge alongside a main road in the New Forest. The path led to a campsite. It was night time and the road was in darkness. The claimant fell into a ditch which ran for a short length adjacent to the path where she was walking, but otherwise the ditch was culverted. The claimant alleged that there was a duty under s 41 of the Highways Act 1980 to make the path safe, the ditch amounting to a hole in the highway. The Court of Appeal concluded that the complaint related to the layout of the road while the duty to maintain was concerned with the 'structure' of the road. Rix LJ said:

'The duty is not a general duty to ensure, subject to the section 58 defence, that a highway is not dangerous to traffic, but no more than a duty to repair the structure of the highway if it is out of repair.'

7.32　The extent of the duty to maintain a footpath was considered in *Hereford & Worcester County Council v Newman*.[4] Footpaths were obstructed by vegetation and, in one case, by a barbed wire fence. It was held that the local authority had failed to maintain the footpaths affected by a substantial growth of vegetation rooted in the surface of the footpaths, because this meant that the footpaths were out of repair, but on the other hand the barbed wire fence was a mere obstruction, and therefore not a failure to maintain the highway.

Pavement tripping cases

7.33　The most commonplace highways claims concern pedestrian tripping accidents. The current judicial interpretation of what amounts to 'failure to maintain' a pavement can be traced back to the so-called 'Liverpool trilogy'[5] of cases. In *Griffiths v Liverpool Corporation*[6] there was a rocking paving slab which gave rise to a trip of

---

1　[2000] 1 WLR 1356.
2　Note, however, s 41(1A) of the Highways Act 1980 which now imposes a duty on highway authorities in regard to snow and ice: see para **7.54**.
3　[2004] EWCA Civ 1016, (unreported) 27 July 2004.
4　[1975] 1 WLR 901.
5　*Griffiths v Liverpool Corporation* [1966] 2 WLR 467, *Meggs v Liverpool Corporation* [1968] 1 WLR 689 and *Littler v Liverpool Corporation* [1968] 2 All ER 343.
6　[1966] 2 WLR 467.

half an inch. The judge held this to be dangerous, a finding not contested at the appeal which the highway authority lost (the Court of Appeal considering that the council had not established its statutory defence under what was then s 1 of the Highways (Miscellaneous Provisions) Act 1961). However, the Court of Appeal did express a view that such a defect did not necessarily amount to a failure to maintain. Sellers LJ said:

> 'We are all of us accustomed to walk on uneven and irregular surfaces and we can all of us trip on cobblestones, cat's-eyes, studs marking pedestrian crossings, as well as other projections. If the finding that the half-inch projection of a solitary flagstone in a wide pavement has to be accepted because of the technicalities of this case, as my brethren think, I have perhaps said enough to indicate that it is a standard which in my view should not become a precedent or guide in ordinary circumstances.'

7.34   In *Meggs v Liverpool Corporation*,[1] a trip of three-quarters of an inch was not regarded as dangerous by the council's highways department although repairs were carried out after the accident. The trial judge held that there was no breach of duty and the Court of Appeal agreed. Lord Denning MR said:[2]

> 'It seems to me, using ordinary knowledge of pavements, that everyone must take account of the fact that there may be unevenness here or there. There may be a ridge of half an inch or three quarters of an inch occasionally, but that is not the sort of thing which makes it dangerous or not reasonably safe.'

7.35   *Littler v Liverpool Corporation*,[3] was the third case to be heard. The plaintiff fell, catching his toe on a half-inch triangular depression 3 inches long, whilst running along the pavement. Giving judgment for the highway authority, Cumming Bruce J said:[4]

> 'The test in relation to a length of pavement is reasonable foreseeability of danger. A length of pavement is only dangerous if, in the ordinary course of human affairs, danger may reasonably be anticipated from its continued use by the public who usually pass over it. It is a mistake to isolate and emphasise a particular difference in levels between flagstones unless that difference is such that a reasonable person who noticed and considered it would regard it as presenting a real source of danger. Uneven surfaces and differences in level between flagstones of about an inch may cause a pedestrian temporarily off balance to trip and stumble, but such characteristics have to be accepted. A highway is not to be criticised by the standards of a bowling green.'

7.36   What has been the position following the three Liverpool cases? In *Lawman v Waltham Forest London Borough Council*,[5] an argument that a trip of 20 mm (just over three-quarters of an inch) amounted to a failure to maintain was firmly rejected by the Court of Appeal.

7.37   In *Mills v Barnsley Metropolitan Borough Council*,[6] the trial judge found for the plaintiff who had fallen and injured herself when her shoe heel caught in a triangular hole that was 2 inches across at its widest and 1¼ inches deep. The defendant's appeal was allowed on the grounds that the defect in question was minor

---

1   [1968] 1 WLR 689.
2   Ibid at 692.
3   [1968] 2 All ER 343.
4   [1968] 2 All ER 343 at 345.
5   (Unreported) 23 January 1980, CA.
6   [1992] PIQR 291.

and of a nature which normal pedestrians must expect. At the end of his judgment Steyn LJ said:[1]

> 'Finally, I add that in drawing the inference of dangerousness in this case the Judge impliedly set a standard which if generally used in the thousands of tripping cases which come before the courts every year, would impose an unreasonable burden upon Highway Authorities in respect of minor depressions and holes in streets which in a less than perfect world the public must simply regard as a fact of life. It is important that our tort laws should not impose unreasonably high standards, otherwise scarce resources would be diverted from situations where maintenance and repair of the highways was more urgently needed. This branch of the law of tort ought to represent a sensible balance or compromise between private and public interests. The Judge's ruling in this case, if allowed to stand, would tilt the balance too far in favour of the woman who was unfortunately injured. The risk was of low order and the cost of remedying such minor defects all over the country would be enormous. In my Judgment the Plaintiff's claim fails on this first point.'

7.38   It is clear that there is no rigid rule or mechanical test based upon the precise dimensions of a given defect which will decide whether or not it amounts to a breach of s 41 of the Highways Act 1980. A trial judge must hear the evidence and take into consideration such matters as the size and nature of the defect and the position in which it is located. Thus in *James and Thomas v Preseli Pembrokeshire District Council*,[2] the Court of Appeal refused to interfere with the discretion of the judge who had tried the case and, after applying the correct test of whether or not the highway had been in a dangerous condition, reached his conclusion that a 25 mm trip did not require urgent repair.

7.39   In the associated appeal in *James and Thomas v Preseli Pembrokeshire District Council*[3] it was also held that a plaintiff must prove that the particular spot which caused the accident was dangerous and it was insufficient to show merely that the pavement as a whole was in poor condition.

7.40   *James and Thomas* should be compared with the approach of the Court of Appeal in *Dibb v Kirklees Metropolitan Borough Council*.[4] The claimant tripped on, or adjacent to, a drainage grating which was situated in a roadway gully next to a narrow piece of pavement. The grating also encroached into the pavement by the width of a kerbstone. The Court of Appeal had little difficulty in agreeing with the judge that the intrusion of the drainage grating into what was already a narrow pavement, and the difference in height of about three-quarters of an inch between the adjacent kerbstone and the grating, represented a danger, even taking into account Steyn LJ's view in *Mills* that the courts should not set unreasonably high standards. The Court of Appeal then went on to consider the highway authority's argument that the claimant had not proved where or how she fell so as to satisfy the test in *James and Thomas*.[5] The claimant's evidence was inconsistent with the particulars of claim and, at one point, the trial judge said:

---

1   [1992] PIQR 291 at 295.
2   [1993] PIQR 114.
3   [1993] PIQR 114.
4   (Unreported) 15 April 1999.
5   See also *Whitworth v The Mayor Alderman and Burgesses of the City of Manchester* (unreported) 17 June 1971.

'There is a certain doubt which is raised in one's mind as to exactly where she was, or how it was, or what she trod on when she went over ...'

The Court of Appeal recognised the difficulty, but found in favour of the claimant. Swinton Thomas LJ considered that the judge had been entitled to find in favour of the claimant as follows:

'In a case such as the present case, where the plaintiff undoubtedly fell on a piece of pavement which was plainly dangerous it is, in my judgment, clearly open to the Judge on the facts of the case, and on the facts of this particular case, to draw the inference on the evidence that the plaintiff's fall and her consequent injuries were indeed caused by the defective pavement. The Judge found as a fact that it was likely that the plaintiff fell by reason of the serious defects in the pavement. In other words he found on the balance of probabilities that the plaintiff had fallen because of the defective state of the highway and the defendants were, accordingly, negligent or in breach of their statutory duty.'

7.41 *Dibb* should be compared with *Edwards v Clwyd County Council*,[1] where it was alleged that the plaintiff's foot slipped into a drainage gulley at the side of the road which was a minor classified rural road in North Wales. The plaintiff alleged that the depth of the drainage gulley at the relevant point was 6 inches whereas elsewhere the gulley had a depth of no more than 2 or 3 inches. The county court judge dismissed the plaintiff's claim and held that this was a standard form of drainage channel used over wide areas of the country and that a depth of 6 inches was neither unusual nor unsafe. It would be entirely impracticable on economic grounds alone for the highway authority to be expected to inspect every inch of the drainage channels within its area and reduce the depth of such channels to 3 inches or less.

7.42 It is also worth noting the decision of the Court of Appeal in *Winterhalder v Leeds City Council*[2] where again, although noting the tests laid down in *Mills v Barnsley Metropolitan Borough Council* and *James v Preseli Pembrokeshire District Council*, the Court of Appeal held against the highway authority in favour of a claimant who caught her foot in a gap of at least 2½ inches between two kerbstones. Swinton Thomas LJ, overruling the trial judge, said:

'A case such as this must be decided on its own particular facts. As appears very clearly from the authorities ... it is difficult for a claimant to succeed in a tripping case where he or she has tripped on the highway because it is of great importance that the court should not impose an unreasonable burden on the highway authority. However, in this particular case there was a gap of no less than 2½" between the two kerbstones, right on the very edge of the road at the point where a person such as the appellant is likely to step off. It was obvious, so it seems to me, that this was a very real danger and that there was a real danger that a pedestrian would catch his or her heel in that gap and fall and sustain an injury.'

7.43 An example of a more restrictive approach in similar circumstances is that of Eady J in *Galloway v The London Borough of Richmond Upon Thames*.[3] The claimant had tripped in a gap created by a broken kerbstone forming part of a cross-over linking the road with a passageway behind the adjacent houses and therefore crossing the pavement. The gap tapered from 31 mm to 10 mm across the width of the kerbstone. The highway authority was aware of the defect, but did not

---

1 [1997] CLY 3784.
2 (Unreported) 18 July 2000.
3 (Unreported) 20 February 2003.

regard it as a danger. Accordingly, no repairs had been carried out. Eady J said that although the gap represented a foreseeable risk of harm to users of the highway, this did not, by itself, necessitate repair:

> 'That is only the first hurdle a claimant has to surmount. The next essential step is to ask whether that particular risk of harm is of a low order and where the balance between private and public interest should be struck. Would a reasonable person regard it as presenting a real source of danger?'

The judge, relying on *Mills*, concluded that the gap in the kerbstone was 'unremarkable' and not such as to give rise to 'a real source of danger'.

7.44   Another case where the Court of Appeal considered *Mills* is *Brett v Mayor and Burgesses of the London Borough of Lewisham*.[1] The claimant tripped on an uneven tarmac strip which had a raised edge although there seems to have been no evidence about the height of the trip. The highway authority submitted that the judge, in finding for the claimant, had applied a test of danger which was unrealistic, having regard to the standard of repair to which the public is entitled. The Court of Appeal was referred to *Mills* and *James v Preseli Pembrokeshire District Council* and noted that, in drawing the inference of dangerousness, the court must not set too high a standard. Chadwick LJ said:

> 'I am content to adopt the test, established in the *Barnsley* and *Preseli* cases in the context of failure to maintain, that dangerous, in a misfeasance case, means something which in the ordinary course of human affairs may reasonably be anticipated to cause harm from continued use of the highway by the public; and that it is not foresight of every risk, however remote, that gives rise to liability.'

In deciding in favour of the claimant, however, the Court of Appeal noted that the uneven tarmac had been laid by the highway authority and Chadwick LJ went on as follows:

> 'It seems to me that, once someone has embarked on a work of repair, both public and private interests require that the work should be carried out competently. And if the work is carried out in such a way that it may reasonably be anticipated that harm will result, the party responsible for that work should be liable in damages to the person harmed.'

The Court of Appeal concluded that the judge had been correct to hold that the point at which the claimant tripped was not just an uneven surface, but was a dangerously uneven surface, and reasonably foreseeable as such. It is suggested that had the highway authority not created the trip, the Court of Appeal might have followed *Mills* and found in its favour.

7.45   In *Hartley v Burnley Borough Council*[2] the plaintiff slipped when descending a steep hill in the local town centre where, at the lower end of the hill, the construction of the footpath changed from flagstones to tarmac. Although the tarmac had broken off and had different textures, one having ridges on the surface and another area being simply uneven, there was no defined trip as such or undulation. The judge held that in all the circumstances the pavement was in a dangerous condition and that this had been caused by failure of the council to fulfil its duty to maintain the highway. It is

---

1   [2000] LGR 443.
2   [1998] CLY 5670.

perhaps significant to note that this was a steep street located close to the town centre with a heavy volume of pedestrian traffic.

Transient defects

7.46 Difficult questions have arisen as to whether transient defects such as ice, snow, floodwater or mud on a highway can amount to a failure to maintain such as to amount to a breach of duty under s 41 of the Highways Act 1980. Flooding was first addressed in *Burnside v Emerson*.[1] This case involved a collision between two cars caused by a pool of water which was halfway across the road as a result of which one vehicle went across the road into the path of the other vehicle. It was an occasion of very heavy rainfall but the Court of Appeal did not interfere with the judge's decision that the flooding had resulted from a failure to maintain the drainage system because the drain cover was not positioned at the lowest point of the road and because the highway authority had not cleared the gutters. This amounted to a failure to maintain the highway under the predecessor to s 41 of the Highways Act 1980. Nevertheless, Lord Denning MR sought to limit the effects of the decision when he said:

'I would say that an icy patch in winter or an occasional flooding at any time is not in itself evidence of a failure to maintain. We all know that in times of heavy rain our highways do from time to time get flooded. Leaves and debris and all sorts of things may be swept in and cause flooding for a time without any failure to repair at all.'

7.47 A similar situation arose in *Pritchard v Clwyd County Council and Another*.[2] The plaintiff fell when crossing a street which was under 3–9 inches of floodwater following substantial rainfall. The Court of Appeal held that there was no evidence of a failure to maintain by the highway authority and that the collection of stormwater was a temporary event which might have been caused by debris being carried by the rain and causing a blockage of which the highway authority had no knowledge. The Court of Appeal held that the plaintiff had failed to establish any circumstance which was more consistent with a failure by the highway authority to carry out its statutory obligations than it was with one of those transient events when rainfall was so heavy that the sewers could not carry it off immediately.

7.48 It should also be mentioned that at common law it is the responsibility of the adjoining landowner to scour and cleanse roadside ditches which he owns to prevent the highway being flooded.[3] In *Thoburn v Northumberland County Council*,[4] however, the Court of Appeal held the highway authority liable for an accident caused by flooding of a road by water from a ditch crossing the neighbouring farmer's land. This ditch was a continuation of a ditch which ran alongside the road and was maintained by the authority as part of the highway to protect the road from flooding. Over its last 8 feet, however, before entering a culvert running beneath the road, the ditch turned away from the road and crossed land owned by the neighbouring farmer. A blockage in the last part of the ditch caused water in the ditch to back up and overflow onto the road. The Court of Appeal held that a failure to maintain that part of the ditch crossing the farmer's land could not make the authority liable as the

1   [1968] 1 WLR 1490.
2   [1993] PIQR 21.
3   *Attorney General v Wearing* (1899) 66 JP 789.
4   (1999) 1 LGLR 819.

Highways Act 1980 did not place any duty on the highway authority to maintain any land other than the highway. Nevertheless it decided that, referring to *Burnside v Emerson*, there was a failure to maintain the highway because the blockage of the farmer's ditch meant that the length of ditch which did form part of the highway no longer acted as a drainage system and collected the water from where it flowed onto the road. Aldous LJ said:

> 'The blockage caused an adequate system of drainage to become a system for filling the road. No doubt the fault was caused by the failure of the farmer to clear his ditch, but the result was that the highway had become impassable as the system designed to prevent flooding did not work. This was not a case of transient danger due to the elements. It was a case of the length of the ditch which was part of the highway not acting as a drain as designed. It acted as a funnel.'

7.49 The Court of Appeal then decided that the authority had not made out its defence under s 58 of the Highways Act 1980 because its officer knew that flooding could occur if the ditch blocked, had cleared the ditch on occasions and the clearing of the ditch was a straightforward exercise. The Court of Appeal stressed that its decision was based on the unusual facts of the case and did not enlarge or extend the liability of highway authorities as laid down in the established cases. The principle that the statutory duty under s 41 of the Highways Act 1980 does not extend to work on land not forming part of the highway remains intact.

7.50 It is suggested that if the claimant had also sued the neighbouring farmer, the court could, subject to the precise circumstances, have made a finding of liability against the farmer and then apportioned responsibility between him and the highway authority in accordance with general principles depending upon the parties' respective culpabilities.

7.51 The highway authority's knowledge of a particular continuing problem being caused by a transient defect is also relevant. In *Misell v Essex County Council* [1] the highway authority was held liable to a motorcyclist who suffered an accident as a result of slippery mud on the highway caused by lorries from a nearby landfill site. The court heard that the council knew of the particular problem and swept the road once a week, but considered that this was inadequate to keep the road safe and clean. Once the council knew of the particular problem at this location there was a foreseeable danger and the court held that the highway authority had taken inadequate steps to deal with the problem.

7.52 It is also worth noting *Bybrook Barn Centre Ltd and Others v Kent County Council*. [2] A culvert built by the defendant highway authority many years previously had become inadequate because of the increased flow of water upstream of the culvert. This caused flooding of the claimants' property. The Court of Appeal accepted that the culvert had been adequate when constructed. Nevertheless the court held the highway authority liable because, having built the culvert, the authority was under a 'high obligation' to see that the culvert could still take the flow of water. The authority knew that flooding had occurred, and could have enlarged the culvert easily and at limited cost.

---

1   (1994) 93 LGR 108.
2   [2001] LGR 239.

7.53   A different result is to be found in *Enion v Sefton Metropolitan Borough Council.*[1] The claimant slipped on seaweed which had been deposited on the footpath by a high tide, the road in question running along the seafront. The local authority knew that the road was flooded by high tides about 12 times a year and, knowing when high tides were likely to occur, put up warning signs indicating that the road was closed and diversions were in operation. Nevertheless the road was not entirely blocked by barriers, to allow access for emergency vehicles, and the local authority made little or no attempt to prohibit pedestrian access. Although the local authority would clean the pavement once the high tides had receded, the cleaning process had not commenced when the claimant slipped on seaweed. The trial judge considered the local authority negligent for failing to close off the road and, even more importantly, giving no signal at all to pedestrians of the dangers on the pavement. The Court of Appeal upheld the local authority's appeal. It considered that the state of the pavement was quite clear to pedestrians who could see the seaweed on the pavement. There was nothing further that any warning notice could have advised pedestrians. The claimant had failed to make out her case that the road was not reasonably safe and there was no breach of the duty to maintain under s 41 of the Highways Act 1980.

Ice and snow on the highway

7.54   The position is now covered by s 41(1A) of the Highways Act 1980 which adds the following to the existing requirement to maintain the highway:

> 'In particular, a highway authority is under a duty to ensure, so far as is reasonably practicable, that safe passage along a highway is not endangered by snow or ice.'

Section 41(1A) of the Highways Act 1980, which was inserted by s 111 of the Railways and Transport Safety Act 2003, came into force on 31 October 2003.

The position before 31 October 2003

7.55   In *Haydon v Kent County Council*,[2] the Court of Appeal held that the statutory obligation to maintain did include clearing snow and ice, or providing temporary protection by gritting. Whether there had been a breach of duty was a question of fact and degree on the facts of each particular case. In particular, the Court of Appeal considered that the time which had elapsed was relevant in deciding whether the highway authority had unreasonably failed to take remedial measures. This decision was followed by the Court of Appeal in *Cross v Kirklees Metropolitan Borough Council*,[3] where the court considered that although the duty to maintain was absolute, it was not a duty to keep the highway at all times entirely clear of surface water, snow and ice. Significantly, Cross LJ expressed the view that the duty to maintain included taking 'preventive measures'.

7.56   In *Goodes v East Sussex County Council*,[4] the House of Lords ruled that both *Haydon* and *Cross* had been wrongly decided. The claimant suffered a very severe injury when his car skidded on a patch of black ice. The case concerned the alleged

---

1   (Unreported) 9 February 1999.
2   [1978] 2 WLR 485.
3   [1998] 1 All ER 564.
4   [2000] 1 WLR 1356.

failure of the highway authority to salt the road before the accident occurred. The House of Lords noted that, at common law, the duty to maintain the highway, whether imposed upon the inhabitants at large, or transferred to highway authorities by statute, was not considered to include a duty to remove ice or snow. Still less was there a duty to take steps in advance to prevent ice forming. Their Lordships considered that the Highways Act 1959 had simply transferred the existing duty to maintain the highway from the previous highway authorities, or the inhabitants at large, to the highway authorities constituted by the 1959 Act. It was significant that the duty to maintain was absolute (the majority of the Court of Appeal in *Haydon* had been wrong to consider otherwise) and was a duty, as expressed by Diplock LJ in *Burnside v Emerson*,[1] to enable the road to be used without 'danger caused by its physical condition'.

7.57 Because of the absolute duty to maintain under s 41 of the Highways Act 1980, if it included a duty to keep the highway free of ice then no highway authority could avoid being from time to time in breach of its duty. For this reason, the House of Lords in *Goodes* considered that the duty to maintain under s 41 of the Highways Act 1980 could not include a duty to keep the highway free of ice. The majority in the Court of Appeal in *Haydon* had been in error because, in deciding that the highway authority would be in breach of duty only if it failed to take remedial measures within a reasonable time, it had ignored the absolute character of the duty to maintain and, in effect, had imported considerations more appropriate to the statutory defence under s 58 of the Highways Act 1980 (see paras **7.67** et seq).

7.58 In *Goodes* the House of Lords expressed the view that it was a matter for Parliament to consider whether the duty to maintain roads should include a duty to keep them free of ice and snow. Parliament subsequently enacted s 111 of the Railway and Transport Safety Act 2003.

Position after 31 October 2003

7.59 The new duty under s 41(1A) of the Highways Act 1980 is not an absolute duty. Parliament presumably had in mind the views of the House of Lords in *Goodes* (see para **7.56**). It remains to be seen how the courts will interpret the new duty under s 41(1A). It seems likely that the best guidance is to be obtained from the Court of Appeal decision in *Cross v Kirklees Metropolitan Borough Council*. The plaintiff slipped and fell on an icy pavement. The Court of Appeal held (at that time incorrectly) that the duty to maintain the highway included a duty to keep the highway clear of snow and ice, and take preventive measures which were sufficient to keep the surface reasonably safe. What measures were sufficient would depend in part on what use of the highway could be anticipated, and by whom. If no or insufficient measures were taken within a reasonable time and injury was caused thereby, then the plaintiff might establish at least a prima facie breach of duty under s 41. The correct question for a judge was whether the evidence established that sufficient time had elapsed to make it prima facie unreasonable for the highway authority to have failed to take remedial measures to clear snow and ice. It seems likely that this will be the test under the new s 41(1A) of the Highways Act 1980. On the facts of the case in *Cross*, the Court of Appeal decided that the highway authority was not in breach of duty.

---

1   [1968] 1 WLR 1490.

7.60 Even before the introduction of the new s 41(1A) of the Highways Act 1980, a highway authority could face liability for failing to clear ice if caused by excessive surface water which should not have been allowed to accumulate.[1]

7.61 It should be noted that s 150(1) of the Highways Act 1980 states that:

'If any obstruction arises in a highway from accumulation of snow or from the falling down of banks on the side of the highway, or from any other cause, the highway authority shall remove the obstruction.'

It is important to note, however, that the sanction for failure to comply with this section is a complaint to the magistrates' court, seeking an order requiring the highway authority to remove the obstruction. Section 150 does not confer a private law right to damages.

7.62 Section 150 of the Highways Act 1980 was considered in *Devon County Council v Webber and Another*.[2] The highway authority cleared a quantity of soil and debris from the highway, this having washed onto the road from fields owned by the defendants. The highway authority's attempt to claim the cost of removal of this debris from the defendants failed. There had been an unprecedented storm and the defendant could not reasonably have foreseen that soil from their fields would wash onto the road.

Is there a duty to clear snow and ice or take preventive measures other than under s 41(1A) of the Highways Act 1980?[3]

7.63 In *Sandhar and Another v Department of Transport, Environment and the Regions*,[4] the Court of Appeal was asked to consider one of a handful of cases where the claimant was neither able to rely on establishing a duty under s 41 of the Highways Act 1980 because of the decision in *Goodes v East Sussex County Council*,[5] nor, because of the date of the accident, to rely on the new duty under s 41(1A). The claimant's husband had died when he lost control of his car on an icy road. The Secretary of State had delegated his responsibility in respect of trunk roads to Bedfordshire County Council. On the day in question, the council relied on Met Office forecasts and decided not to arrange that roads be salted. There was available to the council a system known as 'ICELERT' which provided information from various sensors around the county. Had this system been used, the judge considered that the council would have anticipated the fall in temperature and would have ordered the roads to be salted. In the circumstances, it was likely that the accident would not have occurred.

7.64 The Court of Appeal was asked to consider whether the highway authority could be liable, in spite of the decision in *Goodes* which meant that the claimant could

1   See *Burnside v Emerson* [1968] 1 WLR 1490.
2   [2002] EWCA Civ 602, [2002] 18 EGCS 153.
3   It should be remembered that employers owe a duty of care to employees to take reasonable care to remove snow and ice where it may endanger the safety of their employees and, similarly, landowners have a duty under the Occupiers Liability Act 1957. For example, a local authority would be expected to take reasonable steps to clear snow and ice from a car park for which it was responsible.
4   [2004] EWCA (Civ) 1440, [2004] All ER (D) 105.
5   [2000] 1 WLR 1356.

not rely on alleging a failure to maintain the highway under s 41 of the Highways Act 1980.

7.65   Because of the decision in *Goodes*, s 41 of the Highways Act 1980 did not, at the time of the accident, give rise to a duty to take preventive steps by spreading salt on roads to avoid the formation of frost and ice. With some hesitation, the Court of Appeal agreed with the judge that the power to salt the highway is encompassed within work for the improvement of the highway under s 62(2) which provides as follows:

> '[A highway authority] may ... carry out in relation to a highway maintainable at the public expense by them, any work (including the provision of equipment) for the improvement of the highway.'

The Court of Appeal then went on to consider whether a common law duty of care arose in the context of the statutory framework. Guidance was to be had from the House of Lords' decision in *Gorringe v Calderdale Metropolitan Borough Council.*[1] In that case, the House of Lords considered that a common law duty could not be founded simply upon the failure to provide some benefit which a public authority has power to provide.

7.66   In *Sandhar*, the Court of Appeal accepted that before 31 October 2003, when s 41(1A) of the Highways Act 1980 came into force, there was no statutory duty giving rise to a private right of action for failure to prevent or remove ice. It then went on to consider whether there could be a common law duty of care. The relevant principles to consider were first, whether the highway authority could be taken to have assumed a general responsibility to all road users to ensure that trunk roads would be salted in freezing conditions and, secondly, whether the claimant could establish the necessary element of reliance. The Court of Appeal considered that there was no assumption of responsibility. May LJ said:

> 'It is the primary responsibility of motorists to take care for their own safety and that of their passengers and other road users.'

Similarly, the deceased was not entitled to assume that the road had been salted and there was no evidence that he had relied on an expectation that the road had been salted. Cases in which the Court of Appeal had held that a common law duty of care arose, such as *Kent v Griffiths*[2] and *Watson v British Boxing Board of Control*,[3] were cases where the defendants had assumed responsibility to a particular claimant. This was not the case in *Sandhar* and, accordingly, the Court of Appeal held that no common law duty of care arose.

THE STATUTORY DEFENCE

7.67   The old common law position was that the duty to maintain the highway lay on the inhabitants at large, namely the highway authority, but a private individual who suffered damage as a result of a highway being out of repair could not recover

---

1   [2004] UKHL 15, [2004] 2 All ER 326, and see paras **7.95–7.101**.
2   [2001] QB 36.
3   [2001] QB 1134.

damages in a civil action if the lack of repair was due to mere failure to repair, namely non-feasance. This situation continued, even when the common law duty was converted into a statutory duty to maintain the highways. However, by s 1(1) of the Highways (Miscellaneous Provisions) 1961, the exemption from liability for non-repair of a highway was removed. Had this statutory duty stood alone then the liability of the highway authority for non-feasance as well as misfeasance in maintaining the highways in its area would have been absolute. A plaintiff who proved in a civil action against the highway authority the presence of a danger in the highway which caused him to sustain damage would have been entitled to succeed without proving any lack of care on the part of the highway authority. It is for this reason that there was also provided the so-called 'statutory defence' under s 1(2) and (3) of the Highways (Miscellaneous Provisions) Act 1961. The provisions are now contained in s 58 of the Highways Act 1980 and such is the importance of this section that it is reproduced in full below:

'58. Special defence in action against a highway authority for damages for non-repair of highway

(1)   In an action against a highway authority in respect of damage resulting from their failure to maintain a highway maintainable at the public expense it is a defence (without prejudice to any other defence or the application of the law relating to contributory negligence) to prove that the authority had taken such care as in all the circumstances was reasonably required to secure that the part of the highway to which the action relates was not dangerous for traffic.

(2)   For the purposes of a defence under subsection (1) above, the court shall in particular have regard to the following matters:

(a)   the character of the highway, and the traffic which was reasonably to be expected to use it;

(b)   the standard of maintenance appropriate for a highway of that character and used by such traffic;

(c)   the state of repair in which a reasonable person would have expected to find the highway;

(d)   whether the highway authority knew, or could reasonably have been expected to know, that the condition of the part of the highway to which the action relates was likely to cause danger to users of the highway;

(e)   where the highway authority could not reasonably have been expected to repair that part of the highway before the cause of action arose, what warning notices of its condition had been displayed.

But for the purposes of such a defence it is not relevant to prove that the highway authority had arranged for a competent person to carry out or supervise the maintenance of the part of the highway to which the action relates unless it is also proved that the authority had given him proper instructions with regard to the maintenance of the highway and that he had carried out the instructions.

(3)   This section binds the Crown.'

7.68   The onus is on the highway authority to prove the defence on the balance of probabilities.

7.69   When ss 41 and 58 of the Highways Act 1980 are juxtaposed, a question arises as to what the correct approach of a court should be. This was dealt with by Steyn LJ in

Mills v Barnsley Metropolitan Borough Council[1] when he explained that in order for a plaintiff to succeed against a highway authority in a claim for personal injury for failure to maintain or repair the highway, the plaintiff must prove that:

(1) the highway was in such a condition that it was dangerous to traffic or pedestrians;
(2) the dangerous condition was created by the failure to maintain or repair the highway; and
(3) the injury or damage resulted from such a failure.

Steyn LJ then went on:

> 'Only if the Plaintiff proves these "facta probanda" does it become necessary to turn to the Highway Authority's reliance on the special defence under Section 58(1) of the 1980 Act, namely, that the authority had taken such care as in all the circumstances was reasonably required to secure that the particular part of the highway was not dangerous to traffic. On this aspect the burden rests on the Highway Authority.'

7.70   In *Griffiths v Liverpool Corporation*,[2] the majority of the Court of Appeal held that the defendants had failed to make out their statutory defence in circumstances where the highway authority admitted that it had no system of inspection because it had insufficient workmen to repair the pavements in its area even though it could have employed sufficient highway inspectors. The Court of Appeal was no doubt understandably unimpressed with this argument and even more so when the highway authority admitted that it could have made safe the particular defect concerned had it been discovered.

7.71   Guidance as to the requirements to establish the statutory defence was provided by the Court of Appeal in *Pridham v Hemel Hempstead Corporation*.[3] The plaintiff caught her foot in a hole in the pavement of a residential road and suffered injury. At first instance, Mocatta J held that the condition of the footpath where the plaintiff tripped was defective so as to establish a breach of duty to maintain on the part of the highway authority. He also held that the highway authority had failed to establish its statutory defence under what was then s 1(2) of the Highways (Miscellaneous Provisions) Act 1961. The evidence was that the council had, in conjunction with other councils, consulted as to the way in which highway inspections should be carried out. As a result, it appointed a full-time highway inspector and divided the highways in its area into different classes: those on which a lot of traffic would normally be expected to travel, both vehicular and pedestrian, were to be examined monthly; the less frequented roads were to be inspected once every 2 months; still less frequently, roads, of which this particular road was one, were to be examined quarterly.

7.72   The judge, and, initially, the Court of Appeal, were concerned that the highway authority had called no evidence to establish whether the inspection regime decided upon by the highway authority was reasonable. Thereafter, as was pointed out by the Court of Appeal, the judge appeared to conclude that the system decided upon was a good one, but he had gone on to consider whether the highway inspector could, in fact,

---

1   [1992] PIQR 291.
2   [1966] 2 WLR 467. See also para **7.33**.
3   (1971) 69 LGR 523.

have carried out more frequent inspections. The judge decided that as it was practicable that the highway inspector could have carried out inspections on a more frequent basis, the highway authority system was not reasonable. The Court of Appeal did not agree. The Court of Appeal also concluded that it did not need expert evidence to establish that the system was reasonable and could look at the matter broadly when deciding how often a particular road should be inspected. Davies LJ said:

> 'It seems to me that it is wrong to depart from the words of the section,[1] the test there being reasonableness, and to substitute practicability. Of course it would be practicable to inspect more often than once every three months. It would, I suppose, be practicable to have these streets inspected once a month or once a week or, I suppose, putting it in the extreme, once a day, if it were practicable to get and pay the men to do it. But nobody I think would say that was reasonable. In my view, if it was a reasonable system (as I think it was), then the fact that it was practicable to do more does not make the system not reasonable.'

7.73 The courts have also made it clear that when considering the statutory defence it is necessary to consider whether the highway authority has established its defence in relation to the location of the accident rather than considering the highway authority's system as a whole. Therefore, in *Jacobs v Hampshire County Council*,[2] Skinner J held that a 6-monthly inspection of a highway the surface of which was susceptible to water penetration which could have caused holes to appear within 2 months did not enable the highway authority to succeed with its statutory defence. The judge said that in determining the regularity of highway inspections, the highway authority should take account of the sort of traffic which would foreseeably use the highway and the character of the road itself. It should also take account of the actual design of the carriageway concerned. In this particular case there was no tarmac adjoining the cobbles at the edge of the carriageway, rendering it particularly vulnerable to water penetration.

7.74 By contrast, in *Allen v Elmbridge Borough Council*,[3] the judge considered that the defendant's system of classification of the road as a 'local access road' was reasonable. Mr Recorder R Hunt QC, sitting as a deputy High Court judge said:

> 'I find that a twelve-monthly inspection of such a road as this was reasonable, and that a policy of otherwise reacting to specific individual complaints, and taking reports from staff, police and public, was operating and was operated reasonably. In short, the statutory defence under s 58 of the Highways Act is available to the Defendants.'

7.75 In *Allen v Newcastle City Council*,[4] a decision in the Newcastle-upon-Tyne County Court, the plaintiff tripped while descending steps where paving slabs had been dislodged, creating a danger. The court heard that the section of footpath had been inspected on three occasions in the 16 months prior to the plaintiff's accident. On the first inspection a defect in the steps had been reported which was repaired and the defect did not appear on the two further inspection reports prior to the accident. The judge held that there was a regular system of inspection in the area which was being carried out properly. It was submitted on the plaintiff's behalf that there were only five highway inspectors working for the authority and that this could not be sufficient to

---

1 Highways (Miscellaneous Provisions) Act 1961, s 1(2).
2 (1994) *The Times*, May 28.
3 [1999] LGR 65.
4 [1995] CLY 3664.

cover the authority's highways adequately. The judge held, however, that it was necessary only to determine whether the area in which the plaintiff's accident occurred was inspected regularly. He found that the system of inspections was reasonable and that the local authority had established its statutory defence.

7.76   In *Williams v Knowsley Borough Council*,[1] the highway authority succeeded in establishing a defence under s 58 of the Highways Act 1980 in spite of evidence that its system of inspection was inadequate. The claimant tripped over a paving stone in May 1992. The council had no regular system of inspection, but there had been an isolated inspection only 7 weeks before the accident. The judge found that the defect was so substantial that it must have been observed had it been present at the time of this inspection. He therefore concluded that the defect had not existed at that stage. The plaintiff argued that the highway authority could not establish a defence under s 58 because its system of inspection was inadequate. However, in the Court of Appeal, Otton LJ did not agree:

> 'The failure to inspect annually did not preclude the defendant from proving that they did, in fact, inspect before the accident and that the seven weeks interval was a reasonable interval. In other words, the fact that the system of inspection was unreasonable or inadequate did not preclude the defendant from raising the statutory defence and relying upon the evidence of the last inspection.'

The Court of Appeal accepted the judge's finding that the defect had not existed 7 weeks before the accident and accordingly the highway authority could not be in breach of duty for having failed to repair a defect about which it had no knowledge.

7.77   What then is the evidence required to establish that the system of maintenance and repair is adequate in all the circumstances, and upon what basis will a court decide upon that adequacy? The court will want to know how the highway authority uses its resources for routine maintenance and repair. Depending upon the circumstances of each case, the evidence will have to include details of the classification of highways, the inspection frequency of each classification of highway, the criteria for what amounts to 'lack of repair' and the prioritisation of the repairs. However, the system must be such that it is reasonable and adequate in all the circumstances taking into account national criteria and what is generally acceptable through the country.

7.78   In 1970, the *Report of the Committee on Highway Maintenance*[2] was published, which set out detailed recommended standards for highway maintenance. That report has been succeeded by *Highway Maintenance: A Code of Good Practice*[3] published from time to time which sets out up-to-date recommended standards. Although none of these publications has any statutory force, they do represent the best evidence available of what those concerned with highway maintenance nationally regard to be good practice and acceptable standards. Additionally, the Department of Transport has issued its own 'Code of Good Practice' for the maintenance of trunk and similar roads. It is also open to highway authorities to issue their own standing instructions for the standards to be adopted as regards the highways within their own

---

1   (Unreported) 17 January 1996.
2   HMSO, 1970, ISBN 0 11 550155 X (the so-called 'Marshall Report').
3   The latest version was published by the Association of County Councils, Association of District Councils, Association of Metropolitan Authorities and the Convention of Scottish Local Authorities.

area, which can be based upon the various Codes of Good Practice, but adapted to local requirements.

7.79 The second limb of the defence will entail proof of the operation of the system in the circumstances of the particular case. Clearly that will involve evidence from the highways inspector as well as evidence of how and when any defects were repaired. Of crucial importance also will be the question of knowledge. If the highway authority either did have or should have had knowledge of a particular defect or need for repair, then the s 58 defence will fail. Such knowledge can derive not only from the highways inspector, but also from other relevant council employees who might be aware of any particular problems, complaints from the public, other accidents, and complaints from the police or parish council. Knowledge of other accidents can derive not only from the official accident statistics maintained by the highway authority, but also from less formal reports of perhaps damage-only accidents of which the council might have notice by virtue, for example, of the finance department seeking to recover the costs of damage to road signs or street furniture.

7.80 The courts' approach to the various Codes of Practice is illustrated by *Rance v Essex County Council*[1] (see para **7.7**). The problem in this case was the existence of ruts in the grass verge caused by heavy lorries leaving a construction site. The evidence was that the highway authority was aware of the problem and had decided to wait until the volume of heavy traffic had abated before repairing the damage to the ruts. There was evidence from a witness called by the council that it was familiar with the fact that there was a publication of good practice to be applied by highway authorities. The guide recommended monthly inspections for the type of road concerned while the last inspection of the stretch of road had occurred some 18 months prior to the accident. There was also evidence that the council's system of recording complaints was not working. In dealing with the statutory defence Otton LJ said:

> 'It is true that the Code of Practice sets down stringent obligations upon Highways Authorities, but it must be borne in mind that they are recognised as guidelines only and do not impose a rigid regime for the inspection and maintenance of roads. It does not follow that the breach of the code, however technical, automatically creates a situation of negligence on the part of the Highway Authority, or, conversely, as Counsel for the Plaintiff seems to suggest, deprives them of the benefit of that defence even though such a breach was not causative of the accident complained of.

> It may be that their system of recording complaints was defective. That would only be relevant if the Highway Authority tried to prove that they were unaware of the existence of the danger in question. Here it was clear that they knew about the existence of the ruts, they had discovered it for themselves, and that they were monitoring the ruts on a frequent basis. Their inspectors and others within the relevant department were frequent users of the road and were aware of the existence of the ruts, the presence of mud upon the road and the fact that the ruts were getting deeper. They were also aware that some complaints were being made, albeit primarily targeted at the presence of the mud upon the road to such an extent that there was danger of skidding. There can be little doubt that the Local Authority did consider the situation, kept it under observation and made a deliberate decision that in the light of the progress of the construction works any remedial work should be held back until the heavy construction work had been completed, and that they could then reinstate or repair the works at that time.

---

1   (Unreported) 21 February 1997.

The Judge took into account that the road was a secondary feeder and came to the conclusion that he accepted the Defendant's explanation and that in so doing they had discharged the burden of proof and could avail themselves of the statutory defence.'

Otton LJ went on to confirm that the judge was entitled to reach the conclusion that he did based on the evidence before him.

7.81 In *Stringer v Bedfordshire County Council*,[1] the claimant alleged that the highway authority had failed to maintain the surface of an 'A' road where resurfacing had been carried out on either side of the site of her accident, but there was a gap of about 30 m where no resurfacing had been carried out. Burton J held that on the facts there had been no failure to maintain. He went on, however, to deal, obiter, with the statutory defence. The defendant had records showing that there had been two personal injury accidents and one damage-only accident at the location in the 3 years prior to the accident. The highway authority followed a system of considering further investigations if there were three or more personal injury accidents in a highway location in any 3-year period. Burton J considered that the authority's system of considering further investigation only if there were three personal injury accidents in a period of 3 years was reasonable and he noted that an even less stringent policy of a need for five personal injury accidents in 3 years before special attention was merited had been referred to without criticism by Lord Hoffmann in *Stovin v Wise*.[2]

Position of contractors and statutory bodies

7.82 A person who carries out work in the highway is under a common-law duty to take reasonable care to avoid injury to members of the public as a result. Ordinarily, the carrying-out of works in the highway will be governed by Part III of the New Roads and Street Works Act 1991 which contains provisions, inter alia, for the issuing by the contractor or undertaker of an advance notice, a starting notice, a notice of interim reinstatement (works clear notice) and a notice of permanent reinstatement.

7.83 An undertaker with apparatus in a highway must make sure that it is maintained to the reasonable satisfaction of the highway authority under s 81 of the New Roads and Street Works Act 1991.

7.84 The position where a pedestrian trips over apparatus which is the responsibility of one of the various utility companies was considered by the Court of Appeal in *Nolan v Merseyside County Council and Another*.[3] The plaintiff tripped over a hole in the pavement which was about 8 inches square and 4½ inches deep where a cover to a hydrant point owned by North West Water Authority should have been present, but was missing. The Court of Appeal agreed with the judge that the highway authority was in breach of its duty to maintain the highway. The water authority was held liable for a failure to carry out any necessary works of maintenance or repair as required by the Water Act 1945. The matter came before the Court of Appeal on an argument as to the correct apportionment between the water authority, on the one hand, and the highway authority, on the other. The judge had held that the highway authority was entitled to a full indemnity from the water authority. The Court of Appeal disagreed

---

1   (Unreported) 27 July 1999.
2   [1996] AC 923.
3   (Unreported) 15 July 1982.

and held that liability to the plaintiff should be apportioned between the defendants on a 50/50 basis. May LJ said:

> 'If one remembers that the plaintiff was entitled to succeed against each of the defendants in this case on the ground of a breach by each of them respectively of an absolute statutory duty without otherwise any moral or legal "fault" or turpitude on either side, then we do not see how one can differentiate in any way between their several "responsibilities" for the plaintiff's damage.'

7.85 Section 82(1) of the New Roads and Street Works Act 1991 provides that an undertaker must compensate the appropriate person with apparatus in the street for damage to that apparatus caused by his work, irrespective of negligence, provided that there has been no negligence on the part of the owner of the apparatus. This therefore provides a method by which, for example, an electricity or water company can recover the cost of repairing cables or pipes damaged by works in the highway. Even if the Act does not apply, there may still be liability if negligence can be proved.

7.86 The position of the highway authority where another party is also under a duty to maintain part of the highway was considered in *Roe v Sheffield City Council and Others*.[1] The Court of Appeal was asked to decide whether a highway authority continues to have a duty to maintain the highway pursuant to s 41 of the Highways Act 1980 following the installation of a tramway. The claimant was injured when the wheels of the car he was driving came into contact with tram rails and he lost control of the car through no fault of his own. The highway authority argued that its duty under s 41 of the Highways Act 1980 was displaced by the duties imposed on the tramway operator by ss 25 and 28 of the Tramways Act 1870, as incorporated into the South Yorkshire Light Rail Transit Act 1988. The Court of Appeal decided that the highway authority's duty was not displaced. Although the 1870 Act did give rise to a private law cause of action against the tramway operator, nevertheless this did not displace the duty on the highway authority under s 41 of the Highways Act 1980. The tramway operator was obliged to comply with inspections by the highway authority and take action to the satisfaction of the highway authority. This provided certain safeguards for the highway authority. Furthermore, the Court of Appeal considered that the statutory provisions reflected what was sensible in terms of public needs and safety by retaining the highway authority's duty to road users.

CONTRIBUTORY NEGLIGENCE

7.87 Where a breach of duty under s 41 of the Highways Act 1980 has been established and there is no defence under s 58, the courts must still consider whether, depending upon the circumstances, the claimant's damages should be reduced by reason of his own contributory negligence. Allegations of contributory negligence against a claimant might include such matters as the wearing of unsuitable footwear, running or hurrying, not looking where he was going and previous knowledge of the defect in question. In an extreme case it has been held that a claimant, who knew of the defect outside her front gate because she had been reporting it repeatedly to the highway authority, was guilty of contributory negligence to the extent of 100 per

---

1   [2003] LGR 389.

cent.[1] The Court of Session in Edinburgh reduced an award of damages by one-third where the claimant tripped over a raised kerb and fell into the path of a van. He had been asked to leave a bar after drinking six pints of beer. Lord Osborne[2] said:

> 'The roads authority ought reasonably to foresee that pedestrians who may be to some extent under the influence of alcohol may walk along the footpath without paying too close attention to the form of the footpath.'

7.88   In carriageway accidents, it can always be argued that the motorist should drive at a safe speed and in a safe manner appropriate in all the circumstances. Thus if the highway authority is liable under s 41 because a particular section of highway was substandard in relation to skid resistance, the plaintiff's damages can be reduced if it can be established that he was travelling at an excessive speed for the wet weather conditions and that had he been travelling at a proper speed the accident would not have occurred. Similarly, where there is an accident between two motorists, with an allegation by the defendant motorist that the condition of the highway was a contributory factor, then normally even if there is liability on the highway authority, that liability will only be for a minority proportion of the plaintiff's damages. Thus in *Bird v Pearce and Somerset County Council*,[3] where warning signs and white line markings at a 'T' junction had been obliterated by resurfacing works, the highway authority was held to be in breach of s 41 but only to the extent of one-third of the plaintiff's damages. The primary responsibility still rested with the motorist approaching the junction along the minor road. Similarly, in *Burnside v Emerson*,[4] where the highway authority had failed to maintain the highway, and the road was flooded by heavy rainfall, the Court of Appeal considered that the motorist, who had lost control of his vehicle in the floodwater, still carried the greater responsibility. The highway authority again only had to pay one-third of the plaintiff's damages.

7.89   In *Sandhar v Department of Transport, Environment and the Regions*,[5] where the motorist had lost control of his car in icy conditions, Newman J indicated that he would have held the motorist one-third to blame for driving at an excessive speed in known frosty conditions. In *Great North Eastern Railway Limited v Hart*,[6] where the motorist fell asleep and his vehicle came to rest on the main railway line, Morland J said that if he had found that the highway authority should have extended the protective safety barriers, he would have apportioned liability between the highway authority and the motorist on a 50:50 basis. Finally, in *Thompson v Hampshire County Council*,[7] the Court of Appeal approved a finding of contributory negligence of one-third in circumstances where the claimant had fallen in a ditch while walking in darkness without carrying a torch.

---

1   *McClurrey v Copeland Borough Council*, Workington County Court 1998. (This case is not, of course, authority but merely an example.)
2   *Kemp v Scottish Secretary* 1999 Rep LR 110.
3   (1979) 77 LGR 753.
4   [1968] 1 WLR 1490.
5   [2004] EWHC 28 (QB), (unreported) 19 January 2004.
6   (Unreported) 30 October 2003.
7   [2004] EWCA Civ 1016, (unreported) 27 July 2004.

COMMON LAW NEGLIGENCE

7.90   Normally the liability of a highway authority will arise under its statutory duty under the Highways Act 1980. Nevertheless, an example otherwise is *Cassin v Bexley London Borough Council and Another*.[1] The claimant rode his motor bicycle over the plinth of a 'keep left' sign on the highway. The London Borough of Bexley had agreed with the police to remove potential missiles from the route of a march. Accordingly the local authority agreed to remove bollards, but only once the road could not be used, or users had been alerted to the danger. The bollards were removed by contractors on behalf of the London Borough of Bexley, but the local authority did not find out if the road had been closed by the police or if notices had been erected notifying road users of the lack of adequate traffic signs. The Court of Appeal relied on *Donoghue v Stevenson*[2] in deciding that there was a duty of care on the highway authority where the road remains in use. The highway authority had no power to close the road and only the police could do so. Either the local authority should have ascertained that the road was closed or it should have ascertained that adequate signs were in place. Roch LJ said:

'There is no issue here but that the duty on the highway authority was to take reasonable care to see that persons using the highway could do so safely. In this instance the discharge of that duty required that bollards should not be removed until motor vehicles could no longer use the road.'

Peter Gibson LJ said:

'Bexley London Borough Council, as the highway authority, had the responsibility for the state of the highway so long as the highway was in use by motorists . . .'

It should be noted that the Court of Appeal refused to interfere with the trial judge's apportionment of responsibilty on the basis of one-third to the highway authority and two-thirds to the police.

7.91   A highway authority's common-law duty of care was also considered by the House of Lords in *Gorringe v Calderdale Metropolitan Borough Council*.[3] Although there was no question of a breach of any common-law duty of care in *Gorringe*, Lord Hoffmann appeared to accept that such a duty can exist when he said:

'But I would certainly accept the principle that if a highway authority conducts itself so as to create a reasonable expectation about the state of the highway, it will be under a duty to ensure that it does thereby create a trap for the careful motorist who drives in reliance upon such an expectation.'

7.92   Lord Hoffmann was considering the Court of Appeal decision in *Bird v Pearce*,[4] where the court had decided that a highway authority was liable for failing to replace warning signs which it had removed from a road junction. Lord Rodger's analysis of the same case was that the Court of Appeal had taken the view that by failing to repaint the warning sign, the highway authority had negligently created a danger to motorists which would not otherwise have existed. He then went on:

1   [1999] LGR 694.
2   [1932] AC 562.
3   [2004] UKHL 15, [2004] 2 All ER 326, and see paras **7.95–7.101**.
4   (1979) 77 LGR 753.

'Assuming that this was correct, on ordinary common law principles the council were liable to the plaintiff who suffered injury due to the danger which they had created. The fact that the authority had been exercising a statutory power when they created the danger was irrelevant, since there was nothing in the statute to provide them with a defence against their common law liability.'

DOES A COMMON LAW DUTY OF CARE ARISE OUT OF THE HIGHWAY AUTHORITY'S DISCRETIONARY POWERS?

7.93   The cases dealt with above have all arisen out of the duty to maintain the highway found in s 41 of the Highways Act 1980. There have, however, been cases arising out of various powers given to highway authorities. For example, in *Lavis v Kent County Council*,[1] the court was concerned with an accident at a junction where the plaintiff, who was riding a motorcycle, failed to stop and finished in the grass verge on the other side of the junction, suffering very serious injuries. It was the plaintiff's case that the highway authority was liable for failing to erect signs or put markings on the road to warn of the junction in addition to the transverse double broken white lines indicating 'Give Way' at the junction. The relevant statutory provision, s 65 of the Road Traffic Regulation Act 1984, simply gives the highway authority a power to erect traffic signs, but imposes no duty. The case came before the Court of Appeal which allowed an appeal against an earlier decision striking out the claim as disclosing no cause of action.[2] In dealing with the appeal, however, Steyn LJ made it clear that the Court of Appeal considered that the duty under s 41 of the Highways Act 1980 did not cover the erection of traffic signs.

7.94   When the matter came for hearing before the trial judge,[3] he considered that a highway authority should not completely shut its eyes to the possibility that through momentary inadvertence a motorist might not adhere to the provisions of the Highway Code and that some allowance should be made for this when considering whether, and if so what, road signs should be placed on a road or at a junction, but he held that any such duty did not extend to motorists who were plainly disregarding the provisions of the Highway Code by, for example, driving at an excessive speed. The judge referred in passing to *Levine and Another v Morris and Another*[4] where the Court of Appeal considered that there was a duty on the Ministry of Transport to take care, when siting what was described as a 'massive traffic sign', so as not to select a site which involved materially greater hazard to the motorist than would another site with equally good visibility. However, the Court of Appeal in *Levine* was dealing with the actual positioning of the sign and not with the discretion as to whether or not to erect a sign. It is also significant to note that the Court of Appeal refused to interfere with the trial judge's finding that the driver should bear 75 per cent of the responsibility for the accident.

7.95   A highway authority's duties in relation to the placing of signs has now been considered by the House of Lords in *Gorringe v Calderdale Metropolitan Borough*

---

1   (1992) 90 LGR 416.
2   Arguably, the Court of Appeal would have decided differently if the case had come before it following the House of Lords' decision in *Stovin v Wise*, which is dealt with below.
3   (1994) *The Times*, November 24.
4   [1970] 1 All ER 144.

Council.[1] The claimant was injured when she drove her car head-on into a bus. The bus was hidden behind a sharp crest in the road until just before the claimant reached the top of the crest. When she first caught sight of the bus, a curve on the far side of the crest may have given her the impression that the bus was actually on her side of the road. In any event she applied her brakes and skidded into the bus. The claimant alleged that the council caused the accident by failing to give her proper warning of the danger presented by the sharp crest in the road. In particular she alleged that the council should have painted the word 'SLOW' on the road surface at some point before the crest. There had been such a marking in the past, but it had disappeared, probably when the road was mended 7 or 8 years before.

7.96 The House of Lords was in no doubt that the duty to maintain the highway under s 41 of the Highways Act 1980 did not extend to the provision of information, whether by street furniture or painted signs.

7.97 *Gorringe* turned on whether a common-law duty had been created by, or in parallel with, s 39 of the Road Traffic Act 1988 which states:

'(2)   Each local authority must prepare and carry out a programme of measures designed to promote road safety . . .

(3)   Without prejudice to the generality of sub-section (2) above, in pursuance of their duty under that sub-section each local authority –

(a) must carry out studies into accidents arising out of the use of vehicles on roads . . . within their area;

(b) must, in the light of those studies, take such measures as appear to the authority to be appropriate to prevent such accidents, including the dissemination of information and advice relating to the use of roads, the giving of practical training to road users or any class or description of road users, the construction, improvement, maintenance or repair of roads for which they are the highway authority . . . and other measures taken in the exercise of their powers for controlling, protecting or assisting the movement of traffic on roads . . .'

Although the House of Lords accepted that the provisions of s 39 impose statutory duties on highway authorities, they are typical public law duties expressed in wide and general terms and, as Lord Hoffmann said:

'No-one suggests that such duties are enforceable by a private individual in an action for breach of statutory duty. They are enforceable, so far as they are justiciable at all, only in proceedings for judicial review.'

7.98 The claimant relied on the decision of the Court of Appeal in *Larner v Solihull Metropolitan Borough Council,*[2] a case which was similar on its facts to that of *Gorringe*. Although the Court of Appeal had decided the case in favour of the highway authority, nevertheless it had not ruled out the possible existence of a duty of care in the circumstances alleged. According to Lord Woolf CJ:

'However, so far as section 39 of the 1988 Act is concerned, we would accept that there can be circumstances of an exceptional nature where a common law liability can arise. For that to happen, it would have to be shown that the default of the authority falls outside the ambit of discretion given to the authority by the section. This would happen if an authority acted wholly unreasonably . . . As long as any common law duty is confined in this way,

---

1   [2004] UKHL 15, [2004] 2 All ER 326.
2   [2001] LGR 255.

there are no policy reasons which are sufficient to exclude the duty. An authority could rely on lack of resources for not taking action and then it would not be in breach ... These difficulties in the way of claimants mean that the existence of the residual common law duty should not give rise to a flood of litigation. On the other hand for the desirability of a duty in the exceptional case we adopt the reasons of Lord Nicholls of Birkenhead in *Stovin*.'

7.99   The House of Lords in *Gorringe* was clear in its view that in *Stovin v Wise*:[1]

'The majority (of the House of Lords) rejected the argument that the existence of the statutory power to make improvements to the highway could in itself give rise to a common law duty to take reasonable care to exercise the power or even not to be irrational in failing to do so.'

Lord Hoffmann summarised his view as follows:

'Speaking for myself, I find it difficult to imagine a case in which a common law duty can be founded simply upon the failure (however irrational) to provide some benefit which a public authority has power (or a public law duty) to provide.'

7.100   It is important to note that *Gorringe* was concerned with a case in which the council was not alleged to have done anything to give rise to a duty of care. The House of Lords distinguished the Court of Appeal decision in *Bird v Pearce*,[2] a case, at first sight, involving facts similar to those in *Gorringe* and *Larner*. The highway authority had removed and failed to repaint the warning lines which customarily indicated to drivers that they were emerging from a minor road onto a major road. Four weeks after the road markings had been obliterated, the first defendant, driving his car, emerged from the minor road and collided with a vehicle travelling along the major road, injuring the plaintiff in the action. The Court of Appeal decided that the highway authority was liable. The Court of Appeal appears to have approached the case on the basis that the council had created an expectation on the part of users of the major road that there would be lines to warn people on side roads that they were entering a major road. In *Gorringe* Lord Hoffmann wondered if this was a 'rather artificial assumption' and he expressed no view as to whether *Bird v Pearce* had been correctly decided. However, he then said:

'I would certainly accept the principle that if a highway authority conducts itself so as to create a reasonable expectation about the state of the highway, it will be under a duty to ensure that it does not thereby create a trap for the careful motorist who drives in reliance upon such an expectation.'

7.101   Lord Rodger justified the decision in *Bird v Pearce* on ordinary common law principles:

'In other words, the council had exercised their power under section 55(1) of the Road Traffic Regulation Act 1967 to paint signs on the road to assist drivers but, by failing to repaint and so breaking the pattern, had negligently created a danger to motorists which would not otherwise have existed. Assuming that this was correct, on ordinary common law principles the council were liable to the plaintiff who suffered injury due to the danger which they had created. The fact that the authority had been exercising a statutory power when they created the danger was irrelevant, since there was nothing in the statute to provide them with a defence against their common law liability.'

---

1   [1996] AC 923.
2   (1979) 77 LGR 753.

7.102 In the earlier case of *West v Buckinghamshire County Council*,[1] Caulfield J held that decisions taken by the council as to the circumstances in which lines prohibiting overtaking should be placed on the road in question, the frequency of inspections, the keeping of accident statistics and the consideration of complaints about the road, were policy decisions which the council was entitled to take in the exercise of its discretion under the relevant statutory provision.[2]

7.103 In *Bustill v Leeds City Council*,[3] the court dealt with an accident in which a pedestrian was struck by a car. It was alleged that the accident had occurred because three nearby street lights were unlit. The judge, in fact, gave judgment for the highway authority on the basis that it had an adequate system of inspections and that these inspections had been carried out. In the course of his judgment, however, McKinnon J considered s 97(1) of the Highways Act 1980 which provides the highway authority with a discretion as to the construction and maintenance of lamps and lamp posts. The question of whether there was a duty on the highway authority to inspect and maintain street lighting was not fully argued and was not essential to the judge's decision; however, he expressly doubted whether there is a duty on the highway authority to inspect and maintain the street lighting.

Stovin v Wise

7.104 The House of Lords has now made clear in *Stovin v Wise*[4] that there will be few, if any, cases in which the courts will impose liability for a negligent failure to exercise a statutory power. The plaintiff was injured when his motorcycle collided with a car driven by the defendant at a junction where the view from the plaintiff's direction of the side road from which the defendant emerged was obscured by an earth bank which was adjacent to the road and on land owned by the railway. The court heard that the highway authority was aware that the presence of the bank made the junction dangerous and that it had approached the railway authority with an offer to remove the bank and pay the cost, but at the time of the accident no further action had been taken.

7.105 Under s 79 of the Highways Act 1980, the highway authority has a power to require the owner or occupier of land to alter any wall, fence, tree or other vegetation on the land so as to prevent danger arising from obstruction from the view of persons using the highway. This was held by the court to include a power to require the removal of the bank on the railway land.

7.106 The courts were concerned that the imposition of liability on the highway authority would involve imposing liability for an omission which normally the courts are reluctant to do. Lord Hoffmann said:

'In the case of positive acts, therefore, the liability of a public authority in tort is in principle the same as that of a private person but may be *restricted* by its statutory powers and duties. The argument in the present case, however, is that whereas the private person would have owed no duty of care in respect of an omission to remove the hazard at the junction, the duty of the Highway Authority is *enlarged* by virtue of its statutory powers.

1   (1984) 83 LGR 449.
2   Road Traffic Regulation Act 1967, s 55(1).
3   (Unreported) 21 December 1994.
4   [1996] 3 WLR 388.

The existence of the statutory powers is said to create a "proximity" between the Highway Authority and the highway user which would not otherwise exist.'

7.107 Lord Hoffmann went on to say that he was not prepared to hold that a statutory power could never give rise to a common law duty of care but he considered that the fact that Parliament had conferred a discretion must be some indication that the policy of the statute conferring the power was not to create a right to compensation. Summarising his views he said:

'I think that the minimum pre-conditions for basing a duty of care upon the existence of a statutory power, if it can be done at all, are, first, that it would in the circumstances have been irrational not to have exercised the power, so that there was in effect a public law duty to act, and secondly, that there are exceptional grounds for holding that the policy of the statute requires compensation to be paid to persons who suffer loss because the power was not exercised.'

7.108 Lord Hoffmann then went on to consider the question of particular and general reliance. He referred to the argument that a statutory power can never generate a common law duty of care unless the public authority has created an expectation that the power will be used and the plaintiff has suffered damage from reliance on that expectation. Lord Hoffmann made it clear that he did not consider that *Stovin v Wise* fell within such a category, but he went on to say:

'It appears to be essential to the doctrine of general reliance that the benefit or service provided under statutory powers should be of a uniform and routine nature, so that one can describe exactly what the public authority was supposed to do ...

Another way of looking at the matter is to say that if a particular service is provided as a matter of routine, it would be irrational for a public authority to provide it in one case and arbitrarily withhold it in another.'

7.109 Turning to the facts of the particular case, Lord Hoffmann noted that the council had agreed to remove the bank, but had not yet done so before the accident occurred. Nevertheless he did not consider that this showed that it would have been unreasonable or irrational for the council not to have done the work. The timing of the work was in his view as much a matter of discretion as the decision in principle to do it and his Lordship asked why the council should be in a worse position than if the council officers had left the relevant report at the bottom of the in-tray and forgotten about it. His Lordship went on:

'It seems to me, therefore, that the question of whether anything should be done about the junction was at all times firmly within the area of the Council's discretion. As they were therefore not under a public law duty to do the work, the first condition for the imposition of a duty of care was not satisfied.

But even if it were, I do not think that the second condition would be satisfied. Assuming that the Highway Authority ought, as a matter of public law to have done the work, I do not think that there are any grounds upon which it can be said that the public law duty should give rise to an obligation to compensate persons who have suffered loss because it was not performed. There is no question here of reliance on the Council having improved the junction. Everyone could see that it was still the same. Mr Stovin was not arbitrarily denied a benefit which was routinely provided to others. In respect of the junction, he was treated in exactly the same way as any other road user. The foundation for the doctrine of general reliance is missing in this case, because we are not concerned with provision of a uniform identifiable benefit or service. Every hazardous junction, intersection or stretch of road is different and requires a separate decision as to whether anything should be done to improve it.'

7.110   Finally, Lord Hoffmann stated:

'Denial of liability does not leave the road user unprotected. Drivers of vehicles must take the highway network as they find it. Everyone knows that there are hazardous bends, intersections and junctions. It is primarily the duty of drivers of vehicles to take due care and if, as in the case of Mrs Wise, they do not, there is compulsory insurance to provide compensation to the victims. There is no reason of policy or justice which requires the Highway Authority to be an additional Defendant.'

7.111   Lord Hoffmann had the opportunity to look again at *Stovin v Wise* in the case of *Gorringe v Calderdale Metropolitan Borough Council*,[1] where it was alleged that the council should have placed a warning sign on the road advising motorists to slow down before a sharp crest in the road. The House of Lords rejected a claim that a common law duty had been created by s 39 of the Road Traffic Act 1988. Lord Hoffmann said:

'Speaking for myself, I find it difficult to imagine a case in which a common law duty can be founded simply upon the failure (however irrational) to provide some benefit which a public authority has power (or a public law duty) to provide. . . . my Lords, in this case, the council is not alleged to have done anything to give rise to a duty of care. The complaint is that it did nothing. Section 39 is the sole ground upon which it is alleged to have had a common law duty to act. In my opinion the statute could not have created such a duty.'

7.112   Lord Hoffmann considered that this followed the decision of the majority in *Stovin v Wise*. He expressed the view that a misunderstanding appeared to have arisen because the majority in *Stovin v Wise*, having concluded that the council owed no duty to road users which could have required the council to improve the intersection, then went on to discuss the nature of such duty which might be said to exist. Noting the suggestion in *Stovin v Wise* that liability might arise if it would have been irrational in a public law sense not to exercise the statutory power to do the work, Lord Hoffmann said:

'The suggestion that there might exceptionally be a case in which a breach of a public law duty could found a private law right of action has proved controversial and it may have been ill-advised to speculate upon such matters.'

7.113   *Stovin v Wise* was considered by the Court of Appeal in *Kane v New Forest District Council*.[2] The local planning authority required the developer of a housing estate to construct a footpath. The footpath crossed a busy main road at a dangerous location which provided limited visibility for motorists. There were discussions with the local highway authority and a local landowner which were intended to result in the provision of improved sightlines, making the location of the footpath safer. However, before any work could be carried out, the claimant was seriously injured when emerging from the footpath onto the main road. Relying, inter alia, on *Stovin v Wise*, the claim had been struck out as disclosing no reasonable prospect of success. The Court of Appeal, however, upheld the appeal and reinstated the claim. The court distinguished *Stovin* on the basis that in *Kane* the council had created the source of the danger by requiring the footpath to be constructed. The court considered that the local

1   [2004] UKHL 15, [2004] 2 All ER 326.
2   [2001] EWCA Civ 878, [2001] 3 All ER 914.

planning authority should have required the developer to keep the footpath closed until the work to improve the sightlines on the main road had been completed.

7.114 *Stovin v Wise* was also considered by Morland J in *Great North Eastern Railway Limited v Hart*.[1] The defendant fell asleep while driving along the M62 motorway and his vehicle ended up on the main railway between Newcastle and London, causing a serious rail disaster. The defendant made a claim against the Secretary of State for Transport, Local Government and the Regions alleging that a longer safety barrier should have been erected at the railway bridge and that this would have prevented the accident. Morland J accepted that *Stovin v Wise* had decided that the failure of the highway authority to exercise its statutory powers to require the adjoining landowner to take the necessary action to get rid of the dangerous bank could not be used to found an action in tort for negligence. Although the Department had had the opportunity to renew and therefore lengthen the safety fencing before the accident, *Stovin v Wise* was an answer to any claim based on an alleged failure to exercise the power to alter the safety fencing. *Stovin v Wise* was not an answer to the claim based on the original construction of the safety fencing because, as in *Kane v New Forest District Council*, the danger represented by the conjunction of the motorway and the railway line had been created by the Department.

7.115 In fact Morland J decided that there had been no negligence on the part of the Department when the safety fencing was originally constructed because it had complied with the relevant minimum standards at the time of construction and the judge accepted evidence that the site would not have been identified as representing a risk which was out of the ordinary.

7.116 Morland J also had to consider the apparently novel question whether a highway authority can owe a duty of care to prevent the egress of a vehicle from the carriageway to avoid either physical injury or property damage to those off the highway. In the absence of obvious authority on the point, the judge decided that if the effective cause of the vehicle leaving the carriageway is created by the highway authority there is no reason of policy why the law should not impose a duty of care on the highway authority not only to users of the highway but also to those who are or whose property is on neighbouring land. Even if the vehicle leaves the highway partly through negligent driving and partly from a danger created by the highway authority and causes damage to someone off and beyond the highway, that person could recover damages from the highway authority.

---

1   (Unreported) 30 October 2003.

Chapter 8

ENVIRONMENTAL LIABILITIES

INTRODUCTION

8.1 Environmental law impacts on local authorities in a number of ways, both directly and indirectly. Environmental legislation has woven its way into almost every aspect of a local authority's functions. But to what extent has the regulatory framework increased the potential liability of local authorities to claims by third parties?

8.2 This chapter will address the two key aspects where claims might arise in an environmental context. First, it will look at the extent to which a local authority may incur a direct liability for damage caused to a third party arising out of its day-to-day activities. Secondly, it will look at the extent to which liability may arise during the performance of its regulatory functions. This second aspect has come more sharply into focus with the introduction of the Environment Act 1995 and, in particular, the provisions relating to contaminated land. Paragraphs **8.127–8.171** will focus directly on those concerns.

8.3 Any legal entity, including a local authority, may incur the following environmental liabilities arising out of its day-to-day activities:

(1) At common law, under one or more of the following heads:

    (a) nuisance;

    (b) the rule in *Rylands v Fletcher*;

    (c) negligence.

(2) Under statute, for example under the Environmental Protection Act 1990, the Health and Safety at Work etc Act 1974 and the Water Resources Act 1991.

NUISANCE

Basic principles of nuisance

8.4 In order for a local authority to understand its potential environmental liabilities, it is necessary to have a grasp of the fundamental principles of nuisance and the rule in *Rylands v Fletcher*. This section sets out those principles, with particular emphasis on cases involving local authorities.

Private v public nuisance

8.5   It is important to distinguish between a public nuisance and a private nuisance. A public nuisance is a criminal offence, whereas a private nuisance is a common law liability. A person is guilty of the offence of public nuisance:[1]

> '... if the effect of the act or omission is to endanger the life, health, property, morals, or comfort of the public, or to obstruct the public in the exercise or enjoyment of rights common to all Her Majesty's subjects.'

A public nuisance could include selling food unfit for human consumption or obstructing the highway by rendering it dangerous and inconvenient to pass.

8.6   Various matters have been declared to be nuisances by statute, in particular under the Environmental Health Act 1990, Part III, and the Clean Air Act 1993.

Private nuisance defined

8.7   In public nuisance, the acts complained of are unlawful acts. Private nuisance, on the other hand, commonly arises when an individual does something on his own land which is lawful, but becomes a nuisance when it interferes with the use or enjoyment of a neighbour's land. Clerk and Lindsell sum up the position as follows:[2]

> 'His conduct only becomes a nuisance when the consequences of his act are not confined to his own land but extend to the land of his neighbour by (1) causing an encroachment on his neighbour's land, when it closely resembles trespass, (2) causing physical damage to his neighbour's land or building or works or vegetation upon it, or (3) unduly interfering with his neighbour in the comfortable and convenient enjoyment of his land.'

Encroachment on neighbour's land

8.8   In *Fay v Prentice*,[3] a man built a cornice on his own house which overhung his neighbour's garden and caused rainwater to flow onto the neighbour's garden. This was held to constitute an actionable nuisance. The other obvious example of an encroachment is tree root damage, which is dealt with in detail in Chapter 11.

Causing physical damage to land

8.9   In *Sedleigh-Denfield v O'Callaghan*,[4] a pipe became blocked and caused water to overflow onto the neighbouring property. This was held to constitute a nuisance. Vibrations created on a defendant's own land have also been held to constitute a nuisance when they cause damage to his neighbour's buildings.[5]

Interference with enjoyment

8.10   Where physical damage has been caused to land or property, the nature of the loss is easy to determine. It is less easy where there has been an interference with enjoyment, which is defined as:[6]

---

1   *Archbold: Criminal Pleading, Evidence and Practice 1994*, para 31–40.
2   *Clerk and Lindsell on Torts* 18th edn (Sweet & Maxwell, 2000), para 19.06.
3   (1845) 1 CB 828.
4   [1940] AC 880.
5   *Hoare & Co v McAlpine* [1923] 1 Ch 167.
6   *St Helen's Smelting Co v Tipping* (1865) 11 HLC 642.

'. . . the personal interference with one's enjoyment, one's quiet, one's personal freedom, anything that discomposes or injuriously affects the senses or the nerves.'

Reasonableness

8.11 When it comes to considering whether or not an activity amounts to a nuisance, the court will look at the degree of reasonableness. In *Thomas v Lewis*,[1] the defendant owned land, part of which he worked as a quarry. He allowed the plaintiff grazing rights over another part of the land. The defendant had worked his quarry for a number of years before this agreement. The court concluded that it was an implied condition of the agreement to allow grazing rights that the defendant would continue to work the quarry and consequently there was no actionable nuisance.

8.12 In *Arscott and Others v The Coal Authority and Another*,[2] Tuckey LJ identified three themes running though the law of nuisance, namely natural use of land, reasonable use of land and reasonable foreseeability of damage. Broadly speaking a landowner will not be liable for natural use of his land unless the quality or extent of that use was unreasonable. However, non-natural use of land cannot be excused by any argument of reasonableness. The latter point is made clear by the rule in *Rylands v Fletcher* which will be dealt with below.

8.13 In *Arscott* Merthyr Tydfil County Borough Council placed spoil from coal tips on a recreation area which was susceptible to flooding. The result was that when the river overflowed, the claimants' property suffered flooding which had not occurred previously. The claimants alleged that the placing of spoil represented a nuisance because it interfered with the use and enjoyment of their land. Against the background of the law of nuisance, which Tuckey LJ had identified, the Court of Appeal had to consider what it referred to as the 'common enemy rule' which allows a landowner to erect defences whose effect will be that water which would otherwise have flowed onto his land will be diverted on to his neighbour's land. The Court of Appeal noted that there are limits on the rule, namely that there should be no interference with an established watercourse, and no discharge of water from one person's land on to another. Deciding that the defendants were not guilty of nuisance, in the view of Tuckey LJ:

> '[The limits on the common enemy rule] are mechanisms to achieve the balance which has to be maintained between the right of the occupier to do what he likes with his own, and the right of his neighbour not to be interfered with. So it is at this point, as it seems to me, that the common enemy rule can be seen to conform with the general law of nuisance. It represents a resolution of the balance between self interest and duty to neighbour which, in the broad context of land use of which it is a particular instance, makes up the body of law called nuisance.'

The Court of Appeal considered that the position might have been different had the claimants been able to show that the defendants' actions were excessive, for example if by placing spoil on the recreation ground they had raised the level to a height in excess of what was needed to prevent that area being flooded, and that the extra height was an independent cause of damage to the claimants' property. That was not the case here.

---

1   [2004] EWCA Civ 892, (unreported) 13 July 2004.
2   [1937] 1 All ER 137.

8.14   For similar reasons the Court of Appeal ruled out any breach of either Article 8 (respect for one's home) or Article 1 of the First Protocol (right to the peaceful enjoyment of one's possessions) of the European Convention on Human Rights (ECHR). The law of nuisance represented a resolution of the balance between private right and public interest.

8.15   In *Gillingham Borough Council v Medway (Chatham) Dock Co*,[1] Buckley J stated:

> 'Where planning consent is given for a development or change of use, the question of nuisance will thereafter fall to be decided by reference to a neighbourhood with that development or use and not as it was previously.'

In other words, the grant of planning permission effectively altered the character of a neighbourhood, in that case precluding an action in nuisance.

8.16   This point fell to be decided in *Wheeler and Another v J J Saunders Ltd and Others*.[2] The plaintiffs and defendants were neighbours. The defendants operated a pig farm. They applied for planning permission to build two pig housing units on their land. Prior to obtaining planning permission, they had cut off a means of access to the plaintiffs' property by building a wall. The plaintiffs brought an action in nuisance, to prevent the defendants blocking their right of access to the property and restraining the defendants from keeping pigs in housing units. The defendants argued that as they had obtained planning permission for the pig housing units, any smell emanating therefrom could not amount to a nuisance. Staughton LJ in the Court of Appeal concluded:[3]

> 'It would in my opinion be a misuse of language to describe what has happened in the present case as a change in the character of a neighbourhood. It is a change of use of a very small piece of land, a little over 350 square metres according to the dimensions on the plan, for the benefit of the applicant and to the detriment of objectors in the quiet enjoyment of his house. It is not a strategic planning decision affected by considerations of public interest. Unless one is prepared to accept that any planning decision authorises any nuisance which must inevitably come from it, the argument that the nuisance was authorised by planning permission in this case must fail. I am not prepared to accept that premise.'

8.17   Still on the question of reasonableness, in *Dymond v Pearce and Others*,[4] the Court of Appeal held that, in principle, leaving a lorry on the highway for a considerable period for the driver's convenience constituted a nuisance by obstruction, actionable if that obstruction caused damage to a member of the public. In the particular case, the plaintiff's case failed because it was found, as a matter of fact, that the accident was caused wholly due to the plaintiff's own negligence.

8.18   David Hughes summarises the position surrounding reasonableness as follows:[5]

---

1   [1993] QB 343.
2   [1995] 2 All ER 697.
3   Ibid at 706.
4   [1972] 1 QB 496.
5   David Hughes *Environmental Law* 3rd edn (Butterworths, 1996), p 42.

'In any nuisance action the real issue will usually be, not whether there has been an interference, but whether the land usage goes beyond acceptable bounds of mutual give and take, live and let live.'

Construction: demolition and building

8.19   Noise resulting from demolition or building work will be actionable only if it is caused by unreasonable activities or if the defendant takes no proper steps to avoid inconvenience to neighbours. Vaughan Williams J summarised the position as follows, as long ago as 1891:[1]

'A man who pulls down his house for the purpose of building a new one no doubt causes considerable inconvenience to his next door neighbours during the process of demolition; but he is not responsible for a nuisance if he uses all reasonable skill and care to avoid annoyance to his neighbour by the works of demolition. Nor is he liable to an action even though the noise and dust and the consequent annoyance be such as would constitute a nuisance if the same, instead of being created for the purpose of demolition of the house, had been created in sheer wantonness, or in the execution of works for a purpose involving permanent continuance of the dust and noise. For the law, in judging what constitutes a nuisance, does take into consideration both the object and the duration of that which is said to constitute the nuisance.'

Natural nuisances

8.20   In certain circumstances, the courts have held that a defendant was under a duty to prevent a nuisance caused, not by his own making, but from the natural condition of the land. On appeal from the court in Australia, the Privy Council in *Goldman v Hargrave*[2] concluded that the defendant was under a duty of care to abate a fire which started on his own land when lightning struck a tree, but which subsequently spread to his neighbour's land. Lord Wilberforce held[3] that there is a duty of care upon occupiers in relation to hazards occurring on their land, whether natural or man-made, to prevent those hazards going onto the neighbouring property. He defined the scope of the duty as follows:[4]

'How far does it go? What is the standard of the effort required? What is the position as regards expenditure? It is not enough to say merely that these must be "reasonable", since what is reasonable to one man may be very unreasonable, and indeed ruinous, to another: the law must take account of the fact that the occupier on whom the duty is cast has, ex hypothesi, had this hazard thrust upon him through no seeking or fault of his own ... One may say in general terms that the existence of a duty must be based upon knowledge of the hazard, ability to foresee the consequences of not checking or removing it, and the ability to abate it.'

Hence:[5]

'... the owner of a small property where a hazard arises which threatens a neighbour with substantial interest should not have to do so much as one with larger interests of his own at stake and greater resources to protect them. If the small owner does what he can and

---

1   *Harrison v Southwark and Vauxhall Water Co* [1891] 2 Ch 409.
2   [1967] 1 AC 645.
3   Ibid at 661.
4   Ibid at 663.
5   Ibid at 663.

promptly calls on his neighbour to provide additional resources, he may be held to have done his duty: he should not be liable unless it is clearly proved that he could, and reasonably in his individual circumstances should, have done more.'

8.21 A further important case on this point is *Leakey and Others v National Trust for Places of Historic Interest or Natural Beauty*.[1] The plaintiffs' property was on land situated at the foot of a large mound, which was on the defendant's land. For a number of years, soil and rubble had fallen from the mound onto the plaintiffs' land. Subsequently, the mound slipped causing further damage to the plaintiffs' land. The Court of Appeal concluded that:[2]

(1) an occupier of land owes a general duty of care to a neighbouring occupier in relation to a hazard occurring on his land, whether such a hazard is natural or man-made;
(2) the duty is to take such steps as are reasonable in all the circumstances to prevent or minimise the risk of injury or damage to the neighbour or his property of which the occupier knows or ought to have known;
(3) the circumstances referred to include the knowledge of the hazard, the extent of the risk, the practicability of preventing or minimising the foreseeable injury or damage, the time available for doing so, the probable cost of the work involved and the relative financial and other resources, taken on a broad basis, of the parties.

8.22 The issue of reasonableness in the context of natural nuisance has been considered by the Court of Appeal in *Bybrook Barn Centre Limited and Others v Kent County Council*.[3] The claimants owned land through which a natural watercourse flowed. The watercourse was interrupted by a highway, under which had been constructed a culvert. Kent County Council was responsible for the maintenance of the highway. At the time of construction, in 1950, the culvert was adequate; however, subsequent development in the catchment area had had the effect of diverting a greater flow of water towards the culvert so that it could no longer cope with the capacity of the watercourse. Flooding of the garden centre and surrounding land occurred in 1996.

8.23 It was conceded by the council that it had been aware of problems concerning the capacity of the culvert in or around 1990. The question for the court was whether the council was liable for the flooding, bearing in mind that, when constructed, the culvert had neither created a nuisance, nor was it a potential nuisance. In fact the nuisance had arisen gradually. The Court of Appeal decided that a duty was owed by the council in circumstances once it was aware of the risk of flooding and where there was no suggestion that the increased flow of water in the culvert was due to any wrongdoing by those upstream. The test was that of reasonableness laid down in *Leakey*.

8.24 Delivering the judgment of the court, Waller LJ said:

'The factors which in my view point in favour of liability are the following. The defendants' predecessors must have chosen to construct a culvert to put the natural stream

---

1   [1980] QB 485.
2   Ibid, headnote, at 486.
3   [2001] LGR 239.

under the highway. It is common ground that the defendants are to be treated as in no better position than their predecessors. Even if, as I have suggested, it does not place on the defendants a strict liability for all eventualities thereafter, it places on them a high obligation to see that the natural stream can continue to flow under the highway. This is not a case of an inadequate sewage system and the plaintiff rate payer seeking to get the local authority to do its public duty. This is a case where a private land owner has suffered damage from flooding caused by a culvert built by and under control of the highway authority. The highway authority had the means of preventing the flooding by enlarging the culvert at some cost, but basically without great difficulty ... it would not in such circumstances be an answer for them to say that they did not have the money to do it having regard to more pressing matters.'

8.25   In the course of its judgment, the Court of Appeal distinguished the earlier decisions in *Dear v Thames Water and Others*,[1] *Glossop v Heston and Isleworth Local Board*,[2] and *Smeaton v Ilford Corporation*,[3] on the basis that those had been cases concerned with alleged breach of statutory duty. They were cases[4] where the claimants had been members of the public for whose benefit the sewers or sewage system had been installed, and what the claimants, in effect, had been trying to do was to seek an order to compel the local authorities to carry out their statutory duties to provide an adequate system. The Court of Appeal in *Bybrook Barn Centre Limited* accepted that liability would not attach in such circumstances, but did not consider that the cases were relevant to the facts surrounding the flooding of the garden centre.

8.26   The House of Lords has confirmed the relevance of the existence of a statutory scheme in *Marcic v Thames Water Utilities Limited*.[5] A claim in nuisance, arising out of flooding of the claimant's property because of an inadequate sewerage system, failed because Thames Water's obligations in respect of the sewers could not sensibly be considered without regard to the statutory scheme under which the sewers were vested in Thames Water. According to Lord Nicholls:

'The common law of nuisance should not impose on Thames Water obligations inconsistent with the statutory scheme. To do so would run counter to the intention of Parliament as expressed in the Water Industry Act 1991.'

Foreseeability

8.27   In *The Wagon Mound (No 2)*,[6] the Privy Council concluded that whilst in nuisance proof of negligence was not necessary, it was usually necessary to prove fault and 'fault generally involves foreseeability'.[7] The question was considered again by the House of Lords in *Cambridge Water Co Ltd v Eastern Counties Leather plc*.[8] Eastern Counties Leather plc operated a tannery from a site in Cambridgeshire. As part of the tanning process, it used perchloroethane (PCE). From time to time, PCE spilt onto the ground. It seeped through the soil and into the aquifer below.

---

1   (1992) 33 Con LR 43.
2   (1879) 12 ChD 102.
3   [1954] Ch 450.
4   See paras **8.90–8.98**.
5   [2003] UKHL 66, [2003] 3 WLR 1603.
6   *Overseas Tankship (UK) Ltd v Miller Steamship Co Pty (The Wagon Mound (No 2))* [1967] 1 AC 617.
7   Ibid at 640.
8   [1994] 1 All ER 53.

Approximately 1½ miles away, Cambridge Water operated a bore hole, from which it extracted water. In 1984, water safety standards altered and it was discovered that the water in the aquifer used by Cambridge Water contained unsatisfactory levels of PCE. Cambridge Water was forced to close down the bore hole and relocate. It sued Eastern Counties Leather plc in negligence, nuisance and under the rule in *Rylands v Fletcher*, to recover the cost of relocation.

8.28 On the question of fault and 'reasonableness', Lord Goff stated: [1]

'... it is still the law that the fact that the Defendant has taken all reasonable care will not of itself exonerate him from liability, the relevant control mechanism being found within the principle of reasonable user.'

8.29 Turning to the issue of foreseeability, it was important that Eastern Counties Leather had stopped using PCE in the tanning process in 1976. Against this background, Lord Goff went on to observe: [2]

'But it by no means follows that the Defendant should be held liable for damage of a type which he could not reasonably foresee; and the development of the law of negligence in the past 60 years points strongly towards a requirement that such foreseeability should be a prerequisite of liability and damages for nuisance, as it is of liability and negligence. For if a Plaintiff is in ordinary circumstances only liable to claim damages in respect of personal injuries where he can prove such foreseeability on the part of the Defendant, it is difficult to see why, in common justice, he should be in a stronger position to claim damages for interference with the enjoyment of his land where the Defendant was unable to foresee damage.'

The House of Lords concluded that where the use of PCE ceased in 1976 and the contamination did not come to light until 1984, the damage was not foreseeable to Eastern Counties plc and consequently it was not liable in nuisance.

8.30 From the point of view of local authorities, the most relevant case, in considering both foreseeability and continuing nuisances, is *Sedleigh-Denfield v O'Callaghan*.[3] The case is considered in Chapter 1, but the principles are important. The defendant owned land on which was located a ditch. Before the defendant purchased the land, a pipe had been inserted for carrying off rainwater. A grating had been placed at the opening of the pipe, to prevent blockage. The pipe was maintained from time to time by the local authority, and the defendant was not personally aware of the existence of the pipe. During a heavy rainstorm, the pipe became blocked and water overflowed onto the neighbouring property, causing damage.

8.31 The defendant was found liable notwithstanding that he was not personally aware of the existence of the pipe, on the basis that he was taken to have knowledge of its existence through his servants – in this case the local authority – and yet did nothing to remedy it. Lord Wright stated: [4]

'... the gist of the present action is the unreasonable and unjustified interference by the Defendant in the use of his land with the Plaintiff's right to enjoy his property ... the difficulty is that the respondents did not create the offending structure and in that sense create the nuisance. It was created by the Middlesex County Council, which was or has

---

1   [1994] 1 All ER 53 at 71, 72.
2   Ibid at 72.
3   [1940] AC 880.
4   Ibid at 904.

been treated as being a trespasser . . . it has I think been rightly established in the Court of Appeal that an occupier is not prima facie responsible for a nuisance created without his knowledge and consent. If he is to be liable a further condition is necessary, namely, that he had knowledge or means of knowledge, that he knew or should have known of the nuisance in time to correct it and obviate its mischievous effects. The liability for a nuisance is not, at least in modern law, a strict or absolute liability.'

He concluded: [1]

'In the present case it is in my opinion clear on the facts . . . that the respondents, by their servant knew or at least ought to have known of the nuisance.'

Who can successfully sue?

8.32 The key question in the environmental context is whether it is necessary for the plaintiff to have a possessory right in land in order to establish a cause of action.

8.33 *Hunter and Others v Canary Wharf Ltd; Hunter and Others v London Docklands Development Corp* [2] restricted the scope of nuisance by confirming that only a person with a right to the land affected by a nuisance could bring an action in private nuisance. In the *Canary Wharf* case, the plaintiffs sued for interference with their television reception following construction of the Canary Wharf Tower. In the *London Docklands* case, the same plaintiffs sued for damage caused by excess dust from road construction work.

The House of Lords concluded that interference with television reception caused by the mere presence of a building was not capable of constituting an actionable private nuisance. In the second action, whilst excessive dust could in itself constitute a nuisance, in the particular case the plaintiffs had no right to the land affected by the nuisance and consequently they had no right to sue.

Lord Goff stated: [3]

'It follows that, on the authorities as they stand, an action in private nuisance will only lie at the suit of a person who has a right to the land affected.'

He went on:

'The question therefore arises whether your Lordships should be persuaded to depart from established principle, and recognise such a right in others who are no more than mere licensees on the land. At the heart of this question lies a more fundamental question, which relates to the scope of the law of private nuisance.'

And concluded: [4]

'I can see no good reason to depart from the law on this topic as established in the authorities. I would therefore hold that *Khorasandjian v Bush* must be overruled in so far as it holds that a mere licensee can sue in private nuisance . . .'

8.34 *Khorasandjian v Bush* [5] concerned harassment by a defendant of a young girl. The Court of Appeal concluded that it did have the jurisdiction to grant an injunction

---

1   [1940] AC 880 at 908.
2   [1997] 2 All ER 425.
3   Ibid at 437.
4   Ibid at 438.
5   [1993] 3 All ER 669.

in nuisance. Commenting on that decision in *Hunter and Others v Canary Wharf et al*, Lord Goff stated:[1]

> 'In truth, what the Court of Appeal appears to have been doing was to exploit the law of private nuisance in order to create by the back door a tort of harassment which was only partially effective in that it was artificially limited to harassment which takes place in her home.'

8.35   The case of *Masters v London Borough of Brent*[2] addressed the situation where a person acquired a proprietary interest in property which was subject to a continuing nuisance. This case, and the subsequent decision in *Delaware Mansions Ltd v Westminster City Council*,[3] are considered in relation to tree roots in Chapter 11. The judge concluded that the interest of Delaware at all material times was contractual, not proprietary. It therefore had no possessory right and the claim failed on the principles outlined in *Hunter v Canary Wharf Ltd*.[4]

Who is liable?

8.36   The starting point on liability is *Pride of Derby and Derbyshire Angling Association v British Celanese Ltd*.[5] In that case, Lord Denning stated:[6]

> '. . . liability for nuisance has been applied in the past to sewage and drainage cases in this way. When a local authority take over or construct a sewage and drainage system which is adequate at the time to dispose of the sewage and surface water for their district, but which subsequently becomes inadequate owing to increased building which they cannot control, and for which they have no responsibility, they are not guilty of the ensuing nuisance.'

8.37   The issue of a local authority's liability where it takes over responsibility for a sewerage and drainage system which was adequate when constructed, but which becomes inadequate subsequently, was considered in the case of *Dear v Thames Water and Others*.[7] In distinguishing the cases of *Goldman v Hargrave*,[8] *Leakey and Others v National Trust for Places of Historic Interest or Natural Beauty*[9] and *Russell v London Borough of Barnet*,[10] Judge Bowsher QC concluded that no duty was owed in these circumstances where the drain became inadequate owing to increased development outside the local authority's control.

8.38   *Gilson v Kerrier District Council*,[11] looked at a similar point, and was decided on its own particular facts. However, the judgment makes it clear that the courts will look closely at the arrangements between the regulatory authorities and decide which authority had overall responsibility at the particular time. The case concerned a watercourse which flooded, causing damage to the plaintiff's property. The local authority had been responsible for the watercourse until 1968 when, by virtue of the

---

1   [1997] 2 All ER 426 at 437.
2   [1978] 2 All ER 664.
3   [1998] EGCS 48.
4   [1997] 2 All ER 426.
5   [1953] 1 All ER 179.
6   Ibid at 203.
7   (1992) 33 Con LR 43.
8   [1967] 1 AC 645.
9   [1980] 1 QB 485.
10   (1984) 271 EG 699.
11   [1976] 1 WLR 904, CA.

South Cornwall Water Board Order 1967, responsibility was transferred to the water board. The plaintiff sought a declaration that the rural district council was under a duty to maintain the watercourse, and failed.

Are damages for personal injury recoverable in nuisance?

8.39 The general proposition is that an action for private nuisance is not a proper remedy for personal injury.[1] However, confusion was created by the decision of *Woolfall v Knowsley Borough Council*[2] where damages were given for an action in nuisance arising out of a fire in a pile of rubbish on land. It was held that the local authority was liable in nuisance because it should not have left the rubbish by the highway.

8.40 The point came before the court in *Hunter and Others v Canary Wharf Ltd; Hunter and Others v London Docklands Development Corp.*[3] In concluding that an action in private nuisance will lie only at the suit of a person who has a right in the land affected (see paras **8.32–8.35**), Lord Hoffmann stated:[4]

> 'So far as the claim is for personal injury, it seems to me that the only appropriate cause of action is negligence. It would be anomalous if the rules for recovery of damages under this head were different according to whether, for example, the Plaintiff was at home or at work. It is true, as I have said, that the law of negligence gives no remedy for discomfort or distress which does not result in bodily or psychiatric illness. But this is a matter of general policy and I can see no logic in making an exception for cases in which the discomfort or distress was suffered at home rather than somewhere else.'

In other words, the court concluded that an action in nuisance was a proprietary right, rather than an individual right.

Statutory authority

8.41 In the environmental context, this potential defence to an action in nuisance and/or under the rule in *Rylands v Fletcher* is critical, in view of the regulatory role performed by local authorities in the environmental context. The proposition is that a local authority – or any other body exercising a statutory duty – is not liable at common law in the absence of negligence. This is important because, as will be seen later,[5] establishing a duty of care in negligence can be a difficult hurdle to overcome.

8.42 A potential defence of statutory authority was first raised by Lord Blackburn in *Geddis v Proprietors of Bann Reservoir,*[6] where he stated:

> '... it is now thoroughly well established that no action will lie for doing that which the legislature has authorised, if it be done without negligence, although it does occasion damage to anyone; but an action does lie for doing that which the legislature has authorised, if it be done negligently. And I think that if by a reasonable exercise of the powers, either given by statute to the promoters, or which they have at common law, the

---

1 See David Hughes *Environmental Law* 3rd edn (Butterworths, 1996), p 39, and FH Newark in the Boundaries of Nuisance (1949) 65 LQR 480.
2 [1992] 4 LMELR 124.
3 [1997] 2 All ER 425.
4 Ibid at 452.
5 At paras **8.86–8.123**.
6 (1878) 3 App Cas 430 at 455–456.

damage could be prevented it is, within this rule, "negligence" not to make such reasonable exercise of their powers.'

8.43 This point was taken up by Lord Wilberforce in *Allen v Gulf Oil Refining Ltd.*[1] His interpretation of the defence of statutory authority was unequivocal:[2]

'It is now well settled that where Parliament by express direction or by necessary implication has authorised the construction and use of an undertaking or works, that carries with it an authority to do what is authorised with immunity from any action based on nuisance. The right of action is taken away.'

Lord Wilberforce went on to explain that a cause of action *may* lie where the statutory powers are exercised 'negligently'. This argument was taken up by Webster J at first instance in *Department of Transport v North West Water Authorities*,[3] where he summarised statutory authority as a defence in cases of nuisance as follows:

'(a) in the absence of negligence, a body is not liable for a nuisance which is attributable to the exercise by it of a *duty* imposed by statute;

(b) it is not liable in those circumstances even if by statute it is expressly made liable, or not exempted from liability, for nuisance;

(c) in the absence of negligence, a body is not liable for a nuisance which is attributable to the exercise by it of a *power* conferred by statute if, by statute, it is neither expressly made liable, nor expressly exempted from liability, for nuisance;

(d) a body is liable for a nuisance by it attributable to the exercise of a *power* conferred by statute even without negligence, if by statute it is expressly either made liable, or not exempted from liability, for nuisance.'

8.44 This summary was adopted and approved by the House of Lords in the same case.[4] At first instance, Webster J went on to say:[5]

'References to nuisance are to be taken as references either to liability in nuisance simpliciter, or to liability under the rule in *Rylands v Fletcher*.'

8.45 In the *North West Water* case, it was agreed between the parties that the burst of a water main which was the subject of the dispute happened without 'negligence' – or carelessness – on the part of the water authority. The question that fell to be considered was whether the statutory provision, s 18(2) of the Public Utility Street Works Act 1950, was intended to create liability for nuisance in these circumstances. At first instance, Webster J concluded that it was; the House of Lords overturned this part of the decision on appeal.

In approving the test of statutory authority as annunciated by Webster J, Lord Fraser went on to say:[6]

'The word "negligence" is used in these propositions in the special sense explained by Lord Wilberforce in *Allen v Gulf Oil Refining Ltd* ... of requiring the undertaker, as a condition of obtaining immunity from action, "to carry out the work and conduct of the operation with all reasonable regard and care for the interests of other persons ..."'

---

1   [1981] AC 1001.
2   Ibid at 1011.
3   [1984] 1 AC 336.
4   Ibid at 359–360, per Lord Fraser.
5   Ibid at 344.
6   Ibid at 359–360.

8.46   The defence of statutory authority was considered, in the context of a claim in negligence, by Lord Wilberforce in *X (Minors) v Bedfordshire County Council*.[1] Having reviewed the decisions of *Geddis* and *Allen*, and the decision in *Home Office v Dorset Yacht Co Ltd*,[2] Lord Browne-Wilkinson concluded his findings on this point as follows:

> 'In my judgement the correct view is that in order to found a cause of action flowing from the careless exercise of statutory powers or duties, the Plaintiff has to show that the circumstances are such as to raise a duty of care at common law. The mere assertion of the careless exercise of a statutory power or duty is not sufficient.'

8.47   In summary, the correct approach to adopt in considering the defence of statutory authority in cases of nuisance and/or the rule in *Rylands v Fletcher* is this. First, it is appropriate to consider whether, on the facts of the case, a liability in nuisance and/or under the rule in *Rylands v Fletcher* may arise. If not, it is not necessary to proceed to consider the defence of statutory authority. If a cause of action may arise, the next stage is to look at whether the incident arose out of the exercise by a local authority of its statutory powers or duties. If so, the defence of statutory authority may well arise, depending on the precise wording of the statute. If the defence applies, a cause of action can arise only in negligence and, following the decision in *X (Minors)*, a duty of care in negligence will arise only from the manner in which the statutory duty has been implemented in practice.[3]

THE RULE IN *RYLANDS v FLETCHER*

Basic principles

8.48   The rule in *Rylands v Fletcher* is commonly regarded as simply another strand of nuisance. However, the rule does have certain distinct features which warrant special consideration, particularly in the context of environmental damage. The extent to which the rule in *Rylands v Fletcher* is indeed a separate cause of action has been confirmed by the House of Lords in *Transco Plc v Stockport Metropolitan Borough Council*.[4] Their Lordships confirmed that the rule survives in English law in spite of the fact that:

(a)   the rule does not apply in Scotland (see *RHM Bakeries (Scotland) Limited v Strathclyde Regional Council*[5]);
(b)   in Australia, the rule is treated as absorbed by the principles of ordinary negligence (see *Burnie Port Authority v General Jones Property Limited*[6]).

8.49   In nuisance, the need to prove fault is enshrined in the principle of reasonableness: in order to establish a claim, the plaintiff must show that the defendant acted unreasonably and was, to that extent, at fault. The rule in *Rylands v*

---

1   [1995] 3 All ER 353.
2   [1970] 2 All ER 294.
3   See paras **8.141–8.146**, and see the judgment of Lord Wilberforce in *Allen v Gulf Oil Refining Ltd* [1981] AC 1001 at 1011.
4   [2003] UKHL 61, [2004] 2 AC 1.
5   1985 SLT 214.
6   (1994) 120 ALR 42.

Fletcher is stricter, in that it provides for liability *without proof of fault* in certain circumstances. In the case of *Rylands v Fletcher*,[1] Blackburn J (at first instance) stated:[2]

> 'We think that the rule of law is, that the person who for his own purposes brings on his lands and collects and keeps there anything likely to do mischief if it escapes must keep it in at his peril, and, if he does not do so, is prima facie answerable for all the damage which is the natural consequence of its escape.'

This test was approved by the House of Lords, but Lord Cairns restricted the rule to circumstances where the use of the land was 'non-natural use'.[3]

8.50　Thus a defendant will be liable without proof of fault where:

(1)　he brings or collects material on his land;
(2)　the accumulation is for the defendant's own purposes;
(3)　the matter is something likely to do mischief if it escapes;
(4)　there is an escape from the place of accumulation to some other place outside the defendant's control.

'Accumulation for defendant's own purposes'

8.51　In the past, local authorities have tried to argue that the rule in *Rylands v Fletcher* does not apply to them where they are carrying out their statutory functions for the public benefit, in view of the requirement that the material must be accumulated for the defendant's 'own purposes'.

8.52　However, this argument was expressly rejected in the case of *Smeaton v Ilford Corporation*,[4] which is considered in more detail at paras **8.54** and **8.58**.

In his judgment, Upjohn J reviewed the rule in *Rylands v Fletcher* insofar as it had been applied to local authorities in the past.[5] He quoted Buckley J in *Hobart v Southend on Sea Corporation*:[6]

> 'The Plaintiff is entitled to the enjoyment of a several fishery; he has a right to enjoy the land for the purpose of laying oysters there. That right of his in the land is interfered with by nuisance caused by the discharge by the Defendants from their pipes of offensive matter in such a way as that it reaches the Plaintiff's layings. Upon the principle of *Fletcher v Rylands* and the decisions upon which that case is founded, the Defendants must keep their noxious matter from trespassing upon their neighbour's land.'

8.53　In *Jones v Llanrwst Urban District Council*,[7] Parker J stated:

> 'I am of the opinion that anyone who turns faecal matter or allows faecal matter collected by him or under his control to escape into a river in such manner or under such conditions that it is carried, whether by the current or the wind, onto his neighbour's land is guilty of a trespass.'

1　(1866) LR 1 Ex 265.
2　Ibid at 279, and see Chapter 1.
3　*Rylands v Fletcher* (1886) LR 3 HL 330 at 338–340.
4　[1954] 1 All ER 923.
5　Ibid at 930.
6　(1906) LJKB 305.
7　[1911] 1 Ch 393 at 402.

In *Jones*, the sewer had discharged onto the plaintiff's land. Phillips J went on to say: [1]

> 'On these findings of fact I do not think that if the Defendants were private individuals, and if the Plaintiff were in actual occupation of the fields adjoining the river, there could be any defence to this action.'

8.54 In *Smeaton v Ilford Corporation*,[2] on the narrow point of whether the local authority could be described as having accumulated the sewage for its own purposes, Upjohn J concluded:

> '... the Defendants are under a duty to provide sewers and a sewage disposal system. The sewers vest in them, and they are bound to permit owners and occupiers of premises to discharge sewage into their sewers. I have already referred to the relevant sections of the Public Health Act 1936, which re-enacted sections to the same effect in the Public Health Act 1875. It is said that, in those circumstances, it is not correct to speak of the Defendants as collecting sewage on their own land. I reject that contention. The Defendants do collect, although they may be under a duty to do so, and they collect it into a sewer vested in them.'

The 'non-natural user' principle

8.55 Since the rule in *Rylands v Fletcher* was first formulated in 1886, the courts have shown a reluctance to apply it, chiefly out of a general reluctance to impose strict liability at common law. Thus, no sooner had the principle been formulated by Blackburn J, than it was qualified by Lord Cairns in the House of Lords with his stipulation that the use of the land in question must be 'non-natural use'. This qualification was picked up by Lord Moulton in *Rickards v Lothian*,[3] who in commenting on the rule in *Rylands v Fletcher* stated:

> 'It is not every use to which land is put that brings into play that principle. It must be some special use bringing with it increased dangers to others, and must not merely be the ordinary use of land or such a use as is proper for the general benefit of the community.'

8.56 In *Read v Lyons*,[4] Lord Porter stated:

> 'Each case seems to be a question of fact subject to a ruling of the Judge as to whether ... the particular use can be non-natural, and in deciding this question I think that all the circumstances of the time and place and produce of mankind must be taken into consideration so that what might be regarded as ... non-natural may vary according to those circumstances.'

8.57 In *Pride of Derby and Derbyshire Angling Association Ltd v British Celanese Ltd*,[5] Denning LJ made the following observation:

> 'In this case, negligence is not alleged. The only cause of action available to the Plaintiffs is an action for nuisance. I pause here to say that I doubt whether the doctrine of *Rylands v Fletcher* applies in all its strictness to cases where a local authority, acting under statutory authority, builds sewers which afterwards overflow, or sewage disposal works which later pour out a polluting effluent, for the simple reason that the use of land for drainage

---

1   [1911] 1 Ch 393 at 403–404.
2   [1954] 1 All ER 923 at 931.
3   [1913] AC 263 at 280.
4   [1947] AC 156 at 169.
5   [1953] 1 All ER 179 at 202.

purposes by the local authority is "such a use as is proper for the general benefit of the community", and is on that ground exempt from the rule in *Rylands v Fletcher*.'

8.58 In *Smeaton v Ilford Corporation*,[1] Upjohn J reviewed the various authorities which considered the principle of non-natural user and concluded:

'Those observations do, at all events, show that what is or is not a natural user of land for the purposes of the rule awaits authoritative determination.'

On the facts of the case before him, he concluded:[2]

'Whatever may be the law, however, as regards use of land for ordinary domestic purposes, in my judgement, different considerations arise when a local authority collects, even though under a duty to do so, large quantities of sewage which they are bound to dispose of. To collect into a sewer a large volume of sewage, inherently noxious and dangerous and bound to cause great damage if not properly contained, cannot be described, in my judgement, as a natural user of land. Accordingly, in my judgement, a local authority cannot claim exemption from the rule on this point.'

8.59 Megaw LJ addressed the question of non-natural use in *Leakey and Others v National Trust for Places of Historic Interest or Natural Beauty*.[3] He highlighted the problems in determining the meaning of the phrase 'non-natural use' as follows:[4]

'It is notorious that those cases involve apparent anomalies and grave difficulties of reconciliation with one another.'

In *Sedleigh-Denfield v O'Callaghan*,[5] Viscount Maugham said:

'My Lords I will begin by saying that in my opinion the principle laid down in *Rylands v Fletcher* does not apply to the present case. That principle applies only to cases where there has been some special use of property bringing with it increased danger to others, and does not extend to damages caused to adjoining owners as a result of the ordinary use of land: see *Rickards v Lothian* [1913] AC 263–280.'

That in turn lead Megaw LJ to conclude in *Leakey*:[6]

'If *Rylands v Fletcher* was thus irrelevant in the *Sedleigh-Denfield* case, it is not relevant in this case.'

8.60 The result of these various decisions over the last 100 years was that – with the exception of claims relating to tree roots – almost every kind of activity had been defined by the courts as amounting to a 'natural' use of land or as being 'for the benefit of the community', including the building of houses and the operation of a chemical factory.

8.61 However, the legal position was significantly revised by the House of Lords in *Cambridge Water Co Ltd v Eastern Counties Leather plc*[7] (see paras **8.27** and **8.66–8.69**). Having reviewed the question of foreseeability in negligence, nuisance and under the rule in *Rylands v Fletcher*, the House of Lords went on to comment

---

1   [1954] 1 All ER 923 at 932.
2   Ibid at 933.
3   [1980] 1 QB 485.
4   Ibid at 521.
5   [1940] AC 880 at 888.
6   [1980] 1 QB 485 at 519.
7   [1994] 1 All ER 53.

upon the non-natural user principle in *Rylands v Fletcher* (although that issue did not directly affect the outcome of the case). Lord Goff commented:[1]

> 'I feel bound to say that the storage of substantial quantities of chemicals on industrial premises should be regarded as an almost classic case of non-natural use; and I find it very difficult to think that it should be thought objectionable to impose strict liability for damage caused in the event of their escape.'

8.62   Lord Goff concluded by saying that the term 'natural' should have its ordinary meaning and expressed the hope that 'the courts may feel less pressure to extend the concept of natural use ... and in due course it may become easier to control this exception'.[2]

Having thus opened the door for more claims under the rule in *Rylands v Fletcher*, the House of Lords in *Cambridge Water* declined to be more specific in its definition of the term 'non-natural' use.

8.63   The decision at first instance in *Ellison v Ministry of Defence*[3] demonstrated that there will be continuing difficulty on this point. Mr and Mrs Ellison were the owners and occupiers of land adjacent to the Greenham Common airfield. The Ministry of Defence were the occupiers of the airfield and contractors were carrying out work for them on site. The contractors created two large berms on the site, near the boundary with the Ellison's property. A storm on 10 August 1986 caused severe flooding at the Ellison's property, which they claimed was caused because the berms diverted the natural flow of water from Greenham Common. In discussing the 'non-natural use' principle, Judge Peter Bowsher QC, in the Official Referees Division, concluded that the rainwater was naturally on the MOD's land and that, if the flows had been diverted by the berms, the construction works were an ordinary use of land which were not essentially dangerous in themselves.

8.64   The point has been considered again by the House of Lords in *Transco Plc v Stockport Metropolitan Borough Council*.[4] The defendant council owned a tower block to which water was supplied through a large pipe, also owned by the council. A leak developed in the water pipe which led to the partial washing away of an embankment where the claimant's gas pipeline was situated. The gas pipe was left unsupported and exposed. Transco claimed the cost of the works required to restore support and cover the pipe. The House of Lords considered that although the leak had occurred in a water pipe, which was substantially larger than an ordinary domestic supply, nevertheless the council had not brought onto its land something likely to cause danger or mischief if it escaped and that it was an ordinary user of the council's land. Lord Bingham summarised the position:

> 'It is of course true that water in quantity is almost always capable of causing damage if it escapes. But the piping of a water supply from the mains to the storage tanks in the block was a routine function which would not have struck anyone as raising any special hazard. In truth, the council did not accumulate any water, it merely arranged a supply adequate to meet the residents' needs. The situation cannot stand comparison with the making by

---

1   [1994] 1 All ER 53 at 78.
2   Ibid at 78–79.
3   (1996) 81 BLR 101, QBD.
4   [2003] UKHL 61, [2004] 2 AC 1.

Mr Rylands of a substantial reservoir. Nor can the use by the council of its land be seen as in any way extraordinary or unusual. It was entirely normal and routine.'

8.65 Lord Hoffmann agreed and commented on two features which he considered to be relevant:

(1) The effect of s 209 of the Water Industry Act 1991,[1] which in the case of a pipe vested in a water undertaker, makes that undertaker liable for damage caused by an escape of water from that pipe, might suggest that it was intended to exclude the rule in *Rylands v Fletcher*.
(2) As the rule is only concerned with damage to property, it is to be anticipated that the owner of the property could reasonably be expected to have insured himself against such damage.

Foreseeability

8.66 Prior to 1993, there was some doubt as to whether foreseeability was a relevant consideration in a case brought under the rule in *Rylands v Fletcher*. Based upon the original rule as enunciated by Blackburn J at first instance, it was felt that the reference to a party being 'answerable for all the damage'[2] meant that the defendant would be liable without proof of fault and irrespective of whether or not the damage was foreseeable. Neither the judge at first instance nor the House of Lords made reference to foreseeability.

8.67 This point was argued before the House of Lords in *Cambridge Water Company Co Ltd v Eastern Counties Leather plc*,[3] and their Lordships firmly concluded that foreseeability was an essential ingredient, not just of claims in negligence and nuisance, but also under the rule in *Rylands v Fletcher*. Thus, Eastern Counties Leather's claim failed under all three heads because the House of Lords concluded that it was not foreseeable that the use of PCE up to 1976 might cause the damage suffered by Cambridge Water Company at a site 1½ miles away, which was first identified in 1984. Referring to the speech of Blackburn J in *Fletcher v Rylands*, Lord Goff stated:[4]

> 'The general tenor of this statement of principle is ... that knowledge, or at least foreseeability of the risk, is a pre-requisite of the recovery of damages under the principle; but that the principle is one of strict liability in the sense that the Defendant may be held liable notwithstanding that he has exercised all due care to prevent the escape from occurring.'

Thus, foreseeability of damage of the relevant type is a *prerequisite* of liability in damages under the rule in *Rylands v Fletcher*.

8.68 In *Cambridge Water*, whilst extending the potential scope of situations to which the rule in *Rylands v Fletcher* may apply, Lord Goff at the same time appeared to restrict the overall applicability of that rule by commenting that in principle the rule should be seen as little more than 'an extension of the law of nuisance to cases of

---

1   Note that Transco could not rely on this section because liability for damage sustained by a gas supplier is excluded under s 209(3).
2   (1866) LR 1 Ex 265 at 279.
3   [1994] 1 All ER 53.
4   Ibid at 72.

isolated escapes'.[1] As a matter of policy, he was of the view that it was not desirable to extend the applicability of strict liability beyond the narrow scope of the rule. He indicated that it was for Parliament, and not the courts, to create fresh areas of law. Since the judgment was delivered, in December 1993, Parliament has shown a disinclination to get involved.

8.69 The House of Lords' conclusion on this point has confirmed the view, held by many, that the rule in *Rylands v Fletcher* forms part of the law of nuisance, and is not properly a separate cause of action in its own right. The nuisance 'unreasonableness' can be explained by the stipulation that the defendant must accumulate material for his own purposes which is *likely to do mischief if it escapes.*

Who can sue?

8.70 The rule in *Rylands v Fletcher* is an extension of the law of nuisance, and the principles surrounding the entitlement to sue are the same as those in relation to nuisance.[2] The key case is *Hunter v Canary Wharf Ltd.*[3] The aggrieved party must have a possessory right in the land in order to establish a cause of action.

8.71 Liability does not attach where the escape comes from something which is for the joint benefit of the plaintiff and defendant. In *Kiddle v City Business Properties Ltd,*[4] the defendant leased a shop to the plaintiff. The shop was situated in an arcade and the glass roof of the shop was the property of and under control of the defendant. Rainwater from the roof ran into a gutter over the plaintiff's shop, and was carried to the sewer by a gutter which ran down the side of the shop. Rubbish accumulated in the piping and the gutter overflowed, causing damage to the plaintiff's shop. There was an adequate system of inspection and consequently the defendant was not liable in negligence. Goddard LJ summarised the position as follows:[5]

> 'It is now settled law that where the Plaintiff and the Defendant occupy parts of the same building, whether it be two floors of a warehouse, two sets of offices, or two flats, and water which is laid onto the building escapes and does damage, the person from whose part the escape takes place is not liable in the absence of negligence.'

8.72 The point came before Goddard LJ again in *Peters v Prince of Wales Theatre (Birmingham) Ltd,*[6] in which he stated:

> 'The contractual relationship between landlord and tenant, or the willingness of the Plaintiff to take a lease of part of a house so constructed that at the time when he takes his lease other occupiers are being supplied with water, removes the case from the severities of the common law doctrine laid down in *Rylands v Fletcher.*'

8.73 In *A Prosser and Son Ltd v Levy and Others,*[7] freehold owners of a large block granted the plaintiff a lease of the ground floor lock up shop, with the right to use lavatories on the second floor in common with other tenants. Other tenants in the block had rights of passage over common ways. A stop tap from a redundant pipe,

---

1   [1994] 2 AC 264 at 306.
2   See paras **8.32–8.35**.
3   [1997] 2 All ER 426.
4   [1942] 2 All ER 215.
5   Ibid at 216–217.
6   [1942] 2 All ER 533 at 538.
7   [1955] 1 WLR 1224, CA.

situated in one of the corridors, accidentally switched on causing extensive flooding to the plaintiff's premises. In a curious interpretation of the law, Singleton LJ in the Court of Appeal reviewed the possible exceptions to the rule in *Rylands v Fletcher* and summarised the position as follows:[1]

> 'From these Judgments it appears that there are two important elements for consideration, namely, negligence and consent. In the case of an ordinary water supply in a block of premises each tenant can normally be regarded as consenting to the presence of water on the premises if the supply is of the usual character. It cannot be said that he consents to it if it is of quite an unusual kind, or is defective or dangerous, unless he knows of that.'

He concluded:[2]

> 'The leaving of the copper pipe in the position, and in the condition in which it was was something which no reasonable person would do, and the damage to the Plaintiff's goods was damage of a kind which might naturally follow from it.'

In consequence, the defendants were liable under the rule in *Rylands v Fletcher*.

8.74 In relation to local authorities, the point came up in *Gilson v Kerrier District Council*.[3] The plaintiff owned a farm, across which flowed an artificial watercourse. The watercourse supplied water for the inhabitants of a nearby village. In 1969, the watercourse blocked and the plaintiff's land was flooded following heavy rain. In discussing the *Rylands v Fletcher* point, Buckley LJ concluded as follows:[4]

> 'In the present case, for reasons already indicated, I consider that the proper inference from the nature of the works is that the owner of Trebarvah at that time consented to the water course being constructed across his land because of the benefits he would obtain from being able to get access to the water.'

Consequently, the claim under the rule in *Rylands v Fletcher* was bound to fail.

Are local authorities exempt from the rule in *Rylands v Fletcher*?

8.75 There are two aspects to this argument. First, it is suggested that in the majority of instances where local authorities exercise a duty under statute, they do so for the general benefit of the community rendering the use of land in every case a 'natural' use. This point is dealt with in paras **8.54** and **8.58**, and Upjohn J concluded in *Smeaton v Ilford Corporation*[5] that there was no such exemption.

8.76 The second limb to the argument is slightly different. The argument is that where a local authority performs a function pursuant to its statutory duty, and the statute in question makes no provision for damages in nuisance or under the rule in *Rylands v Fletcher*, then the local authority is exempt from liability. Statutory authority as a defence is considered, as a general proposition, under nuisance, above.[6]

---

1   Ibid at 1233.
2   Ibid.
3   [1976] 1 WLR 904, CA.
4   Ibid at 913.
5   [1954] 1 All ER 923.
6   At paras **8.41–8.47**.

8.77   In *Jones v Llanrwst Urban District Council*,[1] the specific problems arising in relation to the rule in *Rylands v Fletcher* were considered by Parker J. He concluded:[2]

'If A, the owner of a cess-pit, grants to B, or B acquires by prescription, a right to turn B's sewage into A's pit, I cannot myself see how A can escape liability for letting the sewage out on his neighbour's land merely because of the rights of B. It would be different if B's prescription had been to turn his sewage through A's pipe onto his neighbour's land. I come to the conclusion that the existence of the statutory rights affords no defence to the claim for an injunction.'

8.78   In reaching his decision, Parker J was forced to deal with the earlier decision of *Glossop v Heston and Isleworth Local Board*.[3] That case concerned the operation of a sewer under s 13 of the Public Health Act 1875. In *Jones v Llanrwst Urban District Council*, Parker J distinguished that case on the following basis:[4]

'... the action was in substance not an action based on a private wrong, but an action for a mandatory injunction to compel the Defendant board to carry out their statutory duty to provide a proper system of sewerage, relief which could only be obtained by prerogative writ of mandamus.'

He concluded:[5]

'I think it clear that the principle of *Fletcher v Rylands* would apply to the owner of a sewer, whether he made the sewer or not ... His duty at common law would be to see that the sewage in his sewer did not escape to the injury of others, and mere neglect of his duty would give any person injured a good cause of action.'

8.79   The point came before the Court of Appeal in *Pride of Derby and Derbyshire Angling Association v British Celanese*.[6] In that case, the first plaintiff owned a fishery and the second plaintiff, the Earl of Harrington, owned a stretch of one of two rivers concerned. The defendant operated a factory on the banks of the same river. The river became polluted by:

(1)   effluent from the sewer operated by Derby Corporation; and
(2)   organic matter from the factory operated by British Celanese.

The point of particular interest in the context of local authorities surrounds the potential liability of Derby Corporation.

8.80   Section 109(1) of the Derby Corporation Act 1901 provided:

'The sewage disposal works constructed on the lands acquired under the powers of this Act shall at all times hereafter be conducted so that the same shall not be a nuisance and in particular the Corporation shall not allow any noxious or offensive effluvia to escape therefrom or to do or permit or suffer any other act which shall be a nuisance ... and this Act shall not exempt or be deemed to exempt the Corporation from any liability for any nuisance arising from such sewage disposal works or from any proceedings which might but for this Act be taken against them under the provisions of the Public Health Acts or

---

1   [1911] 1 Ch 393.
2   Ibid at 410.
3   (1879) 12 ChD 102.
4   [1911] 1 Ch 393 at 405.
5   Ibid at 405.
6   [1953] 1 All ER 179.

otherwise and the County Council may take any proceedings they may think fit for the purpose of enforcing or giving effect to these provisions.'

In considering the construction of this statutory provision, Sir Raymond Evershed, MR concluded:[1]

'... what the Corporation are doing, as I follow it, is pumping or otherwise diverting into the river, by such mechanical or other means as may be there, the effluent after treatment in the beds and tanks of the disposal works on their land ... if the Public Health Acts apply to this case, or if, contrary to the view which I have expressed, the Act of 1901 ought to be construed as equivalent, in effect, to the Public Health Act, there would be no statutory defence available to the Corporation for what they are doing in discharging effluent through this pipe into the Derwent River.'

8.81   In concluding that the local authority was liable, the judge went on to say that this action could not be considered one 'obliquely directed to commanding a local authority to perform a public duty'.[2] In *Smeaton v Ilford Corporation*, the local authority maintained the sewer pursuant to the Public Health Act 1936. Section 31 of the Public Health Act 1936 provides:

'A local authority shall so discharge their functions under the foregoing provisions of this part of the Act as not to create a nuisance.'

Upjohn J concluded:[3]

'That section necessarily implies, in my judgement, that provided the Defendants do not "create a nuisance" in carrying out their duties, they are to be absolved from liability.'

Dealing with the decision in *Pride of Derby*, the judge observed:[4]

'... they were not directly concerned with escape and the point I have to consider was not directly before them. The Public Health Act 1936, Section 31, seems to me clearly to absolve the Defendants from liability for the escape of sewage complained of. It is, therefore, unnecessary to express a concluded view on the question whether a local authority exercising its statutory duties is altogether outside the rule in *Rylands v Fletcher* ... the question will turn on the construction of the relevant statute.'

8.82   The other relevant case in this context is *King and King v London Borough of Harrow*.[5] Judge Humphrey Lloyd QC, in considering the potential liability of London Borough of Harrow in connection with a blocked culvert, stated:[6]

'In my judgement the Defendants by constructing a culvert entrance which was liable to be blocked and, if blocked, would lead to flooding were not for their own purposes bringing on their land and collecting and keeping there the water so retained. There was no accumulation or even an intention to accumulate and, as I have found, no negligence on the part of the Defendants in constructing or clearing the grille or in failing to do so, as a result of which there was the overflow.'

He went on to conclude:[7]

---

1   [1953] 1 All ER 179 at 197.
2   Ibid.
3   [1954] 1 All ER 923 at 936.
4   Ibid at 936.
5   [1994] 39 Con LR 21.
6   Ibid at 48.
7   [1994] 39 Con LR 21.

'Here the Defendants did not **use** the water in the water course in any ordinary sense of that word.'

8.83   In other words, the courts would be reluctant to impose liability under the rule in *Rylands v Fletcher* where the local authority is performing a function pursuant to its statutory duty, unless the statute in question makes provision for damages in nuisance under the rule in *Rylands v Fletcher*. This ties in with the defence of statutory authority, dealt with under nuisance, above.[1]

Other defences include:

(1)   act of God;
(2)   consent, express or implied (see *Gilson v Kerrier District Council*, at para **8.74**);
(3)   contributory negligence;
(4)   act of a stranger caused the escape;
(5)   act or default of the plaintiff led to the damage;
(6)   statutory authority (see paras **8.41–8.47**).

Remedies in nuisance and under the rule in *Rylands v Fletcher*

8.84   In *Rylands v Fletcher* Blackburn J said that the defendant who is liable under the rule 'is prima facie answerable for all the damage which is the natural consequence of its escape'. Furthermore, liability is owed to those 'damnified'[2] by the escape: they need not be the occupiers of adjoining land or indeed any land.

In nuisance, if the claimant establishes liability he is entitled to an injunction to prevent the nuisance from continuing; and/or to prevent further escapes under the rule in *Rylands v Fletcher*; and/or damages to compensate for the losses suffered. *Transco Plc v Stockport Metropolitan Borough Council*[3] confirms that damages for personal injury are not recoverable under the rule in *Rylands v Fletcher*. Lord Hoffmann said:

'But I think that the point is now settled by two recent decisions of the House of Lords: *Cambridge Water Co. v Eastern Counties Leather Plc*, which decided that *Rylands v Fletcher* is a special form of nuisance and *Hunter v Canary Wharf Limited* which decided that nuisance is a tort against land. It must, I think, follow that damages for personal injuries are not recoverable under the rule.'

8.85   In *Pride of Derby and Derbyshire Angling Association v British Celanese*[4] – which involved ongoing pollution from a sewer and factory – Sir Raymond Evershed MR commented on the potential remedy against Derby Corporation as follows:

'It is, I think, well settled that, if A proves that his proprietary rights are being wrongfully interfered with by B and that B intends to continue his wrong, then A is prima facie entitled to an injunction and he will be deprived of that remedy only if special circumstances exist, including the circumstances that damages are an inadequate remedy for the wrong that he has suffered. In the present case, it is quite plain that damages would be a wholly inadequate remedy for the plaintiff association. The general rule which I have stated applies, in my opinion, to local authorities as well as to other citizens. Equally, of course, the court will not impose on a local authority, or on anyone else, an obligation to do something which is impossible, or which cannot be enforced, or which is unlawful.'

---

1   At paras **8.41–8.47**.
2   *British Celanese Ltd v AH Hunt (Capacitors Ltd)* [1969] 1 WLR 959 at 963, per Lawton J.
3   [2003] UKHL 61, [2004] 2 AC 1.
4   [1953] 1 All ER 179.

Thus, in *Pride of Derby* the plaintiffs were entitled to an injunction to prevent future pollution, and damages to compensate them for the cost of remedying the damage.

NEGLIGENCE

Background

8.86   The principal torts in the area of environmental damage are nuisance and the rule in *Rylands v Fletcher*. This is because where damage has been caused to land or property by flooding or pollution, it is generally easier to establish that the defendant was liable in nuisance and/or under the rule in *Rylands v Fletcher*.

8.87   The explanation for this can be found in the definition of negligence. In order to establish negligence, a plaintiff must show:

(1)   that the defendant owed the plaintiff a duty of care;
(2)   that there has been a breach of the duty of care;
(3)   that the breach has resulted in damage which was a reasonably foreseeable consequence of the breach.

The stumbling block to proving negligence is usually establishing a duty of care and/or that there has been a breach of that duty.

8.88   In most straightforward cases, a local authority *may* be liable in negligence directly, for damages resulting from its day-to-day activities. Thus, for example, in *A Prosser and Son Ltd v Levy and Others*[1] – in which a pipe in the corridor of a property burst, causing damage to the plaintiff tenant's office – it was held that the local authority was liable in negligence for failing to take reasonable steps to prevent the escape of water, the authority being aware of the existence and condition of the pipe in question.

8.89   However, claims in negligence are more likely to arise where the damage has not resulted from local authority land, but rather has been caused indirectly as a result of a local authority performing its statutory duties. There are three main areas where claims have arisen:

(1)   damage resulting from the exercise by a local authority of its statutory duties;
(2)   damage resulting from alleged failure by a local authority to take proper steps to protect an individual or company from the tortious activities of a third party;
(3)   damage resulting from negligent advice or negligence in the performance of a regulatory duty.

Liability where the local authority is exercising a statutory duty

8.90   The starting point for any discussion in this area is *Stovin v Wise*.[2] This case is considered in Chapters 1 and 7. Lord Hoffmann concluded that the minimum conditions for establishing a duty were:[3]

---

1   [1955] 1 WLR 1224, CA.
2   [1996] 3 All ER 801.
3   Ibid at 828.

'... first, that it would in the circumstances have been irrational not to have exercised the power, so that there was in effect a public law duty to act, and secondly, that there are exceptional grounds for holding that the policy of the statute requires compensation to be paid to persons who suffer loss because the power was not exercised.'

It should, however, be noted that Lord Hoffmann, commenting in *Gorringe v Calderdale Metropolitan Borough Council*,[1] cast doubt on the above quotation from *Stovin v Wise*. He expressed the following view:

'The suggestion that there might exceptionally be a case in which a breach of a public law duty could found a private law right of action has proved controversial and it may have been ill-advised to speculate on such matters.'

In *Gorringe* Lord Hoffmann stressed that there is a difference between cases in which a local authority has a statutory power, but does nothing which can be said to give rise to a duty of care on the one hand and cases where a local authority performs an act which does create a common law duty.

8.91 One area where a local authority may incur a liability in negligence for environmental damage is where the damage flows, for example, from a drain which is operated as part of the local authority's statutory duty. In *Dear v Thames Water and Others*,[2] the plaintiff suffered damage to his property caused by foul and storm water from two sources: (a) a brook which ran through the plaintiff's land; and (b) a culvert. The judge found that the drainage system at the plaintiff's property had become inadequate as a result of building development. The plaintiff sued the London Borough of Harrow, Thames Water and Thames Water Utilities Limited in negligence and/or nuisance.

8.92 In considering liability of each of the defendants in negligence, Judge Bowsher QC first addressed the question of whether the defendants owed the plaintiff a duty of care. He concluded that, at the relevant time, none of the defendants were under a statutory duty to maintain either the brook or the culvert. In considering the liability of London Borough of Harrow, the judge concluded:[3]

'Any claim for negligence or nuisance in relation to any non-exercise of powers under the Water Act 1989 should have been brought against the National Rivers Authority rather than the First Defendants.'

This was because, under the Water Act 1989, responsibility for land drainage transferred from the local authority to the National Rivers Authority. Similarly, Thames Water and Thames Water Utilities Limited were under no obligation to maintain the culvert and/or the brook, under the Public Health Act 1936. Consequently, the judge held that none of the defendants owed the plaintiff a duty of care, because they were not the responsible party under statute.

The judge went on to deal with the question of a possible breach of duty and concluded that there was no evidence of a breach of duty in any event. He commented as follows:[4]

---

1   [2004] UKHL 15, [2004] 2 All ER 326.
2   [1992] 33 Con LR 43.
3   Ibid at 52.
4   Ibid at 62.

'The case of the Plaintiff seems to be "I complained for a long time and nothing was done therefore you should compensate me." I have great sympathy for that view, but it is not enough to found an action at common law.'

8.93 In *Glossop v Heston and Isleworth Local Board*,[1] the court dealt with the situation where the local authority was under a statutory duty to act, and failed to do so. The court in *Glossop* concluded that an action in negligence at common law will not lie against a statutory body for non-feasance, as distinct from misfeasance. In *Dear*,[2] Judge Bowsher QC referred to the fact that a sewerage authority's duty to act under the predecessor of s 14 of the Water Act 1973 was a duty to the public and was not a duty owed to individuals. The proper remedy was to seek judicial review. This general principle was, of course, confirmed in *O'Reilly v Mackman*.[3]

8.94 The judge in the same case also decided that, in the light of the decision in *Murphy v Brentwood District Council*,[4] local authorities owed no private law duty to secure compliance with regulations in any event.

8.95 The same point fell for consideration in *King and King v London Borough of Harrow*,[5] which has already been considered in relation to nuisance and the rule in *Rylands v Fletcher*.[6] In that case, the Kings suffered a series of floodings at their property, the latest from foul sewage surcharging from sewers in the road. Judge Humphrey Lloyd QC approved the decision in *Dear* and concluded that under s 23 of the Public Health Act 1936, as applied by s 14(1) and (2) of the Water Act 1973, responsibility for the sewer at the relevant time lay with Thames Water Authority, and not with the local authority. Section 14(1) of the Water Act 1973 made it the duty of every water authority to provide:

'... such public sewers as may be necessary for effectually draining the area and to make such provision ... as may be necessary for effectually dealing with the contents of their sewers ...'

Section 14(2) stated that functions conferred on local authorities by ss 15–24 and 27–31 of the Public Health Act 1936 should be exercisable by the water authorities. The judge concluded that, even though the water authority had been given a statutory power to delegate performance to a local authority, the duty ultimately remained with the water authority.

8.96 In *King*, the judge went on to consider whether or not the plaintiffs might be able to establish negligence, even if a duty of care was owed by the local authority. After considering the argument in some detail, he concluded that they could not, a decision which highlights the difficulty in all such cases in proving that a local authority has been negligent over a period of time in any event.

8.97 *Dear* and *King* cover the more straightforward position where the local authority was not the statutory body responsible for maintaining the drain or sewer. What is the position where the authority does have a statutory duty to maintain the

---

1   [1874–80] All ER Rep 836.
2   [1992] 33 Con LR 43 at 58.
3   [1983] 2 AC 237.
4   [1990] 2 All ER 908; see Chapter 1.
5   [1994] 39 Con LR 21.
6   See paras **8.82–8.83**.

sewers, and does so negligently? In that event, a duty of care probably will arise *unless* the remedy is defined by the statute. Where the remedy is so defined, the cause of action will be for a breach of statutory duty only and the claimant's remedy will be confined to the remedies prescribed by statute.

8.98 Following the decision in *X (Minors) v Bedfordshire County Council*,[1] a local authority does not owe a duty of care in exercising a discretion conferred on it by statute – for example whether or not to carry out improvements to a drain – but does owe a duty of care for the manner in which those works are carried out, a decision having been taken to act. Thus, in *King* it is easy to envisage that, had the local authority been under a statutory duty to maintain the sewer in question, and not Thames Water Authority, a duty of care might have arisen for the manner in which the authority chose to carry out that duty. Judge Humphrey Lloyd QC spent some time considering the potential liability of the authority on this basis, before concluding that it had not been negligent. His review covered a number of works carried out to the drain by the local authority between 1973 and 1990, when further flooding occurred.

8.99 Liability for inadequate drainage has now been considered by the House of Lords in *Marcic v Thames Water Utilities Limited*.[2] The claimant's house was at a low point of the drainage system and suffered flooding from both surface water and foul water sewers. The sewers had been acceptable when originally constructed, however, subsequent housing development in the area meant that they became overloaded in times of heavy rainfall. The claimant put forward claims in nuisance and under the Human Rights Act 1998 that Thames Water, as a public authority, had acted incompatibly with the claimant's rights under Article 8 of the European Convention on Human Rights (ECHR) (respect for family life and home) and Article 1 of the First Protocol to the Convention (protection of property). The House of Lords rejected both claims.

8.100 It was essential, when considering Thames Water's obligations and liabilities, to have in mind the statutory scheme under which it operates. The powers and duties of water undertakers and sewerage undertakers are set out in the Water Industry Act 1991. The exercise of their functions under the Act is subject to supervision and control by the Director General of Water Services. The Director must ensure that companies appointed as sewerage undertakers are able, by securing reasonable returns on their capital, to finance the proper carrying-out of their functions. At the same time he is required to protect the interests of customers. The Director is empowered to make enforcement orders if, for example, he considers that the undertaker is failing to ensure that its area is properly drained; however, this is a question of degree. Analysing the statutory provisions from the point of view of the claimant, the House of Lords pointed out that he could bring proceedings against the sewerage undertaker in respect of failure to comply with an enforcement order if such an order had been made. Alternatively he could take judicial review proceedings against the director for failure to make an enforcement order. In *Marcic*, no enforcement order had been made and no judicial review proceedings commenced.

---

1   [1995] 3 All ER 353.
2   [2003] UKHL 66, [2003] 3 WLR 1603.

8.101   The Court of Appeal had decided in favour of the claimant, relying on cases such as *Sedleigh-Denfield v O'Callaghan*,[1] and *Leakey v National Trust for Places of Historic Interest or Natural Beauty*,[2] establishing that an occupier must do whatever is reasonable in all the circumstances to prevent hazards on his land, however they may arise, from causing damage to a neighbour. The House of Lords held, however, that this line of cases could not apply to Thames Water, in which sewers are vested by statute. Lord Nicholls said:

> 'The common law of nuisance should not impose on Thames Water obligations inconsistent with the statutory scheme. To do so would run counter to the intention of Parliament as expressed in the Water Industry Act 1991. In my view the cause of action in nuisance asserted by Mr Marcic is inconsistent with the statutory scheme.'

8.102   Thames Water was not able to control the volume of water entering the sewers. Nor could it refuse to accept new connections to the sewers. The claimant alleged that he had a cause of action in respect of Thames Water's failure to construct more sewers; however, this ignored the statutory limitations on the enforcement of sewage undertakers' drainage obligations. It was clear, said the House of Lords, that a feature of the statutory enforcement scheme under the Water Industry Act 1991 was that individual householders should not be able to launch proceedings in respect of failure to build sufficient sewers. The taking of enforcement proceedings lay with the Director General of Water Services who would consider the position of an individual householder, but in the context of the wider consideration as set out in the statute. Lord Nicholls, said:

> 'Individual householders may bring proceedings in respect of inadequate drainage only when the undertaker has failed to comply with an enforcement order made by the Secretary of State or the Director. The existence of a parallel common law right, whereby individual householders who suffer sewer flooding may themselves bring court proceedings when no enforcement order has been made, would set at nought the statutory scheme. It would effectively supplant the regulatory role the Director is intended to discharge when questions of sewer flooding arise. For this reason I consider there is no role in this case for a common law cause of action in nuisance as submitted by Mr Marcic.'

8.103   The claimant also alleged breaches of Article 8 (the right to respect or private and family life) and Article 1 of the First Protocol (the right to the enjoyment of possessions) to the ECHR. However, the House of Lords rejected this claim for the same reason, namely that it failed to take into account the statutory scheme under which Thames Water operated the offending sewers. At the same time the House of Lords confirmed that it considered that the statutory scheme was compatible with the ECHR.

Failing to take proper steps to protect an individual or company from the tortious activities of a third party

8.104   This question is considered in detail in Chapter 1.

8.105   In *King v Liverpool City Council*,[3] the plaintiff was a tenant of a block of flats owned by the defendant. The flat above became vacant and, despite requests from the

---

1   [1940] AC 880.
2   [1980] 1 All ER 17.
3   [1986] 1 WLR 890.

plaintiff, the defendant took no effective steps to secure it. Vandals broke in and damaged water pipes on three occasions. The plaintiff claimed damages from the defendant in negligence, alleging that the defendant owed a duty of care to secure the vacant flat so as to prevent vandals gaining access.

Purchas LJ quoted both Robert Goff LJ and Waller LJ in *P Perl (Exporters) Ltd v Camden London Borough Council*[1] and then went on to comment on the decision of the judge at first instance as follows:[2]

'The Judge considered the general system adopted by the Council in the context of the extensive area of their responsibility and the regrettable, but established, social climate at present being experienced in that city, and indeed in other cities. The Judge considered with great care the effectiveness, or lack of effectiveness, of "boarding up" as being one of the courses which admittedly the Council from time to time took as they could ...; nevertheless flooding was a recognised result.'

He concluded:[3]

'... in my judgement the Judge was right to hold the Council owed no duty to the Plaintiff in respect of the acts of the vandals in this case and accordingly I would dismiss this Appeal.'

Liability for negligent advice or negligence in the performance of a regulatory duty

8.106 In *Tidman v Reading Borough Council*,[4] the court held that the local authority did not owe a duty of care when giving advice to the general public about planning matters. In *Philcox v Civil Aviation Authority*,[5] it was held that the CAA's supervisory role was intended for the protection of the public and did not give rise to a duty of care of owners of aircraft to ensure that those aircraft were maintained carefully. And in *Gaisford v Ministry of Agriculture, Fisheries and Food*,[6] it was held that the Ministry did not owe a duty of care to subsequent purchasers to discover the presence of disease in imported animals before their release from quarantine.

8.107 All of these cases support the view that a public body does not, as a general principle, owe a duty of care to the public at large when carrying out its regulatory functions. In environmental matters, this general principle is of direct relevance to environmental health officers and health and safety officers, as well as those officers charged with enforcing the contaminated land provisions under the Environment Act 1990.[7]

8.108 That said, the authority may well owe a duty of care to an individual when performing its regulatory function to the detriment of that individual. This point was raised in *Welton v North Cornwall District Council*.[8] This case, and the

---

1   [1984] QB 342, CA.
2   [1986] 1 WLR 890 at 901.
3   Ibid at 901.
4   [1994] 3 PLR 72.
5   (1995) 92(27) LSG 33.
6   [1996] TLR 444.
7   See paras **8.168–8.169**.
8   [1997] 1 WLR 570.

related decision of *Lam v Brennan and the Borough of Torbay*,[1] are also dealt with in Chapter 9, in relation to negligent advice and misstatement. Nevertheless, the case is an important one in considering the potential liability of environmental health officers specifically, and those performing regulatory functions more generally. This chapter will therefore review the principles, in the specific context of environmental law.

8.109   The general principle, as outlined in Chapter 9, is that the courts will be reluctant to impose liability for advice or information given by local authorities provided they do so in the course of and in accordance with their statutory functions. Mr and Mrs Welton ran a guest house. Mr Evans was the environmental health officer for North Cornwall District Council. He attended at the guest house in 1990 and set out 13 requirements which he said the Weltons had to meet in order to comply with the law relating to environmental health. He threatened to close down the business if they were not met. The Weltons incurred what the Court Appeal described as 'substantial and unnecessary expense'[2] in consequence.

8.110   The Weltons sued the local authority in negligence, alleging that the local authority owed a duty of care because there was a special relationship between Mr Evans and Mrs Welton which gave rise to a duty to take reasonable care in the statement he made as to the extent of the alterations required to comply with the law.

8.111   The relevant statutes were the Food Safety Act 1990 and the Food Act 1984. It was accepted by both parties that Mr Evans was an 'authorised officer' within the meaning of that legislation. The Court of Appeal concluded that the local authority were liable for three principal reasons:

(1)   Mr Evans was not involved in 'conduct specifically directed to statutory enforcement' and consequently there was no tendency to discourage due performance of the statutory duty, within the principles set out by Lord Browne-Wilkinson in *X (Minors) v Bedfordshire County Council*.[3]

(2)   The local authority was not involved in offering an advisory service which could be said to form part of the defendant's system for discharging its statutory duties.

(3)   Mr Evans' conduct was at the heart of the case, namely his imposition of detailed requirements enforced by threat of closure and close supervision, which were 'outwith the legislation'.[4] Rose LJ concluded:[5]

> '... in my Judgment, the existence of their statutory powers and duties affords no reason why the Defendant should not be liable at common law for this type of conduct by their servants, which is otherwise well within the Hedley Byrne principle. If, which I doubt, it is material, at this stage, to consider policy and what is fair, just and reasonable, these considerations could not, in my judgement, lead to any conclusion other than that the conduct in the third category gives rise to a duty at common law.'

8.112   On first reading, this judgment will give concern to environmental health officers. However, a closer analysis of the judgment reveals that the Lord Justices reaffirmed the general legal position and decided this case on its own particular facts,

---

1   See para **8.113**.
2   [1997] 1 WLR 570, per Judge LJ.
3   [1995] 3 All ER 353.
4   [1997] 1 WLR 570 at 581.
5   Ibid.

where the individual in question was not performing his statutory functions in the manner in which he was authorised to do.

8.113 This stance is confirmed by the judgment in *Lam v Brennan and the Borough of Torbay*.[1] In concluding that the local authority was not liable Potter LJ stated that the functions of planning and environmental health officers were exercised by local authorities in the interests of the public at large and not individual members of it. In considering an argument that the defendant council had assumed responsibility to the plaintiffs to take steps under planning and environmental health legislation to bring an alleged nuisance and breach of planning condition to an end, Potter LJ stated:

> 'Nor does it seem to us that the [Plaintiff's] position can be improved by some alternative formulation of his cause of action on the basis of "assumption of responsibility". Where an allegation of "assumption of responsibility" is made against a person or body carrying out a statutory function, there must be something more than the performance (negligence or otherwise) of the statutory function to establish such assumption of responsibility: see for instance the case of *Welton v North Cornwall District Council* ...'

8.114 Perhaps the decision in *Welton* can best be explained by the comment of Ward LJ, who put a slightly different interpretation on the public policy argument when he stated:[2]

> '... from the point of view of the public at large, public safety is important but in the special circumstances of this case it does not seem to me that it would be imperilled if the need for justice to Mrs Welton was given its proper place. So I conclude that fairness, reasonableness and justice and all the material aspects of policy inextricably wrapped in those concepts leads me to uphold the duty of care imposed upon the local authority in this particular case.'

8.115 Where a local authority acts in a regulatory function, therefore, the general principle is that it will not owe a duty of care in negligence to members of the public. Certainly, a duty of care will not be owed for negligent omissions, ie for any failure to act pursuant to statute.

8.116 A local authority will not generally owe a duty of care even where it does act pursuant to its statutory functions, provided that it acts in accordance with those prescribed powers. However, a duty of care may arise where the enforcing officer acts outside its statutory powers, as in *Welton*, or where specific advice is given to an individual which gives rise to proximity and reliance, within the principles of *Caparo v Dickman* (see below), *provided that* the advice in question is not given as part of the authority's statutory functions.

Economic loss

8.117 As a general principle, damages for pure economic loss – as distinct from personal injury or physical damage to property – are not recoverable in negligence *unless* the claimant can establish a degree of proximity and reliance within the

---

1   [1997] PIQR 488.
2   [1997] 1 WLR 570 at 586.

principles of *Hedley Byrne v Heller and Partners*[1] and *Caparo Industries Plc v Dickman.*[2] This point is discussed in more detail in Chapter 1.

8.118	In reality, most claims involving environmental damage will involve damage to land or property which would, in normal circumstances, be recoverable. However, *Welton v North Cornwall District Council* was a claim for pure economic loss, concerning as it did recovery of costs unnecessarily incurred as a result of the environmental health officer's onerous requirements. For that reason, the Weltons could succeed in their claim only if they were able to establish the requisite degree of proximity within *Hedley Byrne* principles, and the court in that case concluded that they could.

8.119	The point of particular concern for local authorities is in relation to contaminated land. This may apply to circumstances such as those in *Welton* but also, perhaps more significantly, where a local authority requires land to be cleaned up pursuant to its statutory duties.[3]

8.120	If a local authority is sued, either for failure to carry out its statutory function, or possibly for contributing towards the contamination in the first place, the cost of clean-up would almost certainly be recoverable as being loss resulting from physical damage to property. However, would any diminution in value or blight resulting from such failure also be recoverable?

8.121	This point came before the Court of Appeal in *Ministry of Defence v Blue Circle Industries plc.*[4] In that case, rain caused ponds situated on the land of the atomic weapons establishment (AWE) to overflow. The overflow passed down a stream into a lake which was situated on land owned by Blue Circle Industries plc. The marsh land became contaminated with radioactive material. The Ministry of Defence was liable to Blue Circle pursuant to s 7(1)(a) of the Nuclear Installations Act 1965. The issues in relation to damages, however, were similar to those in negligence, nuisance and under the rule in *Rylands v Fletcher*.

8.122	There were two key elements to the claim for damages:

(1)	the cost of clean-up (put at £143,963);
(2)	loss in value (assessed at £6.28 million). This arose due to a fall in value of the land between the time the contamination was discovered and the date of completion of the clean-up (January 1993 to December 1994).

It was argued for the defendant that this loss of value constituted pure economic loss, to be distinguished from the actual physical damage to a small proportion of the land. This argument was rejected by the Court of Appeal. Aldous LJ stated that, once actual physical damage to land had been established, the defendant should be liable for all losses that flowed naturally therefrom. He stated:

'The damage in the present case was not mere economic damage and therefore the reasoning in such cases as *Murphy v Brentwood District Council* [1991] AC 398 does not apply. The land itself was physically damaged by the radioactive properties of the

1	[1964] AC 465.
2	[1990] 2 AC 605.
3	See paras **8.133** and **8.153**.
4	[1999] Ch 289.

plutonium which had been admixed with it. The consequence was economic, in the sense that the property was worth less and required the owner to spend money to remove the top soil, but the damage was physical.'

He went on to say:

'Having concluded that the marsh land was damaged by radioactive properties, the only remaining question is – how much compensation should be paid by virtue of Section 12 of the 1965 Act [the Nuclear Installations Act]? The answer must be: all losses of BCI caused by the damage which were reasonably foreseeable and not too remote. Such losses are not limited to the damage to the marsh land ... In my view the Judge was right to conclude that it was a foreseeable consequence of the contamination that BCI would be unable to sell the estate until remedial work had been completed.'

8.123 Perhaps the key point in relation to contaminated land is that blight, whilst on the face of it amounting to pure economic loss, will on the basis of *Ministry of Defence v Blue Circle Industries* be deemed to flow directly from the physical damage to the property – the contamination – and would therefore normally be recoverable upon proof of liability.

Limitation

8.124 This point is relevant to a consideration of the remedies available to a claimant in cases involving environmental damage. Limitation runs from the date the cause of action accrues. In negligence, the limitation period is 6 years from the date of the breach of duty of care (3 years in actions involving personal injury). The key question in any argument on limitation in negligence will be: when did the breach of duty of care arise?

8.125 In cases where the damage or defect in question is hidden, or latent, then under ss 1 and 2 of the Latent Damage Act 1986 the limitation period is 3 years from the date of the claimant's 'knowledge' or 6 years from the date of breach, whichever is the earliest. The Latent Damage Act 1986 covers all actions, save those involving personal injury. The Latent Damage Act 1986 has given some comfort to claimants, but nevertheless in the context of environmental damage and contaminated land the time-limits can present serious difficulties for the claimant.

8.126 Contrast limitation in negligence actions with the position in nuisance, where the limitation period is 6 years from the date the nuisance occurred. Where there is an ongoing or continuing nuisance, every fresh continuance of the nuisance is a fresh cause of action and consequently the injured party who sues after cessation of the wrong may recover for such portions of the nuisance as lie within the limitation period.

STATUTORY FRAMEWORK

Background

8.127 Local authorities are appointed as regulators pursuant to the following provisions of the Environmental Protection Act 1990 (EPA 1990):

(1)　Part I, which creates the regime known as local authority air pollution control (LAAPC);
(2)　Part II in relation to the disposal of waste;
(3)　Part III covering statutory nuisance;
(4)　Part IIA (as enacted by s 57 of the Environment Act 1995) in relation to contaminated land.

Part I of EPA 1990: LAAPC

8.128　Part I of EPA 1990 creates the regimes known as integrated pollution control (IPC) and LAAPC. The Act defines certain 'prescribed processes'. It is unlawful to carry on a prescribed process without authorisation from the enforcing authority. IPC covers the most environmentally hazardous processes. The enforcing authority is the Environment Agency.

8.129　LAAPC covers the remaining processes and is administered by local authorities. The principle behind granting authorisation is to ensure that companies authorised are using the 'best available techniques not entailing excessive costs' (BATNEEC). Under LAAPC, 12,000 industrial plants in England and Wales are regulated by 400 district and borough councils and port health authorities.

Part II of EPA 1990: Waste

8.130　This covers anyone who has control of or responsibility for waste at any stage, from its production to its disposal. The body responsible is under a duty to ensure that the waste is disposed of safely. The obligation affects more bodies, not just those involved in the waste industry, with the exception of householders in relation to household waste.

8.131　Waste is managed in accordance with a licensing system, and a waste management licence is necessary to authorise the treatment, keeping or disposal of controlled waste and landfills or by specified mobile plants. In England, the waste regulation authorities are the county councils. In Greater London and other metropolitan areas, they are the district councils.

Part III of EPA 1990: Statutory nuisance

8.132　This covers control over pollution emanating from industrial, commercial and domestic premises, and from vehicles. The sanction is normally by way of a prosecution in the magistrates' court, giving rise to a fine. Again, the regime is administered by the district and borough councils and port health authorities.

Part IIA of EPA 1990: Contaminated land

8.133　This is enacted by s 57 of the Environment Act 1995. The contaminated land provisions came into force on 1 April 2000.

For local authorities, the provisions are critical in terms of assessing the future role of local authorities in the environmental sphere; therefore, the provisions are worth considering in some detail. A full summary of the Guidance Notes is set out at para **8.174**.

Implications of the contaminated land provisions: claims and third party liabilities

8.134   The point that falls for consideration is the extent to which a liability may arise for local authorities for the manner in which they exercise, or fail to exercise, their duties under the contaminated land provisions. Of concern is the fact that s 78 of the EPA 1990 provides that the local authority *shall act* in order to identify areas of contaminated land within its area, as defined by statute.

8.135   Any person served with a remediation notice has 21 days to appeal against it (s 78L of EPA 1990). In England and Wales, appeal is to a magistrates' court if the notice was served by a local authority, and to the Secretary of State if it was served by the Environment Agency. The notice is suspended pending the outcome of the appeal.

8.136   Where a local authority fails to act pursuant to s 78 of EPA 1990, the proper course for an individual who wishes to compel an investigation and/or who wishes to object to an investigation is to apply by way of judicial review. The Act itself gives no entitlement to a third party to recover damages for breach of statutory duty.

8.137   Aside from these provisions, the appropriate remedy is to apply by way of judicial review. Section 78B(1) and (3) of EPA 1990 provides that the local authority *shall* act, thus creating a positive obligation. This may prove to be crucial, following the Court of Appeal decision in *R v Carrick District Council, ex parte Shelley and Another*.[1] The case concerned sewage on a beach in Cornwall. A local body known as Surfers Against Sewage complained that the local district council had failed to take positive action to clean up the beach pursuant to s 79(1)(e) of EPA 1990, which provides that councils are under a duty to investigate 'any accumulation or deposit which is prejudicial to health or a nuisance'. The court held that, under this section, the council was under a positive duty to decide whether or not a nuisance was being caused and consequently that a decision simply to 'monitor' the situation was insufficient.

8.138   In consequence, there is an avenue that can be pursued against a local authority by a party that feels aggrieved by a local authority's failure to act pursuant to the statute. This could be particularly significant in connection with contaminated land, where the high profile national pressure groups could well have a significant part to play.

8.139   To what extent might a third party be entitled to recover private law damages, in nuisance or negligence?

Nuisance

8.140   EPA 1990 is silent on the question of damages in the context of contaminated land. Thus the principles set out in *Department of Transport v North West Water Authority*,[2] will apply. A claim in nuisance or under the rule in *Rylands v Fletcher* will normally not apply in such circumstances, and the claimant would need to establish that a duty of care was owed in negligence. In order to do so, he would need to establish carelessness in the manner in which the local authority carried out its statutory function.

---

1   [1996] Env LR 273.
2   [1984] 1 AC 336, and see paras **8.41–8.47**.

Negligence

Policy and statutory discretion

8.141　To succeed in negligence, the claimant must establish that the defendant owed the claimant a duty of care. The core principles are outlined in Chapter 1. In the case of *X (Minors) v Bedfordshire County Council*,[1] the House of Lords reiterated the general principle that local authorities do not owe a duty of care when exercising a discretion conferred on them by statute. The House of Lords held that the exercise of that discretion would necessarily involve taking decisions that are subjective. The exception to that rule is where the exercise of the discretion results in a decision which is so unreasonable that no reasonable local authority could have made it (the 'unreasonableness' argument).

8.142　If a third party pursues an 'unreasonableness' argument, the court will also look at the following questions.

(1)　Are public policy considerations involved? These will include, for example, the allocation of resources or the determination of general policy in the performance of public duties. If matters of public policy are involved then, again, the local authority does not owe a duty of care.

(2)　Is it 'just and reasonable' to impose a duty of care at common law? This would involve arguments such as whether the court should develop novel categories of negligence (see *X (Minors)*); whether other factors were involved in reaching the decision whether or not to act; or whether by imposing a duty of care the courts may encourage a cautious and defensive approach to the exercise of the local authority's duties.

8.143　In relation to contaminated land, s 78 of EPA 1990 creates two main areas of potential exposure for a local authority to a third party claim for damages:

(1)　in relation to the maintenance of registers; and

(2)　where a local authority takes action to clean up a site and does so in such a way that it causes damage.

8.144　It is anticipated that the courts would conclude that the failure to maintain a register does not give rise to a duty of care, either because it would involve the exercise of a discretion conferred by statute or because, in certain circumstances, the local authority's ability to act may be directly influenced by the allocation of resources and the determination of general policy in the performance of its public duties. That said, it is quite conceivable that the third party could claim that a decision not to include an area of land on a register was so unreasonable that no reasonable local authority could have made it and that the decision did not directly involve the allocation of resources. Whether a court would consider that it is 'just and reasonable' to impose a duty of care in relation to registers will no doubt be determined in due course.

Operational duties

8.145　Where a local authority takes action to clean up a site and does so in such a way that it causes damage, this would in most instances be what is known as an

---

1　[1995] 3 All ER 353.

'operational' matter and would therefore give rise to a duty of care. This point is discussed in Chapters 1, 3 and 10, and reference should be made in particular to the decision in *Capital and Counties v Hampshire County Council*.[1]

8.146 It is clear that any private law claim in damages against a local authority arising out of its duties under the Act will need to be looked at carefully on its own particular facts. It is sufficient to bear in mind that before the court will impose a duty of care in negligence, it will have to be satisfied that a third party has overcome the difficult hurdles outlined in *X (Minors)* and other subsequent decisions. It is highly unlikely that an attempt to impose a general duty of care on local authorities for failing to act under s 78 of EPA 1990 would succeed.

Legal implications: other key factors

Resources

8.147 The Government announced that it would make funds available to assist local authorities in implementing the new provisions. This would meet part, but not all, of the total cost of setting up an appropriate scheme. Local authorities must still consider funding to cover the following.

(1) the cost of maintaining and administering the registers;
(2) the 'upfront' cost in the event that the appropriate person fails to remedy contaminated land and the local authority is obliged to do so in its place;
(3) where it does intervene, the possibility of recovering its outlay.

8.148 Further questions remain in relation to interpretation of the Act. For example, how will the courts view the local authority's obligations? In particular, how will they interpret the word 'shall' under s 78B(1) and (3)?

8.149 Turning to liability issues, similar principles apply as in relation to third party liabilities, outlined at paras **8.134–8.146**. In nuisance and/or under the rule in *Rylands v Fletcher*, the defence of statutory authority would normally be available. In negligence, it was confirmed by the House of Lords in *X (Minors)* that the allocation of resources was a significant factor to take into account in considering whether or not the local authority owed a duty of care when exercising a discretion conferred on it by statute. On this point, Lord Browne-Wilkinson commented as follows:[2]

> '... in seeking to establish that a local authority is liable at common law for negligence in the exercise of a discretion conferred by statute, the first requirement is to show that the decision was outside the ambit of the discretion altogether: if it was not, a local authority cannot itself be in breach of any duty of care owed to the plaintiff.
>
> In deciding whether or not this requirement is satisfied, the court has to assess the relevant factors taken into account by the authority in exercising the discretion. Since what are under consideration are discretionary powers conferred on public bodies for public purposes the relevant factors will often include policy matters, for example social policy, the allocation of financial resources between the different calls made upon them or ... the balance between pursuing desirable social aims as against the risk to the public inherent in doing so.'

1   [1997] 2 All ER 865.
2   [1995] 3 All ER 353 at 369.

Planning

8.150 Local authorities must appreciate the importance of the interaction between the planning department and the enforcement authorities. Planning is, of course, in itself an integral part of the environmental debate. It is also worth noting the Government's 1997 commitment to build 4.4 million new homes in the South East of England on brown field sites, some of which may well be contaminated.

8.151 The potential liability of planning officers is considered in detail in Chapter 9. In this context, it is worth noting the judgment of Newey J in *Ryeford Homes v Sevenoaks District Council*,[1] in which even before the decision in *Murphy v Brentwood District Council*,[2] the court held that there was no duty of care on the part of a planning officer, under the principle of *Anns v Merton Borough Council*,[3] where planning permission was granted for the building of homes which subsequently became flooded when the natural drainage to the land was barred by a neighbouring proprietor. As a general principle, therefore, it is clear that establishing a duty of care on the part of a planning officer will be difficult.

It should be noted, however, that the Court of Appeal, in *Kane v New Forest District Council*,[4] rejected an argument that planning officers enjoyed a blanket immunity. A planning decision had resulted in the placing of a footpath in a dangerous position which resulted in the claimant sustaining a serious injury when he was hit by a car. The Court of Appeal held that the planning officers owed a duty of care.

8.152 The relevant government policy relating to planning and contaminated land is set out in *Planning Policy Guide Note No 23* (p 23) for England, in *Planning Guidance (Wales)* for Wales, and in *Planning Advice Note on Planning and Environmental Protection* for Scotland. The guidance indicates that contamination of land may be a material planning consideration to be taken into account at various stages in the planning process. Account should be taken of both the actual and intended uses of the land. Thus the local authority must take account of potential future contamination from the proposed use, as well as possible risks arising from the current use of the land (which is covered by Part IIA of EPA 1990).

Negligent advice

8.153 Where a local authority employee gives specialist advice which goes beyond the statutory obligations, then, in theory, that individual may owe a duty of care, giving rise to a claim in negligence. This principle was perhaps most clearly demonstrated in *Welton v North Cornwall District Council*.[5] The situation may arise where a landowner has been served with a remediation notice and requires advice on the extent of the clean-up required. For this reason, enforcement officers would be well advised to be aware of their statutory obligations in relation to contaminated land and not to exceed them. They should also act within the guidance issued to them by their employers.

---

1 [1989] 16 Con LR 75.
2 [1991] AC 398.
3 [1978] AC 728.
4 [2001] EWCA Civ 878, [2001] 3 All ER 914.
5 [1997] PNLR 108.

8.154 For a more detailed discussion on this area, see paras **8.106–8.116** and Chapter 9.

8.155 In the context of duty of care and damages, the House of Lords' judgment in *South Australia Asset Management Corporation v York Montague Ltd*[1] should also be noted. In considering the liability of valuers of a commercial property, the House of Lords concluded that the valuer should be liable only for consequences which have a 'sufficient causal connection with the subject matter of the duty'. This is akin to the 'assumption of responsibility' argument, which has been considered elsewhere in this book.[2] In general, a professional person will be liable only for those damages flowing directly from the advice he or she was qualified to give, as a professional person. Lord Hoffmann concluded:[3]

> 'In my view the damages should have been limited to the consequences of the valuation being wrong, which were that the lender had £700,000 or £650,000 less security than he thought. The Plaintiffs say that the situation produced by the over valuation was not merely that they had less security, but also that there was a greater risk of default. But the valuer was not asked to advise on the risk of default, which would depend upon a number of matters outside his knowledge, including the personal resources of the borrower.'

Liabilities of third parties

8.156 In implementing the statutory provisions, local authorities are likely to seek independent advice from environmental consultants and lawyers. Contractors employed by local authorities will also need to be aware of their obligations surrounding contaminated land and waste. Where advice is sought, the local authority may well be able to recover any losses it suffers from the advisers. However, local authorities would be well advised to ensure that the relevant professional has appropriate insurance in place. It is now commonplace to seek such insurances from contractors on large construction projects.

Registers

8.157 Since the introduction of the EPA 1990, the issue of contaminated land registers has been a vexed one. The initial scheme for maintaining registers, under s 143 of EPA 1990, was abandoned. However, s 78R of EPA 1990 (introduced by s 57 of the Environment Act 1995) provides that a local authority is obliged to keep a register containing details of remediation served by the authority or other criminal prosecutions brought pursuant to the Act. However, there is no requirement for different authorities to pool their information into a national register save where a site designated as a 'special site' is notified to the Environment Agency. Further, different authorities will interpret their obligations in different ways, so that the accuracy and extent of available data will differ from area to area.

8.158 There are other concerns as follows.

(1) If a local authority is diligent in serving remediation notices, there is a danger that it will drive industry from the area. Thus, it may be in the authority's interest not to identify the potential problems in its area, which would need to be

---

1   [1996] 3 All ER 365.

2   See Chapters 1, 4 and 9.

3   [1996] 3 All ER 365 at 379.

published on a register. Conversely, it could be argued that once an area has been cleaned up it would encourage industry to set up there safe in the knowledge that there are unlikely to be any outstanding environmental problems. However, getting to that situation will inevitably take time.

(2) Local authorities have effectively become the watch dogs in identifying contaminated land, leaving them open to criticism if, say, a purchaser of land subsequently establishes that a particular site is not on the register. It is not entirely clear how the interrelationship with the Environment Agency will work but the principal duty for designating special sites rests with the local authority.

(3) At present, many local authorities simply do not have the funds to carry out their duties relating to contaminated land. However, as the provisions of the Act begin to bite might they not find themselves compelled to act by local residents and/or pressure groups?

(4) Purchasers and sellers of property will in time come to rely on the registers of contaminated land. Might local authorities incur a liability to third parties if they fail to keep those registers up to date and/or if the registers are inaccurate?

(5) Industry has criticised the fact that an area of land will remain on the register despite the fact that it may have been cleaned up. The very fact of being on a register may in itself be seen as 'taboo', making a site difficult to sell. Might a local authority incur a liability for including an area of land on its register which should not be there?

8.159   As the law currently stands, the answer to the last two questions should be 'no'. However, it is possible to envisage a court seeking to get round the established legal principles, in particular where inclusion or failure to include on the register comes about as a result of an 'operational' failure, rather than as a result of an initial policy decision whether or not to include a piece of land on the register.

Insurance

8.160   As a general rule, prior to 1991 most public liability (PL) insurance policies covered claims by third parties for environmental damage. In the UK, concern over the potential increase in insurers' exposure led to a recommendation in 1991 from the Association of British Insurers (ABI) aimed at deleting cover for so-called 'gradual' pollution from PL policies altogether. The recommended ABI exclusion to be included in all such policies from 1991 reads:

> 'This policy excludes all liability in respect of pollution or contamination other than that caused by a sudden identifiable, unintended and unexpected incident which takes place in its entirety at a specific time and place during the period of insurance.'

8.161   The clause excludes cover for all environmental damage, and places the onus on the insured to establish that the damage was caused by a 'sudden identifiable, unintended and unexpected incident'. The intention is to allow cover for the one-off accidental incident but not for liabilities arising out of gradual pollution over time.

8.162   The effect of the ABI clause has been to reduce significantly the availability of cover for gradual pollution risks and, broadly speaking, the situation remains the same today. The implications could be significant if, as anticipated, there is an increase in claims surrounding land which has been contaminated in the past.

8.163 Part of the problem here is that the precise scope of the so-called pollution exclusion is yet to be determined by the courts. It is well documented that in the US some bizarre interpretations of a similar policy wording which was introduced by insurers in the 1980s have led to most incidents falling within the scope of insurance policies. In effect, the courts in the US have bent over backwards to apply cover. The result was the introduction of a blanket pollution exclusion in all PL policies. It has for some time now been anticipated that a similar exclusion will be introduced in the UK, although to date it has not happened. This is largely because the incidence of claims has not increased in the proportions anticipated.

8.164 The conclusions to be drawn for local authorities grappling with this area are equivocal. The majority of one-off incidents giving rise to contamination are likely to be covered under the standard policy wording. However, where an argument can be made out that the incident was gradual, coverage cannot be guaranteed. Where the land in question has been contaminated for some time, such that it may fall within a pre-1991 PL policy, the exclusion is unlikely to apply in any event. On balance, claims are more likely than not to be covered but the risks are there and are likely to increase over time, as awareness of the issues and the potential for causing damage also increases.

Environmental insurance: implications of the Environment Act 1995

8.165 Although the policies do vary, most local authority public liability policies issued since 1991 contain the ABI recommended pollution exclusion, or a variant thereof. The majority of policies issued before 1991 will contain no pollution exclusion.

8.166 For claims after 1991, the key question is: to what extent might the potential liabilities identified above fall within the definition 'sudden and unintended'?

8.167 As far as registers are concerned, it is doubted whether a claim that the authority had failed to maintain a register would fall within the definition 'sudden and unintended'. Most insurers will argue that it falls outside the scope of such a policy. However, it is arguable that the 'sudden and unintended' incident would not be the negligent act of the local authority in failing to maintain the register (if proved), but rather the incident which gave rise to the pollution in the first place. If that is correct, then whether or not a failure in respect of a register is covered under a public liability policy will depend upon the nature of the incident and, in particular, whether it involves the recent discovery of a long-standing contamination or a one-off incident.

8.168 Where a local authority takes action to clean up a site and does so in a way that causes damage, then whether such an incident would be described as 'gradual' or 'sudden and unintended' would depend on the circumstances of each case. It is thought that most incidents of this nature would fall within the definition 'sudden and unintended', thus affording the local authority cover.

8.169 The other interesting question that arises in respect of insurance policies, which could indirectly affect local authorities, is where a local authority cleans up and seeks to recover the costs of that clean-up from the 'appropriate person'. Would a claim by the local authority in those circumstances be covered under the appropriate person's public liability policy, whether or not there is a pollution exclusion? It is anticipated that a recovery would not be covered in these circumstances; otherwise, it would be in the interests of the appropriate person not to respond to a remediation notice when first served, but to wait until sued by the local authority and then claim the cost of clean-up from his or her insurers. This would surely be against public policy.

Conclusions in relation to contaminated land

8.170 EPA 1990 imposes regulatory obligations on local authorities in connection with the environment. The Environment Act 1995, by creating s 78 of EPA 1990, imposes significant obligations on local authorities in relation to contaminated land. In particular, local authorities are obliged to act to compel clean-up of certain sites within their area. The consequences of failing to do so are as yet unclear.

8.171 The new statutory duties, and in particular those in relation to contaminated land, may give rise to claims by individuals affected, as they seek to recover the costs of contamination from a third party. In reality, local authorities are unlikely to owe a duty of care when exercising the discretion conferred on them by statute. However, some concern remains surrounding the setting-up and maintenance of the contaminated land registers. Local authorities could also expose themselves to potential liability where they take action to clean up a site and to recover the cost of doing so from a third party, pursuant to the statute. On a more general level, s 78 of EPA 1990 may well result in an increase in claims in the long term. Where it incurs the cost of clean-up, a party is likely to seek to recover some or all of those costs, particularly where the owner or occupier is not the polluter. Parties are also more likely to act themselves to clean up a site where there is a risk of being placed on the local authority register. This pressure may well increase the overall number of claims relating to the environment. In some circumstances, local authorities are likely to find themselves on the receiving end of litigation, as owners of a significant quantity of land nationwide. In that context, questions of foreseeability of damage are likely to prove critical.

SECTION 78 OF THE ENVIRONMENTAL PROTECTION ACT 1990 (AS ENACTED BY SECTION 57 OF THE ENVIRONMENT ACT 1995): A SUMMARY

8.172 Of the most significance to local authorities is s 57 of the Environment Act 1995, which creates an amendment to s 78 of EPA 1990. The section puts local authorities under a positive duty to:

(1) identify areas of contaminated land (s 78B(1));
(2) designate certain areas as 'special sites' (ss 78B(1) and 78C); and
(3) give notice of that fact to:
    (a) the appropriate agency;
    (b) the owner of the land;
    (c) any person who appears to the authority to be in occupation of the whole or any part of the land;
    (d) the person who appears to the authority to be the 'appropriate person' (s 78B(3)).

Section 78 goes on to create the following duties.

(1)   The local authority must identify and designate 'special sites' (s 78C).
(2)   Where land has been designated as a special site, the local authority must serve on the 'appropriate person' a remediation notice specifying what the person must do by way of remediation and the time within which he or she must do so (s 78E).
(3)   Where the 'appropriate person' fails to carry out remediation within the appropriate time-limit, the local authority has the power to carry out the remediation itself and to recover the cost of that remediation from the appropriate person (ss 78M and 78N).
(4)   The local authority is obliged to keep a register containing details of remediation notices served by the authority or other criminal prosecutions brought pursuant to the Act (s 78R).

8.173   The 'appropriate person' is, of course, defined in the statute but still leaves considerable scope for argument. Section 78F(2) defines the appropriate person as:

'... any person, or any of the persons, who caused or knowingly permitted the substances, or any of the substances ... to be in, on or under that land.' (Class A person)

However, under s 78F(3), where the person who causes or knowingly permits the pollution cannot be found, then the appropriate person:

'... is the owner or occupier for the time being of the contaminated land in question.'

Guidance Notes

8.174   The key points arising out of the Guidance Notes are as follows:

(1)   The notes provide that a local authority should prepare, publish and implement a *written strategy* for its area. The strategy should be published within 15 months of the issue of the Guidance Notes and should be kept under review.

As part of its strategy, the local authority should include the following.

(a)   Procedures for the periodic review of assumptions made, of any information previously used to assess potential problems and for managing new information.
(b)   Appropriate time scales for the inspection of different parts of its area, identifying the most pressing and serious problems and reflecting local circumstances.
(c)   Procedures for handling information on the possibility of problems associated with individual land provided by businesses, voluntary organisations and members of the public.

(2)   In determining whether or not land falls within the *definition of 'contaminated land'*, the local authority should consider whether one of the following grounds applies:

(a)   significant harm is being caused;
(b)   there is a significant possibility of significant harm being caused;
(c)   pollution of controlled waters is being caused;

(d)   pollution of controlled waters is likely to be caused.

In making a determination as to whether or not land is contaminated, the local authority should take all relevant evidence into account and carry out an appropriate scientific assessment. It should then prepare a written record of the determination.

(3)   In *assessing risk*, the Notes provide that risk can be defined as a combination of:

(a)   the probability, or frequency, of occurrence of a defined hazard; and
(b)   the magnitude (including the seriousness) of the consequences to a specific receptor.

Local authorities should follow the concept of *source–pathway–receptor*, where they should in each case identify the following:

(a)   a contaminant or potential pollutant (the source);
(b)   a receptor (the target);
(c)   a pathway.

(4)   In considering whether there is a possibility of *significant harm*, local authorities should consider the following:

(a)   the nature and degree of harm;
(b)   the time scale within which the harm might occur; and
(c)   the vulnerability of the receptors to which the harm might be caused.

(5)   In looking at whether or not remediation of contamination is required, the *standard of remediation* is that the land should be 'suitable for use'. The standard is that which is:

'achievable ... by the use of a remediation package which forms the best practicable techniques of remediation for:

(a)   dealing with any one or more of the pollutant, pathway or receptor ...
(b)   remedying the effect of any significant harm or pollution of controlled water which is resulting, or has already resulted from, the significant pollutant linkage.'

In considering whether or not a remediation action is reasonable, the authority should carry out an assessment of the costs likely to be involved and the resulting benefits. They should be satisfied that the benefits are worth incurring the costs.

In assessing the benefits of a remediation action, 'the authority should have regard for the seriousness of any significant harm or of any pollution of controlled waters to which the action relates'.

(6)   In considering whether a person is an *appropriate person* to bear responsibility for a remediation action, the Guidance Notes go into significant detail. The authority should first of all identify those persons who 'caused or knowingly permitted' the pollution (Class A persons). If there are two or more Class A persons, then liability should be apportioned between them in accordance with the Guidance Notes. Only if a Class A person cannot be found should the local authority proceed against a Class B person, who is defined as: '... the owner or occupier'.

There will no doubt be arguments in due course as to what constitutes 'causing or knowingly permitting' the damage, but see *Alphacell Ltd v Woodward*.[1] The Guidance Notes also quote the following reference from *Hansard*:

'The test of "knowingly permitting" would require both knowledge that the substances in question were in, on or under the land and the possession of the power to prevent such a substance being there.' (House of Lords, *Hansard* [11 July 1995] col 1497)

(7) The Guidance Notes go on to create *six exclusions to Class A*. Effectively, these deal with circumstances where the person was not the person who directly caused or knowingly permitted the damage.

(8) If the authority carries out the remediation and then seeks to *recover the cost of remediation* from the appropriate person, it shall have regard:

'... to any hardship which the recovery may cause to the person from whom the cost is recoverable ...'

The Guidance Notes state that 'hardship' should have its ordinary meaning. Where the authority waives or reduces recovery of remediation costs in accordance with this provision, it becomes responsible for those costs.

HUMAN RIGHTS ACT 1998 AND ENVIRONMENTAL LIABILITIES

8.175 An example of the potential effect of the Human Rights Act 1998, as it relates to the environment, is the possible development of the law of nuisance following the judgment in *Lopez Ostra v Spain*.[2] A neighbour was affected by noxious fumes from a nearby site. The public authority had granted planning permission for the building of a factory on the site. The Spanish court held that the use of the factory with planning permission was 'reasonable'. The neighbour's appeal to the European Court of Human Rights on the grounds of a breach of Article 8 of the European Convention on Human Rights (ECHR) (the right to respect for private and family life) was successful.

8.176 A claim for a breach of Article 8 can now be brought under s 6 of the Human Rights Act 1998, on the basis that the public authority was in breach of the ECHR. However, it is likely that a claim would also proceed in nuisance and the courts will need to deal with the interrelationship between Article 8 and the law of nuisance in this country. Furthermore, the courts will need to consider Article 8 in relation to the rule in *Rylands v Fletcher*. It is arguable that Article 8 provides a basis for a successful claim for compensation, which might not be available under the rule in *Rylands v Fletcher*.

8.177 A further point to note in relation to the Human Rights Act 1998 concerns noise pollution. In *Powell and Rayner v United Kingdom*,[3] applicants living near Heathrow Airport succeeded in persuading the European Court that Article 8 could

---

1   [1972] 2 All ER 475.
2   (1994) 20 EHRR 277.
3   (1990) 12 EHRR 355, and see paras **2.40–2.41**.

apply in relation to noise pollution. However, the European Court, sitting as a Grand Chamber, later overturned this decision.

8.178   In the domestic courts, the decision in *Southwark London Borough Council v Mills; Baxter v Camden London Borough Council (No 2)*,[1] dealt with inadequate sound proofing and concluded that the tenants of flats owned by the local authority could not pursue a claim in negligence as the neighbours were not doing anything unreasonable. The claim in nuisance also failed. In order for a claim in statutory nuisance to succeed under s 79(1)(g) of EPA 1990, the claimants would need to show that the nuisance was prejudicial to health, ie 'injurious or likely to cause injury to health'.[2] It is submitted that a claim by the tenants under s 6 of the Human Rights Act 1998 for a breach of Article 8 would have failed because the House of Lords considered that the complaint related to what was only normal domestic noise; however, the potential for such a claim exists.

---

1   [1999] 4 All ER 449, HL, and see Chapter 5.
2   EPA 1990, s 79(7).

Chapter 9

ADVICE AND INFORMATION

INTRODUCTION

9.1   Local authorities have many statutory functions, some of which are powers and some duties. These functions at one time or another will touch the lives or business of every member of the public. In addition, local authorities are storehouses of information about property and other matters which are kept on statutory registers. It is a common feature of everyday life for members of the public to ask a local authority for advice or information about the exercise of its functions or for information from one of its registers. This chapter considers the liability of local authorities in these areas.

THE BASIC LAW

9.2   Liability for economic loss caused by negligently given advice or information entered the law of England and Wales in the case of *Hedley Byrne & Co Limited v Heller & Partners Limited*,[1] which has already been discussed in Chapter 1.

There has never been any reason in principle why local authorities should not be liable under the *Hedley Byrne* doctrine. Although *Murphy v Brentwood District Council*[2] removed from them a substantial area of liability, nothing said in the speeches in that case affected its application. Lord Oliver of Aylmerton, referring to *Dutton v Bognor Regis Urban District Council*,[3] and *Anns v Merton London Borough Council*,[4] said:[5]

> 'In neither case was it possible to allege successfully that the Plaintiffs had relied upon the proper performance by the Defendant of its ... duties so as to invoke the principles expounded in *Hedley Byrne & Co Limited v Heller & Partners* ...'

Lord Bridge was more explicit:[6]

> '... since the function of a Local Authority approving plans or inspecting buildings in the course of construction is directed to ensuring that the builder complies with building bye-laws or regulations, I cannot see how, in principle, the scope of the liability of the authority for a negligent failure to ensure compliance can exceed that of the liability of the builder for his negligent failure to comply.

---

1   [1964] AC 465.
2   [1991] 1 AC 398.
3   [1972] 1 QB 373.
4   [1978] AC 728.
5   [1991] 1 AC 398 at 483C.
6   Ibid at 481C.

There may, of course, be situations where, even in the absence of contract, there is a special relationship of proximity between builder and building owner which is sufficiently akin to contract to introduce the element of reliance so that the scope of the duty of care owed by the builder to the owner is wide enough to embrace purely economic loss. The decision in *Junior Books Limited v Veitchi Co Limited* [1983] 1 AC 520 can, I believe, only be understood on this basis.'

Such a special relationship of proximity could in theory arise between a building owner and a local authority. However, he continued:[1]

'In *Council of the Shire of Sutherland v Heyman*, 157 CLR 424 . . . the central theme . . . is that a duty of care of a scope sufficient to make the authority liable for damage of the kind suffered can only be based on the principle of reliance and that there is nothing in the ordinary relationship of a local authority as statutory supervisor of building operations, and the purchaser of a defective building capable of giving rise to such a duty. I agree . . .'

9.3 In two cases, *Henderson v Merrett Syndicates Limited*,[2] and *Spring v Guardian Insurance Plc*,[3] Lord Goff of Chieveley based the principle underlying the *Hedley Byrne* doctrine upon the assumption of responsibility by the person giving the advice or information to the person receiving it. In the former case, he said:[4]

'. . . though *Hedley Byrne* was concerned with the provision of information and advice, the example given . . . of the relationship between solicitor and client and . . . [the] statements of principle show that the principle extends beyond the provision of information and advice to include the performance of other services . . . although in the case of the provision of information and advice, reliance upon it by the other party will be necessary to establish a cause of action . . . , nevertheless there may be other circumstances in which there will be the necessary reliance to give rise to the application of the principle . . . [A]s cases concerned with solicitor and client demonstrate, where the plaintiff entrusts the defendant with the conduct of his affairs, in general or in particular, he may be held to have relied on the defendant to exercise due skill and care in such conduct . . .'

He continued:[5]

'The question has frequently arisen whether the plaintiff falls within the category of persons to whom the maker of the statement owes a duty of care. In seeking to contain that category . . . there has been some tendency on the part of the Courts to criticise the concept of "assumption of responsibility" as being "unlikely to be a helpful or realistic test in most cases" (see *Smith v Eric S. Bush* [1990] 1 AC 831, 864–865, per Lord Griffiths . . .). However . . . there seems to be no reason why recourse should not be had to the concept, which appears after all to have been adopted in one form or another, by all of their Lordships in *Hedley Byrne* . . . Furthermore, especially in a context concerned with a liability which may arise under a contract or in a situation "equivalent to contract" it must be expected that an objective test will be applied when asking the question whether, in a particular case, responsibility should be held to have been assumed by the defendant to the plaintiff . . . It follows that, once the case is identified as falling within the *Hedley Byrne* principle, there should be no need to embark upon any further enquiry whether it is "fair, just and reasonable" to impose liability for economic loss . . . The concept indicates too that in some circumstances, for example where the undertaking to furnish the relevant

---

1   [1991] 1 AC 399 at 481E.
2   [1995] 2 AC 145.
3   [1995] 2 AC 296.
4   [1995] 2 AC 145 at 180E.
5   Ibid at 180G.

service is given on an informal occasion, there may be no assumption of responsibility; and likewise that an assumption of responsibility may be negatived by an appropriate disclaimer. I wish to add in parenthesis that ... an assumption of responsibility by, for example, a professional man may give rise to liability in respect of negligent omissions as much as negligent acts of commission, as for example when a solicitor assumes responsibility for business on behalf of his client and omits to take a certain step ... which falls within the responsibility so assumed by them.'

9.4 An important discussion of this principle is contained in *Williams v Natural Life Health Foods Ltd and Another*.[1] The claimants entered into a franchise agreement with the defendant company. In due course they sued the company for negligent advice contained in its financial projections. They also sued Mr Mistlin, the managing director and principal shareholder of the defendant company. They claimed that the defendant company's promotional literature referred to and relied upon the skill of Mr Mistlin and that as a result he had assumed personal responsibility to them for the accuracy of the projections. Although that claim was upheld by Langley J and the Court of Appeal, the House of Lords rejected it.

9.5 Lord Steyn referred to what he called 'the extended *Hedley Byrne* principle',[2] and continued:

'It is clear ... that the governing principles are stated in the leading speech of Lord Goff ... in *Henderson v Merrett Syndicates Ltd* [1995] 2 AC 145. First, in Henderson's case it was settled that the assumption of responsibility principle ... is not confined to statements but may apply to any assumption of responsibility for the provision of services. ... Secondly, it was established that once a case is identified as falling within the extended *Hedley Byrne* principle, there is no need to embark on any further enquiry whether it is "fair, just and reasonable" to impose liability for economic loss. Thirdly, ... it was made clear that

"reliance upon [the assumption of responsibility] by the other party will be necessary to establish a cause of action (because otherwise the negligence will have no causative effect) ..."

Fourthly, it was held that the existence of a contractual duty of care between the parties does not preclude the concurrence of a tort duty in the same respect.'

9.6 In applying those principles, he said:[3]

'The touchstone of liability is not the state of mind of the Defendant. An objective test means that the primary focus must be on things said or done by the Defendant or on his behalf in dealings with the Plaintiff ... The primary focus must be on exchanges (in which term I include statements and conduct) which cross the line between the Defendant and the Plaintiff ... The enquiry must be whether the director, or anybody on his behalf, conveyed directly or indirectly to the prospective franchisees that the director assumed personal responsibility towards the prospective franchisees.'

He continued:[4]

---

1   [1998] 1 WLR 830.
2   Ibid at 834D.
3   Ibid at 835F.
4   Ibid at 837B.

'The test is not simply reliance in fact. The test is whether the Plaintiff could *reasonably* rely on an assumption of personal responsibility by the individual who performed the services on behalf of the company.'

He then concluded: [1]

'In the present case there were no personal dealings between Mr Mistlin and the Plaintiffs. There were no exchanges or conduct crossing the line which could have conveyed to the Plaintiffs that Mr Mistlin was willing to assume personal responsibility to them. ... I am also satisfied that there was not even evidence that the Plaintiffs believed that Mr Mistlin was undertaking personal responsibility to them.'

This case will be of some assistance in considering whether a local authority has assumed a private as opposed to a public responsibility to the person to whom it has provided advice or information.

9.7   Two relevant points emerge from this analysis: first, whether in any situation the giver of advice or information has assumed a duty of care to the receiver contains an objective element which is for the court to assess; secondly, a duty of care in relation to an omission to advise or inform or take any other step is unlikely to arise between a local authority and members of the public since the latter do not in general entrust the conduct of their affairs to the former.

9.8   The objective element in the assumption of responsibility is illustrated in the speech of Lord Oliver of Aylmerton in *Caparo Industries Plc v Dickman*: [2]

'... it is not easy to cull from the speeches in the *Hedley Byrne* case ... any clear attempt to define or classify the circumstances which give rise to the relationship of proximity on which the action depends ... The nearest that one gets to the establishment of a criterion for the creation of a duty in the case of a negligent statement is the emphasis to be found in all the speeches upon "the voluntary assumption of responsibility" by the defendant. This is a convenient phrase but it is clear that it was not intended to be a test for the existence of the duty for, on analysis, it means no more than that the act of the defendant in making the statement or tendering the advice was voluntary and that the law attributes to it an assumption of responsibility if the statement or advice is inaccurate and is acted upon. It tells us nothing about the circumstances from which such attribution arises.'

9.9   Later in his speech, Lord Oliver set out the components of the duty: [3]

'What can be deduced from the *Hedley Byrne* case ... is that the necessary relationship between the maker of a statement or giver of advice ("the adviser") and the recipient who acts in reliance upon it ("the advisee") may typically be held to exist where

(1)   the advice is required for a purpose, whether particularly specified or generally described, which is made known, either actually or inferentially, to the adviser at the time when the advice is given;

(2)   the adviser knows, either actually or inferentially, that his advice will be communicated to the advisee, either specifically or as a member of an ascertainable class, in order that it should be used by the advisee for that purpose;

(3)   it is known either actually or inferentially, that the advice so communicated is likely to be acted upon by the advisee for that purpose without independent enquiry, and

(4)   it is so acted upon by the advisee to his detriment.'

---

1   [1998] 1 WLR 830 at 838C.
2   [1990] 2 AC 605 at 637E.
3   Ibid at 638B.

Components (2) and (3) indicate that the reliance in (4) must be reasonable in all the circumstances.

9.10   Local authorities, unlike solicitors, accountants and others, do not carry on the business of giving advice or information for reward or even gratuitously. They must perform their statutory functions: indeed, they must perform no functions which are not statutory or incidental to their statutory functions. If they give advice or information, possibly in the form of guidance and assistance to members of the public, it is likely that they do so only to assist themselves and the public in the performance of those functions.

9.11   It is for this reason that in assessing the objective element contained in the concept of assumption of responsibility the courts have considered the statutory framework within which advice or information has been given by a local authority. Although *X (Minors) v Bedfordshire County Council*[1] was not primarily concerned with liability for advice or information, the speech of Lord Browne-Wilkinson emphasised the importance of the statutory framework in the court's consideration of the three components of a duty of care. He said:[2]

> '... the question whether or not there is a common law duty of care falls to be decided by applying the usual principles ... Was the damage to the plaintiff reasonably foreseeable? Was the relationship between the plaintiff and the defendant sufficiently proximate? Is it just and reasonable to impose a duty of care? ... However the question whether there is such a common law duty and if so its ambit, must be profoundly influenced by the statutory framework within which the acts complained of were done. ... a common law duty of care cannot be imposed on the statutory duty if the observance of such common law duty of care would be inconsistent with, or have a tendency to discourage, the due performance by the local authority of its statutory duties.'

9.12   In *Welton v North Cornwall District Council*,[3] the Court of Appeal applied these words to a claim based directly on the *Hedley Byrne* doctrine. Although the case will be discussed further below there are several statements of principle in the judgments which are relevant to a general discussion. The facts appear in the headnote:

> 'The plaintiffs owned a guesthouse ... an environmental health officer employed by [the defendant] ... entered the plaintiffs' premises to inspect them ... he told the plaintiffs to execute substantial building works purportedly to comply with [relevant legislation] and threatened to close the premises if the plaintiffs failed to meet his requirements. Despite repeated requests, and in contravention of [the defendant's] policy, the requirements were never confirmed in writing ... upon discovering that the officer's requirements were vastly in excess of those which could properly have been required ... the plaintiffs brought an action against [the defendant] claiming damages for the unnecessary expenditure incurred as a result of the negligent misstatements of their officer ... the judge found that the plaintiffs had undertaken the work as a result of the threat of closure and that 90% of the work which the officer had required ... was unnecessary to comply with [the relevant legislation].'

9.13   Rose LJ said:[4]

---

1   [1995] 2 AC 633.
2   Ibid at 739A.
3   [1997] 1 WLR 570.
4   Ibid at 581H.

'. . . it seems to me that there are at least three categories of conduct to which the existence of the defendants' statutory enforcement duties might have given rise. First, there might be conduct specifically directed to statutory enforcement, such as the institution of proceedings before the justices, the service of an improvement notice and the obtaining of a closure order . . . such conduct, even if careless, would only give rise to common law liability if the circumstances were such as to raise a duty of care at common law . . . and such a duty is not raised if it is inconsistent with, or has a tendency to discourage due performance of, the statutory duty . . . secondly, there is the offering of an advisory service: insofar as this is merely part and parcel of the defendants' system for discharging its statutory duty, liability will be excluded so as not to impede the due performance of those duties . . . But insofar as it goes beyond this, the advisory service is capable of giving rise to its duty of care; and the fact that the service is offered by reason of the statutory duty is immaterial . . . Thirdly, there is the conduct which is at the heart of this case, namely the imposition by [the environmental health officer] outwith the legislation, of detailed requirements enforced by threat of closure and close supervision.'

9.14 Rose LJ in describing the first category referred to the remarks of Lord Browne-Wilkinson (set out at para **9.11**). In relation to the second category, he referred to the speech of Lord Browne-Wilkinson in *X (Minors)*, where he said: [1]

'The claim is based on the fact that the authority is offering a service (psychological advice) to the public. True it is that, in the absence of a statutory power or duty, the authority could not offer such service. But once the decision is taken to offer such a service, a statutory body is in general in the same position as any private individual or organisation holding itself out as offering such a service. . . . I can see no ground on which it could be said at this stage [ie on an application to strike out for failing to disclose a reasonable cause of action] that the defendant authority, in providing a psychology service, could not have come under a duty of care to the plaintiff . . . it may well be that when the facts are fully investigated at trial it may emerge that, for example, the alleged psychology service was merely part and parcel of the system established by the defendant authority for the discharge of its statutory duties. . . . If so, it may be that the existence and scope of the direct duty owed by the defendant authority will have to be excluded or limited so as not to impede the due performance by the authority of its statutory duties.'

9.15 *Welton* was considered by the Court of Appeal in *Harris v Evans and Health and Safety Executive*.[2] Mr Harris owned a bungee jumping business. He complained that Mr Evans, an inspector employed by the Health and Safety Executive (HSE), and the HSE itself owed him a duty of care which they had broken by Mr Evans' allegedly negligent advice given to local authorities who in consequence had served improvement and prohibition notices on him. As a result, he had suffered economic loss.

9.16 Sir Richard Scott V-C (as he then was), concentrated on the statutory framework created by the Health and Safety at Work etc Act 1974. He said: [3]

'The important features of the statutory scheme . . . seem to me to be the following:

(i)   The purpose of the 1974 Act is to protect the safety of members of the public, whether employees or others.

(ii)   The statutory duties imposed on employers and on entrepreneurs, such as Mr Harris . . . are imposed for that purpose.

---

1   [1995] 2 AC 633 at 762H.
2   [1998] 1 WLR 1285.
3   Ibid at 1296B.

(iii) The very extensive powers that are available to inspectors are made available to them for that same purpose. Whether in giving advice to local authorities about safety requirements . . . or in deciding whether to issue an improvement notice . . . or in deciding whether to issue a prohibition notice, inspectors are exercising discretionary powers given to them for the purpose of protecting the safety of members of the public.'

9.17 He gave reasons for finding against the duty of care claimed by Mr Harris. First, he held that such a duty would cut across the statutory system created by the 1974 Act and regulations made under it. He placed particular emphasis on the availability of alternative remedies open to any person who considered that an improvement or prohibition notice should not have been issued: [1]

'The system includes provision for appeals against acts taken by enforcing authorities . . . If an appeal against an improvement notice or a prohibition notice succeeds, the error on the part of the enforcing authority is corrected. If the appeal fails, how then can it be open to the aggrieved entrepreneur to recover via a negligence action the damage caused to his business by the notice that has been upheld . . . ?'

The Vice-Chancellor thought it a strong argument against a duty of care that enforcing authorities might adopt a cautious or defensive approach to their duties if they were liable for damages in private law. He also placed emphasis on the words of Lord Browne-Wilkinson in *X (Minors)*, where he said: [2]

'In my judgment, the Court should proceed with great care before holding liable in negligence those who have been charged by Parliament with the task of protecting society from the wrongdoings of others.'

9.18 Counsel for Mr Harris relied on *Welton*. The Vice-Chancellor distinguished it on the basis that Mr Harris received no direct advice from either of the defendants. In addition, the actions of the local authorities which served the notices could have been challenged under statutory procedures provided by the 1974 Act, whereas in *Welton* nothing had been done by the officer that could be challenged under comparable procedures.

9.19 Nonetheless he considered the reasoning of Rose LJ and said: [3]

'. . . if [the officer in *Welton*] had served an improvement notice on the Plaintiffs requiring them to carry out the excessive works, or had given advice to some other enforcing authority who had then served the improvement notice, the question whether a duty of care was owed would have depended upon whether the imposition of the duty of care would have tended to discourage the performance of the statutory duty. I respectfully agree that that question would have so depended. But that question, critical in the present case, was not answered . . .'

He continued: [4]

'I must confess, however, that I find some difficulty with the decision. I do not understand how it was possible to come to the conclusion that the Plaintiffs' claim, based on the principles in the *Hedley Byrne* case, was "incontrovertible" . . . without considering whether the duty of care contended for was consistent with the statutory framework of the

---

1   [1998] 1 WLR 1285 at 1297H.
2   [1995] 2 AC 633 at 751F.
3   [1998] 1 WLR 1285 at 1300H.
4   Ibid at 1301C.

two Acts. The only reason ... why the Plaintiffs had followed the officer's recommendations was because he was an environmental health officer under the Acts and, as
such, in a position to serve an improvement notice on them if they did not follow his
recommendations. I find it very difficult to accept that the result of the negligence action
could depend upon whether the officer's advice that the plaintiffs had followed had been
given without the service of an improvement notice or had been incorporated into an
improvement notice. It seems to me that in either case the question whether the duty of
care was owed should have depended on whether the imposition of the requisite duty was
consistent with the statutory scheme and the statutory duties lying on the officer, as to
which the various considerations expressed by Lord Browne-Wilkinson in *X (Minors) v
Bedfordshire County Council* would arise. If the imposition of the duty was not consistent
with the statutory scheme, there should have been no liability under the *Hedley Byrne*
principle or under any other common law duty of care principle.'

9.20   The Vice-Chancellor concluded:[1]

'It is implicit in the 1974 Act that improvement notices and prohibition notices may cause
economic loss or damage to the business enterprise in question. It would, in my view, be
seriously detrimental to the proper discharge by enforcing authorities of their responsibilities in respect of public health and safety if they were to be exposed to potential liability
in negligence at the suit of the owners of the business adversely affected by their
decisions. The 1974 Act itself provides remedies against errors or excesses on the part of
inspectors in enforcing authorities. I would decline to add the possibility of an action in
negligence to the statutory remedies.'

He did, however, add a qualification:[2]

'It could be that a particular requirement imposed by an inspector, whether expressed in
an improvement notice or prohibition notice or expressed in advance advice, might
introduce a new risk or danger not present in the business activity as previously
conducted. The new risk or danger might materialise and result in economic damage to
the business itself as well as physical damage to person or property. We do not need to
decide the point but I would not be prepared to rule out the possibility that damage thus
caused could be recovered by means of a negligence action. *Capital & Counties plc v
Hampshire County Council* [1997] 2 All ER 865 seems to me to provide support to such
an action.'

The nature and limits of this qualification or exception can only be worked out on a
case-by-case basis.

9.21   In *W v Essex County Council and Another*,[3] children whose parents had an
agreement with Essex County Council to become foster-parents alleged sexual abuse
by a 15-year-old boy who had been placed with them by the council. It was pleaded
that an employee of the council had assured the parents that the boy had no history as a
sexual abuser and that no person with such a history would be placed with them. These
assurances were said to be incorrect. The Court of Appeal by a majority (Stuart-Smith
LJ dissenting) dismissed the council's appeal against Hooper J's refusal to strike out
the children's claims in negligence against it. They considered it arguable that the
council was not immune under the guidelines in *X (Minors)* from liability for breach
of the assurances, although given in relation to performance of their statutory
obligations.

---

1   [1998] 1 WLR 1285 at 1301H.
2   Ibid at 1302A.
3   [1998] 3 WLR 534.

9.22   Judge LJ said:[1]

'... the Local Authority assumed responsibility for the accuracy of its positive assurances to the parents about [the boy]. Relying on these assurances they accepted [the boy] into their home. ... Even if contrary to the conclusion expressed earlier the policy considerations in this case were otherwise indistinguishable from those identified in *X (Minors)* the express assurance that a sexual abuser would not be placed in the foster parents' home would have led me to conclude that this particular claim was arguable, either on the basis that in accordance with the authorities the policy grounds for exclusion were qualified, or because these additional features undermine the public policy argument in favour of ... immunity ...'

He considered the discrete claim based on negligent misstatement:[2]

'If the plaintiffs relied on the accuracy of the information given to them by the local authority that [the boy] was not a sexual abuser, the local authority knew, first, that the plaintiffs were indeed relying on the accuracy of this information before making their decision to accept [the boy] into their home and, second, that the information given to the plaintiffs was wrong. ... The ingredients for a claim under *Hedley Byrne & Co Limited v Heller & Partners Ltd* [1964] AC 465 are established ... it is at least arguable that "immunity" would not extend far enough to exclude it.'

9.23   In the House of Lords, Lord Slynn of Hadley, with whom the other members of the panel agreed, said:[3]

'... it cannot be said here that the claim that there was a duty of care owed to the parents ... is unarguable ... On the contrary whether it is right or wrong on the facts found at the end of the day, it is on the facts alleged plainly a claim which is arguable. In their case the parents made it clear that they were anxious not to put their children at risk by having a known sex abuser in their home. The council and the social worker knew this and also knew that the boy placed had already committed an act or acts of sex abuse. The risk was obvious and the abuse happened. Whether the nature of the council's task is such that the Court should not recognise an actionable duty of care, in other words that the claim is not justiciable, and whether there was a breach of their duty depends, in the first place, on an investigation of the full facts known to, and the factors influencing the decision of, the defendant.'

9.24   In examining claims that local authorities have assumed responsibility to members of the public for advice or information, the courts have accordingly been careful to consider the statutory framework within which that advice or information was given and sometimes the effect of the imposition of a duty of care on the performance of those functions and the interests of the public at large. This is particularly true in the cases discussed below where members of the public have claimed duties of care arising from planning advice or information given by local authorities.

---

1   [1998] 3 WLR 534 at 560A.
2   Ibid at 560D.
3   [2000] 2 WLR 601 at 605C.

EFFECT OF THE HUMAN RIGHTS ACT 1998

9.25 The cases of *Osman v United Kingdom*,[1] and *Barrett v Enfield London Borough Council*,[2] have been considered in Chapters 1, 2 and 3 above. They are relevant in this area of local authority liability as in others. Where public policy considerations are raised in the way envisaged by Lord Browne-Wilkinson in *X (Minors)* (set out at para **9.14**), any consideration of whether it is fair, just and reasonable for a duty of care to be imposed must involve an investigation of the facts and a balance struck between the individual interest of the claimant in favour of a duty of care and the public interest in favour of its absence. Lord Browne-Wilkinson said:

> 'In a wide range of cases public policy has led to a decision that the imposition of liability would not be fair and reasonable in the circumstances, e.g. some activities of financial regulators, building inspectors, ship surveyors, social workers dealing with sex abuse cases. In all these cases and many others the view has been taken that the proper performance of the defendant's primary function for the benefit of society as a whole will be inhibited if they are required to look over their shoulder to avoid liability and negligence. In English law the decision as to whether it is fair, just and reasonable to impose a liability in negligence on a particular class of would-be defendants depends on weighing in the balance the total detriment to the public interest in all cases from holding such class liable in negligence as against the total loss to all would-be plaintiffs if they are not to have a cause of action in respect of the loss they have individually suffered.'

It is evident that the public policy component of any *Hedley Byrne* liability must be treated in this way, although it is likely to be rare.[3] *Z v United Kingdom*,[4] however, also discussed in Chapter 3, suggests that the issue of whether it is fair, just and reasonable for a duty to be owed is one of substantive domestic law and does not fall within the scope of Article 6 of the ECHR.

9.26 In *Palmer v Tees Health Authority and Another*,[5] the Court of Appeal held that *Osman* and *Barrett* did not apply to the question whether there was proximity between the defendant and the claimant. This conclusion is likely to govern the decision whether there is a special relationship between the parties where *Hedley Byrne* liability is alleged.

9.27 The effect of *Osman* and *Barrett* where it is alleged that a local authority has assumed responsibility in private law for the accuracy of advice and information about its statutory functions was considered in *Qazi and Qazi v The London Borough of Waltham Forest*.[6] The claimants alleged that the council was liable in negligent misstatement for advice and information about the availability of grants under Part VIII of the Local Government and Housing Act 1989. The council published what it called a 'grant information pack' which invited applicants or potential applicants for grants 'to contact someone for more information'. In addition the council corresponded with the claimants.

---

1   [1999] 1 FLR 193.
2   [1999] 2 FLR 426.
3   See *Phelps v London Borough of Hillingdon* [2000] 3 WLR 776, and see para **9.78**.
4   [2001] 2 FLR 612.
5   [2000] PIQR 1.
6   (2000) 32 HLR 689.

9.28   The claimants complained, for the most part, of the absence of appropriate advice. They alleged that as a consequence of advice given and not given they lost the right to a grant when the Housing Grants, Construction and Regeneration Act 1996 came into effect.

9.29   The council applied to strike the claim out. At first instance it was successful. On the claimants' appeal, Richards J referred to the authorities set out above. He also referred to *Tidman v Reading Borough Council*,[1] which is considered below. In response to the claimants' submissions that *Osman* and *Barrett* precluded their claim from being struck out he said:[2]

> 'Whilst the need for caution is obvious, the considerations referred to by Lord Browne-Wilkinson apply with less force to . . . the present case. This case does not engage any difficult question as to whether it is fair, just and reasonable to impose a duty of care in relation to the exercise of statutory functions. The exercise or purported exercise of statutory functions by the defendant is of course an important feature of the case. But the specific question is whether there was a voluntary assumption of responsibility by the [council] such as to give rise to a duty on the *Hedley Byrne* principle. This is a well-established category and does not in itself require separate consideration whether it is fair, just and reasonable to impose a duty of care. Nor is it contended by the [council] that, if there was a voluntary assumption of responsibility, the [council's] statutory functions were such that a duty should be excluded for reasons of public policy or because it would not be fair, just and reasonable to impose it. The approach I have indicated seems to me to accord with what was said by Lord Goff in [*Henderson v Merrett Syndicates Ltd*] and by the Court of Appeal in [*Welton*] about the relationship between the *Hedley Byrne* duty and the "fair, just and reasonable" test.
>
> For similar reasons [*Osman*] does not in my view pose significant problems. In determining whether a factual situation arguably fits within the category into which the claimants seek to fit it, the Court is not applying any exclusionary rule. No question arises of balancing private hardship against considerations of public policy, as in determining whether it is fair, just and reasonable to impose a duty of care.'

9.30   Richards J held that he was entitled to determine whether the claimants had an arguable case that the council owed them a private law duty of care. He emphasised the fact that most of the evidence was in documentary form and before the court. He concluded:

> '. . . I see nothing in the matters pleaded to warrant the conclusion that the [council] assumed responsibility towards the claimant. Whether the system that it adopted in relation to the payment of grants was compatible with the 1989 Act is for this purpose immaterial. The fact is that the [council] did adopt a system, in purported if not in actual discharge of its statutory functions. It was a normal and legitimate incident of the [council's] statutory functions to provide information and advice about the system to those making enquiries about the availability of grants or applying for grants. I do not see how, by providing such information or advice, the [council] could be said to have assumed a responsibility in private law towards would-be or actual applicants. [Counsel for the claimant] accepted that a local authority is not generally subject to a duty of care in private law in relation to the provision of information or advice about the discharge of its statutory functions. This case does not have special features that could make it an exception to the general rule.

1   [1994] 3 PLR 72.
2   Transcript at p 21.

The main thrust of the pleaded case relates not to the giving of positively misleading advice but to the failure or omission to give advice about the effect of the statutory provisions. Yet the first claimant did not request advice... In my view the nature of the duty that the first claimant seeks to impose upon the [council] would require exceptional circumstances to establish it; and those circumstances simply do not exist. I see nothing to distinguish this case from others where a local authority gives information or advice about the way in which it seeks to discharge its statutory functions, and nothing to distinguish the first claimant from any other person who enquired about or applied for grants. There was no special relationship, nothing from which a voluntary assumption of responsibility could be inferred.

The reasoning that led to the dismissal of the claim in *Tidman v Reading Borough Council* applies *a fortiori* in relation to the present claim.'

ENQUIRIES OF LOCAL AUTHORITIES

9.31 There is, however, an area where local authorities have accepted a responsibility for the accuracy of information given, that is enquiries of local authorities made usually by prospective purchasers of an interest in land.

9.32 Any prospective purchaser of an interest in land will know the importance of discovering the existence of local land charges and other information kept on statutory registers or otherwise by local authorities.[1]

Local Land Charges Act 1975

9.33 Much of the information relating to property falls within the definition of a local land charge in s 1 of the Local Land Charges Act 1975 (LLCA 1975):

'(1) A charge or other matter affecting land is a local land charge if it falls within any of the following descriptions ... :

(a) any charge acquired either before or after the commencement of the Act by a Local Authority, Water Authority or New Town Development Corporation [under specified statutes] or any similar charge acquired by a Local Authority under any other Act ... being a charge that is binding on successive owners of the land affected;

(b) Any prohibition of or restriction on the use of land –
   (i) imposed by a Local Authority ... or
   (ii) enforceable by a Local Authority under any covenant or agreement made with them ...
   being a prohibition or restriction binding on successive owners of the land affected;

(c) Any prohibition of or restriction on the use of land –
   (i) imposed by a Minister of the Crown or Government Department ... or
   (ii) enforceable by such a Minister or Department under any covenant or agreement made with him or them ...
   being a prohibition or restriction binding on successive owners of the land affected;

---

1   For a full discussion of the subject, see JF Garner *Local Land Charges* 11th edn (Shaw & Sons, 1992) and Pugsley *Enquiries of Local Authorities* 3rd edn (Tolley, 1994).

(d) Any positive obligation affecting land enforceable by a Minister ... Government Department or Local Authority under any covenant or agreement made with him or them ... and binding on successive owners of the land affected;

(e) Any charge or other matter which is expressly made a local land charge by any statutory provision not contained in this section.'

9.34 It is necessary to refer to the LLCA 1975 to discover whether any particular matter is a local land charge.

9.35 The scheme of the LLCA 1975 is to require local authorities to keep registers of local land charges. Section 8 gives any person a right to search the register on payment of a fee. Section 9 provides that any person may require an official search of the register by the local authority. Section 10 contains a statutory scheme of compensation for non-registration of a local land charge or for a defective official search certificate. It also provides that a charge will be effective despite non-registration or omission from an official search certificate:

'(1) Failure to register a local land charge ... shall not affect enforceability of the charge but where a person has purchased any land affected by a local land charge, then –

(a) in a case where a material personal search ... was made ... if at the time of the search the charge was in existence but not registered ... ; or

(b) in a case where a material official search of the appropriate ... register was made in respect of the land in question ... , if the charge was in existence at the time of the search but (whether registered or not) was not shown by the official search certificate as registered in that register;

the purchaser shall ... be entitled to compensation for any loss suffered by him in consequence.'

9.36 The meaning of the compensation provisions in s 10 was considered in *Pound v Ashford Borough Council*.[1] When the claimant purchased his property the council failed to disclose that it was listed as a building of architectural or historic interest. Subsequently, the claimant unsuccessfully objected to the grant of planning permission for the development of the neighbouring property. Several years later the claimant discovered that his property was listed. He brought a claim against the council alleging that had this fact been disclosed to him when he purchased, as it should have been, he would have drawn this to the attention of the planning authority which would not, or might not, have granted planning permission for the development of the neighbouring property. The claimant alleged that the development of the neighbouring property had reduced the value of his own property and that he had suffered a nuisance while the development of the neighbouring property proceeded. The claim was struck out on the basis that it is a prerequisite of a claim to compensation under s 10 that the claimant's land is affected by an enforceable charge. Laddie J made the position clear:

'What the section is doing is making charges enforceable, but putting in place a right to compensation when an un-registered charged is enforced *against* the purchaser. In other words, the right to compensation is a response and tied to the fact that the charge is enforceable against the purchaser ... Compensation is given only because the charge is

---

1   [2003] EWHC 1088 (Ch), [2003] All ER (D) 222 (May).

enforceable, and is given to compensate for the loss which results from that enforceability.'

Here, there had been no attempt to enforce the listed building charge against the claimant. Accordingly, his claim did not fall under s 10.

9.37 Section 10 contains other relevant provisions:

'(4) Any compensation for loss under this section shall be paid by the registering authority ... and where the purchaser has incurred expenditure for the purpose of obtaining compensation under this section, the amount of the compensation shall include the amount of any expenditure reasonably incurred by him for that purpose ...'

If the fault is that of the local authority originating the local land charge the registering authority may obtain payment from it. Otherwise:

'(6) Where any compensation for loss under this section is paid by a registering authority, no part of the amount paid ... shall be recoverable by the registering authority or the originating authority from any other person except ... under a policy of insurance or on grounds of fraud.'

9.38 By s 10(7) the limitation period begins to run when the local land charge comes to the notice of the purchaser. Section 10(8) provides that claims may be made in the courts. In accordance with general principles of law it is likely that the statutory scheme for compensation excludes any common law remedy in respect of a failure to register a local land charge or to include it on the official certificate of search. A claim under s 10 favours the claimant since he does not have to prove negligence, the limitation period is favourable and by s 10(9):

'If in any proceedings for the recovery of compensation under this section the court dismisses the claim for compensation, it shall not order the purchaser to pay the registering authority's costs unless it considers that it was unreasonable for the purchaser to commence the proceedings.'

9.39 In addition to the register of local land charges, local authorities keep a number of other registers including a register of planning applications under s 69 of the Town and Country Planning Act 1990, public highways under the Highways Act 1980, public sewers under ss 199 and 200 of the Water Industry Act 1991, and contaminated land under s 143 of the Environmental Protection Act 1990.

9.40 In general, these registers are required by statute to be made available for public inspection. The accuracy of any personal search will be a matter for the person carrying out the search. As a matter of practice local authorities respond in writing to enquiries relating to these registers and other information within their knowledge such as development plans and road schemes. There is a standard form of enquiry produced by the Law Society and known as Conveyancing 29 or Con 29 which will be familiar to local authorities and solicitors. It sets out a number of questions for answer by local authorities and most relevantly contains a note as follows:

'The replies will be given after the appropriate enquiries and in the belief that they are in accordance with the information at present available to the officers of the replying Councils, but on the distinct understanding that none of the Councils, nor any Council Officer, is legally responsible for them, except for negligence. Any liability for negligence shall extend for the benefit of not only the person by or for whom the enquiries are made but also a person ... who or whose agents have knowledge, before the relevant time ... of the replies to these enquiries.'

This clause was added as the result of the decision of Bean J in *Coats Paton (Retail) Limited v Birmingham Corporation*,[1] where he held that a local authority could not disclaim liability for inaccurate answers if it had negligently failed to make appropriate enquiries and searches.

9.41   Local authorities have therefore assumed responsibility for the accuracy of answers given by them to enquiries contained in Conveyancing 29 although they will only be in breach of their duty of care if they have been negligent. It is possible to imagine a case where they give incorrect information without negligence. Nonetheless incorrect information will always require an explanation so that the evidential if not the probative burden will be upon the local authority to justify its errors.

9.42   An example of the position in practice is *Gooden v Northamptonshire County Council*.[2] In response to the claimant's enquiry, the council incorrectly stated that a footpath was maintainable at the public expense. This reply encouraged the claimant to believe that he could develop the property which was the subject of his enquiry. When the truth came to light his development could not be completed and the project became unprofitable. He sued the council for his losses. The Court of Appeal confirmed that when answering the usual enquiries in conveyancing transactions, councils must be taken to be aware that the purpose of the enquiries is that of acquiring an interest in land. In this case it was within the contemplation of the council that the claimant would rely on the reply in deciding to purchase the property. Loss resulting from the purchase of the property would be recoverable. This was not, however, the subject of the claim. To enable the claimant to recover his development losses, he would have to show that the council was actually made aware that he proposed to acquire the property for development. There was no evidence that the council was aware of this. Accordingly, the council was not liable to pay damages reflecting the claimant's development losses.

9.43   The Court of Appeal also rejected the claim in negligence. The council had relied on a map which it maintained as part of its statutory list of highways maintained at public expense. This was the map which could have been inspected by someone carrying out a personal search. The map indicated that the highway was maintainable at public expense and this was the information given to the claimant. It transpired that the highway was not, in fact, maintainable at public expense. It also transpired that the council had in its possession a further map which showed the correct position. Nevertheless, the Court of Appeal decided that in the absence of a differently pleaded case, the council could not be held to have been negligent in answering the enquiry in the way it did.[3]

9.44   This case applies standard principles of damages in tort. Damages recoverable for breach of the duty discussed in para **9.40** will normally be confined to overpayment for the property and wasted expenditure. The Court of Appeal seems to have taken the view, however, that other loss such as development losses could be recoverable if the council was put on notice that a property was being purchased for development purposes.

---

1   (1971) 69 LGR 56.

2   [2001] EWCA Civ 1744, [2002] PNLR 18,440.

3   It is submitted that the issue of negligence might have been decided against the council had the case been pleaded differently, eg alleging that the council was negligent in its belief that its statutory list of highways maintainable at public expense was accurate.

9.45   The date at which damages should be assessed was considered in *Smith and Another v South Gloucestershire Council*.[1] The claimants purchased a property in February 1995. The official local authority certificate of search failed to reveal that the property was subject to an agricultural occupancy condition. In November 1998, the claimants learned of the existence of the occupancy condition. They unsuccessfully attempted to get the condition lifted. In December 2000 the judge made an order that the claimants were entitled to compensation to be assessed. When the assessment was made in September 2001 the judge valued the diminution in market value suffered as at November 1998. In the absence of direct precedent the Court of Appeal decided that to adopt November 1998 as the date on which compensation should be assessed would produce injustice to the claimants. The existence of the occupancy condition made it very difficult for the claimants to sell their property. Furthermore, without being able to sell the property the claimants were not in a position to purchase another property. It was also significant that the period between November 1998 and September 2001 had seen a substantial rise in property prices which meant that the claimants would suffer a substantial loss if damages were assessed at the earlier date.

9.46   What is significant in relation to enquiries of local authorities is that it is a formal procedure where the request for information is in writing and the local authority, by replying in writing, is taken to accept the obligation set out in para 9.40.

Accrual of cause of action

9.47   Unlike the accrual of a cause of action for statutory compensation under s 10 of LLCA 1975, a cause of action for the negligence of local authorities in answering enquiries will generally accrue when, in reliance upon the answers, the claimant acts to his financial detriment. This will usually be when he enters into a contract to purchase property, although liability may be incurred earlier if, for example, the prospective purchaser is allowed to enter the premises before contracts are exchanged to carry out building works.

DUTY OF CARE NOT ACCEPTED

9.48   It is now appropriate to examine those areas where local authorities have not accepted responsibility in private law for advice or information in relation to their statutory functions. As discussed in para **9.2**, there is no bar in principle to local authorities being liable for negligent misstatement. In *Davy v Spelthorne Borough Council*,[2] the plaintiff claimed that he had suffered loss as a result of relying on negligent planning advice given to him by the defendant council. He claimed an injunction restraining it from implementing an enforcement notice, and damages for negligence. The issue in the case was whether the claimant was seeking to enforce a public law or a private law right. The House of Lords held that it was the former. Nonetheless, Lord Wilberforce said:[3]

> 'It is necessary to define the claim . . . as pleaded . . . it is that the appellant council owed to the respondent a duty of care in, through its officers, advising him as to his planning

---

1   [2002] All ER 502.
2   [1984] AC 262.
3   Ibid at 276A.

application; that the council was negligent in so advising him; that by reason of this negligence he suffered damage, namely the loss of the chance of successfully appealing against the enforcement notice ... To say that such a claim, so formulated, ought to be, or indeed can be, struck out as an abuse of the process of the court seems on the face of it a remarkable proposition. There is no doubt that, side by side with their statutory duties, local authorities may in certain limited circumstances become liable for negligence at common law in the performance of their duties ...'

9.49 Although it is easy to say that in principle local authorities may assume responsibility for the accuracy of advice or information given by them, it is difficult to assess in any given case whether such a duty exists. The principles have already been set out.[1] In general, it can be said that if an officer or officers of a local authority who give advice or information do so in the course of performing the local authority's statutory functions and act within their own authority and any guidelines or policies imposed on them, there will be at least a factual presumption against such a duty. This will be all the more so if the circumstances in which the advice or information was given were informal and it was not recorded in writing.

9.50 A number of areas where such claims have been made will now be considered.

Planning functions

9.51 Most owners of property come into contact with the planning regime created by the Town and Country Planning Act 1990 whether by making or opposing an application for planning permission or by seeking information about the planning history of property to be purchased or leased. As stated above, local authorities are required to keep a register of planning applications. Details of planning permissions are kept on the register of local land charges.

9.52 There have been several cases where plaintiffs have claimed that, in giving advice or information relating to planning matters, local authorities have come under a duty of care to them.

9.53 In *JGF Properties Limited v Lambeth Borough Council*,[2] the plaintiff's solicitors obtained answers to their written enquiries from the defendant council in accordance with the procedure described in paras **9.39**–**9.46**. A director of the plaintiff subsequently spoke to someone in the defendant council's planning department who, it was said, gave incorrect information which caused the plaintiff to suffer financial loss. Rubin J had to consider whether the contents of that telephone conversation gave rise to a duty of care. He referred[3] to a case in the Supreme Court of Australia, *L Shaddock and Associates Pty v Parramatta City Council*.[4] In that case there had been an oral enquiry followed by a written enquiry. Gibbs CJ said:[5]

'The nature of the [written] enquiry – made by a solicitor, for conveyancing purposes, on a form commonly used and prepared by law stationers – made clear the gravity of the enquiry and the importance attached to the answer. The council therefore owed a duty of care to [the solicitor's] clients ... in answering the written enquiry. It would not, however,

---

1 See paras **9.2**–**9.24**.
2 (1986) 277 EG 646.
3 Ibid at 650.
4 [1981] 36 ALR 385.
5 Ibid at 393.

have been reasonable for [the claimants] to have relied on an unconfirmed answer given by an unidentified person in response to an enquiry made over the telephone. The council therefore owed no duty of care in making a response to such enquiry.'

Stephen J said:[1]

'The [claimants] through their solicitor ... made two enquiries of the council. The first, by telephone, should not in my view, be regarded as giving rise to any consequences in law. It was marked by informality: the person in the council office to whom [the solicitor] spoke remained unidentified and the advice which the person then and there gave over the telephone remained unconfirmed by any writing. It must be but rarely that information conveyed by unidentified voices answering a telephone at the offices of municipal councils will render those councils liable in damages for negligence if the information should prove to be incorrect. In my view neither a council nor an enquirer would in the absence of *quite special* circumstances regard the response to such an enquiry as carrying with it liability in damages if incorrect: this must *especially* be the case when there exists a customary and more formal means of obtaining from a council the information which is sought.' (emphasis added)

Rubin J continued:

'One has here an informal telephone conversation to an officer of the council (if it was an officer), unidentified, who has answered a question whose precise terms are not clear, after consulting with apparently some unidentified other person in the same room, in circumstances where these matters are normally dealt with by way of formal enquiry made by solicitors to the council and indeed had been made in this very case and had in fact been answered. I cannot help thinking that the officer ... either did not understand the question which was being put ... or ... was not a person who was competent to deal with these matters ... It seems to me that the telephone conversation cannot be relied upon as proving negligence against the council.'

9.54 It is worth emphasising Rubin J's point that in a telephone conversation or even in a meeting face to face there is a considerable risk of the wrong facts being given or the wrong question asked by the enquirer so that incorrect advice or information is likely to be given.

9.55 A similar case came before Buxton J in *Tidman v Reading Borough Council*.[2] In that case the claimant, who wished to sell his business premises, telephoned the defendant council on more than one occasion to seek advice whether his prospective purchaser's change of use of the premises had or required planning permission. He alleged that he had been told that planning permission was required. When it subsequently turned out that it was not, he claimed damages from the defendant council for loss of his sale caused by the delay occasioned by his unnecessary planning application. He also complained that the defendant council's officers did not inform him that there was a summary statutory procedure, then s 53 of the Town and Country Planning Act 1971, for determining whether a particular use of property was lawful. In his judgment, Buxton J, having cited *Henderson v Merrett Syndicates Limited* and *Spring v Guardian Assurance Plc* (see para **9.3**), said:[3]

1   Ibid at 395.
2   [1994] 3 PLR 72.
3   [1994] 3 PLR 72 at 90A.

'The essence of the *Hedley Byrne* principle is the concept of reliance by the plaintiff and acceptance of responsibility by the defendant. That seems to me to give rise to three questions:

1. Was the relationship between the plaintiff and the defendants a relationship of a type from which reliance by the plaintiff upon the defendants, together with the acceptance of responsibility for that reliance by the defendant, would normally be assumed?
2. If the answer to question 1 is "no", were there nonetheless particular considerations obtaining between the plaintiff and the defendants from which the defendants should have realised that the plaintiff was relying upon them?
3. In any event, did the plaintiff in fact rely upon the defendants?

I add two further considerations:

(a) It is now recognised in the law of negligence generally that the overall question for the Court in deciding whether a duty of care exists is as stated by Lord Bridge of Harwich in *Caparo Industries Plc v Dickman* ... [at 617H to 618B]:

"... the situation should be one in which the court considers it fair, just and reasonable that the law should impose a duty of a given scope upon the one party for the benefit of the other."

Considering this aspect of the law of negligence ... Lord Goff ... said it followed that, once the case is identified as falling within the *Hedley Byrne* principle, there should be no need to embark upon any further enquiry whether it is fair, just and reasonable to impose liability for economic loss ... it follows from this that the overriding question whether the imposition of a duty is fair, just and reasonable is taken up in, and must be referred to in, the preliminary question of whether the situation is not merely one of reliance but one of reliance such as properly falls within the law of negligence.

(b) ... it is clear that the nature of the responsibility, or more precisely the nature of the circumstances from which the law will infer an assumption of responsibility, is a matter of judgment to be assessed according to the guidance provided ... nevertheless the two guiding considerations are, in my view:

(i) whether reliance by the plaintiff would be reasonably inferred from the relationship between the plaintiff and the defendant; and
(ii) the assumption that a guide in deciding that question is whether the relationship could be said to be equivalent to a contract. ... It would, in my view, be taking too narrow a view of the *Hedley Byrne* principle ... to say that it can only arise where one can point to all the indicia of a contractual relationship, save for the presence of consideration. Nonetheless, the concept remains an important one because it demonstrates that the relationship of reliance will only arise when there is something resembling the direct and conscious relationship between the two parties that is characteristic of the existence of a contract. Therefore ... it will always in my judgment be appropriate at least as a check on any conclusion the court might otherwise reach, to ask if the relationship between plaintiff and defendant, whether it be a general or a special relationship, can legitimately be described in broad terms as being equivalent to a contract.'

9.56 Although this guidance is in general terms it may provide some help to those who have to consider whether on the facts before them a private law duty of care has come into existence. The judgment in *Tidman* was given before the speeches in *X*

(Minors) v Bedfordshire County Council.[1] Nonetheless, Buxton J considered the impact of a private law duty of care upon the defendant council's performance of its planning functions. He referred[2] to a leaflet put out by the defendant council which contained the following:

'ARE YOU SURE THAT YOU NEED PLANNING PERMISSION?

It is not always necessary for you to apply for planning permission. If you are in any doubt ... you should consult the Council's Planning Department. You may be given a leaflet on this subject or an appointment may be made for you to see the Planning Officer.'

This was clearly an explicit invitation by the defendant council to members of the public to seek advice or information from it. Nonetheless, Buxton J said:[3]

'... I am quite unable to agree that a person who seeks advice or guidance from a local authority about the planning application that he has it in mind to make thereby necessarily places the local authority in a position where they owe him a duty of care under the *Hedley Byrne* rule ... there are a number of considerations which force the court in any case to be, at lowest, very cautious before concluding that a local authority has assumed responsibility ... for planning advice. ... The case here ... is based solely on the advice given, or omitted to have been given ... In respect of that part of their activities, it is argued that the local authority stepped outside statutory planning functions. They volunteered advice, as shown by the booklet, which they did not need to have done. So it is argued that they are potentially at least ... caught by the general *Hedley Byrne* rule, like any other adviser. Nevertheless, even granted that analysis of the facts, the local authority, unlike an ordinary professional adviser ... owe a public duty to apply the planning law and also a public duty to exercise their judgment and discretion in the general public interest. It would be inconsistent with those duties to recognise an overriding obligation to give advice in the interests of particular individuals who are engaged in the planning process. The private interest of that particular individual cannot be allowed to override the interests of the public at large in the proper performance of the planning process. ... Even if one leaves aside those general considerations ... [t]he approach here was informal, over the telephone, and on the basis of very slight information given by the applicant. It cannot reasonably be thought that in such cases, if the planning officers respond to the enquiry to give such help as they are able, they are immediately placing the local authority under obligations springing from the law of negligence. Indeed it would be seriously contrary to the public interest if such were held to be the law, since the likely outcome would be that local authorities would be forced to cease to give any guidance at all ... [in addition] it is entirely reasonable to suppose that in any case where the view of the local authority is crucial to the interests of the applicant and certainly where a matter as grave as a contract for £650,000 is alleged to turn on a planning decision, an applicant would not simply rely on what the local authority said but would also have the benefit of proper advice of its own.'

Having given his reasons why no duty of care arose on the facts before him Buxton J considered the circumstances in which a duty might arise:[4]

'It is not inconsistent with these considerations that the local authority should give initial and general guidance ... but that such guidance is sought and is available is very different from saying that the seeking and giving of such guidance creates a relationship of

---

1   [1995] 2 AC 633.
2   [1994] 3 PLR 72 at 92A.
3   [1994] 3 PLR 72 at 92C.
4   [1994] 3 PLR 72 at 93D.

foreseeable reliance and responsibility ... or that it is fair, just and reasonable in the interests of all parties that that should be so. I accept that it might be possible that a formal approach to a local authority, which was known by the local authority to have serious implications, which was put on a formal basis, and to which the local authority chose to respond, might conceivably generate a duty of care on their part. But I would want to reserve, in a case where that did occur, careful consideration of the implications of such a finding.'

9.57 Although Buxton J referred to a failure to give advice as well as to giving incorrect advice it would require strong facts for a local authority performing planning or other statutory functions to be responsible not only for incorrect advice and information negligently given but for a negligent failure to give advice or information. The remarks of Lord Goff in *Henderson v Merrett Syndicates Limited* (set out at para **9.3**) draw a distinction between a particular relationship created by the giving of advice and information and a general relationship such as that of solicitor and client where the latter entrusts the former with the general conduct of his affairs. A relationship with a local authority (if it exists at all) is likely to be particular rather than general.

9.58 In *Fashion Brokers Ltd v Clarke Hayes and Cannock Chase Council*,[1] solicitors sought to pass on to the council responsibility for damages which the solicitors had agreed to pay to their clients for their failure to discover that their clients' proposed use of leasehold property which they wished to acquire was contrary to an existing planning permission.

9.59 Contact between the relevant solicitor and the council had been confined to a short conversation between the solicitor and an unidentified person in the council's planning department who informed him that the proposed use was lawful. The solicitor acted in this way because he thought that there was a deadline for completion. In fact, completion occurred several days later during which time further, more detailed enquiries could have been made.

9.60 At first instance the solicitors' claim was dismissed. On appeal Gage J, with whom Roch and Ward LJJ agreed, dismissed the appeal. He referred to the judgment of Lord Steyn in *Williams v Natural Life Health Foods Limited and Another*,[2] which is considered at **9.4** above. He referred to the passages quoted at **9.6** and said:[3]

'Lord Steyn's speech has, of course, to be seen in the context of a case which involved the alleged personal liability of a director of a company for advice given by a company to the plaintiffs in that case. Nevertheless, in my judgment, his remarks on the test of reasonableness which must be applied to reliance is plainly of wider application.'

He concluded:[4]

'In my judgment, the judge's reasoning ... cannot be faulted. It seems to me that a solicitor who rings up a local authority out of the blue, and obtains information over the telephone, in the course of a conversation lasting a few minutes, without identifying his informant, and without seeking any faxed confirmation can, in my opinion, have no complaint if the court refuses to find that any duty of care exists between him and the local

1   [2000] PNLR 473.
2   [1998] 1 WLR 830.
3   [2000] PNLR 473 at 480D.
4   [2000] PNLR 373 at 481E.

authority. I have no difficulty in accepting as correct the judge's holding that it was not reasonable for [the solicitor] to rely on the information given to him. In my judgment it is not without significance that [the solicitors] in their pleading ... pointed out that the dangers of relying on an oral reply by an informant from the local planning authority was self-evident.

If one adds to that the fact that, in this case, [the solicitor] could, had he so chosen, have made arrangements to get the information properly authenticated before completion, the argument that he reasonably relied on the information given to him becomes quite untenable.'

9.61   In all the cases discussed so far, contact between the claimant and officers of the defendant council was by telephone and with unidentified persons. In two cases, contact was in a series of meetings with an identified officer. In *Hewings v Teignbridge District Council*,[1] the claimants complained that the defendant's officer had incorrectly informed them that a property which they wished to buy fell within a development area where planning permission for construction of a dwelling on part of the garden was likely to be obtained. In fact, the property did not fall in such an area and planning permission was unlikely. The claimants and the officer discussed the matter face to face on three occasions.

9.62   The judge found that the officer, in giving the incorrect information, also informed the claimants that:

'... her advice was informal advice; that they should write in order to obtain a more formal statement of the position; that whether the property was in a development area was only one of many relevant considerations; that there were no guarantees and that the only ultimate test would be the actual grant of permission.'

The judge held that:

'... on the findings of fact which I have already made it must follow that there was no duty of care ... It seems to me that this case is basically on all fours with *Hedley Byrne v Heller* where there was an effective disclaimer of responsibility.'

Nonetheless, he considered whether a duty would otherwise have been owed. He held that the third of Lord Oliver's requirements (set out in para **9.9**) had not been satisfied: the officer did not expect the advice given to be acted upon without the claimants writing in to make a formal enquiry which would have led to more research. He therefore found that the claimants' reliance was unreasonable. In answer to the argument that the officer was giving information and not advice, the judge said:

'[Counsel for the claimant] has pointed out that he is not complaining of wrong advice but of incorrect information. I do not think that there is any such relevant distinction to be drawn in this case. I think that what [the council's officer] was taking part in was the offering of an advisory service. I do not think that it makes any difference that when she made a mistake she made it in the form of a piece of information. It is very difficult to draw distinctions between information and advice in cases such as these. The defendant was clearly acting under statutory powers ... what the ... defendant here was offering was an advisory service which was merely part and parcel of the defendant's system for discharging its statutory duties.'

---

1   (Unreported) 15 November 1995.

9.63 In *Haddow v Tendring District Council*,[1] the claimant claimed that the defendant council assumed a duty of care to her as a result of advice and information given to her by one of its officers at a meeting. The advice and information related to an existing planning application in respect of which there had been considerable contact and discussion between the claimant and the officer. The deputy High Court judge considered the authorities cited above and, additionally, *Welton v North Cornwall District Council*,[2] before finding that no duty of care was owed. Among his reasons was the fact that the claimant had her own professional advisers. In addition he said:

'The evidence adduced before me of the manner in which applicants for planning permission and local planning officers . . . discuss applications informally seems to me to demonstrate an entirely sensible and practical method of proceeding . . . [the claimant] has attempted to persuade me that such informal discussions achieved a formality that entitled her to claim damages. I have found that they did not do so. I would, in any event, have been extremely reluctant, save on the basis of exceptional facts . . . to have found that . . . [the defendant council] was liable to [the claimant] for negligent misstatement . . . It would, in my judgment, be detrimental to the whole planning process if . . . the local authority had continually to balance the private law *rights* of individual applicants against their public law duties. The whole planning process is one of balancing public rights and private *interests*. If . . . a local authority were potentially to be liable to actions in negligence when performing that balancing exercise, the whole process of carrying out important planning functions in the public interest would be jeopardised. It would, in my judgment, be a serious matter if that were the law. Even in a quite exceptional case, where liability might be found . . . it might well be (as Buxton J said in *Tidman*) that a court would want to consider carefully the implications of such a finding, which would undoubtedly cause serious damage to the whole relationship between planning officers and members of the public, and to the planning process itself.'

9.64 These words indicate the apparent reluctance of the courts to impose liability for advice or information given by local authorities, provided they do so in the course of and in accordance with their statutory functions.

9.65 In *Haddow v Secretary of State for the Environment*,[3] the same claimant alleged that an officer of the Department of the Environment gave her negligent advice about the need for an environmental assessment of a planning application which had been made. At first instance her claim was dismissed. The same deputy High Court judge found no duty or breach of duty.

9.66 On appeal Kennedy LJ, with whom Mummery and Mantell LJJ agreed, said:[4]

'Legally, there are a limited number of issues which . . . arise in relation to this matter. First of all, although there can be liability in law for negligent misstatement, that liability only arises when the relationship between the maker of the statement and the person to whom it is addressed is such as to give rise to a duty of care. As to that, see [*Hedley Byrne*] . . . Such a duty can arise when advice is sought in relation to a planning matter, but, as Buxton J (as he then was) indicated in [*Tidman v Reading Borough Council*] . . . it is only likely to arise in exceptional circumstances. The ordinary process of giving routine advice to an applicant for planning permission and answering such questions as he or she may

1 (Unreported) 6 February 1998, QBD.
2 [1997] 1 WLR 570.
3 [2000] Env LR 212.
4 Ibid at 219.

raise, especially when the applicant is one known to have her own professional advisers, does not give rise to any duty of care.'

9.67 It is important to note that there will be no protection for a local authority if the advice or information is not 'part and parcel' of the performance of its statutory functions; or if the officer concerned, as in *Welton v North Cornwall District Council* discussed further below, is acting outside his role or contrary to his employer's instructions. An example of the latter is the case of *Lambert v West Devon Borough Council*.[1] The claimant had considerable contact with one of the defendant's building control officers who had authority to administer the regime created by the Building Act 1984 and Building Regulations but did not have authority in planning matters. Overend HHJ found that the officer informed the claimant that he was entitled to carry out building works despite the fact that he had not received a relevant planning permission. The judge said that the officer had been guilty of 'making decisions outside his proper sphere'. He continued:[2]

'It follows in my judgment that the defendants were in breach of their duty of care by telling the plaintiff that he could go ahead, when they knew or ought to have known that the question of the amendment of the existing planning permission was still unresolved ... and [the officer] had himself no authority to deal with it.'

9.68 The liability of planning officers in connection with the grant of planning permission was considered in *Lam v Brennan and Borough of Torbay*.[3] The court considered that the Town and Country Planning Act 1971 was not intended to create a duty of care at common law which would make the planning authority liable to pay compensation for foreseeable loss caused by the exercise or non-exercise of the power conferred on it to grant or refuse planning permission. *Lam* was considered by the Court of Appeal in *Kane v New Forest District Council*.[4] Relying, inter alia, on the decision in *Lam*, the claim had been struck out as disclosing no reasonable prospect of success. The Court of Appeal, however, upheld the claimant's appeal and decided that the claim could proceed. The court did not consider that *Lam* provided planning authorities with immunity from liability. Therefore, in *Kane*, the claim could proceed in circumstances where the planning department had required the construction of a footpath in a dangerous situation. Simon Brown LJ said:

'It seems to me far from clear on these authorities that a planning authority would be immune from liability if they permitted (still less if they required) the construction of a foreseeably dangerous footpath or (which is perhaps the better way of putting the present case) if they failed when granting the planning permission (or requiring the work) to impose a condition forbidding the footpath to the public until the sightlines had been cleared.'

The above principles and discussion will apply to all statutory functions of local authorities and the same considerations will determine whether or not a duty of care was assumed. A summary of the relevant negative considerations will include the following:

---

1   [1997] 1 FLR 103.
2   Ibid at 118A.
3   [1997] PIQR 488, and see **9.71–9.72**.
4   [2001] EWCA Civ 878, [2001] 3 All ER 914.

(1) the advice or information was given on the telephone, whether or not by an unidentified person and not confirmed in writing by the adviser or the advisee;

(2) if given informally there was a more formal method of seeking and giving that advice or information such as enquiries of local authorities;

(3) the advisee had or should have had his own advisers;

(4) the adviser made it clear actually or inferentially that the advice was given informally and was subject to confirmation or to formal procedures which could not be pre-empted;

(5) the advice or information was part and parcel of the local authority's method of discharging its statutory functions;

(6) the officer or officers concerned were acting within their authority and in compliance with the local authority's policies and procedure;

(7) the imposition of a duty of care would prejudice and interfere with the local authority's performance of its statutory functions and would or might be against the interests of the public;

(8) the statutory framework within which the local authority was operating itself provided a means by which its actions or failure to act could be challenged.

The more of these considerations that are absent, the more likely it will be that a duty of care exists.

Environmental health functions

9.69 Despite the above propositions it may be helpful to consider several particular applications of the principles to other areas. *Welton v North Cornwall District Council* [1] has already been referred to (at para **9.12**). It is important to note a number of further points from the judgments. Rose LJ rejected the argument that the local authority in exercising 'police or quasi-police' functions was entitled to the public policy immunity then granted to the police by *Hill v Chief Constable of West Yorkshire.* [2] He also rejected the argument that it was not fair, just or reasonable to impose a duty of care since the local authority was exercising statutory functions (see the passage set out at para **9.10**), after which he continued: [3]

'It is, for present purposes, unnecessary further to analyse the advisory service offered in the present case. For ... the existence of ... statutory powers and duties affords no reason why the defendant should not be liable at common law for this third type of conduct by their servants ...'

9.70 The defendant council had a policy which had not been followed by its officer of confirming its requirements in writing and of drawing a distinction between requirements and recommendations. Ward LJ referred to the policy and continued: [4]

'... it is in my judgment necessary to see precisely what [the officer] was doing, or rather what he was not doing. He was entering the premises under his [statutory] power ... but he was not exercising the power to launch a prosecution, which was the only vehicle for obtaining a closure order. Nor was he carrying out the defendant's policy of differentiating in writing between requirements ... and recommendations ... He was

---

1   [1997] 1 WLR 570.
2   [1989] AC 53.
3   [1997] 1 WLR 570 at 581C.
4   Ibid at 584C.

acting both outside the [statutory] powers and also outside the informal enforcement practice of the defendants. In the scale and detail of the directions he gave, and the degree of control he exerted, he was conducting himself in a manner which was exceptional. These circumstances make this case special on its own facts and I would not wish my conclusions to be thought certain to govern, for example, a negligent misstatement of defects in premises which are then made the grounds of a prosecution, or even those which are then asserted in a letter of the kind the local authority do send. A duty of care may still arise, on the other hand it may not.'

In this case, as in *Lambert v West Devon Borough Council*, [1] the officer concerned could not claim that he was performing the defendant council's statutory functions in the manner in which he was authorised or required to do so. Judge LJ rejected the argument that the officer had not been giving advice or information: [2]

'It is . . . irrelevant to the question for decision that the language used by [the officer] could probably be described as a recommendation, exhortation or instruction rather than "advice". The duty may arise whatever the description applied to the words used. Indeed to the extent that the words are clothed with the voice of authority and the hint of compulsion, the more important that they should be included within the normal ambit of the duty to take reasonable care.'

He also considered the argument that the officer was performing statutory functions and continued: [3]

'The circumstances in which local authorities may be held liable in private law claims for damages have been repeatedly considered in the House of Lords. Nothing in the decisions suggest that the *Hedley Byrne* principle has been undermined merely because advice has been given by employees of local authorities carrying out their statutory duties.'

He referred to the speech of Lord Bridge of Harwich in *Murphy v Brentwood District Council*, [4] which is in the following terms:

'In *Council of the Shire of Sutherland v Heyman*, 157 CLR 424 the critical role of the reliance principle as an element in the cause of action . . . is the subject of close examination. . . . The central theme of [the majority judgments] is that a duty of care of a scope sufficient to make the authority liable for damage of the kind suffered can only be based on the principle of reliance and that there is nothing in the ordinary relationship of a local authority, a statutory supervisor of building operations, and the purchaser of a defective building capable of giving rise to such a duty. I agree with these judgments. It cannot, I think, be suggested . . . that the approval of plans or the inspection of a building in the course of construction by the local authority in performance of their statutory function and the subsequent purchase of the building by the plaintiff are circumstances in themselves sufficient to introduce the principle of reliance which is the foundation of a duty of care of the kind identified in *Hedley Byrne*.'

Judge LJ continued:

'Both Lord Keith of Kinkel and Lord Oliver of Aylmerton appeared to accept that if the facts so warranted liability under the *Hedley Byrne* principle could be established against the local authority.'

---

1   [1997] 1 FLR 103.
2   [1997] 1 WLR 570 at 587B.
3   Ibid at 589H.
4   [1991] 1 AC 398 at 481E.

Judge LJ considered that it was fair, just and reasonable to impose liability upon the defendant council since its officer gave the claimants:

'... inaccurate information about the true extent of his authority and omitted any reference to their own rights under the statutory provisions.'

9.71 In *Lam v Brennan and the Borough of Torbay*,[1] the claimants claimed that the defendant council owed them duties of care in relation to both planning and environmental health functions. Potter LJ, giving the judgment of the court, stated that such functions were exercised by local authorities in the interests of the public at large and not individual members of it. He emphasised that under the Environmental Protection Act 1990 an individual affected could complain to magistrates that a statutory nuisance was being committed. Of more relevance to this discussion was his treatment of a claim that the defendant council had assumed responsibility to the claimants to take steps under planning and environmental health legislation to bring an alleged nuisance and breach of planning condition to an end. He said:

'Nor does it seem to us that the [claimants'] position can be improved by some alternative formulation of his cause of action on the basis of "assumption of responsibility". Where an allegation of "assumption of responsibility" is made against a person or body carrying out a statutory function, there must be something more than the performance (negligent or otherwise) of the statutory function to establish such assumption of responsibility: see for instance the case of *Welton v North Cornwall District Council* ... in which the plaintiffs were held to have established an assumption of responsibility on the part of a servant of the defendant authority ... The court held that in making ... statements he had acted far outside the ambit of his statutory powers and duties which were said to provide no more than "the backcloth and reason" for the relationship created which gave rise to a duty of care. ... the facts proposed to be pleaded fall well short of establishing any such assumption of responsibility. All relate to matters which arose in the course and scope of the [defendant council's] planning and enforcement functions ... here there is no contract between the [claimants] and the [defendant council] nor any situation equivalent to it ... The matters relied upon are essentially no more than the fact that [the defendant council] on the complaint and at the prompting of the [claimants] and [their] solicitors, set out to remedy the situation but took inadequate steps to do so.'

9.72 *Harris v Evans and Health and Safety Executive*[2] was concerned with the functions of the Health and Safety Executive under the Health and Safety at Work etc Act 1974. It has been fully considered at paras **9.15–9.20**.

Building control functions

9.73 Local authorities have statutory functions which arise under the Building Act 1984 and Building Regulations made under it. Whether careless performance of these functions could give rise to a duty of care has been briefly discussed at para **9.2**. It was considered by the Court of Appeal in *King v North Cornwall District Council*.[3] In 1992 the claimant was considering purchasing premises which had been the subject of the defendant council's approval of plans and inspection in 1985. In October 1992 her solicitors wrote to the council:

---

1   [1997] PIQR 488.
2   [1998] 1 WLR 1285.
3   [1995] NPC 21.

'We act on behalf of the purchasers of the above property and should be grateful if you would confirm that all Building Regulation inspections have been carried out and are satisfactory.'

The council replied:

'I ... would confirm that a final inspection was carried out at the above property on 12th June 1985 and there was no reason to believe that the work did not comply with the Building Regulations which were in force at the time the plans were deposited with the Council.'

9.74 After purchase the claimant found a number of breaches of Building Regulations in the works carried out in 1985. She claimed that the defendant council had assumed a responsibility to her for the carefulness of its approval of plans and inspection of the building works by writing a letter in the above terms. Simon Brown LJ dealt with the principle to be applied: [1]

'I have no doubt that a Local Authority can, in the course of an exchange of correspondence such as this, expose itself to liability to a prospective purchaser for negligent misstatement. Indeed, I have no doubt that such a liability could encompass liability based upon a council's negligent inspection of a building and their failure to note non-compliance with the Building Regulations.'

Henry LJ said:

'As the basic relationship does not give rise to a *Hedley Byrne* situation, the question ... identified is whether there is what I have called 'sufficient value added' in the exchange of correspondence to set up the *Hedley Byrne* relationship ... in *Henderson v Merrett Syndicates Limited* ... Lord Goff indicated, first, the need for a special relationship; secondly, an acceptance of responsibility: that is to say, that by their response the council assumed responsibility for saying that the inspection was not negligent, ie assumed a responsibility over and above that [which] *Murphy v Brentwood District Council* had said they had ... Lord Goff made the point that the test as to whether the responsibility had been assumed was an objective test ...'

9.75 In applying those principles to the facts, Simon Brown LJ nonetheless dismissed the claimant's appeal. He said:

'[Counsel for the claimant] asks us to construe [the council's letter] as an assurance ... that their final inspection had been properly carried out, i.e. carried out in such a way as would have revealed any non-compliance with the Building Regulations. ... I find it quite impossible to construe it in that way. Not only would that be a highly surprising assurance to give – why should a Local Authority so readily surrender the benefit of the ... decision in *Murphy v Brentwood District Council*? – but the letter itself, to my mind, was clearly intended to convey no more than that upon the final inspection where no reason was found, and nothing noted, to suggest the works did not comply with the Building Regulations.'

Henry LJ said:

'... it seems to me that in that exchange of letters no special relationship of proximity is established ... It seems to me that in [the council's] cautious reply no responsibility for a negligent inspection was assumed. ... I can see here no objective reason to find that in that exchange of correspondence the council was accepting a liability that *Murphy v Brentwood District Council* freed them of. ... Lord Goff raises the question whether in all

---

the circumstances it would just and fair to impose the duty. It seems to me that it would not be just and fair to impose a duty on the council on the basis of this exchange of correspondence. If there was any special relationship in these circumstances, it seems to me that *Murphy v Brentwood District Council* would have been decided differently, and that the principle enunciated in *Murphy* cannot be avoided by an exchange of correspondence as bland as these letters, properly construed, are.'

Grant functions

9.76 Liability for advice and information in relation to grant functions was considered in *Qazi and Qazi v The London Borough of Waltham Forest* which is fully considered in paras **9.27–9.30**.

Social services and education functions

9.77 In the speech of Lord Browne-Wilkinson in *X (Minors) v Bedfordshire County Council*,[1] he indicated that there might be circumstances in which a local authority would be vicariously liable for advice given by, for example, a psychiatrist or educational psychologist in its employment.

He said:[2]

'The claim is based on the fact that the authority is offering a service (psychological advice) to the public ... once the decision is taken to offer such a service, a statutory body is in general in the same position as any private individual or organisation ... the position is directly analogous with a hospital conducted, formerly by a local authority now by a health authority, in exercise of statutory powers.'

However, in *Phelps v London Borough of Hillingdon*,[3] the Court of Appeal disagreed. Stuart-Smith LJ said:

'Lord Browne-Wilkinson appears to have thought that in setting up an educational psychology service, the local education authority were offering a service to the public which they could take advantage of, which he likened to a health authority running a hospital. It is quite clear that is not what the defendant's psychology service was. It was set up and used by the local education authority to advise it and its other employees on the discharge of its statutory functions in teaching the plaintiff. It is quite different from, for example, a health authority setting up a clinic where people can come to see doctors and nurses for treatment. In such a case there would be a direct relationship of doctors and patient, and an assumption of responsibility to treat him or her.'

Because the Court of Appeal (unlike the judge at first instance) categorised the loss in *Phelps* as 'economic loss', Stuart-Smith LJ considered that the claimant's claim could only succeed if she could show that the educational psychologist, employed by the local education authority, had voluntarily assumed responsibility for advising the claimant through her parents. Stuart-Smith LJ considered that this was not the case. He said:

'[the duty of the educational psychologist] was to advise the school and the local education authority. Merely because the plaintiff was the object of that advice and the parents were told in effect what the advice was, does not in my judgment amount to such

---

1   [1995] 2 AC 633.
2   Ibid at 762H.
3   [1999] 1 WLR 500. See also paras **4.82**.

an assumption of responsibility . . . [the educational psychologist] was doing no more than discharging her duty to the defendants to enable them to perform their statutory functions. The Court ought to be slow to superimpose on a duty which the employee owed his employer, the defendants, a further duty towards the plaintiff, in the absence of very clear evidence that the employee had undertaken such responsibility.'

Having reviewed the evidence in the case, Stuart-Smith LJ went on:

'In my opinion what happened here went nowhere near establishing such an assumption of responsibility to the plaintiff. It was no more than the discharge of her ordinary duties to the defendants. I derive much assistance from the speech of Lord Steyn (with whom other members of the House of Lords agreed) in *Williams v Natural Life Foods Limited*[1].'

9.78   The House of Lords reversed the decision of the Court of Appeal. Although its decision is fully discussed in Chapter 4, there are passages in the speeches which throw light on the subject matter of this chapter. Lord Slynn of Hadley said:

'I accept that, as was said in [*X (Minors)*] . . . there may be cases where to recognise . . . a vicarious liability on the part of the authority may so interfere with the performance of the local education authority's duties that it would be wrong to recognise any liability on the part of the authority. It must, however, be for the local authority to establish that: it is not to be presumed and I anticipate that the circumstances where it could be established would be exceptional.'

He continued in relation to liability for the advice of an educational psychologist:

'It must . . . be shown that the educational psychologist is acting in relation to a particular child in a situation where the law recognises a duty of care. A casual remark, an isolated act may occur in the situation where there is no sufficient nexus between the two persons for a duty of care to exist. But where an educational psychologist is specifically called in to advise in relation to the assessment and future provision for a specific child, and it is clear that the parents acting for the child and the teachers will follow that advice, prima facie a duty of care arises. It is sometimes said that there has been an assumption of responsibility by the person concerned. That phrase can be misleading in that it can suggest that the professional person must knowingly and deliberately accept responsibility. It is however clear that the test is an objective one: *Henderson v Merrett Syndicates Limited* . . . the phrase means simply that the law recognises that there is a duty of care. It is not so much that responsibility is assumed as that it is recognised or imposed by the law.

The question is thus whether in the particular circumstances the necessary nexus has been shown.'

9.79   Lord Clyde said:[2]

'It is clear on principle that where a professional person gives advice, knowing, or being taken to know, that another will rely on that advice in deciding how to manage his affairs, the adviser may owe a duty of care to that other person. Opinion has differed on the question whether the language of an assumption of responsibility is useful or not. . . . The expression may be descriptive rather than definitive, but the point does not seem to be of significance in the present context.

In principle it is not immediately easy to see why the law should not admit the possibility of the duty of care upon professional employees of an education authority . . . as Lord Browne-Wilkinson observed [in *X (Minors)*], at page 763:

1   [1998] 1 WLR 830.
2   [2000] 3 WLR 776 at 807D.

"Psychologists hold themselves out as having special skills and they are, in my judgment, like any other professional bound both to possess such skills and to exercise them carefully."

In principle the same view should apply to any professional member of the staff of an educational authority. Where a child privately consults an educational psychologist there should be a duty on the latter to exercise due professional care in the giving of advice.... It would be surprising if the same was not also to be possible where the advice is given by one employed by an education authority.'

Lord Millett said:[1]

'At the conclusion of the argument I was inclined to agree with Stuart-Smith LJ in the Court of Appeal that the plaintiff's claim in the *Phelps* case could not hope to succeed on the basis of vicarious liability. Her claim was argued on the *Hedley Byrne* principle ... that is to say, on an allegation that the educational psychiatrist ... gave negligent advice to the plaintiff (or more probably her parents) in the knowledge or expectation that she (or they) would rely upon it. [The educational psychiatrist] was, however, employed by the defendant authority to advise it how best to discharge its statutory duties to the plaintiff ..., not to give advice to the plaintiff or her parents on which they could rely. If this is the correct analysis, then either she was merely communicating to the plaintiff and her parents the gist of the advice she had given or was proposing to give to the defendant, without assuming a separate responsibility *to them* for that advice; or (less probably) she was giving separate though similar advice to the plaintiff and her parents on which they were entitled to rely, in which case she was acting outside the scope of her employment. The fact that everyone had the same end in view, so that there was no conflict between them, does not in my opinion affect this.

I have, however, been persuaded that, even though [the educational psychiatrist] did not give advice to the plaintiff or her parents on which they were entitled to rely, she did owe the plaintiff a duty to take care that the advice which she gave to the defendant was properly given. ... the defendant is vicariously liable for the breach of the duty of care which [she] owed the plaintiff when, in the course of her employment, she gave negligent advice to the defendant on which the defendant acted. Thus the plaintiff's claim does not depend (nor should it) on what [she] told the plaintiff's parents, but on what she told the defendant.'

9.80 A more direct example of assumption of responsibility is the case of *T (A Minor) v Surrey County Council*.[2] The claimant child was injured by a childminder. An officer in the defendant council's social services department had informed the plaintiff's mother that the childminder was registered under the appropriate regulations and that there was no reason why the claimant could not safely be left in her care. In fact, less than 3 months earlier another child in her care had been seriously injured probably through violent shaking.

9.81 The claimant made claims for negligence and for breach of statutory duty which was rejected. In upholding the claim in negligence Scott Baker J said:[3]

'In my judgment the criteria for finding liability for negligent misstatement are met. [The officer] was at all times acting as the Local Authority's nursery and child-minding adviser. When he spoke to [the plaintiff's mother] ... he was consulted and speaking as a

---

1   [2000] 3 WLR 776 at 813G.
2   [1994] 3 All ER 577.
3   Ibid at 600j.

professional officer with special knowledge and responsibility. He knew, or ought to have known, that what he said would be relied upon. What he said related directly to the safety of the infant plaintiff. There was, in these circumstances, a special relationship of proximity.'

9.82 Surrey County Council's officer had in effect given the childminder a reference. In this case personal injury rather than economic loss was the consequence of the breach of duty but it is clear that the same criteria are to be applied to determine whether a duty of care exists whatever the nature of the damage. See also the discussion of *W v Essex County Council and Another*, at para **9.21**, where an employee of the council made an incorrect statement about the history and suitability of a child to be fostered by the parents of the claimant children, whose claim against the council for damages for personal injury was allowed to proceed by the Court of Appeal and the House of Lords. Nonetheless, the dissenting judgment of Stuart-Smith LJ that:[1]

'The giving of information or advice to the foster parents is all part and parcel of the [council's] performance of their statutory powers and duties . . .'

is convincing.

9.83 In *S v Newham London Borough Council*,[2] the claimant sued the defendant council for alleged libel in information it had provided to the Department of Health for inclusion in its index of persons unsuitable to work with children. The Court of Appeal refused to accept at the striking out stage the council's argument that it had a public policy immunity from such a claim.

The 'right to buy' legislation

9.84 In *Blake and Brooks v The London Borough of Barking and Dagenham*,[3] the claimants had exercised their right to buy land owned by the defendant council under the provisions of the Housing Act 1985, of which s 125 required the council to serve a notice containing the following:

'(2) The notice shall describe the dwelling-house, shall state the price at which, in the opinion of the landlord, the tenant is entitled to have the freehold conveyed or . . . the lease granted to him and shall, for the purpose of showing how the price has been arrived at, state –

(a)   the value at the relevant time . . .'

Section 125(5) provided that:

'The notice shall also inform the tenant of . . . his right under section 128 to have the value of the dwelling-house at the relevant time determined or re-determined by the district valuer . . .'

9.85 The defendant council served notices on the claimants. The claimants bought their flats but later complained that the valuations given were incorrect. They claimed that the defendant council came under a duty of care to them in stating a value in the s 125 notices.

---

1   [1998] 3 WLR 534 at 574D.
2   [1998] 1 FLR 1061, CA.
3   [1996] NPC 134.

9.86 Douglas Brown J considered the evidence that approximately 90 per cent of applicants exercising the right to buy did not ask the district valuer to intervene. He gave his conclusion:

> 'A local authority owes no duty of care to a tenant when stating its opinion of the price in the notice served under section 125 ... A duty of care is not raised if it is inconsistent with or has a tendency to discourage the performance of the local authority's statutory duty ... a duty of care in giving an opinion as to price is not inconsistent with the due performance of the local authority's duty but it does have a tendency to discourage it. ... I agree with [the] alternative argument that section 125 imposes no statutory duty on the local authority ... [I]t is difficult to see how a duty of care arises in these circumstances ... Fatal to [the claimants'] argument is the existence of the right to apply to the district valuer for a determination as to price ... [this is] a statutory scheme which provides in clear terms, communicated to the applicant both in the notice and in the ... pamphlet, that he has a right to apply to an independent government valuer. In those circumstances it does not seem to me just or reasonable that there should be a duty of care on the local authority.'

CONCLUSION

9.87 The present state of the law seems to be as follows.

(1) Whether there has been an assumption of responsibility by a local authority to a member of the public for the accuracy of its advice and information is to be assessed objectively on the basis of foreseeability of damage, proximity and whether it is fair, just and reasonable to impose a duty of care.

(2) The statutory framework within which the local authority operates and the context in which it gives any advice or information are important considerations in answering the question in (1) above.

(3) In general, exceptional facts are needed to create a special relationship of proximity between a member of the public and a local authority where the latter provides advice and information to the former. This special relationship is more likely to arise where the advice or information is given by a person who falls into one of the recognised categories of persons who hold themselves out as having expertise.

(4) Considerations of public policy to negative what would otherwise give rise to a duty of care must be specifically raised and proved by the local authority and are likely to be exceptional.

(5) Consideration of the issue in (4) above requires a balancing of public and private interests and of detriment to the claimant, on the one hand, and the public interest, on the other.

Chapter 10

THE EMERGENCY SERVICES

INTRODUCTION

10.1 In recent years, the judiciary has had ample opportunity to consider the principles governing the liability for negligence of the emergency services. This chapter considers the factors which have influenced the response of the judiciary to actions against the police, fire and ambulance services.

GENERAL PRINCIPLES

10.2 In order to establish negligence, a claimant has to establish three premises, namely:

(1) that the defendant owed him a duty of care whose scope includes avoidance of the damage in fact suffered;
(2) breach of that duty, causing
(3) the claimant to suffer damage by reason of that breach.

The same principles apply when considering the liability of the emergency services, although greater attention usually needs to be paid to the first requirement.

10.3 Where there is a negligent act by a member of the emergency services which causes physical injury or damage to property, the position is usually clear-cut. Problems of interpretation arise, however, in relation to a failure or omission to act in a particular situation. As Lord Hoffmann observed in *Stovin v Wise*:[1]

'Omissions, like economic loss, are notoriously a category of conduct in which Lord Atkin's generalisation in *Donoghue v Stevenson* offers limited help. In the High Court of Australia in *Hargrave v Goldman* 1963 110 CLR 40 at 65–66, Windeyer J drew attention to the irony in Lord Atkin's allusion in formulating his "neighbour" test to the parable of the Good Samaritan:

"The priest and Levite, when they saw the wounded man by the road, passed by on the other side. He obviously was a person whom they had in contemplation, and who was closely and directly affected by their action. Yet the common law does not require a man to act as the Samaritan did."

There are sound reasons why omissions require different treatment from positive conduct. It is one thing for the law to say that a person who undertakes some activity shall take reasonable care not to cause damage to others. It is another thing for the law to require that a person who is doing nothing in particular, shall take steps to prevent another from suffering harm from the acts of third parties ... or natural causes.'

---

1   [1996] 3 All ER 801 at 818.

10.4   In general, a person may only be found liable for an omission where the law imposes on him a positive duty to act. The law has not hesitated to impose such a duty on certain relationships such as employer/employee and teacher/pupil.

10.5   The question is whether a duty is imposed upon members of the emergency services in favour of a member of the public. In assessing this question, it is necessary to consider the three-fold requirements of a duty of care, as laid down in *Caparo Industries Plc v Dickman*:[1]

(1)   foreseeability of damage;
(2)   a relationship characterised as one of 'proximity' or 'neighbourhood'; and
(3)   the court considers it fair, just and reasonable that the law should impose a duty of a given scope on one party for the benefit of the other.

THE POLICE

10.6   At common law, police officers owe the general public a duty to enforce the criminal law, as stated in *R v Metropolitan Police Commissioner, ex parte Blackburn*.[2] However, the case illustrates that a chief officer of police has a wide discretion as to the manner in which the duty is discharged.

Negligent acts

10.7   Where a police officer commits a negligent act which directly causes injury to the person or damage to property, problems of liability do not normally arise. Thus a police officer who negligently drives a motor vehicle has the same liability as an ordinary motorist. This is illustrated in *Marshall v Osmond*,[3] where a police officer was driving in pursuit of a stolen car and it was held that the plaintiff in the stolen car was still owed the normal duty of care.

10.8   Other cases illustrate the same point. In *Rigby v Chief Constable of Northamptonshire*,[4] the police, in order to flush out a suspect, fired a CS canister into premises owned by a gunsmith. The police knew that the device might set fire to the shop, as proved to be the case. At the time when the police fired the canister, they knew that fire engines which had previously been in attendance had left because they were needed elsewhere. It was held that the police were liable.

10.9   In *Knightley v Johns*,[5] a police inspector, attending an incident in a tunnel in Birmingham, ordered a police motorcyclist to ride against the traffic in order to close the entrance to the tunnel. The motorcyclist was subsequently involved in an accident. Again, it was held that the police were liable.

10.10   In all the cases referred to above, the police were held liable because they had committed a negligent act.

---

1   [1990] 2 AC 605.
2   [1968] 1 All ER 763.
3   [1983] 2 All ER 225.
4   [1985] 1 WLR 1242.
5   [1982] 1 WLR 349.

Omissions

10.11   It is in cases involving allegations of a failure to act that problems normally arise. To determine whether a duty of care is owed to the claimant, more careful scrutiny of legal principles is required.

Investigating crime

10.12   The starting point in considering whether a duty of care can arise when the police are investigating a crime is *Hill v Chief Constable of West Yorkshire*.[1] It is submitted that this remains the leading case on this aspect, although some doubt has been cast on *Hill* by the decision of the European Court of Human Rights in *Osman v United Kingdom*,[2] which will be dealt with below.[3] *Osman* itself has been put in doubt by the more recent decision of the European Court in *Z and Others v United Kingdom*.[4]

10.13   In *Hill*, the plaintiff was the mother of the last victim of Peter Sutcliffe, the 'Yorkshire Ripper'. In her claim against the Chief Constable of West Yorkshire, she alleged that the police force had been negligent in failing to apprehend Sutcliffe. The causation issue – whether the alleged negligence caused the death of Jacqueline Hill – was not explored. The primary function of the House of Lords was to determine the extent of the duty of care owed to members of the public by police officers. In the House of Lords, Lord Keith accepted that:

> 'There existed reasonable foreseeability of likely harm to such as Ms Hill, if Sutcliffe were not identified and apprehended.'

10.14   However, foreseeability of injury or damage was not enough to enable the House of Lords to find that a duty of care existed. In reaching their decision in favour of the police, their Lordships relied upon the decision in *Home Office v Dorset Yacht Co Ltd*,[5] in which it had been decided that a civil action can be maintained only if the duty owed is one:

> 'Which exposes that person to a particular risk of damage, which is different in its incidence from the general risk of damage from criminal acts of others which he shares with all members of the public.'

In *Hill*, the House of Lords decided that for a duty of care to exist there must be a special relationship of proximity. On the facts of the case, no such special relationship was established. The duty which the police owed – to identify and apprehend the criminal committing the crimes – was owed to the public at large, and not to the deceased as an individual.

10.15   However, the House of Lords did not leave the matter there. It decided that even if such a duty did exist, public policy required that the police should not be liable. Lord Keith said:[6]

---

1   [1989] AC 53.
2   [1999] 1 FLR 193.
3   See para **10.22**.
4   [2001] 2 FLR 612.
5   [1970] AC 1004.
6   [1989] AC 53 at 63.

'In some instances the imposition of liability may lead to the exercise of a function being carried on in a detrimentally defensive frame of mind ... A great deal of police time, trouble and expense might be expected to have to be put into the preparation for the defence to the action, and the attendance of witnesses at the trial. The result would be a significant diversion of police manpower, and attention from their most important function, that of the suppression of crime.'

10.16 The public policy argument was spelled out further by Lord Templeman. He observed:[1]

'If this action lies, every citizen will be able to require the Court to investigate the performance of every policeman. If the policeman concentrates on one crime, he may be accused of neglecting others. If the policeman does not arrest on suspicion a suspect with previous convictions, the police force may be held liable for subsequent crimes. The threat of litigation against the police force would not make a policeman more efficient. The necessity for defending proceedings, successfully or unsuccessfully, would distract the policeman from his duties. This action is, in my opinion, misconceived and will do more harm than good.'

10.17 In *Alexandrou v Oxford (Chief Constable of Merseyside)*,[2] the plaintiff was the owner of a shop connected to the police station by a burglar alarm. The alarm sounded, and a police officer attended the scene. The police officer claimed that everything was secure at the front of the shop, and that he visited the rear on two occasions and again found everything secure. However, the following day the plaintiff discovered that his shop had been burgled. At first instance, Hodgson J found that there was a special relationship between the police and the owners of burglar alarm systems and that there was accordingly sufficient proximity to give rise to a duty of care. However, the Court of Appeal, following *Hill*, decided that there was no such duty. It based its decision on two grounds. First, that there was not a relationship of proximity. Glidewell LJ stated:[3]

'The communication with the police in this case was by a 999 telephone call, followed by a recorded message. If, as a result of that communication, the police came under a duty of care to the plaintiff, it must follow that they would be under a similar duty to any person who informs them, whether by 999 call, or in some other way, that a burglary or indeed any crime against himself or his property, is being committed or about to be committed. In my view, if there is a duty of care, it is owed to a wider group than those to whom the judge referred. It is owed to all members of the public to give information of a suspected crime against themselves, or their property. It follows that on the facts of this case ... there was no such special relationship between the plaintiff and the police.'

10.18 Secondly, the Court of Appeal decided that the observations about public policy expressed in *Hill* were of general application. As a result, it was not 'fair or reasonable' that the police should be under a duty of care in the investigation of suspected crime.

10.19 From the above, it will be seen that the approach of the English courts has been to grant immunity to the police from claims arising from actions carried out in the course of the investigation of crime, no matter how dilatory or careless they have been. This is perhaps best illustrated by *Osman v Ferguson and Chief Officer of the*

---

1   [1989] AC 53 at 65.
2   [1993] 4 All ER 328.
3   Ibid at 338g–j.

Metropolis,[1] where the Court of Appeal granted the application by the police to strike out the plaintiff's claim as disclosing no reasonable cause of action.

10.20   A teacher, Paget-Lewis, became infatuated with a 15-year-old boy, Ahmed Osman. Paget-Lewis was responsible for graffiti alleging a sexual relationship between Ahmed and another boy. An office at the school was broken into and the file relating to Ahmed was removed. Shortly afterwards, Paget-Lewis changed his name by deed poll to Osman. All these matters were made known to Hackney police. Paget-Lewis then committed several acts of vandalism against the boy's home and property. Soon after, he confessed to a police officer that there was a danger that he might do something criminally insane. Half-hearted attempts by the police were made to follow him, but 3 months after giving his warning, the teacher shot both Osman and Osman's father.

10.21   Counsel for the plaintiffs argued that *Osman* could be distinguished from *Hill*, because the culprit had already been identified. Counsel also submitted that no further investigation was needed as the police had only to apprehend the school teacher, to avoid the subsequent crime. The Court of Appeal was not prepared to accept this submission. It decided that there was an arguable case that as between Ahmed Osman and his family, on the one hand, and the police, on the other, there existed a close degree of proximity amounting to a special relationship. However, the Court of Appeal followed *Hill* in deciding that it was contrary to public policy that a duty should arise. McCowan LJ said:[2]

> 'In my judgment, investigation of crime is not meant to be narrowly interpreted, and suppression includes the prevention of crime.'

10.22   As has been said, the decisions in *Hill* and *Osman* have been thrown into some doubt by the decision of the European Court of Human Rights in *Osman v United Kingdom*,[3] in which the European Court was asked to consider the decision by the Court of Appeal to strike out the claim in *Osman v Ferguson and Chief Officer of the Metropolis*. There the court decided that there had been a breach of Article 6(1) of the ECHR which provides:

> 'In the determination of his civil rights and obligations . . . everyone is entitled to a fair and public hearing within a reasonable time by an independent and impartial tribunal established by law.'

The court considered that the conferring of what it described as a 'blanket immunity' on the police for their acts and omissions during the investigation and suppression of crime amounted to an unjustifiable restriction on the claimant's right to have a determination of his or her claim on the merits. When dealing with the policy considerations which had led the House of Lords to reach its finding in favour of the police in *Hill*, the European Court said:

> 'It must be open to a domestic court to have regard to the presence of other public interest considerations which pull in the opposite direction to the application of the rule.'

---

1   [1993] 4 All ER 344.
2   Ibid at 353.
3   [1999] 1 FLR 193.

The effect of the European Court's decision seems to be that in future the police will have to present evidence to the court of any policy considerations supporting an argument that no duty was owed to a particular claimant. The claimant will be entitled to challenge the evidence and present evidence of any countervailing policy considerations. At the end of the day the English courts may still decide cases on the basis of *Hill* and *Osman*, but probably only after hearing evidence, and it is unlikely that any application to strike out a similar claim as disclosing no cause of action will succeed.

10.23   Following *Osman v United Kingdom*, it seemed that the police would have to present evidence to the court of any policy considerations supporting an argument that no duty was owed to a particular claimant. It is submitted that this may no longer be the case in the light of the decision of the European Court of Human Rights in *Z and Others v United Kingdom*.[1] It should be noted, in particular, that the European Court, in *Z and Others* said:

> 'The Court considers that its reasoning in the *Osman* judgment was based on an understanding of the law of negligence ... which has to be reviewed in the light of the clarifications subsequently made by the domestic courts and notably in the House of Lords. ... In the present case, the Court is led to the conclusion that the inability of the Applicants to sue the local authority flowed not from an immunity, but from the applicable principals governing the substantive right of action in domestic law. There was no restriction on access to the Court.'

Other police duties

10.24   *Hill*, *Alexandrou* and *Osman* all concerned the duty of the police in the detection and suppression of crime. However, the judiciary has been prepared to take the matter further, and restrict the liability of police forces in cases where there are allegations of omission, in areas that are essentially the general public duties of the police. For example, in *Clough v Bussan*,[2] the plaintiff was a passenger in a motor car which was in collision with a car at a crossroads. The traffic lights were malfunctioning, and the police had been informed of the malfunction some 35 minutes earlier. It was alleged by the defendant in third party proceedings that the police had not responded to that information as they should have done. The third party notice was struck out by Kennedy J. He said:[3]

> 'The police were under a duty to preserve law and order, and to protect life and property, because that is their continuing obligation. But nothing, as I find, happened, so as to give rise to a particular duty of care towards the first defendant on which he can now rely in response to the claim for damages from the plaintiff. The fact that a police station received information that the traffic lights at a particular junction were malfunctioning could not, in my judgment, be sufficient to impose on the police a duty of care to every motorist who might thereafter use the junction. If there was a breach of duty, that is a matter of public law which it might be possible to investigate by means of judicial review, but not in third party proceedings, such as have been instituted in this case. Were it necessary to do so, I would also hold, as a matter of public policy, that the police authority should not be exposed to this type of litigation for the reasons given ... in *Hill*.'

---

1   [2001] 2 FLR 612.
2   [1990] RTR 178.
3   Ibid at 182E.

10.25 This restrictive approach was reaffirmed by the Court of Appeal in the case of *Ancell v McDermott*.[1] A coupling fell from the unsecured toolbox of an oil tanker onto the carriageway of a main road. A taxi driver ferrying passengers to Luton Airport drove over the coupling. This caused his fuel tank to rupture, leading to an oil spillage on the carriageway. The taxi did not stop until it ran out of fuel, half a mile further on. A police car came upon the spillage and the officers decided to pursue the trail to its source. When they came upon the taxi, they helpfully offered to take the passengers to Luton Airport. They did not return to erect warning signs at the head of the trail of oil.

10.26 Mrs Ancell drove her car onto the spillage, causing it to skid into an articulated lorry coming in the opposite direction. Proceedings were issued against the owners of the oil tanker, the taxi driver and the police. The police applied to strike out the claim, as disclosing no reasonable cause of action and succeeded before the Court of Appeal. It was decided by Beldam LJ and Sir John Megaw that:

> 'The police were under no duty of care to protect road users from, or to warn them of, hazards discovered by the police, while going about their duties on the highway, and there was in the circumstances no special relationship between the Plaintiff and the police, giving rise to an exceptional duty to prevent harm from dangers created by another. The extreme width and scope of such a duty of care would impose on a police force a potential liability of almost unlimited scope, and it will be against public policy because it would divert extensive police resources and manpower from, and hamper the performance of, ordinary police duties. Accordingly, the police officers did not owe the plaintiffs a duty of care in the circumstances.'

Assumption of responsibility

10.27 Thus far all the cases discussed in relation to alleged failures to perform a duty have resulted in the police avoiding liability. However, liability has been imposed by the courts even for alleged omissions in circumstances where the police have assumed some measure of responsibility for the claimant. In *Kirkham v Chief Constable of Manchester*,[2] the police knew that an arrested man was a suicide risk. They did not pass on this information to the prison authorities. Lloyd LJ observed[3] that:

> 'The common law frequently imposes liability for a pure omission, where the defendant is under a duty to act, or, as the case may be, a duty to speak ... The question depends in each case on whether, having regard to the particular relationship between the parties, the defendant has assumed a responsibility towards the plaintiff, and whether the plaintiff has relied on that assumption of responsibility.'

Similarly, in *Reeves v Commissioner of Police of the Metropolis*,[4] the House of Lords held that the police have a duty to take reasonable care to prevent prisoners in custody from harming themselves, or committing suicide where they are known suicide risks. In this instance, the duty was breached by the failure to shut the wicket hatch in the cell door.

---

1   [1993] 4 All ER 355.
2   [1990] QB 283.
3   Ibid at 289A.
4   [2000] 1 AC 360.

10.28 The decisions in *Kirkham* and *Reeves* can be contrasted with the Court of Appeal judgment in *Orange v Chief Constable of West Yorkshire Police*.[1] The claimant was arrested for being drunk and disorderly. He was placed in a cell, monitored by closed circuit television. However, the camera did not cover the area around the cell which was recessed. Inside the door was a steel gate. The horizontal bar on the gate provided a ready means whereby a prisoner could hang himself. The claimant was found hanging by his belt from the bar. The Court of Appeal acknowledged that the police owe a duty to take reasonable care of any person in their custody and that such duty undoubtedly encompasses the duty to take reasonable steps to prevent a person from committing suicide if he is a known suicide risk. On the facts of the case, there was nothing to indicate that the claimant presented a suicide risk. The Court of Appeal said that it would not be fair, just or reasonable to impose on the police a general obligation to treat every prisoner as a suicide risk.

10.29 The Court of Appeal has also held that the police have no duty to ensure that a man they have arrested as a suspect is not injured in an attempt to escape. In *Vellino v Chief Constable of Greater Manchester*,[2] the claimant, in an attempt to escape, jumped from a window of his second floor flat. He fractured his skull, suffering serious injury. It was common ground that, prior to pronouncing the words 'I arrest you', the police owed the claimant no duty to prevent him hurting himself while trying to escape. While the Court of Appeal was content to assume, without so deciding, that when a police officer arrests a citizen, he puts himself in a relationship with that prisoner which could involve the police officer owing a duty of care to the prisoner, in each case it is necessary to identify the particular duty which is said to have been broken. Where, however, a man breaks away from the arresting officer, he commits a crime, and is no longer in the immediate power of the officer. If the police were not, at the moment of arrest, under a duty owed to the claimant to take care that he did not hurt himself whilst escaping, the Court of Appeal failed to see how it could be said that the police had such a duty thrust on them at the moment he broke free.

10.30 In *Cowan v Chief Constable of Avon and Somerset Constabulary*[3] it was held that the police do not have a duty of care to prevent an offence being committed against a tenant under the Prevention from Eviction Act 1977. The claimant had called for assistance from the police, when he had been threatened with violence if he did not leave his rented property as the landlord had requested. The claimant brought proceedings in negligence, alleging that the officers owed him a duty to take steps to prevent a crime being committed under the 1977 Act. The Court of Appeal stated that it did not accept that the mere presence of the officers at the scene was in the circumstances sufficient to give rise to the special relationship necessary for a duty of care to arise. Their Lordships found it impossible to discern any sufficiently weighty counter-balancing public interest which would make a duty of care appropriate in the circumstances, or render it just or reasonable to impose such a duty.

10.31 In giving its judgment, the Court of Appeal approved the propositions as laid down by May LJ in *Costello v Chief Constable of Northumbria Police*.[4] In that case the chief constable was held liable to the claimant, a police officer, in circumstances

1   [2001] EWCA Civ 611, (2001) 98 (24) LSG 44.
2   [2001] EWCA Civ 1249, (2001) 151 NW 1441.
3   [2001] EWCA Civ 1699, [2002] HLR 44.
4   [1999] ICR 752.

where the officer's colleague had stood by whilst a prisoner assaulted the claimant officer. The Court of Appeal said that on the facts of this case a sufficiently close relationship existed between the claimant and the other police officer to justify a duty of care being imposed.

10.32 Liability was, however, imposed in *Wilson v Chief Constable Lothian Borders Constabulary*,[1] when a man who was paralytic with drink was taken for a ride in a police car, and released in the countryside. He was only lightly clothed and was left exposed in sub-zero temperatures. He died of exposure. Liability was imposed, the court deciding that the police had assumed responsibility for the man's well-being. They had thereafter failed in their duty.

10.33 The police were also held liable in *Swinney v Chief Constable of Northumbria Police*.[2] The plaintiff received information which helped to identify the driver of a vehicle which had hit and killed a police officer. The information was passed to the police on the strict understanding that confidentiality was to be preserved, the plaintiff fearing retaliation if his identity became known to the perpetrator of the original crime. The police left the information in a police vehicle which was stolen. The information came into the hands of the suspect. The plaintiff was threatened and suffered considerable psychological damage. The police argued that no duty was owed. Furthermore, there was no proximity and on grounds of public policy the claim should be dismissed. The Court of Appeal found for the plaintiff deciding that the police did not have a blanket immunity. There were other considerations of public policy including the protection and encouragement of informants, without fear of their identity becoming known to the criminal fraternity.

10.34 In *Clarke v Chief Constable of Northamptonshire Police and Another*,[3] the Court of Appeal held that the police owed a duty of care to a prisoner to inform the Prison Service accurately of the date of his arrest when he was handed over by the police into the custody of the Prison Service. Any misinformation by the police which led to the prisoner being detained beyond the proper term would make the police liable in damages to the prisoner for his unlawful detention.

Vicarious liability

10.35 An issue sometimes arises as to whether acts committed by a serving police officer are committed within the course of his or her employment, thus making the chief constable vicariously liable for those tortious acts. In *Weir v Chief Constable of Merseyside Police*,[4] the Court of Appeal was asked to decide such a point in circumstances where a police officer had identified himself as such, although off duty. He assaulted the claimant, forcibly removing him from a building, and locking him in a police van. The claimant brought proceedings against the chief constable. On the question of vicarious liability, the Court of Appeal held that the claimant had to show that the alleged tort was committed at a time when the police officer was apparently acting in his capacity as a constable. On the facts of this case, it was held that from the moment the constable put the claimant out of the building, he was apparently

1   1989 SLT 97.
2   [1996] 3 All ER 449.
3   (1999) 96(24) LSG 38.
4   [2003] EWCA Civ 111, [2003] ICR 708.

exercising his authority as a constable, having confirmed that he was a police officer. Therefore, the chief constable was vicariously liable for the assault and for the injuries caused. This claim was brought against the chief constable alleging assault, and false imprisonment and, as such, falls outside the ambit of this book. However, it is submitted that the principles as to whether a chief constable is liable for negligence would be the same, in appropriate circumstances.

Liability of the police for damage to property

10.36 All of the cases discussed thus far have been concerned with liability for injury to the person. There is, however, a growing body of cases concerned with liability for damage to property. The police have powers both at common law and under statute to obtain or retain custody of the property of individual members of the public. At common law, the police have the power to seize property where they have reasonable grounds for believing that a serious offence has been committed; that the property is the 'fruit' or 'instrument' or 'material evidence' of the crime; and that the person in possession has himself committed the crime, or is implicated in it, or is an accessory to it 'or at any rate that his refusal (to hand over the property), must be quite unreasonable'.[1] Extensive powers are provided under the Police and Criminal Evidence Act 1984. For example, s 19(2) gives the police powers to seize property obtained in consequence of the commission of an offence which it is necessary to seize in order to prevent it being concealed, lost, damaged, altered or destroyed.

10.37 Examples where the police may be considered to have 'assumed a responsibility' to the owner for the care and safety of his property include a custody officer taking personal property of an arrested person for safe keeping or a person who, on arrest, is deprived of his ability to control and care for the safety of his own property.

10.38 It is often argued that the police not merely owe a duty of care in negligence to the owners of the property where they have taken it into their custody, possession or control, but also owe a common law duty as bailee. The duty of care was conceded by the police in *Sutcliffe v Chief Constable of Yorkshire*.[2] The police had seized a car under s 19 of the Police and Criminal Evidence Act 1984, and kept it in a compound at the rear of a police station. The vehicle was attacked and damaged by vandals. On the facts, it was held that the duty had not been breached.

10.39 More recently, the Court of Appeal refused to strike out claims in negligence and bailment by the owner of stolen property, where the police had arrested the thief and placed the stolen property in their yard, from which it had again been stolen.[3] A similar approach was adopted by the Court of Appeal in *Lervold v Chief Constable of Kent*.[4] Mr Lervold was in transit down the English Channel en route from Scandinavia to the Caribbean. The engine of his boat failed and he drifted ashore. On arrival, police and customs officials were involved, and Mr Lervold was detained in custody. While he was being held, his boat was looted and also damaged by natural causes. He sued Kent Police on the basis that, having arrested him, and thereby depriving

---

1   *Ghani v Jones* [1970] QB 693.
2   [1996] RTR 86, CA.
3   *Goldie-Scott v Chief Constable of Kent* (unreported) 22 November 1995, CA.
4   [1995] CLY 3687.

him of any ability to guard or protect his property, he was owed a duty of care. The Court of Appeal refused to strike out the claim on an application brought on behalf of the chief constable on grounds of absence of proximity and public policy.

10.40 As yet, it has not been argued on behalf of the police in such cases that public policy militates against the duty, which is effectively a duty to 'care for' or act as guardian of such property. It could be argued on behalf of the police that their imposed duty to take possession of property in certain specified circumstances deprives them of the freedom to choose whether or not to take possession of the property. They are in effect involuntary bailees of the property, and should not be subjected to the ordinary duties of care which attach to volunteers.

THE FIRE BRIGADE

10.41 The Fire Services Act 1947 provided for the transfer of firefighting functions from the National Fire Service to fire brigades maintained by local authorities.

10.42 In *Kilbey v South Eastern Fire Area Joint Committee*,[1] it was held that the members of a fire brigade were servants of the statutory fire authority which was responsible for any negligence of its members established on the part of the officer or fireman of the brigade.

10.43 Section 1 of the 1947 Act provides that:

'It shall be the duty of every fire authority ... to make provision for fire fighting purposes and, in particular, every fire authority shall secure –

(a)   the services for their area of such a fire brigade and such equipment as may be necessary to meet efficiently all normal requirements;

...

(c)   efficient arrangements for dealing with calls for the assistance of the fire brigade in the case of fire and for summoning members of the fire brigade.'

10.44 The Act has a number of other provisions relating to every fire authority. The statute does not expressly, or by any obvious implication, suggest that a remedy lies in the hands of an individual to sue for damages for breach of the statutory duties contained in the Act.

10.45 In *Stovin v Wise*,[2] Lord Hoffmann considered an argument that a statutory power could not generate a common law duty of care, unless the public authority had created an expectation that the power would be used, and the plaintiff had suffered from reliance on that expectation. In relation to this argument, Lord Hoffmann observed:[3]

'I will only note in passing that its application may require some very careful analysis of the role which the expected exercise of the statutory power plays in community behaviour. For example, in one sense it is true that the fire brigade is there to protect people in situations in which they could not be expected to be able to protect themselves.

---

1   1952 SC 280.
2   [1996] 3 All ER 801.
3   [1996] 3 All ER 801 at 829j.

On the other hand, they can and do protect themselves by insurance against the risk of fire. It is not obvious that there should be a right to compensation from a negligent fire authority, which will ordinarily enure by right of subrogation to an insurance company. The only reason would be to provide a general deterrent against inefficiency. But there must be better ways of doing this, than by compensating insurance companies out of public funds. While premiums, no doubt, take into account the existence of the fire brigade, and the likelihood that it will arrive swiftly upon the scene, it is not clear that they would be very different, merely because no compensation was paid in the rare cases in which the fire authority negligently failed to perform its public duty.'

10.46 Notwithstanding Lord Hoffmann's view, there have in recent years been a number of cases in which the owner or occupier of premises has sued the fire brigade for damages for negligence as a result of its attendance at a fire. In *Capital and Counties Plc v Hampshire County Council*,[1] the Court of Appeal considered three such cases and had to consider in what circumstances a fire brigade owed a duty of care.

Does the fire brigade owe a duty of care?

10.47 In one of the three cases, *John Munroe (Acrylics) Limited v London Fire Brigade and Civil Defence Authority*,[2] a company specialising in creating special effects for film and television caused a deliberate explosion on wasteland near the plaintiff's industrial premises. Burning debris was scattered over a wide area, and small fires broke out. Some of the debris was seen to fall onto the plaintiff's premises and smoke was observed coming from a corner of the plaintiff's yard. Members of the public made emergency calls to the fire brigade which responded within a short time by sending four fire engines to the scene. When they arrived, the fire had already been extinguished by employees of the special effects company. There was no visible evidence of any continuing conflagration. The fire brigade's officers took steps to satisfy themselves that all fires had been extinguished and that there was no residual danger. They left the scene about 20 minutes after the initial explosion, without inspecting the plaintiff's premises. Later that evening, a fire broke out at the plaintiff's premises which were severely damaged.

10.48 In the second of the three cases, *Church of Jesus Christ of Latter Day Saints v West Yorkshire Fire and Civil Defence Authority*,[3] the fire brigade arrived to put out a fire in a classroom next to a chapel. Owing to the absence of a proper water supply the fire brigade was unable to fight the fire properly for some time. Of the seven water hydrants surrounding the chapel, four failed to work, and the three remaining were not located in time to be of any assistance. Water had to be obtained from a mill dam over half a mile away.

10.49 At first instance, in *Munroe*, Rougier J had observed:[4]

'There is a growing belief that every misfortune must, in pecuniary terms at any rate, be laid at someone else's door, and after every mishap, every tragedy, the cupped palms are outstretched for the solace of monetary compensation.'

---

1   [1997] 2 All ER 865.
2   [1996] 4 All ER 318, QBD.
3   [1997] 3 WLR 331.
4   [1996] 4 All ER 318.

10.50 Not surprisingly, Rougier J gave judgment for the fire brigade and the judgment was upheld on appeal. Indeed, the fire brigade was successful in the first two of the three cases to be considered by the Court of Appeal.

No general immunity

10.51 The fire brigade was found liable in the third of the cases, *Capital and Counties Plc v Hampshire County Council*. A fire officer ordered the sprinkler system to be turned off. When the sprinklers were disabled the fire brigade had not yet found the seat of the fire and were not effectively fighting it. The sprinklers were therefore at that stage the only operative means of fighting the fire. With the sprinklers out of action, the fire rapidly grew out of control. The Court of Appeal held that there was sufficient proximity. There had been an increase in the risk of the fire spreading, caused by the positive act of the fire brigade. The court declined an invitation to find that there was some general immunity in favour of fire brigades.

10.52 Although this case was a disappointment to fire brigades, close analysis reveals that there is unlikely to be a flood of claims as a result.

10.53 Stuart-Smith LJ gave judgment in the following terms:[1]

'But where the rescue/protective service itself, by its negligence, creates the danger which caused the Plaintiff's injury, there is no doubt in our Judgment, the plaintiff can recover ... it seems to us that there is no difference in principle, if, by some positive negligent act, the rescuer/protective service substantially increases the risk; he is thereby creating a fresh danger, albeit of the same kind, or of the same nature, namely, fire.'

10.54 Stuart-Smith LJ later elaborated:[2]

'In such circumstances the defendants would at least prima facie be liable for the extra damage, unless they could show – and the burden would be on them – that the damage would have occurred in any event, even if they had never come upon the scene. If they were unable to discharge that burden, then they would be liable.'

10.55 On a simple analysis of the *Capital and Counties* decision, fire brigades would be well advised not to turn up at fires. Indeed, the Court of Appeal specifically held that they are not under a common law duty to answer the call for help, and are not under a duty to take care to do so.[3] If, therefore, they fail to attend, or to attend in time because they have misunderstood the message, got lost on the way or run into a tree, they are not liable. When they do attend upon a fire they should endeavour not to do any positive act which could arguably make matters worse. The Court of Appeal observed that a fire brigade does not enter into a sufficiently proximate relationship with the owner or occupier of premises to come under a duty of care merely by attending at the fire ground and fighting the fire.

1   [1997] 2 All ER 865 at 880.
2   Ibid at 882.
3   The approach of the English judiciary can be contrasted with that adopted by the Scottish courts. In *Duff v Highlands and Islands Fire Board* 1995 SLT 1362, it was decided that since the attendance of a fire brigade to put out a fire at a house was in performance of a statutory duty, in terms of the Fire Services Act 1947, rather than the exercise of a discretionary power, their duties were not restricted to merely ensuring that they did not add to the damage that the householder would have suffered, had they done nothing.

10.56 This could lead to a defensive attitude to firefighting but, in practice, it is unlikely that the fire service will allow considerations of liability to colour its approach to saving life and property.

10.57 The Court of Appeal was at pains to indicate that the facts of the *Capital and Counties* case were unusual, in that they involved a glaring error. The judge found a clear breach of a so-called 'golden rule' of firefighting, that automatic sprinkler machines should not be switched off. It was accepted that the *Bolam* test[1] should be applied to fire brigades, and the Court of Appeal indicated that there was a high threshold to establishing negligence, namely that it must be established that the error was one that no reasonably well-informed and competent fireman could have made. It is submitted that the courts will take into account the difficulties faced by firemen who have to make decisions quickly, without knowing all the facts, and will recognise that there may be more than one reasonable approach to fighting a fire. Furthermore, it will be in comparatively rare circumstances that even if the fire brigade does not fight a fire effectively it can be said to have made matters worse. This is likely to mean that it would only be in the very occasional instance that a property owner can have reasonable prospects of a successful action against a fire brigade.

10.58 The rationale of the Court of Appeal decision in *Capital and Counties* has been tested in *Daly v Surrey County Council*.[2] Mr Daly was working on a building site, when the sides of a trench fell in on him. The fire brigade was summoned and arrived shortly afterwards. When it arrived, the officer in charge witnessed one of Mr Daly's workmates attempting to dig him out with an excavator. The officer ordered the man to stop, because he feared that the attempts would make matters worse, if not kill Mr Daly. The officer then devised and executed a plan which he considered safer both to Mr Daly and to the firemen engaged in the rescue.

10.59 Unfortunately, by the time the fire brigade's men reached the victim, he was dead. It was argued on behalf of the plaintiff that, by preventing workmates from digging him out, the fire brigade had made matters worse, and was thus liable on the basis of the *Capital and Counties* decision. May J rejected this argument. He decided that the fire officer's instructions to the workmates was a positive act, but that on the facts of the case, the instruction was not negligent, but the action of a reasonably competent fire officer attending a trench rescue.

THE AMBULANCE SERVICE

10.60 There are few reported claims against the ambulance service, or indeed doctors or paramedics attending the scene of an accident. However, the position has now been considered by the Court of Appeal in *Kent v Griffiths*.[3] Before this case, liability had been established, at least in part, in *Griffin v Mersey Regional Ambulance*,[4] where it was held that an ambulance responding to an emergency call

---

1   *Bolam v Friern Hospital Management Committee* [1957] 2 All ER 118, when it was decided that the standard required of any professional person is the standard of the ordinary skilled man exercising and professing to have that special skill.
2   (Unreported) 23 October 1997, May J.
3   [2000] 2 WLR 1158.
4   [1998] PIQR 34.

was entitled to cross a road junction where lights were red, provided special care was taken by the driver to ensure the road was clear. In emergency circumstances, the red light was effectively a 'give way' sign.[1]

10.61　The case of *Cattey v St John's Ambulance Brigade*[2] concerned a 15-year-old who had an accident whilst taking part in a motor scrambling event. It was alleged that his spinal injury was made worse by the negligent treatment of the St John's Ambulancemen. On the facts of the case, the judge decided that the plaintiff had been treated in accordance with the ordinary skills to be expected of a trained St John's Ambulance first aider. However, he did consider that there was a duty of care owed by such a volunteer, the appropriate standard being the *Bolam* test,[3] adapted to the circumstances of someone in the position of the ambulanceman.

10.62　The position has now been further clarified by the Court of Appeal in *Kent v Griffiths*. The claimant alleged that she had suffered a miscarriage and brain damage as a result of the delay in the arrival of an ambulance, following an emergency call. The Court of Appeal had earlier refused the defendant's application to strike out the claim as disclosing no cause of action. The case was then tried, with judgment being given in favour of the claimant. The Court of Appeal refused the defendant's appeal against the decision of the trial judge. Lord Woolf MR held that the ambulance service owed a public law duty. They were not volunteers, whose only duty was the requirement not to make the situation worse (see, eg, *Cattey* above). Importantly, Lord Woolf considered that the ambulance service was part of the health service and, as such, owed a duty of care to patients. To this extent, he considered that the ambulance service was not in the same situation as the police and fire brigade. The ambulance had been called for the claimant alone. It was foreseeable that the claimant would suffer further injuries if the ambulance was delayed. The defendant had sufficient resources to provide an ambulance and, in the circumstances, there was no reason to say that no duty of care was owed when the ambulance had been delayed for no good reason. It should be noted that the Court of Appeal viewed *Kent* as an exceptional case and did not anticipate many similar claims arising.

CONCLUSION

10.63　The past decade has witnessed a concerted effort by lawyers and property insurers to increase the extent of liability of the emergency services. In general, the judiciary has responded restrictively. There seems a considerable reluctance to find the police or the fire brigade liable in negligence, either on proximity or fair, just and reasonable grounds. The emergency services do not have immunity from suit, but it is only in the most obvious cases that a police force, fire authority or ambulance service will be deemed liable, and only then in circumstances where a new danger has been brought to the scene by the emergency services. Public policy underpins this

---

1　Fire engines are similarly treated. Special rules exempt them from compliance with speed limits and traffic lights. Again, a red traffic light constitutes a 'give way' sign and not a stop signal, in the case of a fire service vehicle being used for fire brigade purposes: reg 34 of the Traffic Signs Regulations and General Directions 1994, SI 1994/1519.

2　(Unreported) 25 November 1988.

3　*Bolam v Friern Hospital Management Committee* [1957] 2 All ER 118.

approach. The rationale behind the judiciary's thinking was perhaps best explained by May J in *OLL Ltd v Secretary of State for the Home Department*,[1] a case involving the liability of the coastguard. In declining to find a duty of care owed by the coastguard to those in trouble at sea, May J said:[2]

> 'Directly inflicted physical injury is the first building block of the law of negligence because, unless it is excused, it will almost always be a component of a breach of duty.'

10.64   Or, as Stuart-Smith LJ observed in *Capital and Counties*:[3]

> 'The peculiarity of fire brigades, together with other rescue services . . . such as, the police, is that they do not as a rule, create the danger which causes injury to the plaintiff, or loss to his property. For the most part, they act in the context of a danger already created, and damage already caused, whether by the forces of nature, or the acts of some third party, or even the plaintiff himself, and whether those acts are criminal, negligent or non-culpable.'

---

1   [1997] 3 All ER 897.
2   Ibid at 908.
3   [1997] 2 All ER 865 at 879–880.

Chapter 11

TREES

INTRODUCTION

11.1   The 1970s saw at least two developments which led to a massive increase in the number of claims for damage to property caused by tree roots. First, in 1971 the insurance market extended household cover to include subsidence. Secondly, in 1975–76, the UK experienced the worst drought for at least 200 years. Not only did this cause shrinkage of clay sub-soil and therefore a large number of claims for subsidence, but it also brought about an increase in knowledge amongst experts, and among the population as a whole.

11.2   The vast majority of, if not all, claims for subsidence damage to buildings caused by tree roots are brought in nuisance and, accordingly, it is necessary to examine the elements which are required to bring a claim in nuisance.

NUISANCE AND TREES – THE ORIGINAL UNDERSTANDING

11.3   Until 1981 and the Court of Appeal decision in *Solloway v Hampshire County Council* (which is dealt with in the following paragraphs), it was understood that the law was as stated in the judgment of Lord Goddard CJ in *Davey v Harrow Corporation*,[1] where he said, delivering the judgment of the court:

> 'In our opinion, it must be taken to be established law that, if trees encroach, whether by branches or roots and cause damage, an action for nuisance will lie.'

It is interesting to note that much of the time before the Court of Appeal was taken up with the local authority's argument that the plaintiff could not succeed unless it was shown that the offending trees had been planted and were not self-sown and that no action could be maintained where the damage was caused by natural growth or natural causes. The Court of Appeal could see no reason to distinguish between planted and self-sown trees.

Leakey and Others v National Trust for Places of Historical Interest or Natural Beauty

11.4   A significant change in the law of nuisance was brought about by the case of *Leakey and Others v National Trust for Places of Historical Interest or Natural Beauty*.[2] This was not a case of tree root nuisance, but concerned damage caused when a large amount of soil fell from a hill on the National Trust's land onto Mr and

---

1   [1957] 2 All ER 305.
2   [1980] 1 All ER 17.

Mrs Leakey's land. Although the plaintiffs had pointed out the danger to the National Trust, the latter had replied that it was not obliged to do anything about it because the problem was caused by a natural movement of the earth. In the course of his judgment, Megaw LJ laid down what is now accepted as the definitive statement of the law relating to nuisance brought about by natural causes:

> 'The duty is a duty to do that which is reasonable in all the circumstances, and no more than what, if anything, is reasonable, to prevent or minimise the known risk of damage or injury to one's neighbour or to his property. The considerations with which the law is familiar are all to be taken into account in deciding whether there has been a breach of duty, and if so, what the breach is, and whether it is causative of the damage in respect of which the claim is made. Thus, there will fall to be considered the *extent* of the risk; what, so far as reasonably can be *foreseen*, are the chances that anything untoward will happen or that any damage will be caused? What is to be foreseen as to the possible *extent* of the damage if the risk becomes reality? Is it practicable to prevent, or minimise the happening of any damage? If it is practicable, *how simple or how difficult* are the measures which could be taken, how much and how lengthy work do they involve, and what is the probable cost of such works? Was there sufficient time for preventive action to have been taken by persons acting reasonably in relation to the main risk, between the time when it became known to or should have been realised by, the Defendant, and the time when the damage occurred? Factors such as these, so far as they apply in a particular case, fall to be weighed in deciding whether the Defendant's duty of care requires, or required him to do anything, and, if so, what.' (emphasis added)

11.5   The case of *Leakey* therefore confirmed that foreseeability and reasonable care were elements necessary to bring home to a defendant a claim for nuisance arising out of natural causes. The Court of Appeal followed the earlier decision of the House of Lords in *Sedleigh-Denfield v O'Callaghan and Others*,[1] a case of nuisance brought about by human agency, namely the construction of a culvert over a ditch, where the House of Lords confirmed that knowledge on the part of the defendant was an essential element to enable a plaintiff to succeed in a claim of nuisance.

EXISTING LAW OF NUISANCE IN TREE ROOT CASES – *SOLLOWAY v HAMPSHIRE COUNTY COUNCIL*

11.6   It was with the decision of *Leakey* in mind that the Court of Appeal dealt with the case of *Solloway v Hampshire County Council*.[2] The plaintiff was the freehold owner of a house which he had bought in 1967. Outside the house there was a horse chestnut tree, one of a large number growing in the pavement along the avenue in which the plaintiff's house was situated. In 1976, during the long period of drought, the plaintiff observed substantial cracks in the fabric of his house. The area in which the plaintiff's house was situated was slightly unusual in that it was generally an area of gravel, which is not usually affected by tree roots. The plaintiff's house, however, was partly founded on a small outcrop of clay from which the roots had abstracted moisture and thus caused subsidence.

11.7   The issue which came before the Court of Appeal for decision was that of foreseeability. At first instance, Stocker J had dealt with the law as follows:

---

1   [1940] All ER 349.
2   (1981) 79 LGR 449.

'I therefore find that the law which I have to apply to the facts of the present case to be, that the duty in respect of the nuisance created by the roots arises if the encroachment of those roots is known, or ought to be known, to the owner, occupier or other person responsible for the tree and its maintenance, if the encroachment is such as to give rise to a reasonably foreseeable risk that such encroachment will cause damage.'

11.8 The Court of Appeal considered whether Stocker J's formulation had been correct. Dunn LJ gave the decision of the court as follows:

'That formulation of the law [ie by Stocker J], although it had been contested below, was accepted in this court by Mr Smyth, for the plaintiff. I am bound to say that at first I had doubts whether it was an accurate formulation of the law because of the case of *Davey v Harrow Corporation* . . . which makes no reference to foreseeability as an element in the tort of nuisance, where the nuisance is caused by the extrusion of tree roots or branches, but on further consideration I agree that Mr Smyth was right to accept the formulation of the law as made by the Judge.

In *Leakey v National Trust* Megaw LJ reviewed the whole of the law of nuisance not brought about by human agency, and he dealt with the case of *Davey v Harrow Corporation*. He said:

"I have no hesitation in preferring (that) decision as stating the law as it now is: subject to the proviso that the duty arising from a nuisance which is not brought about by human agency does not arise unless and until the Defendant has, or ought to have had, knowledge of the existence of the defect and the danger thereby created."

Although it was not necessary for the decision, the proviso suggested by Megaw LJ puts nuisance by encroachment of tree roots and branches into the same category of any other nuisance not brought about by human agency. It is consistent with *Sedleigh Denfield v O'Callaghan*[1] and confines the strict liability of a nuisance to cases where there has been some unnatural user of the land as stated in *Rylands v Fletcher*.[2] I would accept the proviso as stated by Megaw LJ as applicable to the facts of this case.'

The House of Lords[3] has indicated that foreseeability is now also a requirement for liability under the rule in *Rylands v Fletcher*.

11.9 The law of nuisance which applies to tree root cases has now been established by Dunn LJ in *Solloway v Hampshire County Council*. It is necessary for a claimant to establish the following to prove his case:

(1) causation – roots from the defendant's tree caused the damage about which the claimant claims;

(2) foreseeability – the defendant should have foreseen that the roots were likely to cause damage if nothing was done to prevent it;

(3) a failure to exercise reasonable care – the defendant could have reasonably taken steps to limit the growth of the tree and incursion of the tree roots.

The above matters are dealt with further below.[4]

---

1   [1940] 3 All ER 349.
2   (1868) LR 3 HL 330.
3   See *Cambridge Water Co v Eastern Counties Leather Plc* [1994] 1 All ER 53, and see Chapter 1.
4   See paras **11.39**–**11.53**.

Is the highway authority responsible for the tree?

11.10 The claimant must show that the defendant is the owner of or controls the tree which has caused damage. In most cases, this probably presents no difficulty (although many trees are to be found in hedges marking the boundary of land where there can be doubt as to ownership). The question has, however, caused some difficulty in claims against highway authorities because of doubt as to the ownership of trees situated in the highway.

Common law

11.11 At common law the owner of land over which a public highway ran did not lose any of his rights of ownership whether of the surface or sub-soil. The maxim was that the soil of the highway '*usque ad medium filum viae*' belonged to the owner of land adjoining the highway.[1]

Statutory background

11.12 The Public Health Acts of 1848 and 1875 changed the position. Section 149 of the 1875 Act provided, so far as is material:

'All streets, being or which at any time become highways repairable by the inhabitants at large within any urban district, and the pavements, stones and other materials thereof, and all buildings, implements and other things provided for the purposes thereof, shall vest in and be under the control of the urban authority.'

Similar provisions for the vesting of highways other than those in urban areas were contained in s 29 of the Local Government Act 1929.

11.13 By s 43 of the Public Health Amendment Act 1890, Parliament granted to urban authorities the power to plant trees, provided they did not become a nuisance to the users of the highway or adjacent owners or occupiers. Similar powers were granted to other highway authorities by the Road Improvements Act 1925.

11.14 The various statutory provisions were drawn together by the Highways Act 1959. Section 82(1) of that Act, repeating provisions in the 1925 Act, gave highway authorities the power to do anything expedient to maintain or protect trees which had been planted by the highway authority. That section was amended by the Highways (Miscellaneous Provisions) Act 1961, as a result of which s 82(1) of the 1959 Act read as follows:

'Subject to the provisions of this section, a Highway Authority may, in a highway maintained at public expense by them, plant trees and shrubs and lay out grass verges and may erect and maintain guards and fences and otherwise do anything expedient for the maintenance and protection of trees, shrubs, grass verges planted or laid out (whether or not by them) in a highway.'

Following the 1961 Act, therefore, highway authorities had the power to maintain not only trees which they had planted, but also trees which had been planted before adoption of the road as a highway, or self-sown trees.

11.15 The current statutory provisions relating to highway trees are contained in s 96 of the Highways Act 1980:

---

1   1 Rolle's Abridgement (1668) 392 and *Goodtitle v Alker* (1757) 1 Barr 143.

'(1) Subject to the provisions of this section, a highway authority may, in a highway maintainable at the public's expense by them, plant trees and shrubs and lay out grass verges, and may erect and maintain guards or fences and otherwise do anything expedient for the maintenance or protection of trees, shrubs and grass verges planted or laid out, whether or not by them, in such a highway.'

It therefore remains clear that the highway authorities' power to maintain trees on the highway relates not only to trees which they have planted, but also to trees planted prior to adoption.

Do the statutory provisions vest ownership of trees in the highway authority?

11.16 There have been doubts over the meaning of the vesting provisions in the Public Health Act 1875 and the Local Government Act 1929. In particular, doubts were expressed whether the ownership of trees planted before adoption vested in the highway authority or remained in the ownership of the adjoining property owner. In *Bridges v London Borough of Harrow*,[1] the plaintiffs' houses had suffered subsidence damage caused by roots from trees situated in the pavement outside their properties. Although the London Borough of Harrow was held by the judge, Stuart-Smith J, as he then was, to be beneficial owner of the land on which the trees were situated, the highway authority, on this occasion, was the Greater London Council. The trees had been planted before the land had been dedicated for use as a highway. The London Borough of Harrow argued that, pursuant to s 29(2) of the Local Government Act 1929, property in the trees had passed to the highway authority under the vesting provisions in that section. The plaintiffs argued to the contrary and relied on the statement of the common law as set out in the judgment of Lord Mansfield in *Goodtitle v Alker*,[2] where he said:

'. . . the King has nothing but the passage for himself and his people: but the freehold and all profits belong to the owner of the soil. So do all the trees upon it . . .'

11.17 Having reviewed the earlier cases, and, in particular, *Coverdale v Charlton*[3] and *Stillwell v New Windsor Corporation*,[4] Stuart-Smith J held that the common law position applied and that the statutory vesting positions had not passed the property in the trees to the highway authority.[5] He said:

'This is a case where the trees were planted before the dedication of the highway and, in my judgment, the question is: to whom does the property in the trees belong? It appears to me to belong to the owner of the soil beneath the highway, and that, in my judgment is, and remains the defendant council.'

Ownership of trees planted before adoption of the highway – the concept of control

11.18 Ownership of and responsibility for pre-adoption trees came before the Court in *Russell v London Borough of Barnet*.[6] The judge considered whether

---

1   (1981) 260 EG 284.
2   (1757) 1 Barr 143.
3   (1878) 4 QBD 104.
4   [1932] 2 Ch 155.
5   See, however, his later decision in the Court of Appeal, *Hurst v Hampshire County Council* (1998) 96 LGR 27, where he overruled *Bridges*, and see para **11.26**.
6   (1985) 83 LGR 152.

the vesting provisions in s 149 of the Public Health Act 1875 applied to transfer to the highway authority the ownership or control of trees which had been planted before adoption. Tudor Evans J decided as follows:

> 'The trees in the case were not provided for the purpose of the street; they were planted long before adoption. I hold that Section 149 was not dealing with pre-adoption trees and that the trees in question did not vest in and were not under the control of the Defendants within the meaning of the language of Section 149. The construction that Section 149 only applied to post adoption trees is consistent with the policy in Section 82 of the Highways Act 1959 which, before it was amended by the Highways (Miscellaneous Provisions) Act 1961, limited control over trees to those planted by the Highway Authority.'

11.19 However, this was not the end of the case. The judge went on to consider the plaintiff's contention that from 1961 (when s 5 of the Highways (Miscellaneous Provisions) Act 1961 had amended s 82(1) of the Highways Act 1959), the highway authority had the right to maintain and control the trees; since it had done so it was liable in nuisance for damage caused to an adjoining owner by the roots. It will be recalled that the amendment introduced by the 1961 Act did extend the highway authority's power of maintenance to all trees and therefore not simply those it had planted. Influenced by the view that it would be artificial, particularly in urban areas, to hold that the adjoining owner alone could maintain a tree in the highway so as to avoid a nuisance to his property, Tudor Evans J held as follows:

> 'I entirely agree with Stocker J [in *Solloway v Hampshire County Council*] when he said that Highway Authorities have sufficient interest in and control over a highway tree to make them liable for a nuisance created thereby, bearing in mind that they alone have the power to maintain the tree. I hold that the fact that the Plaintiffs in this case are presumed in law to have been the owners of the trees is not a bar to an action by them in nuisance against the Defendants who were in occupation of the street, save for the sub-soil beneath it, who were in control of the trees and who, as I shall consider later, in fact and, since 1961 with legal authority, exercised control over them.'

11.20 In *Low v R J Haddock Ltd and the Royal County of Berkshire*,[1] Judge Newey QC (sitting as an Official Referee) had to consider whether the highway authority was responsible for a tree which had once formed part of a self-seeded copse. Following the development of an estate the tree was growing in the grass verge forming part of the highway which had been adopted by the highway authority. The judge decided that the tree had been included by the developer in the dedication of the highway; however, he then considered the position if the tree had not been included in the dedication:

> 'In practice, a sensible tree owner would surely consult the Authority in whose highway his tree is set before doing anything which might constitute damage to it. Where the Authority has chosen to exercise powers over the tree, whether legally or not, the owners might well be able to escape liability by proving that they had relied on the Authority to take any necessary action.'

The judge then referred to the decision in *Russell v London Borough of Barnet* and concluded:

> 'I think that if the oak was, as I have held, dedicated as part of the highway, the County had full legal powers and obligations in respect of it. If the tree had not been dedicated, in view

---

1　(1985) EG LR 247.

of the County's assumption of powers by pruning and the like, I should have followed Tudor-Evans J in *Russell v London Borough of Barnet* and held that they could still be liable in nuisance.'

11.21 After *Russell v London Borough of Barnet*, and *Low v R J Haddock Ltd and the Royal County of Berkshire*, therefore, the practical conclusion was that, whatever the true position with regard to the ownership of trees planted before adoption, from 1961 the highway authority had the power to maintain the trees and therefore sufficient control over them to enable a claim in nuisance to succeed. The position has now been clarified by the Court of Appeal in *Hurst v Hampshire County Council*.[1]

11.22 Control, in the absence of ownership, was considered by the Court of Appeal to be sufficient to make the defendant capable of liability and nuisance in *LE Jones (Insurance Brokers) Limited v Portsmouth City Council*.[2] At the relevant time, Hampshire County Council was the highway authority responsible for maintaining street trees in Portsmouth. Under an agency agreement, however, Portsmouth City Council provided an arboricultural service for Hampshire County Council, which included inspection and maintenance of those trees. It was accepted that damage to the claimant's property had been caused by tree root desiccation. The Court of Appeal rejected Portsmouth City Council's argument that Hampshire County Council was the correct defendant. The lawful exercise of control over trees was enough. What mattered was the right and duty to maintain the trees under the agency agreement which gave Portsmouth City Council sufficient control in fact, and in law, to prevent or eliminate nuisance. As for negligence the argument that Portsmouth City Council owed a duty only to Hampshire County Council failed. The fact that Portsmouth City Council owed a contractual duty to Hampshire County Council did not mean that it owed no duty to anyone else. The potential liability of Portsmouth City Council in negligence was not dependent on ownership or occupation of the relevant land. Nor was it excluded by the potential liability for the same negligence of Hampshire County Council as highway authority.

Trees planted or self-sown after adoption

11.23 In *Hurst v Hampshire County Council*, the Court of Appeal was concerned with a tree planted (or possibly self-sown), after the date of adoption, but not by the highway authority under statutory powers. Stuart-Smith LJ considered the vesting provisions under s 149 of the Public Health Act 1875 and referred to the decision in *Coverdale v Charlton*,[3] from which he quoted the judgment of Brett LJ:

'Street means more than the surface, it means the whole surface and so much of the depth as is or can be used, not unfairly, for the ordinary purposes of a street. It comprises of a depth which enables the urban authority to do that which is done in every street, namely to raise the street and to lay down sewers ...

"Street", therefore, in my opinion includes the surface and so much of the depth as may be not unfairly used, as streets are used. It does not include such a depth as would carry with it the right to mines, neither would "street" include any buildings which happen to be built over the land, because that is not a part of the street within the meaning of such an Act as

---

1   (1998) 96 LGR 27.
2   [2002] EWCA Civ 1723, [2003] 1 WLR 427.
3   (1878) 4 QBD 104.

this. *If the enactment gives the local board that property in so much of the land, it gives them the absolute property in everything growing on the surface of the land.*

The legislature have, because the rights of the owners of the soil in a "street" is of so little value, intentionally taken away that right and have given it to the extent I have mentioned to the local board.' (emphasis by Stuart-Smith LJ)

Stuart-Smith LJ considered that the words which he had italicised would clearly include trees. He referred without approval to the judgment of Bramwell LJ in the same case which doubted whether s 149 vested the property in trees in the highway authority.

11.24   Stuart-Smith LJ next considered *Stillwell v New Windsor Corporation*,[1] which concerned trees planted or self-sown after adoption, but not planted under statutory powers. He quoted from the judgment of Clauson J:

'In my view, for all the purposes of exercising the rights of the Highway Authority, these trees are to be treated as the Highway Authority's trees, and if they think it convenient to remove them it is proper that they should remove them. I am not called upon in this action to decide to whom the timber would belong when the trees were removed.'

11.25   Having referred to the decision of Tudor Evans J in *Russell v London Borough of Barnet*,[2] Stuart-Smith LJ gave the decision of the court:

'I have no doubt that so far as post-adoption trees (trees planted or sown after adoption of the road, but not under statutory power) are concerned, the property in them vests in the Highway Authority for all purposes. If they were planted, albeit not under statutory power, as the tree in the present case possibly was, they are planted for highway purposes in that part of the soil which plainly vested. If they are self-seeded, again they are seeded in that part of the highway which vests in the Local Authority. If, as they mature, their roots encroach into the soil which remains the property of the adjoining owner, I do not see how that makes the tree the property of the owner of the sub-soil. I can see no logical distinction between trees and small shrubs, plants or grass.'

Trees planted before adoption of the highway

11.26   Although the above was sufficient to deal with the plaintiff's appeal in *Hurst v Hampshire County Council*, Stuart-Smith LJ went on to consider trees planted before adoption. He noted that, in *Russell v London Borough of Barnet*, Tudor Evans J had held that such trees did not vest in the highway authority but that the highway authority was liable in nuisance since it exercised control over them. He also noted that, in practical terms, it might be difficult for a court to decide precisely when a tree had been planted: the highway authority could not make any distinction in management between trees planted before and after adoption. Dealing with this distinction Stuart-Smith LJ said:

'If there is any logical basis in the distinction it depends upon the fiction that in the case of a pre-adoption tree there is a reservation from the public's right to pass over the full extent of the highway that part of the surface on which the trees is growing and that the owner of the land at dedication intended to reserve the tree from the dedication. This seems to me to be an unreal fiction, in the absence of an express reservation. There are no authorities binding upon this Court which preclude us from holding that pre-adoption trees vest in the

---

1   [1932] 2 Ch 155.
2   (1985) 83 LGR 152; see para **11.18**.

Highway Authority for all purposes, though I appreciate that Bramwell LJ's opinion (in *Coverdale v Charlton* above) was to the contrary. The penal and compensatory provisions in Section 149, as he recognised, suggest that the property of all trees vests in the Highway Authority. I think that the time has come when the Courts should adopt a consistent approach to all highway trees other than those already subject to the statutory scheme now contained in Section 96 of the 1980 Act. And I take this view, notwithstanding that it involves holding that my previous decision in *Bridges v London Borough of Harrow* was wrongly decided.'

11.27 In practical terms, *Hurst v Hampshire County Council* seems to have confirmed the approach which had been adopted at least since *Russell v London Borough of Barnet* that a highway authority could be liable in nuisance for trees whenever planted or self-sown either by virtue of ownership or by virtue of maintenance and control. The Court of Appeal has, however, now made it clear that property in all highway trees vests in the highway authority.

Can the plaintiff sue?

11.28 The above cases dealt with the question whether the highway authority owned or was responsible for the trees and could therefore be sued. Because of the continuing nature of tree root nuisance where a new cause of action may accrue each day during its continuance the courts have had to consider the plaintiff's entitlement to sue where damage has occurred before the plaintiff acquired the property. This issue came before the court in the case of *Masters v London Borough of Brent*.[1] In that case, a house was owned by the plaintiff's father when cracks in the property were noticed and the plaintiff was told that the bay at the front of the house was definitely subsiding. Neither the plaintiff nor his father had enough money to fund the necessary repairs. As a result, the plaintiff's father transferred to him his interest in the premises to enable the plaintiff to raise money by way of a mortgage. It was argued on behalf of the defendants that the plaintiff was not in a position to claim damages based upon the cost of repair of the house because the damage had occurred before he had acquired the leasehold interest from his father. Talbot J gave judgment for the plaintiff on the basis of continuing nuisance as follows:

'The final submission ... is that here is a case where there is a continuing actionable nuisance affecting the land both during the time of the father's ownership and during the Plaintiff's ownership, that there was in fact, not in theory, continuing damage and that the Plaintiff, who has remedied the damage at his own expense, is entitled to recover that cost as his loss for the continuing nuisance. In my judgment, that is a correct submission. Where there is a continuing nuisance inflicting damage upon premises, those who are in possession of the interest will recover losses which they have borne whether the act began before the acquisition of the interest, or whether it began after the acquisition of the interest. The test is:

What is the loss which the owner of the land has to meet in respect of the continuing nuisance affecting his land?'

11.29 The decision in *Masters v London Borough of Brent* was considered, and apparently approved, by the House of Lords in *Delaware Mansions Ltd v Westminster City Council*.[2] This case concerned damage to part of a terrace of mansion flats

---

1   [1978] 2 WLR 768.
2   [2001] UKHL 55, [2002] 1 AC 321.

caused by a plane tree situated in the highway. Although the case was fought on issues of causation, reasonable care and quantum of damages, the defendants also argued that the claimants could not maintain a cause of action because the relevant damage had occurred before their ownership.

Delaware Mansions Ltd v Westminster City Council

11.30   Delaware Mansions Ltd (Delaware) was a company wholly owned by the leaseholders, each of whom owned one share in it. Under the terms of the leases, Delaware covenanted to carry out works of maintenance and repair to the property, both within the individual flats and the common parts, and to the structure. In consideration for performing this obligation, Delaware was entitled to receive contributions from the leaseholders to cover all the costs incurred. In order to perform its obligation, Delaware had the necessary licence to enter the property. It could not enter the property for any other purpose and had no other rights over the property.

11.31   Mr Recorder Derek Wood QC (sitting as a Deputy Official Referee) relied upon the House of Lords' decision in *Hunter and Others v Canary Wharf Ltd*,[1] where their Lordships emphasised that an action in private nuisance is concerned with interference with the enjoyment of rights over land. In general, therefore, only persons with an interest in the land can sue. The judge held that Delaware was simply a licensee and did not have sufficient title to maintain an action:

> 'In order to perform its obligation it has the necessary licence to enter the property. It cannot enter the property for any other purpose, and has no other rights over it. In my judgment that simple bundle of rights and obligations does not amount to an interest in land – much less a right to exclusive possession of land, if that is the test – such as to entitle it to maintain an action in tort, either in negligence or in nuisance. The loss which it claims does not in my judgment represent a diminution in value of an interest in land. It is purely economic loss: an increase in the scope and therefore the cost of its contractual obligation to repair. It would be in my judgment quite artificial to suggest that a bare licence to enter to carry out contractual work is an "interest in land", or that the cost of complying with that contractual obligation is a diminution in the value of any such interest.'

11.32   The block of flats had been owned by the Church Commissioners but, in April 1990, the freehold had been sold to Flecksun Ltd. The judge made two significant findings. First, he held that all, or almost all, of the structural damage which was the subject-matter of the plaintiff's claim had occurred by not later than March 1990, namely before Flecksun Ltd's ownership. In the circumstances the judge accepted the defendant's submission that the cause of action in respect of the damage which had occurred during the Church Commissioners' period of ownership was vested in the Church Commissioners. The Church Commissioners had never assigned their cause of action to Flecksun Ltd which, the judge held, therefore could not claim in respect of damage which had occurred before its ownership of the building. The judge, dismissing Flecksun Ltd's claim, considered that *Masters v London Borough of Brent* had been wrongly decided and refused to follow it. The judge questioned what had happened to the father's potential claim if the son was able to claim for damage which had occurred during the father's ownership. This question has now been answered by the House of Lords. Lord Cooke said:

---

1   [1997] 2 All ER 426.

'One point at least is clear. Double recovery could not be permitted. But there is no question of that in the present case, nor was there in *Masters v Brent London Borough Council.*'

The second important finding by the trial judge was that Flecksun Ltd had acted reasonably in executing the extent of underpinning works undertaken.

11.33 *Delaware Mansions Limited v Westminster City Council* came before the Court of Appeal[1] where the judge's decision was reversed. Although accepting that the relevant damage had occurred before Flecksun Ltd had acquired the block of flats, the Court of Appeal relied upon *Whitehouse v Fellowes*.[2] This was a case where a limitation defence was raised. The trustees of a turnpike road had converted an open ditch by the side of the road into a covered drain, but in consequence of the negligent way in which the catch pits were constructed and kept, the drain was at times of heavy rain insufficient to carry off the water to its accustomed channel. It was consequently diverted onto other land causing damage. In that case, Williams J stated:

'The continuance by the defendants of that negligent and improper condition of the road under their charge, if accompanied by fresh damage to the plaintiff, constitutes a new cause of action.'

In the *Delaware* case, Pill LJ said:

'Thus where there is a continuing nuisance, the owner is entitled to a declaration, to abate the nuisance, to damages for physical injury and to an injunction. He is in my judgment, and on the same principle, entitled to the reasonable costs of eliminating the nuisance if it is reasonable to eliminate it ... a nuisance is present during (Flecksun's) ownership; acceptance of the need for remedial work establishes that. The actual and relevant damage is the costs of the necessary and reasonable remedial work. Underpinning has been held to be a reasonable way of eliminating the nuisance and the owner can recover the cost of doing it. There is no need to prove further physical damage resulting from the nuisance.'

11.34 Hearing Westminster City Council's appeal, the House of Lords[3] noted that there was surprisingly little or no authority in English law about the recoverability of remedial expenditure on damage to buildings caused by the encroachment of tree roots. Lord Cooke said:

'It seems to me therefore that any decision which your Lordships may give in this case must to some extent break new ground in English Law.'

11.35 Lord Cooke considered that the answer to the question whether Flecksun Ltd was entitled to recover the cost of underpinning its property was to be found by applying the concepts of reasonableness between neighbours and reasonable foreseeability. Considering the issues in the case, Lord Cooke decided, first, that there had been a continuing nuisance during Flecksun Ltd's ownership. Moving on, it is important to note that the House of Lords considered that Flecksun Ltd's entitlement to claim damages for the cost of remedial works did not require the occurrence of further damage during their ownership. Lord Cooke explained:

'I think that there was a continuing nuisance during Flecksun's ownership until at least the completion of the underpinning and the piling in July 1992. It matters not that further

1   [2000] BLR 1.
2   (1861) 10 CB (NS) 765.
3   [2001] UKHL 55, [2002] 1 AC 321.

cracking of the superstructure may not have occurred after March 1990. The encroachment of the roots was causing continuing damage to the land by dehydrating the soil and inhibiting rehydration. Damage consisting of impairment of the load-bearing qualities of residential land is, in my view, itself a nuisance.'

11.36 The House of Lords nevertheless considered that it was appropriate to limit the burden on those responsible for trees. Referring to the concept of reasonableness between neighbours, Lord Cooke relied upon *Solloway v Hampshire County Council* in deciding that a building owner should not be entitled to claim substantial costs of underpinning from the person responsible for the tree without giving the latter notice of the damage, and the opportunity to remove the tree. On the other hand, Lord Cooke considered that a refusal to remove the tree could give rise to a claim for the cost of carrying out works which might not only involve the repair of damage occurring before the claimant purchased the property, as in the case of Flecksun Ltd, but also the cost of work to prevent future damage. Lord Cooke said:

'If reasonableness between neighbours is the key to the solution of problems in this field, it cannot be right to visit the authority or owner responsible for a tree with a large bill for underpinning without giving them notice of the damage and the opportunity of avoiding further damage by removal of the tree. Should they elect to preserve the tree for environmental reasons, they may fairly be expected to bear the cost of underpinning or other reasonably necessary remedial works; and the party on whom the cost has fallen may recover it, even though there may be elements of hitherto unsatisfied pre-proprietorship damage or protection for the future. But, as a general proposition, I think that the defendant is entitled to notice and a reasonable opportunity of abatement before liability for remedial expenditure can arise.'

In this case, the House of Lords considered that Westminster City Council had received ample notice, had refused to remove the tree, and was liable for the costs of underpinning carried out by Flecksun Ltd even though Flecksun was repairing damage which had occurred during the ownership of its predecessors, the Church Commissioners.

11.37 Lord Cooke summarised his view of the law as follows:

'In the end, in my opinion, the law can be summed up in the proposition that, where there is a continuing nuisance of which the defendant knew or ought to have known, reasonable remedial expenditure may be recovered by the owner who has had to incur it. In the present case this was Flecksun.'

In *Delaware*, and the earlier case of *Masters*, the claimants' buildings had suffered damage. The House of Lords decided that it did not matter that damage had occurred before the claimants acquired ownership. What arises out of the *Delaware* decision is whether there can be a claim for the cost of deepening foundations when no damage to the building has occurred. Lord Cooke's judgment does seem to allow a claim for the cost of preventative works. Accordingly, it seems arguable that such a claim, where no damage to the building has occurred, might be possible, although there would presumably have to be cogent evidence and, more particularly, the person responsible for the tree would have to be given notice and have the opportunity to abate the nuisance first.[1]

1　The claimant could also seek an injunction. See paras **11.63–11.64**.

When does the cause of action accrue?

11.38 The nature of a tree root claim as a continuing action in nuisance has given rise to the further question whether a claim can be statute-barred when proceedings are commenced before the carrying-out of remedial works (if proceedings are issued more than 6 years after completion of remedial works then the claim in respect of those remedial works will clearly be statute-barred). The result of the House of Lords' decision in *Delaware* would appear to confirm that before the carrying-out of remedial work crystallises the date, the continuing nature of nuisance due to tree root encroachment means that it is unlikely that such a claim will be statute-barred.

ESTABLISHING LIABILITY IN TREE ROOT NUISANCE

11.39 Following *Solloway v Hampshire County Council*,[1] the requirements to establish a claim in nuisance are causation, foreseeability and reasonable care.

How have the courts dealt with these issues?

Causation

11.40 Causation has not proved too difficult a question for the courts. The necessary evidence for establishing causation has normally been present in cases which have come before the courts, ie there has been evidence of the existence of tree roots and the existence of a desiccated clay sub-soil beneath the foundations. However, in *Paterson v Humberside County Council*,[2] Toulson J (then sitting as a deputy High Court judge) did have to consider questions of causation. The case involved a property which had foundations varying from 450 mm to 680 mm below ground level. The property was founded on clay sub-soil and the court heard that the foundations would be regarded as shallow by present day standards. In blaming the trees for damage to his house, the plaintiff relied in particular on the following:

(1) the admitted presence of tree roots under the property;
(2) the nature and history of the damage;
(3) ground investigations;
(4) similar fact evidence relating to other properties.

For its part, the highway authority sought to argue that damage had been caused by:

(1) the likely differential settlement of the foundations due to the imposed loads;
(2) the shallow foundations;
(3) the presence of a chalk aquifer which the defendant contended was sufficient to supply the water demands of the trees.

11.41 The judge rejected the defendant's arguments and reached the following conclusion on causation which is of general application:

'I am satisfied that the trees are an effective and substantial cause of the recent damage. They are not the sole cause. Other causes are the poor foundations of the property and the drought. The superior quality of construction of 42 Park Avenue (a neighbouring

---

1   (1981) 79 LGR 449; see para **11.9**.
2   (1996) 12 Const LJ 64.

property) may well explain why that property has suffered less damage. But it is sufficient to establish causation that the trees were an effective cause of the damage ... the foundations were not so poor that the damage was bound to happen in any event. That is evidenced by the facts not only that the property had stood for over 100 years, but also that the structure was in a stable condition at the time of the Plaintiff's purchase and for several years after. That being so, the fact that the property had shallow foundations and was therefore more susceptible to damage from soil shrinkage caused by invasion of tree roots is no more relevant to liability than the fact that a Plaintiff has a thin skull: cf. *Smith v Leech Brain & Co Ltd*[1] – the roots take their victim as they find it.'

11.42 *Paterson v Humberside County Council* was approved by the Court of Appeal in *Rupert St John Loftus-Brigham v LB Ealing*.[2] It was agreed that the claimant's property had been damaged by the abstraction by vegetation of moisture from the clay sub-soil. The claimant contended that roots from the council's trees were the primary cause of the damage. The council argued that the only vegetation responsible was the large virginia creeper growing on the claimant's property. At trial the judge held that the claimant had not established the burden of proof against the defendant. He considered that the claimant had to establish that the council's trees were probably the dominant cause of the damage.

11.43 The Court of Appeal considered that the judge had erred in his approach. The principles of causation were the same, whether the case fell to be decided in nuisance or negligence. The judge had found that a range of vegetation, including the council's trees, had contributed 'to a greater or lesser degree to what occurred'. On the issue of causation, Chadwick LJ said:

> 'The question that he should have asked himself was that approved by Lord Bingham in *Fairchild v Glenhaven Funeral Services*[3]: whether desiccation from the tree roots materially contributed to the damage.'

The judge's findings were not sufficient to enable the Court of Appeal to substitute its decision on causation and therefore liability. The case was remitted to the court below.

11.44 The decision in *Patel v London Borough of Lambeth*,[4] in favour of the defendant local authority is confirmation that claimants must establish causation, and not simply the presence of tree roots to establish their case. On the other hand, in *Delaware Mansions Ltd v Westminster City Council*,[5] the judge, although finding for the local authority on other issues, nevertheless found causation to have been established in the plaintiff's favour, in spite of there being substantial dispute on the evidence as to whether the ground had been desiccated.

11.45 Highway authorities find it difficult to resist a tree root claim on the issue of causation unless the claimant's evidence will not support a finding that the abstraction by tree roots of moisture from the clay sub-soil caused the damage.

---

1   [1962] 2 QB 405.
2   [2003] EWCA Civ 1490, (unreported) 28 October 2003.
3   [2003] 1 AC 32.
4   (Unreported) December 1996.
5   [1998] EGCS 48; see para **11.29**.

Foreseeability

11.46 This issue fell to be decided by the Court of Appeal in *Solloway v Hampshire County Council*,[1] where the slightly unusual nature of the sub-soil had been described by Stocker J as follows:

> 'Shirley Avenue is situated in an area, the top sub-soil of which is plateau gravel. Insofar as small pockets of clay outcrop may exist, they are of insufficient size to appear at all on the geological plan. A house founded on plateau gravel is unlikely to be affected by intrusion of the roots of trees. The Plaintiff's house was founded upon plateau gravel at the rear and the greater part of the flank wall, but upon an outcrop of Bracklesham-based clay at the front. Differential settlement was therefore likely to occur in any event, even if uninfluenced by external factors, such as dehydration by the roots. However, such settlement would be likely to have revealed its full effect within 10 years of the erection of the house. No structural damage in fact occurred during this period and there was no structural damage of any significance prior to the events of 1976.'

11.47 The Court of Appeal considered that the question was whether the highway authority should reasonably have foreseen that there might be pockets of clay under this house. The geological map showed the sub-soil in the Shirley area to be almost entirely plateau gravel. On the other hand, there was evidence from surveyors and civil engineers working locally that there were also pockets of clay. These pockets of clay were quite small, between 5 and 10 square yards in extent, but this only added to their potential danger if they were under a house because the foundations would not be resting on a homogeneous sub-soil. Stocker J had held that the plaintiff had satisfied the test of foreseeability. The Court of Appeal disagreed. Dunn LJ said:

> 'In considering whether there is a breach of duty, the extent of the risk and the foreseeable consequences of it have to be balanced against the practicable measures to be taken to minimise the damage and its consequences.

> The Judge held that intrusions of clay were likely in the Shirley area. With all respect to the Judge, I cannot, on the evidence, accept that finding. I think that the possibility of an intrusion of clay under the Plaintiff's property, which is the real question, was unlikely. I will hold that it was no more than a vague possibility, not a real risk . . ., but assuming that there was a real risk or chance, I would say that it was an outside chance and that outside chance has to be balanced against the practical steps which could reasonably have been taken by the Defendants to minimise the damage.'

11.48 It is submitted that the Court of Appeal's decision on foreseeability was correct. Nevertheless it was a decision limited to its own somewhat unusual facts.

11.49 *Solloway* was concerned with the question whether the defendants could reasonably have foreseen the ground conditions beneath the plaintiff's property. The other question of foreseeability which has come before the courts is whether a defendant should have foreseen that tree roots could cause damage. In *Greenwood v Portwood*,[2] cracking had occurred to the plaintiff's property between 1975 and 1977. There was no real issue on causation.

11.50 The court heard that the plaintiff had no more knowledge than the defendant that his neighbour's tree might have caused cracking to his property, until his

---

1   (1981) 79 LGR 449.
2   [1985] CLY 2500, Crown Ct.

engineers told him in 1977. The judge heard evidence that although structural engineers had known of the basic problem caused by tree roots since 1947, nevertheless some local authorities had been unaware of the problem prior to 1976. The judge was influenced by the fact that both parties had no technical knowledge and held as follows:

> 'Here the Defendant was an ordinary householder, as was the Plaintiff. The Plaintiff had been in occupation since 1971 and the Defendant since 1965. It would be quite wrong to attribute either the Plaintiff or the Defendant with foresight of the possibility of any real risk existing because of the underlying clay bed ... in my judgment, there was nothing at all to alert them to the possibility of this risk at the time.'

11.51   Although the decision in *Greenwood v Portwood* was probably correct, dealing with events occurring between 1975 and 1977, a similar case would now be decided in favour of the claimant on the basis that ordinary householders now have knowledge that tree roots can cause damage. This view is perhaps supported by the approach of Brandt J in the case of *Butcher v Perkins*.[1] Although, somewhat strangely in the light of *Solloway v Hampshire County Council*,[2] the judge doubted the need to show foreseeability, he said:

> 'A prudent landowner should know that a willow tree or a poplar tree in particular are often responsible for such damage. For a very long time it has been known to the public that such trees can cause damage to buildings by their roots. This tree was 4 metres from the Plaintiff's house and I have seen various publications showing that this was at the very limit of safety. It is clear that the tree was close enough to put the house at risk. Anybody should have known that. Secondly, it is extremely well-known that in the whole of this area there was a stratum of clay either on the surface, under some other layer of ground or that there was clay in the soil. In my Judgment the Defendant knew, or should have known, that there was clay in the soil and that there was potential for disaster. There was plenty of written material on the subject for him to read, there was popular knowledge to listen to and there was advice for him to take had he chosen to do so.'

It would therefore seem that apart from cases where the existence of clay sub-soil cannot reasonably be foreseen, foreseeability will not prove a difficult hurdle for claimants to overcome, particularly in an action against local authorities, which employ engineers and arboricultural experts, but also nowadays against householders.

Reasonable care

11.52   In *Solloway v Hampshire County Council*,[3] the Court of Appeal considered that following *Leakey and Others v National Trust for Places of Historical Interest or Natural Beauty*,[4] it was necessary to decide whether the defendants could reasonably have taken steps to avoid or minimise the damage. In the particular circumstances of that case, where isolated pockets of clay might exist anywhere in Shirley Avenue, there were no reasonable steps open to the highway authority. In particular, the court rejected a submission that the highway authority should have sent circulars to all householders whose houses were adjacent to trees pointing out the dangers and asking

---

1   (1994) 10 Const LJ 67.
2   See para **11.9**.
3   (1981) 79 LGR 449.
4   [1980] 1 All ER 17; see para **11.9**.

them to pay for or share the cost of boreholes. The pragmatic approach of Dunn LJ was as follows:

> 'Householders circulated in this way would be likely to suffer apprehension for the value of their property and probably with no reason. The consequences of such circulation, it seems to me, are unpredictable and unsatisfactory. Balancing the risk of pockets of clay under the Plaintiff's property with the steps necessary to deal with that risk, in my Judgment there was no breach of duty by the Defendants in this case and so no nuisance.'

Reasonableness between neighbours

11.53   The House of Lords, in *Delaware Mansions Ltd v Westminster City Council*,[1] stressed that it could not be right to require a local authority or owner responsible for a tree to pay a large bill for underpinning a building without its being given notice of the damage and the opportunity of avoiding further damage by removal of the tree. This would seem to be an additional requirement to establish liability in tree root nuisance although the House of Lords considered that it followed from the Court of Appeal's decision in *Solloway v Hampshire County Council*.

In *LE Jones (Insurance Brokers) Ltd v Portsmouth City Council*[2] the defendant relied on *Delaware Mansions* to argue that it had not been given an opportunity to abate the nuisance because when it was first notified of the damage, the claimant had already decided to underpin the property. The judge rejected this argument. Although the defendant was not notified as soon as damage from the tree roots was suspected, it did receive notification before the contract to underpin the claimant's property was entered into and the defendant did have time to suggest an alternative remedy. The defendant had had an opportunity at least to ask for a chance to abate the nuisance.

NEGLIGENCE

11.54   Although Tudor Evans J's judgment in *Russell v London Borough of Barnet*[3] dealt principally with a claim in nuisance, he also held that the highway authority was liable in negligence since reasonable foreseeability of damage was present, as was the failure to take reasonable steps to obviate or reduce the risk. Similarly, in *Paterson v Humberside County Council*,[4] Toulson J held:

> 'The Plaintiffs are entitled to succeed in negligence. A risk was foreseeable, and if the Highway Authority did not wish for understandable reasons to remove the trees, it could have removed the risk, or very substantially reduced it, by pruning.'

11.55   In *Delaware Mansions Ltd v Westminster City Council*,[5] the judge also held (although dismissing the claim on other grounds) that the local authority had failed to take reasonable care to protect the plaintiff's property from a foreseeable danger and that as a result it had been negligent.

---

1   [2001] UKHL 55, [2002] 1 AC 321.
2   [2002] EWCA Civ 1723, [2003] 1 WLR 427.
3   (1985) 83 LGR 152; see para **11.18**.
4   (1996) 12 Const LJ 64.
5   [1998] EGCS 48.

11.56 It should be noted, however, that, in *Hurst v Hampshire County Council*,[1] Stuart-Smith LJ expressed doubt as to whether a claim in negligence would have succeeded. His words were obiter as he had made his decision on other grounds, but he said:

> 'Nor is it necessary to deal with any freestanding claim founded in negligence apart from nuisance. In my view such a claim would present great difficulty in the light of *Stovin v Wise*.'

In *Stovin v Wise*,[2] the local authority had no proprietary interest in the land where the obstruction was situated. The highway authority either is the owner of the land where a tree is growing, or, as the judge held in *Low v R J Haddock Ltd and The Royal County of Berkshire*,[3] it is the only person who has sufficient interest to maintain the tree. It is therefore submitted that *Stovin v Wise* is not directly in point, and claims in negligence can, in appropriate circumstances, succeed against a highway authority.

BREACH OF STATUTORY DUTY

11.57 Section 96(6) of the Highways Act 1980 provides as follows:

> 'No tree, shrub, grass verge, guard or fence shall be planted, laid out or erected under this section, or, if planted, laid out or erected under this section, allowed to remain, in such a situation as to hinder the reasonable use of the highway by any person entitled to use it, or so as to be a nuisance, or injurious to the owner or occupier of premises adjacent to the highway.'

It is clear that the above section applies only to trees planted by the highway authority after the adoption of the road as a highway. On the issue of liability for breach of statutory duty, Stuart-Smith LJ expressed the following view in *Hurst v Hampshire County Council*:[4]

> 'So far as planted trees are concerned it is clear that the Highway Authority will be liable under Section 96(6) if the roots of the planted tree cause dehydration to the soil and consequent subsidence in a building adjacent to the highway.'

Later in his judgment, however, Stuart-Smith LJ reserved his opinion as to whether foreseeability was a necessary ingredient for an action for breach of this statutory duty. Nevertheless, it is submitted that foreseeability may not, in fact, be required in the light of s 96(7) which reads:

> 'If damage is caused to the property of any person by anything done in exercise of the powers conferred by this section, that person is entitled ... to recover compensation for it from the authority ... by whom the powers are exercised.'

---

1   (1998) 96 LGR 27.
2   [1996] 3 All ER 801, and see Chapter 7.
3   (1985) EG LR 247, and see para **11.20**.
4   (1998) 96 LGR 27.

LIABILITY IN RELATION TO FALLING TREES

11.58 The position in relation to trees falling on the highway and causing damage or injury to users was considered in the case of *Caminer and Another v Northern & London Investment Trust Ltd.*[1] A large elm tree growing in the defendant's property fell onto the plaintiffs' car damaging it and injuring the plaintiffs. The tree, which was about 130 years old, carried a considerable crown, although not abnormal for a tree of that age, and had never been lopped, topped or pollarded. Evidence was given that elm trees should be inspected every 5 or 7 years and that if the tree had been topped it was unlikely that it would have fallen when it did, but that the tree did not appear to be dangerous before the accident. The House of Lords decided that in the absence of evidence that the defendants had failed in their duty to take reasonable care, they were not liable. External examination of the tree could not have revealed its diseased condition, and their Lordships did not consider that there was any duty on the landowner to bore into the trunk of the tree to ascertain its condition in the absence of any other signs of disease. The claims, whether framed in negligence or nuisance, failed because the necessary elements of foreseeability and knowledge were absent.

11.59 In a similar case, *Chapman v London Borough of Barking and Dagenham,*[2] the Court of Appeal upheld the judge's decision against the highway authority. During a period of very high winds in January 1990, a branch from a tree in the highway fell onto the plaintiff's van, causing him serious injury. A duty to inspect the tree seems to have been accepted by the defendants, and this would seem to follow from the *Caminer* decision above. The judge, therefore, had to decide whether there was a breach of duty, and this question turned on whether a reasonable system of inspection would have revealed that the tree was diseased before the accident occurred. The judge accepted evidence that after the tree had been felled, the stump had shown signs of decay. The presence of active bacteria in the decay showed that there must have been an open wound on the tree. The judge also found that there had been decay at the fork in the tree where the branches grew out of the trunk. It was accepted that this decay could only have been seen by a 'climbing inspection' of the tree.

11.60 The judge held that there was a clear duty on the defendants to conduct a 'systematic expert inspection' of the trees on or close to the highway. In fact, the defendants had not carried out any formal inspection, certainly after the October 1987 gale (which the tree had survived). The judge was satisfied that an inspection from ground level should have been carried out before 1990 when the accident occurred. Liability in the case then depended upon whether such an inspection would have revealed anything which would have shown that a 'climbing inspection' of the tree was necessary. The judge decided in favour of the plaintiff because the tree was in a busy area which should have been high on any tree inspection programme. Various pruning wounds, which the judge held to be a potentially hazardous source of infection, were visible from ground level and were located at the fork in the tree where they would be particularly likely to collect water. Although the Court of Appeal was urged to overturn the decision on the basis that the judge had misinterpreted the evidence, it refused to interfere with the decision.

---

1   [1950] 2 All ER 486.
2   [1998] CLY 4053.

REMEDIES

Damages

11.61   In nuisance, damages are awarded, prima facie, to represent diminution in the value of land, although this will usually represent the cost of remedial works in a case of tree root nuisance. This was, it is submitted, confirmed by Lord Lloyd in the case of *Hunter and Others v Canary Wharf Ltd*,[1] when he said:

> 'But where he claims damages, the measure of damages in cases (1 and 2) (encroachment on a neighbour's land and physical injury to a neighbour's land) will be the diminution in value of the land. This will usually (though not always) be equal to the cost of reinstatement.'

11.62   If the courts can award general damages, the appropriate figure will be low. In the case of *Watts and Another v Morrow*,[2] a case involving an allegation of negligence against a surveyor, the Court of Appeal replaced an award of £4,000 to each plaintiff with an award of £750 to each plaintiff. Ralph Gibson LJ said:

> 'The proper approach is to fix a modest sum for the amount of physical discomfort endured having regard to the period of time over which it was endured.'

Although this was not a case of tree root nuisance, it shows the level of damages which the courts will award in cases where the claimant's claim is for physical discomfort and inconvenience caused by the carrying-out of remedial works.

Injunction

11.63   The court is entitled to grant an injunction in cases to prevent a tree root nuisance. In *Paterson v Humberside County Council*,[3] the judge heard evidence from experts that further damage to the plaintiff's property could be prevented by regular pruning of the tree thus avoiding removal of the tree. As the highway authority was not prepared to offer an undertaking to carry out regular pruning, the judge held that the plaintiff was entitled to an injunction requiring the removal of the tree:

> 'I am therefore left with a choice of refusing an Injunction altogether and ordering the removal of the trees. Since they are a continuing threat to the Plaintiff's property, the Plaintiffs are entitled to an Order for their removal. No doubt a remedial scheme could be devised to make the house safe even if the trees were to stay; and I am sure that many members of the residents association will be sorry to see the trees go. But I do not believe that either of those considerations would entitle me to refuse the Plaintiff's application.'

11.64   In *Elliott v Islington London Borough Council*,[4] the Court of Appeal upheld an injunction requiring the removal of a large oak tree which was causing damage to the plaintiff's boundary wall. The local authority argued that the tree should be preserved in the public interest as a valuable local amenity, with the plaintiff receiving

---

1   [1997] 2 All ER 426.
2   [1991] 4 All ER 937.
3   (1996) 12 Const LJ 64.
4   (1991) 10 EG 145.

damages as compensation for the encroachment of the tree. The Court of Appeal rejected this argument and ordered its removal.[1]

---

1   In fact, subsequent public outcry did lead to discussions between the plaintiff and the local authority which resulted in a compromise whereby only part of the tree was removed.

Index

References are to paragraph numbers.